The Taming of Fate

This book is a product of CODESRIA Book Project.

To Lucy Bonnerjea, my intellectual mentor,
who brought disasters to my attention.

The Taming of Fate

Approaching Risk from a Social Action Perspective
Case Studies from Southern Mozambique

Elísio S. Macamo

Council for the Development of Social Science Research in Africa
DAKAR

© CODESRIA 2017
Council for the Development of Social Science Research in Africa
Avenue Cheikh Anta Diop, Angle Canal IV
BP 3304 Dakar, 18524, Senegal
Website: www.codesria.org

ISBN: 978-2-86978-719-3

All rights reserved. No part of this publication may be reproduced or transmitted in any form or by any means, electronic or mechanical, including photocopy, recording or any information storage or retrieval system without prior permission from CODESRIA.

Typesetting: Djibril Fall
Cover Design: Ibrahima Fofana

Distributed in Africa by CODESRIA
Distributed elsewhere by African Books Collective, Oxford, UK
Website: www.africanbookscollective.com

The Council for the Development of Social Science Research in Africa (CODESRIA) is an independent organisation whose principal objectives are to facilitate research, promote research-based publishing and create multiple forums geared towards the exchange of views and information among African researchers. All these are aimed at reducing the fragmentation of research in the continent through the creation of thematic research networks that cut across linguistic and regional boundaries.

CODESRIA publishes *Africa Development*, the longest standing Africa based social science journal; *Afrika Zamani*, a journal of history; the *African Sociological Review*; the *African Journal of International Affairs*; *Africa Review of Books* and the *Journal of Higher Education in Africa*. The Council also co-publishes the *Africa Media Review*; *Identity, Culture and Politics: An Afro-Asian Dialogue*; *The African Anthropologist, Journal of African Tranformation, Method(e)s: African Review of Social Sciences Methodology*, and the *Afro-Arab Selections for Social Sciences*. The results of its research and other activities are also disseminated through its Working Paper Series, Green Book Series, Monograph Series, Book Series, Policy Briefs and the CODESRIA Bulletin. Select CODESRIA publications are also accessible online at www.codesria.org.

CODESRIA would like to express its gratitude to the Swedish International Development Cooperation Agency (SIDA), the International Development Research Centre (IDRC), the Ford Foundation, the Carnegie Corporation of New York (CCNY), the Norwegian Agency for Development Cooperation (NORAD), the Danish Agency for International Development (DANIDA), the Rockefeller Foundation, the Open Society Foundations (OSFs), TrustAfrica, UNESCO, the African Capacity Building Foundation (ACBF), The Open Society Initiative for West Africa (OSIWA), The Open Society Initiative for Southern Africa (OSISA), Andrew Mellon Foundation, and the Government of Senegal for supporting its research, training and publication programmes.

Contents

Acknowledgment ix
List of Figures and Tables xi
List of Appendices xiii
Transcription Symbols xv

1. Coping with Crises and Disasters in Southern Mozambique 1
   Introduction 1
       The Context of Research 2
       Enter Disasters and Crises 4
       Local Agency 8
   The Structure of the Book 15
       General Structure and Theoretical Chapters 15
       The Case Studies 17
       The Concluding Part 19

Part One
Theoretical and Methodological Issues

2. Studying Africa 25
   Introduction 25
   Studying Africa, Understanding Patrice Lumumba 28
   The Problem of Order 32
       Contingency and Social Action 41
       Social Action and Meaningfulness 46
       The Nature of the (Social) World 51
   African Objects 55

3. Risk and Social Reality 57
   Engaging With Risk 57
   Social Relationships, Trust and Predictability 62
      Encounters and the Fragility of Social Relationships 64
      Interaction and Emerging Properties 70
   Making Risk Relevant 75

4. Methodological Issues: Contexts of Action 79
   Introduction 79
      Excursion: What does it Mean to Say that People Act
      in Order to Act? 80
      Warrants for Empirical Grounding 85
      Mundane Reasoning 88
   Patrice Lumumba Communal Village 89
      The Reality of Uncertainty in Patrice Lumumba 92
      The Lifeworld of Patrice Lumumba 104
   An Analytical Framework: Translating Hazards into Risks 105
      An Analytical Framework for Descriptive Inference 105
      The Operational Dimension of the Framework 107
      The Methodological Tool-box 110

Part Two
Studies in Coping with Disasters and Crises

5. When Disaster Strikes 117
   Introduction 117
      Documenting a Disaster 118
      The Group Interviews 121
   The Process of Socially Constructing Disaster 121
   Analytical Integration 124
      The Object of Discourse 125
      The Drought as the Cause of the Disaster 128

6. Conflicting Interpretations of Reality 137
   Interpreting Reality 137
      Interpretive Hegemony 139

    Descriptive Itinerary 140
    Peasants in the Limpopo Valley 141
    Standard Peasant Reactions 148
Local and External Explanations of the Floods 149
    Social Distribution of Knowledge 149
    The External Problem-solving Structure 151
    The Local Interpretive Diversity 153
Making Life Predictable 159
    An Empirical Illustration 160
    The Code System 163
    Analysis 164
Analytical Integration 173
    Worldviews 174
    Fact and Truth 175
    Struggles Over Interpretive Hegemony 177

7. War Refugees 179
    The Mozambican Civil War as seen by Refugees 179
    Membership Categorisation Devices 180
    Common-Sense Meanings of War 182
        Experiencing the War 183
        Retrieving Social Reality 186
    Analytical Integration 193
        Accounting for Disaster 193
        'Doing' Disaster 195

8. African Christian Converts and the Creation of Locality 197
    Introduction 197
        The World According to Kanana 1 199
        Producing a Biography 202
    Different Biographies 205
        Two Women 205
        Redefining Identities 208
    Analytical Integration 212

Part Three
Conclusion

9. The Taming of Fate 217
      Struggles Over Meaning 217
         Whose Meaning? 218
         The Challenge of Intelligibility 219
      The Taming of Fate: Relevance, Knowledge and Certainty 222
         The Social and Natural Areas of Relevance of Patrice Lumumba
         Village 222
         The Knowledge of Patrice Lumumba Village 223
         The Certainty of Patrice Lumumba Village 224
         Summarising Findings 224
      Daring to Live 231

Appendices 233
Notes 275
Bibliography 287
Index 305

Acknowledgement

I wish to thank CODESRIA, through its former Executive Secretary, Ebrima Sall, but especially the Publications Department for the opportunity that they have given me to reach a broader African readership. The research upon which the book is based was funded by the German Research Council (DFG), to which I am grateful, within the framework of the Humanities Collaborative Research Programme "Local Action in a Global Context" of the University of Bayreuth, in Germany. I thank all the colleagues there for the inspiring discussions and the learning experience. My special thanks go to Prof. Dieter Neubert, my mentor then and the head of the research project which produced this piece of work. I spent wonderful years at the University of Bayreuth, first for my PhD thesis under the extremely enlightening supervision of Prof. Zingerle, for whose generosity and counsel I will be forever grateful, then for my "Habilitation" under Dieter Neubert's supervision who has been a close intellectual friend and a continuing source of inspiration. While I take full responsibility for the shortcomings and omissions in this book, the authorship of most ideas in it is hard to identify because Dieter Neubert and I worked so close together. We had passionate discussions on the field in Mozambique, in the office in Bayreuth and at conferences all over the world. Key insights from those discussions went into this book and make him an unnamed co-author. I am greatly indebted to his friendship, interest in the work, passionate engagement and, of course, the opportunity which he gave me to work as his assistant for eight years at the University of Basel. It is appropriate to seize this opportunity to also thank my family and all the friends and colleagues who put up with me along the way for their support and love. Finally, I also wish to thank Nigel Stephenson for the great copy-editing work.

List of Figures and Tables

Figures

Figure 4.1: A graphic representation of the analytical framework ... 108
Figure 5.1: Perspectives on the disaster in Patrice Lumumba Communal Village ... 130
Figure 6.1: Unusual rainfall in years preceding great floods ... 141
Figure 6.2: Rainfall variation for the month of December between 1951 and 1999 ... 142

Tables

Table 6.1: Rainfall data (1951–2000) ... 143
Table 6.2: Farming activities and main crops ... 146
Table 6.3: The Code System ... 164
Table 6.4: External Actor ... 165
Table 6.5: Local Actor ... 169
Table 6.6a: Local problem solving apparatus ... 172
Table 6.6b: External problem solving apparatus ... 172
Table 6.7: Most frequent predicate ... 173
Table 6.9: Translating hazards into risks in Patrice Lumumba ... 225

List of Appendices

Appendice 1: Maps and Figures

Appendix 1.1: Research site (Xai-Xai city) 233
Appendix 1.2: Livelihood zones 234
Appendix 1.3: Flood zones 235
Appendix 1.4: Water requirement satisfaction 236
Appendix 1.5: Rainfall 237
Appendix 1.6: Limpopo River profile 238
Appendix 1.7: Epidemics and their toll 239
Appendix 1.8: Droughts in recent years 239
Appendix 1.9: Floods and their toll 240
Appendix 1.10: Cyclones / Storms and their toll 240
Appendix 1.11: Age of interview partners 241

Appendice 2: Interview Schedules, Interview Samples, Field Notes and Participant Analysis

Appendix 2.1: Project presentation 242
Appendix 2.2: Narrative interview schedule 243
Appendix 2.3: Interview schedule – Villagers 244
Appendix 2.4: Interview schedule – Institutions 245
Appendix 2.5: Interview Protocols 246
Appendix 2.6: Interview protocol, Sr. Samuel Mondlane, Financial manager, World Vision (Xai-Xai, 9th September 2002) 248
Appendix 2.7: Excerpts from the field diary 250
Appendix 2.8: Participant analysis – Day One 253
Appendix 2.9: Participant analysis – Day Two 256

Appendice 3: Questionnaire

.... 262

Transcription Symbols

Following Bohnsack et al 2001: 363–64, this book uses a transcription system largely borrowed from conversational analysis. Interview partners are indicated through the letters of the alphabet in capitals plus a small f or m for female or male, respectively. The transcription seeks to reflect the flow of speech; for this reason I dispense with punctuation marks. Italics are used to indicate foreign words (in this case, non-English words). The sign : indicates a stretch in the utterance of a word; the repetition of the sign marks the length of the stretch. Everything between the sign @ indicates laughter in speech. Words between the signs ° indicate that they were uttered in a low voice. **Bold** indicates loudness. The sign (.) indicates a pause and the number of dots within the brackets indicates the length of the pause. [indicates the start of an interruption;] indicates the end of an interruption.

1

Coping with Crises and Disasters in Southern Mozambique

Introduction

In this book I describe how a local village community in Southern Mozambique copes with natural and man-made disasters and crises. The point I want to make, however, goes beyond the observation and description of coping mechanisms and strategies. In fact, I argue that the manner in which this local community copes with disasters and crises provides insights of significant theoretical and analytical relevance to the sociology of risk in general and to the study of Africa in particular. To be more specific, the observed coping mechanisms and strategies document a general process, which I describe as translating hazards into risk through the creation of contexts of action. In this sense, these mechanisms appear to be instances of what I intend to call 'the taming of fate', by which I mean the very trivial process through which individuals in society cope with everyday life. This book, therefore, looks at social action from the perspective of cultural sociology as understood and practised by Max Weber.

Indeed, the theoretical and analytical relevance of the findings of the case studies discussed here lie in the opportunity which they provide us to appreciate the extent to which the production of risk – and in contrast to some assumptions within general sociology – is both a universal anthropological constant as well as it is deeply anchored in social action. While the general sociological claim that societies differ in the extent to which they relate to risk and hazards and the roles which both phenomena play within them should be taken seriously if meaningful conceptual categories are to be found in order to describe different empirical realities, I argue that the recognition of common anthropological constants is crucial to furthering the more theoretical project of refining our concepts and approaches in the social sciences. In fact, it is thanks to this recognition that I feel able to suggest, supported by the empirical material presented here, that our notions of social action, and, in particular, Max Weber's ground-breaking conceptual work, have not yet been explored to their full potential in the study of Africa. The concept of social action still offers room for more aspects to be taken into account in both applying its dimensions to research, as well as using it to further elaborate on our theories. In this book it is my aim to do this by grounding my claim on empirical data and theoretical reflection which I have been engaged in for the past decade.

I am particularly interested in engaging the sociology of risk in a discussion of its assumption according to which risk is a particularly modern phenomenon and, in this sense, largely irrelevant, or at any rate marginal, to the description of social phenomena in Africa or, more generally, in technologically less developed societies. In fact, it is my contention that technological risks are particular instances of a more general human tendency to translate hazards into risks. My case rests on the empirical illustrations I have chosen to document how individuals in southern Mozambique, where I carried out my research, organize and structure their social action. I read the evidence as a validation of my contention that the translation of hazards into risks is an anthropological universal, which sociology should seriously take into account if it wants to remain true to its commitment to understanding social phenomena in their full complexity.

The Context of Research

This work brings together research conducted over a period of approximately seven years. It started with a post-doctoral scholarship at the University of Bayreuth's Graduate School for Intercultural Communication in 1997, upon completion of my Ph.D thesis. The scholarship, funded by the German Research Council, allowed me to conduct research in southern Mozambique on the influence of a Protestant Mission (Swiss Presbyterian Mission) on the work ethic of the local African community. Some of the results of this research have been published elsewhere.[1] One preliminary conclusion that I was able to draw from the research, during which I spent a total of five months doing fieldwork, was that the local African community had embraced Christianity for practical, rather than for theological reasons. Indeed, during the colonial period the Swiss Presbyterian Mission had come to be seen by several individuals as a useful resource in their own attempts at coming to terms with changes brought on by Portuguese colonial rule. In this book I include a case study – chapter eight – that draws from the material I collected in the framework of this particular research and use it to show the extent to which the translation of hazards into risks goes beyond the immediate scope of extreme situations and can be fruitfully applied to ordinary everyday life situations.

The idea that local communities embraced Christianity for practical, rather than for theological reasons, gained even more substance following archival research that I conducted in the context of a fellowship at the Institute for

Advanced Studies in Berlin in the academic year 1999/2000. Taking up the theme of work that I had dealt with in my post-doctoral research, I followed up on the significance of the changes introduced by Portuguese colonial rule in Mozambique, with particular emphasis on the role that the regulation of so-called native labour played in structuring the lives of Africans in Mozambique. Again, the issue of social change came to my attention as it became clear from the analysis of available historical material that the regulation of labour was more than the introduction of wage labour into a society that had up until then chiefly relied on barter and social reciprocity for its economic exchanges. In fact, not only did the regulation of labour enable Portugal to formulate its colonial policy,[2] but it also turned Africans into artefacts of colonial intervention, thereby delivering them into a world hitherto unknown to them, which they had to come to terms with. The regulation of labour, as I argued more forcefully at some point (Macamo 2005b), and as many before me had already pointed out,[3] was an ambiguous intervention in the lives of Africans. To the extent that the logic of wage labour would require more mobility and a redefinition of social ties, the regulation of labour promised Africans individual emancipation. At the same time, however, the practice of colonial rule, premised as it was on the delegation of responsibility for the reproduction of labour to a fuzzy notion of 'African traditional society', denied Africans the very promise it seemed to be making. This issue was raised long ago, notably by the Manchester School of Anthropology in the sixties and seventies, which, drawing from a political economy approach to the analysis of mining capital in Southern Africa, sought to show the extent to which ideas of African 'traditional' society were functional to the reproduction needs of the emerging capitalist system. As far as Mozambique is concerned a number of studies confirmed this reading, chief among them Ruth First and her associates' study on the Mozambican semi-proletariat.[4]

It was in this context that the Swiss Presbyterian Mission came to be seen as a resource. Indeed, unlike the colonial state, the Mission offered Africans a *Weltanschauung* that was consistent with their desire for individual emancipation. The Mission's discourse lent legitimacy to the personal striving of individual Africans for emancipation at the same time as it offered them a notion of 'African traditional society' which was more consistent with the changes brought about by colonial rule and the regulation of labour. Subsequent field research funded by Portugal's Foundation for Science and Technology on how a local community in southern Mozambique had dealt with the regulation of labour up to the present increasingly suggested to me that I was on to something that transcended the mere interest in work and missionary activities. In fact, the recurrent theme of social change induced by external forces led me to begin to consider more substantive research on how individuals structure their everyday life. I became interested in the structure of quotidian life by observing with fascination how individuals and local communities seemed to master a truly vertiginous pace of change. How did they do it? What kind of sense did they make of their own lives? How did they go about structuring their lives? How did they think and talk about their lives?

In a nutshell, how did they tame fate?

Enter Disasters and Crises

Between 2001 and 2006 I conducted research on local perceptions of disasters and crises in Southern Mozambique within the framework of the Humanities Collaborative Research Programme funded, again, by the German Research Foundation.[5] This research took me to Southern Mozambique several times, where over this five-year period I spent a total of ten months on the field. In line with the theoretical and analytical concerns of the general research programme the immediate research question was the contrast between local and external interpretations and perceptions of disasters and crises in Southern Mozambique. More than the previous research on the work ethic and the regulation of labour, research on perceptions of disasters and crises brought to my attention the centrality of social action – understood in its broad Weberian sense as the meaning that individuals attach to what they do as they engage with others – to any sociological understanding of what obtains in the world of humans.

Indeed, the more I engaged with villagers, striking friendships, becoming part of their family lives, sharing their problems, worries and hopes concerning the future, the more fascinated did I become by the almost stoic manner in which they faced fate. As I will show in the pages that follow, theirs is a particularly hard life, marked by a recent history of decline in material conditions. Towards the end of the nineteenth century colonial rule had rescued them from a life of insecurity in the face of the despotic rule of the so-called Gaza empire,[6] and amidst the hardships of life as colonial subjects, particularly Portuguese colonial subjecthood, in the run up to Mozambique's independence from Portugal in 1975, their lot had improved somewhat as a result of their integration into the migrant-labour-dominated cash economy of Southern Africa. The immediate post-independence period brought further significant improvements such as easier access to education, bio-medical health care, and local employment. Soon, however, particularly as a result of the civil war that ravaged Mozambique up until 1992, most of the gains of independence eclipsed as life in the village became hostage to nature – floods and droughts – and warring men – the civil war. Their livelihood illustrates the object of what James Ferguson (2000) has quite aptly called the 'ethnography of decline', that is, a progressive reversal of living conditions and material aspirations for the worse.

More importantly, I increasingly became aware of the fact that the lives of villagers in Patrice Lumumba Communal Village did not simply document this progressive decline, but were, in a curious sort of way, a celebration of villagers' tremendous hold on life, at the same time as they documented their attempts at taming their own fate. As I went through the various languages of sociology in search of a vocabulary adequate to make theoretical sense of their experience, the sheer difficulty of finding words broad enough to encompass the size of this experience, but limited enough to account for its singularity, propelled me towards a broader theoretical approach.

In point of fact, rather than simply documenting a local experience, their lives documented both the resilience and ingenuity of the human body and mind in the face of adversity. Theirs were local responses to the hardships of reality, drawing from a universal grammar of human creativity. Their local agency began to look like more than just a local response to local challenges. Increasingly, it appeared to be an instance of what the German sociologist Hans Joas (1996), drawing from the American school of pragmatism, thinks that social action does, namely, bringing into view the ends of what individuals do.

Their magical interpretations of disasters and crises, their sometimes inaccurate understanding of technology and how it functions, their ambivalent attitude towards external institutions, ideas, and individuals and, most of all, their perseverance in the face of such adversity seemed to provide a fertile terrain to test my own ideas about the nature of the social world. Although born and bred in a milieu that was not very different from the one I came to do research on and regardless of the five years it took me to gather material, study sociology, and, particularly, learn to perceive the world on the basis of conceptual tools developed with reference to a world that seemed radically different from my own and from that of the peasants of Southern Mozambique, I was initially not prepared to see the common thread that ultimately gave coherence to my own observations. I plunged into the field in search of difference in order to account for it and probably suggest remedies. When I raised my head to catch air and breathe, I realized, very much in the way Wittgenstein had already remarked upon Frazer's attempts at understanding magical beliefs,[7] that difference was a function of my own ignorance.[8] Local perceptions and interpretations of disasters and crises were instances of social reality made visible and relevant by social action and which cried out for description and theorising. But what kind of theorising should it be?

Two important themes emerged from the more recent research on local perceptions of disasters and crises. First of all, and given the nature of the subject, there emerged the theme of risk. The sociology of risk has gained wide currency over the past decades, particularly as a result of the work of the German sociologist Ulrich Beck (1992) but also of that of several other scholars in response to the general sense of insecurity created by technological progress.[9] The immediate cause for concern was, of course, the fear of the consequences of an atomic war or a nuclear disaster such as Tschernobyl. The sociology of risk drew attention to the importance of security in society and suggested, rather ethnocentrically, that risk might be the privilege of modern, industrial society.[10]

The assumption was, and continues to be, that scientific knowledge about nature is crucial to risk taking, notwithstanding Mary Douglas' very courageous work on risk cultures.[11] The sociological understanding of the notion of risk owes much of its conceptual clarity to a very useful distinction made by Niklas Luhmann (1995) between hazard and risk. This distinction plays a central role in this book (chapter four). Briefly, Luhmann argued that while a hazard was a threat posed by nature on the individual, a risk was a conscious decision by the individual to face a hazard and possibly become its victim. In other words, risk involved knowledge about the nature of the external world, a decision as to how to face it, and the resolve to stick to one's decision. As I hope to argue as we move along, Luhmann's conceptual precision does not warrant the conclusion according to which non-technological societies – whatever is meant by this – cannot take risks. While it is true that certain societal conditions must be met before the need for taking risks in Luhmann's sense arises, it seems nonetheless appropriate to use Luhmann's definition to focus attention on, and operationalise the twin notions of uncertainty and insecurity which, as I see them, can be used as further elaborations of hazard and risk, respectively.

The line separating uncertainty from insecurity is a fine one, especially since the distinction as made in the sociology of risk is premised on the idea that certain types of society may favour one over the other. Yet, if we bear in mind the fact that what defines human communities is their ability to engage meaningfully with their natural and human environment, then we should, at least in principle, entertain the idea that risk, as opposed to hazards, is central to the possibility of any human community. The degree to which communities will be aware of certain hazards and the extent to which they will place risk production at the centre of their lives will surely vary. Risk sociology should be able to go beyond such fine distinctions to identify what is common to human societies, and use insights thereof to inform general sociological understanding of the nature of social action.

Indeed, it was the focus on these twin notions of uncertainty and insecurity during research that enabled me to grasp a wider theoretical significance of the empirical observations that I was making in the field. This observation was to the effect that much of social action probably consists of the translation of hazards into risk. To put it differently, describing and analysing how the villagers of Patrice Lumumba come to terms with a hostile natural and social environment is actually about understanding social action in both its structural and constitutive elements. Meaning, as Max Weber and all sociologists working in his tradition have convincingly remarked upon, is central to social action. I argue here that the innate ability to translate hazards into risks is part and parcel of the constitution of meaning, for this ability is premised on engaging meaningfully with one's environment. The challenge, therefore, is to work out the analytical and theoretical implications of this realisation for social theory in general and for the description of African social reality in particular. Some of these implications will be brought to light in my discussion of the idea of the taming of fate which, as I argue in the concluding chapter, is precisely this never-ending production of risk, regardless of the type of society in which one lives.[12]

The second theme to emerge from the research was that of modernity, a highly problematic notion in the context of African studies.[13] Discussions with colleagues in the context of our Hummanities Collaborative Research Project at the University of Bayreuth in Germany, but also within the wider framework of development sociology, led me to an increasingly greater awareness of the importance of this notion for an adequate understanding of processes of social change in Africa. To be sure, a concern with modernity in Africa cannot be seen under the best theoretical auspices. This is due to several reasons, chief among them, on the one hand, the politically problematic teleological nature of early modernisation theories with their emphasis on the normative idea of the West as the end product of social change in non-Western societies and, on the other, the deep suspicion with which African scholars look at the notion of modernity.[14]

My interest in modernity as a useful category arose from discussions at the Institute for Advanced Studies in Berlin back in 1999 and 2000. While the general tone was critical of modernity and its aftermath, Jürgen Kocka, a social historian who, incidentally, was one of the masterminds behind the defunct Bielefeld school of social history – which engaged seriously with modernisation theories – suggested that one could account for social action by looking into the manner in which individuals negotiated modernity. I understood Jürgen Kocka to be saying that there could be merit in studying how individuals mastered the rough winds of a very specific form of social change. The challenge posed by this invitation to a more open-minded approach to the notion of modernity was, of course, its definition in a manner that would render it less vulnerable to the charges of teleology that had been levelled on modernisation theories.

Discussions on globalisation processes within the framework of the Humanities Collaborative Research Programme at Bayreuth gave me an opportunity to attempt one such definition. In fact, drawing from the work of Anthony Giddens (1995) and Bjorn Wittrock (2000), my attention was directed to the manifestations of modernity, which acquired the label 'products of modernity'.[15] Dieter Neubert and I understood 'products of modernity' to be material and ideational goods that historically emerged in a European philosophical and scientific institutional context and gradually spread across the world in the guise of technology, political ideas, and institutional arrangements. In trying to understand the nature of external influences acting upon local actors and contexts in the region where I conducted my research,

I found it particularly useful to conceptualise them with reference to the notion of 'products of modernity'. This helped me to sharpen my heuristics, as I came to understand that the background against which local individuals and communities sought to produce risk was structured by the presence of these artefacts. Questions concerning how reliable these artefacts were in their availability and how predictable in their use and effects gave me valuable insights into the context within which individuals go about structuring their lives and imbuing them with meaning.[16]

Teorising social action in the context of local perceptions and interpretations of disasters and crises is, in this sense, about identifying the kinds of basic impulses that make meaning within human communities possible. This meaning, I wish to contend, structures the manner in which individuals produce their social world. It is, to use terminology from the Humanities Collaborative Research Programme at the University of Bayreuth, the meaning that makes local agency possible. Before I briefly describe the structure of the book, I would like to offer a few thoughts on 'local agency', as they are central to the theoretical and methodological options that I favoured in collecting, registering, and analysing my data.

Local Agency[17]

'Local' is a relational notion. It acquires its meaning in relation to other notions. In the context of the research on local perceptions and interpretations of disaster the local acquires its meaning in relation to something that is external. Perceptions and interpretations are local because there are perceptions and interpretations that are presumably external. In this sense, therefore, the 'local' is not only to be understood in its relational nature, but also, and perhaps more fundamentally, as the description of a process. Indeed, the 'local' describes the process through which a spatially and temporally limited context of action is constituted. Analytically, the 'local' can be used to describe a very specific type of social action.

To argue that the 'local' qualifies as an analytical concept is to say that it can help us describe the conditions of possibility of social phenomena. Ethnomethodology uses the notion of 'doing' to draw attention to the fact that social action is not the blind and automatic fulfilment of established rules of action, but rather a document of the way in which social situations, actions, and institutions are produced. One *does* going, eating, talking. What structures such 'doings' is not competence in the recognition of social rules, but the ability to negotiate how life should be 'done'. General sociology tends to counterpose structure and agency as if each of them were discrete entities owing little to one another. Ethnomethodology, in contrast, finds it more useful to see each one of them as the outcome of the presence of the other.

Agency takes place against the background of structure and thereby changes it. Structure is, in fact, an interpretive device that acts upon the individual through the manner in which he or she perceives it. Garfinkel and Sacks discuss this issue at length with reference to the notion of reflexivity (1976: 130–31). They draw attention to how individuals assume the existence of structure at the same as they create it through their own action. Social action, in this sense, documents the interpretation that individuals make of structure, and reflexivity brings to light the empirical elements that make action visible.

'Local' agency for the purposes of this book is everything that went into the production of the social world which, I think, I was able to recover from observing what people do, how they speak about what they do or did and, generally, their relationship to one another or, to put it in Weberian terminology, their social relations. 'Local' agency is the foundation of the everyday lifeworld of the peasants who generously gave me their time. It is not an essential category. Rather, it is one that can only be grasped in its full complexity in the very process of its making. 'Local' agency constitutes itself in relation to a range of external influences – some of which, as indicated above, can be usefully defined as 'products of modernity' – and acquires meaning and relevance to its own producers both as a response to the challenges of everyday life – which are perceived as problematic situations[18] – as well as a conscious engagement with the world as it is.

The 'local' agency I attempt to document in this book is the everyday lifeworld of peasants in a village on the periphery of the small city of Xai-Xai in southern Mozambique. I will describe this village in two steps. The first descriptive step will be taken in the first chapter with a brief historical background to the village. The second descriptive step will occur in chapter four on the basis of villagers' own accounts and perceptions. The village has several names. Initially, that is, before independence in 1975, it was known as Mbalalen. This was in reference to the local clan of Mbalan. Etymologically, in the local Tsonga language, 'Mbalalen' means the home of the Mbalan. In anthropological kinship language we could say that the Mbalan are a patrilineal descent group typical of Southern Mozambique, indeed so typical that a missionary-anthropologist, Henri-Alexandre Junod, declared it the vernacular notion of 'nation' among the Tsonga of Mozambique (Junod 1913). As we shall see later on when we come to discuss conflicting accounts of the causes of floods, the original clan of Mbalan plays a crucial role in the perception of natural events.

The emphasis on local agency is, in a sense, also an attempt at coming to terms with the nature of modernity in Africa. In social theory modernity is a hotly debated concept. Scholars differ widely as to whether it can be defined at all, and if so, how and which features should be considered. The more conservative attempts at a definition see modernity as a specific period in European history that can hardly be applied to other parts of the world. It is believed to have ensued from the Enlightenment as the practical fulfilment of the emancipation of reason from the ties of medieval obscurantism and religious fanaticism. The ethnocentric element in this definition consists in the belief that there is something intrinsically European about the development of history, linking the Enlightenment to the origins of Judeo-Christian and Hellenic culture. Hegel's philosophy of history (1959) is a case in point, particularly his much quoted reluctance to contemplate the idea that the 'spirit' may take hold of African imagination in its triumphal march through history.

One consequence of this idea of modernity was the insistence upon the view that modernity could only have occurred in Europe. A rather watered-down version of this is thought by some to be present in the work of Max Weber, the German sociologist, who is interpreted as locating the logic of capitalist development in Europe (2002). While it might be arguable whether capitalism and modernity can be used interchangeably, the way Weber has often been understood and sometimes unfairly criticized for,[19] the view is consistent with the way in which modernity has tended to be described. Such features as a legal bureaucratic state, progressive entrepreneurship, belief in science as opposed to magic and religion, are, among others, both typical of capitalism as they are of modernity. It is indeed easy to read Weber in this vein, especially when one bears in mind that at times he seems to have believed to be describing the process through which men were constructing their own subjection. He described modernity as an 'iron cage'. Adorno's 'Dialectics of the Enlightenment'[20] echoes some of these fears, particularly the introductory chapter equating the evolution of human history with Odysseus' travails.

In *The Consequences of Modernity* (1990), Anthony Giddens makes a useful distinction between modernity and capitalism, which, however, does not go far enough in differentiating the one from the other. In fact, what he sees as the aftermath of modernity, namely the use of symbolic tokens, for instance, expressing new social relationships and practices across time and space, is precisely what most would describe as the main features of capitalism, including Giddens himself.[21] Still, the distinction is useful because it takes us away from the sterile discussion about the origins of modernity, and draws our attention rather to how different societies come to terms with the passing of traditional society, or at any rate, how different societies deal with the world as it is now.

The more recent debates on modernity seem to be structured around these issues. They define modernity in terms of how different societies and cultures change as they come into contact with one another,[22] with the spirit of capitalism, and an ever-encroaching scientific rationality. In the special issue of the journal of the American Academy of Sciences, *Daedalus* (2000), there are several articles which come to the conclusion that it is more appropriate to think in terms of multiple modernities as against a single, Western and all-conquering singular Modernity. Here modernity is understood as an immanent phenomenon that can be, and indeed is, shaped differently in specific contexts. In a way, then, what is important about modernity is not what it looks like, or should look like, but rather how it is differently experienced, and the implications thereof for social theory.

In the same *Daedalus* issue there is an approach to modernity by Bjorn Wittrock (2000), which offers useful insights into ways of accounting for the way individuals experience it. Wittrock finds it less interesting to establish whether there is any European society that, in its institutional patterns, can be adequately described as modern (p. 36). Rather, he finds it more enticing to track down the basic cultural and institutional impulses that led to the formation of modernity. In his analytical quest he suggests that such impulses posited modernity as a series of promissory notes that challenged individuals and communities to reach out for culturally and historically elaborated goals. In other words, Wittrock appears to assume that modernity can be understood as an immanent condition that structures social action in manners that are significantly different from previous epochs.

In his discussion of the notion of promissory notes Wittrock identifies a number of conditions that must be met before the institutional projects of modernity – for example, a democratic nation-state, a liberal market economy, or a research-oriented university (p. 36) – can be realised. It is beyond the scope of my discussion to present these conditions here. Suffice it to say that they refer to the implications which new assumptions about human beings, their rights, and agency have upon social action and how thereby new affiliations, identities, and institutional realities are constituted (Wittrock 2000: 37). As Wittrock puts it,

> … [M]odernity may be understood as culturally constituted and institutionally entrenched. Promissory notes may serve as generalized reference points in debates and political confrontations. However, these generalized reference points not only become focal points in ideational confrontations; they also provide structuring principles behind the formation of new institutions (ibid. p. 38).

I have argued elsewhere (Macamo, 1999) that Africa is a modern construct. This claim is based on the premise that the awareness of an African cultural identity that can lay claim to a single political and economic destiny was the result of a discursive and practical confrontation with existential conditions brought to the continent by its forced integration into European historicity. In other words, it was in the process of coming to terms with slavery and colonialism that a specific kind of African identity was constituted. This identity drew from the experience of slavery and colonialism to argue for the unity of race,[23] the common cultural roots that had brought about the suffering and the community of fate that followed from the realisation of a common African destiny. Returned slaves from America were very instrumental in this, just as, later, Pan-Africanist activists, nationalists, and philosophers became as they wrestled with their own existential condition.

The argument was originally meant to counter some trends in African critiques of the European influence on the continent. These critiques appeared self-defeating in their outcomes. While they rightly pointed to the overbearing presence of Europe in the conditions of possibility of both an African reality and critique of European presence, they took their outrage too far by stripping Africans of any agency in the whole process. V.Y. Mudimbe's deservedly celebrated *The Invention of Africa* (1988) provides a good illustration of this. Much in line with Said's (1979) deconstruction of the 'Orient', Mudimbe argued that the European power of representation had led to the construction of a notion of Africa which did not necessarily represent reality on the ground. In fact, what individuals came to do and think actually perverted that reality, as African social reality became a function of the European will to power. I understood Mudimbe to be suggesting that our idea of Africa was false because it was a European representation and, even more importantly, to be claiming that, given the nature of power relations, it might be difficult to recover genuinely African discourses about Africa. As he pointed out in an earlier work, paraphrasing Michel Foucault's discussion of Hegel,

> As far as Africa is concerned, truly escaping the West implies understanding really well what it costs to break free from it; that in turn implies knowing the extent to which the West, perhaps insidiously, has come close to us; it implies the ability to establish that which is still western in what allows us to critique the West and, furthermore, appreciate how our reaction to it is perhaps still a ruse which the West places before us and at the end of which it is waiting for us, motionless and elsewhere (…). The West which embraces us in this way may perhaps also choke us. We must equally strive in Africa not only to achieve a rigorous understanding of the ways in which we are currently integrated into the myths of the West, but also of the explicit questions which will allow us to be truly critical of this 'body'[24] (Mudimbe 1982:12-13; translation by the author)

A commitment to history as the setting within which social reality is constituted stands in the way of an uncritical acceptance of Mudimbe's claims. To agree with him on this score would mean, in effect, to deny Africans any original role in the constitution of their own social reality and, perhaps more crucially, promoting an essentialist view of reality. It appeared to me more useful to assume that 'real' Africa was the very outcome of what people, both 'African'[25] and non-African, did within the endless flux of history. The argument that Africa is a modern construct was based on the study of the philosophical debate around the issue whether there is an African philosophy. The study found out that the debate could only be understood within the framework of attempts by individuals to negotiate their way into a world made strange by the presence of strangers. To put it differently, the sociology of knowledge of the debate over the existence of an African philosophy suggested that the central issue therein was the definition of an African space and identity. This was done in dialogue – a dialogue at times violent – with colonialism, which had brought to Africa the promissory notes that Björn Wittrock identifies with the immanence of modernity.

In this sense, the debate owed as much to colonialism as to how Africans reacted to it. Starting with the returning slaves who interpreted their predicament as God's 'providence' meant to make them the harbingers of the emancipation of their 'promised land', and continuing with the Pan-Africanist demand for self-determination all the way through to *Négritude*'s and 'ethnophilosophy's' elaboration of an African essence, Africans were responding to the challenge of colonialism by reaching out to the promises that colonial practice denied them: human dignity, emancipation, and progress.

The African experience of modernity is ambivalent precisely in this sense. Colonialism was the historical form through which modernity became a real social project on the African continent. Colonialism, however, was premised on the denial of that same modernity to Africans. Since the onset of colonialism, African social experience has been structured by the ambivalence of promise and denial that was so constitutive of colonialism and, indeed, as we move into what some call a global era, of globalisation. My claim is that for social theory to be relevant to Africa it must be able to offer concepts that can adequately describe and analyse this ambivalence. The description and analysis of Patrice Lumumba Communal Village against the background of modernity and its effects offers a sound opportunity to meet this challenge.

Of course, it is not as if there has never been any attempt to engage colonialism from an analytical perspective that views it as a practical manifestation of modernity. There have been many attempts by Africanist scholars to come to terms with colonialism and how it has shaped African social reality. These attempts can be situated on both sides of the concept of ambivalence. Indeed, while some have seen these attempts as a rejection of the modernity implied by colonialism, others have instead emphasised Africans' eagerness to join the promise of modernity entailed therein. The latter group of approaches falls under the general category of modernisation theories. These were particularly current in the period running from the early waves of independence in Africa in the late fifties and early sixties all the way up to the seventies. The former, in contrast, include a wide range of perspectives on the continent that stress Africans' ability to negotiate modernity in their own terms.

To be sure, modernisation theories were generally upbeat about Africa's development. Much like Karl Marx's optimistic assessment of British colonialism in India (1978),[26] modernisation theorists saw colonialism as a necessary stage in Africa's historical evolution. Their analytical framework gave pride of place to the tension between tradition and modernity. As far as the framework went, the challenge facing African societies consisted in overcoming tradition in order to gain access to the benefits of modernity. Colonialism had introduced into Africa the value of wage labour, entreperneurship, individualism, and empathy (see Lerner 1964 for an early defence of this position). In the view of modernisation theorists, the absence of these values on the continent accounted for Africa's 'backwardness'.

There are instances of colonial policy that represent this attitude very well. One such instance was described by Frederick Cooper, the American historian of Africa, who in his book on decolonisation analyses, among other things, the colonial preoccupation with the 'detribalized African' (Cooper 1996: 168–70). As with almost everything else in colonial policy, this preoccupation was caught up in the contradictory nature of colonial intervention in African society. On the one hand, both French and British colonial establishments were in need of African labour sufficiently mobile, independent, and autonomous to integrate into the world of capitalist labour markets. Yet, they were weary of allowing Africans to lean too far out of the window of their traditional society, not only because they would place demands on the system to treat them as citizens – and not as 'subjects', as Mamdani (1996) convincingly argued – but also because the idea of a primordial African society was functional to the reproduction needs of the colonial economic system.

Critiques of the kind of modernity purveyed by colonialism have tended to stress both African resistance to, as well as selective appropriation, of modernity. Jean and Joan Comaroff, for instance, have shown in their work that the seemingly irrational pattern of African social action over the past decades can be understood as a subtle critique of capitalism. In becoming deliberately unintelligible to the standard discourse of the social sciences, Africans have been resisting the conditions and terms of their integration into the world (Comaroff 1993; see also White 1993, 1995). A slightly different approach is taken by Jean-François Bayart (2000) who puts forward the idea that the encounter between Africans and Europeans has produced a specific logic within African social action. This logic is marked by a kind of instrumental action by Africans, which consists in seeking to take advantage of the chances and opportunities opened up by the continent's contacts to the rest of the world. He calls this 'extraversion', a concept that echoes some of the ideas suggested by the much older notion of 'rentier capitalism' as used by Marxist scholars in the past.

There is, therefore, an ambivalent moment in Africa's experience of modernity and colonialism. While in and by itself this finding does not present a radically new insight into Africa's constitution over the past decades, it does suggest an analytically useful angle from which to approach the continent from a social scientific perspective. Indeed, this ambivalence can be understood as a framework within which Africans negotiate their way into a world of their own making. In other words, Africans produce their own social reality in dialogue with modernity as they move from colonialism into a world defined by themselves and by what they do in their everyday life.

While colonialism provides the larger canvas against which the terms under which modernity is brought to Africans become visible, it is modernity itself that Africans confront headlong. In this sense, therefore, it becomes extremely important to define the intimations of this modernity and the extent to which it plays a central role in the constitution of African social reality. My description of the way in which Patrice Lumumba villagers tame their fate is meant as a contribution towards the long overdue ethnography of African modernity in its full ambivalent, perverse, but promissory nature.

The Structure of the Book

General Structure and Theoretical Chapters

This book consists of three main parts. The first one is theoretical and methodological and is made up of three chapters. In the second chapter on 'Studying Africa' I discuss central theoretical elements of sociology that I would like to tease out as a way of clearing theoretical ground for identifying what is at stake in studying Africa. I take issue with sociology's preoccupation with the problem of order – which may have an influence on the way Africa is approached generally in the social sciences – and I suggest that far from being deviant, African forms of social life are consistent with what should be the central object of sociology as defined by Max Weber, namely social action. In this first chapter I set the issues in a manner that enables me to formulate the problem at hand with reference to contingency. My claim is that the nature of social action in Africa lends itself to analysis drawing from the insights of the sociology of risk which, of late, has pursued the implications of order and contingency much further than any other theoretical school in sociology.

I delve into this further in chapter three, 'Risk and Social Reality', where I am particularly interested in two related issues. First, I try to ground my own concern with contingency firmly within the sociology of risk, which, in my view, has offered some of the most exciting pieces of theorising in recent years. Secondly, I avail myself of Niklas Luhmann's distinction between hazard and risk to suggest that it might be useful to consider social action with reference to the way in which individuals actually produce risk. I conclude this theoretical and methodological part with a discussion of my own notion of 'contexts of action'. Drawing from phenomenological approaches in sociology I suggest that what individuals do when they produce risk is in fact the creation of conditions for them to be able to act. In other words, individuals act in order to be able to act. I develop a simple analytical framework to ground my approach methodologically and theoretically. This framework is derived from a combination of Luhmann's definition of risk and phenomenological views of social reality and is described further below. I use this framework to integrate my empirical data, which I present in four case studies that make up the second part of the book. I stake my explanatory claims with reference to the meaningfulness of social phenomena and the purposeful action that undergirds it.

My aim in this first theoretical part is to set the parameters of my discussion. In so doing, I raise three issues. The first issue concerns the relevance of African studies which, in this book, I define simply as the study of Africa. I am particularly concerned with the sociological justification of studying Africa and, accordingly, I argue that there is more to it than the practical concerns that have come to dominate social scientific approaches to Africa. The relevance of studying Africa should neither be sought in potential practical solutions to the continent's problems, nor in showing how different the social worlds of Africans are from the social worlds of others. Rather, there is, in my view, a sociological relevance to studying Africa; it boils down to the insights that social phenomena and social action constitutive of them allow us to acquire about the general constitution of human action and society. I try to narrow this concern down to my second issue, which is related to approaches and categories in sociology. To the best of my knowledge, discussions within sociology concerning how best to approach the study of society, or social reality, and, particularly, controversies over the relative merits of interpretive as against functionalist approaches[27] have brought out themes and issues of great theoretical and analytical import. Unfortunately, though, these issues do not seem to have been taken up adequately in the further development of special fields of sociology. The trend seems to have been towards taking sides and pursuing one's own programme in splendid ignorance of the other side. Phenomenological critiques of functionalism, for example, appear to have taken flight from Parsons' grand theorising and opted for less ambitious programmes concerned simply with making commentaries on aspects of social reality. This is all the more surprising since theorists working in fields opposite the theoretical divide appear to have come to conclusions that would be worth much greater consideration than there has been a readiness to show.

One such theorist is Niklas Luhmann, especially in his writings on risk, which are extremely insightful and relevant to anyone concerned with understanding and teasing out the properties of social action. I therefore reach out to these diverse programmes and seek to bring them together here in an attempt to make them relevant to a sociological approach to what individuals do in everyday life. I do not attempt integration as such, a claim that would definitely go beyond the more modest aims I have set myself here. However, I do try to make differently grounded approaches fruitful to the study of a single phenomenon. This one phenomenon is the subject of my third issue. Indeed, I endeavour to formulate a problem that should merit the attention of sociologists in particular and social scientists in general. This problem can be generally stated as the challenge of understanding what we can profit from studying extreme situations. In staking the claim in this manner I already hint at the presence of the aim of making different research programmes fruitful to the study of one phenomenon. As a matter of fact, this presence can be ascertained in the notion of 'contexts of action' which I present later on and which forms the backbone of my analytical synthesis. The more concrete statement of the problem flows directly from the centrality of the notion of 'contexts of action' to the extent that I draw from such key notions as uncertainty, insecurity, and risk to argue that both the constitution and the reconstruction of social reality are deeply implicated in the structure of social action itself.

The Case Studies[28]

I present four case studies of coping with disasters and crises and seek to document, through them, my claim that social action consists in the production of risk with a view to creating contexts of action.

The first study is an attempt to understand local definitions of when a disaster takes place. It is based on the discussion of two visualised group discussions drawing from the sociologist Ralf Bohnsack's reconstructive methodology. It offers valuable insights into the elements that villagers summon up to make sense of the world, including the world of natural phenomena. It is local constructionism *avant la lettre*. The group discussions provide useful elements to understand why individuals respond to misfortune in the manner in which they tend to respond. The second study delves deeper into the problem of interpretation by looking into the social distribution of the stock of knowledge. An important finding in this connection, based on sociologist Hans-Georg Soeffner's discussion of what he calls 'problem-solving institutions', is that processes of social differentiation largely go hand in hand with a society's receptiveness to new forms of knowledge and innovation.

In the third study, I look at a rather marginal group in Patrice Lumumba, namely war refugees who settled in the village in the latter half of the eighties. I discuss their war experiences and draw on conversational analytical tools to expose the structure of social relations documented by their accounts with a view to uncovering the strategies they employed to appraise risk and take decisions. Finally, the fourth study discusses how Christian converts use the process of conversion itself to create their own lifeworld. I look at how biographies are constructed in response to challenging changing contexts. I draw from ethnomethodological insights into practical reasoning to argue that knowledge and identity are one and the same when it comes to producing locality. This particular case study does not draw directly from the empirical material collected in Patrice Lumumba Communal Village, but rather from earlier material collected in another village about 10 kilometres away in the context of earlier work on the influence of a Swiss Protestant mission on the work ethic. I include this material in this presentation to draw attention to the usefulness of the analytical approach gained from risk sociology to the study of less extreme situations. I pitch notions of illness against the experience of education to argue that the constitution of biography provides an adequate response which, in turn, is structured very much along the lines discussed in connection with the creation of contexts of action.

In the more methodological chapter in the first part, namely chapter four, I offer an analytical framework that should help me tie up the loose ends offered by the diverse phenomena I look at in this book. One thing that will become apparent is my eclecticism in the choice and use of qualitative methods to prepare the data for analysis. Indeed, as indicated in the previous paragraph, I use ethnomethodological approaches such as those of Melvin Pollner (mundane reasoning) and Harvey Sacks (membership categorisation devices), as well as German hermeneutical approaches such as those of Hans-Georg Soeffner (problem-solving apparatuses) and Ralf Bohnsack (documentary method), and the contrastive propositional discourse analysis of Rodolphe Ghiglione and Alain Blanchet to make sense of the data I collected on the different phenomena.

As I hope to make explicit in detail later on, there are two main reasons for this methodological eclecticism. First of all, the decision to observe diversity in the choice of methodological approaches was borne out of the nature of the research itself, which proceeded somewhat along the lines of Glazer and Strauss' (1967) grounded theory approach. The data that I use is the result of fieldwork in the true sense of the word, that is, an open-ended research process that allowed me flexibility in the choice of methods and interpretive schemes in the field and away from it. Indeed, all through the research process my approach was heuristic in the sense that I was mainly concerned with finding out the right kinds of questions to ask in ways that would be understandable to my interview partners, but also to myself. The general picture of risk production by way of creating contexts of action emerged out of this heuristic exercise. It appeared, therefore, to be extremely important to be open to what the data could yield and not limit its scope and content by means of a pre-established and universal data analysis system. The choice of approach was determined by the nature of the data itself. I will come back to these issues in due course. Suffice it to say that at the end of each chapter that presents empirical findings I have sought to integrate them into the general analytical framework through summaries that go beyond the specific methodological tools employed to make sense of the data.

Secondly, I am taking seriously the interpretative sociological injunction to treat the social world as one that is grounded in individuals' own attempts to make sense of their world. In this sense, therefore, eclecticism itself became a method to caution me against assuming a familiarity with the researched social world, lest it becomes an obstacle to treating the field as a meaningfully constructed one. I was concerned not to foreclose avenues of inquiry by a strict adherence to one particular methodology and favoured, therefore, an attitude of openness to the assumed richness of the social world which could only be adequately accessed through a concern with the detailed documentation of single cases, in the hope of yielding enough information to warrant typifications in the phenomenological tradition that informs qualitative research.

There is a methodological tension in the choice of tools. Considerable weight is thrown on tools such as those from ethnomethodology and hermeneutical approaches which tend to view social reality in constructionist terms as something that is not prior to action, but is actually produced by it. The reconstructive and structural tools of Bohnsack, on the one hand, and Ghiglione and Blanchet, on the other, suggest however that social reality is prior to action. In other words, in the first instance, namely constructionist, the challenge of description rests on the researcher's ability to identify emerging structures in accounts, whereas in the second instance, that is, reconstructive and structural, the challenge consists in articulating accounts that parallel the reality they document. This is a tension worth maintaining for the sake of illustrating empirically what I mean by the need to reach out to differently grounded research programmes to focus attention on a social phenomenon. For what it is worth, my procedure shows that, independently of how we view social reality and the methods we find appropriate to documenting it, once we decide to focus on the creation of contexts of action it becomes irrelevant whether we are constructionists or reconstructivists. Data gain pride of place and provide the background against which our conclusions can be challenged, or accepted. The possibility of an empirically grounded discussion of issues seems paramount and worth an apparent epistemological inconsistency.

The Concluding Part

The third and final part of this book is the conclusion. Under the title 'The Taming of Fate' I draw together the several strands which make up the research. More specifically, I present and then discuss the relevance of my findings for the social scientific study of Africa. I indicate, without going to any considerable length at attempting a stronger theoretical integration to beat new paths, that the way in which the villagers of Patrice Lumumba tame their fate holds very important theoretical and analytical insights, which are of practical relevance to sociology in general, and development work in particular.

For too long social theory has premised the plausibility of its knowledge on a relevant distinction between societies on the basis of levels of technological development. The work of the founding fathers, especially Durkheim's and

Weber's, was particularly instrumental in this regard and has given social scientists important theoretical and conceptual tools to go about making sense of the worlds that human beings have created for themselves. Working out the specificities of modern society has been a useful and necessary exercise to sharpen concepts and develop theoretical frameworks that are sensitive to context and to what determines context. To briefly give examples, Durkheim's distinction between organic and mechanical solidarity, or Weber's concern with types of action enabled social scientists to develop an appreciation of differences that have proven to be constitutive of social worlds. Yet, as critiques of colonial anthropology have brought to light,[29] driven to the extreme, such distinctions have tended to create African social realities which appear to be more of an artefact of power differentials between Europe and Africa than they could be reduced to conceptual precision.

Not surprisingly, my research confirms the existence of fundamental differences between African and European forms of social organization. I contend, however, that this finding is in itself trivial for the reasons I briefly introduced further above and I explore in more detail in the conclusion. The research also draws attention to what the two have in common, namely the simple fact that the social world draws from culture and values, provides context for action, and yields the categories that social scientists need in order to be able to account for social relations. The following descriptions of how individuals and communities in this village cope with disasters and crises bring this to the fore. They show that the same impulses that are at the root of action everywhere else are also present in this context.

Drawing from the very exciting and promising work that the sociology of risk has initiated, and seeking methodological inspiration in sociological schools of thought which give pride of place to the analysis of properties of action as documents of social reality, I suggest that we can profitably understand the nature of modern society and the dangers which it faces, but also the nature of African social reality, if we spend some time in seeking to understand how individuals act in order to be able to act. After all, if there is anything basic about social life, surely, this is one of them.

I spend some time discussing the notion of 'taming fate' which figures prominently in the title. The choice was both stylistic as well as programmatic. Stylistically, I sought a poignant way of summarising what research in Southern Mozambique gave me to understand about the constitution of everyday life. Life in Patrice Lumumba Communal Village is an engagement with a narrative within which individuals figure centrally as heroes, but one which appears to steer aimlessly in history. The village and its inhabitants are caught in the structures of this narrative and seek to interpret their role within them at the same time as, in so doing, they interpret it anew, give the story new twists, and make it truly their own. I found the idea of fate that is tamed alluring precisely because it drew my attention to the extent to which the very possibility of social life rests on individuals' ability to engage their own worlds. Programmatically I wanted to stress the tension between structure and agency and make it fruitful to an epistemologically and methodologically eclectic approach to a singular social phenomenon that draws most of its coherence from my belief in the idea that our ability to describe and analyse social reality stands and falls with the place we accord to social action.

I hope that the overall result of my efforts will show that the notion of risk combined with that of social action can help us make extreme situations methodologically and analytically fruitful to the analysis of ordinary everyday life situations. While the larger context within which ordinary everyday life situations occur may vary according to the degree of technological progress, use of and reliance on science, and freedom from material want and the whims of nature, the single most important guide to the constitution of social reality remains social action. My attention in the following chapters is focussed on this guide.

Part One

Theoretical and Methodological Issues

2

Studying Africa

Introduction

African studies can be depressing, as Gavin Kitching (2000) suggested in a personal account describing the reasons that led him to abandon the field.[30] The ensuing controversy showed, however, that not all those who operate within the field of African studies develop similar frames of mind. The Malawian scholar Paul Zeleza (2003) suggested in a long and thick indictment of the political economy of 'African studies' that self-serving and paternalist attitudes towards the African continent stood in the way of an adequate understanding of African reality. As the very title of his book made clear, namely *Manufacturing African Studies*, Zeleza argued that the knowledge that passed for an academic account of the social reality of the continent was, in fact, an artefact of a combination of personal and political interests owing little to genuine scientific inquiry. The case seems overstated, but there is something to it.

In this chapter I want to discuss the problem of studying Africa in the social sciences. My discussion will bear on a claim, which is not at all new, to the effect that a fundamental problem besetting African studies consists in the use of theoretical and analytical approaches developed for the study of societies structurally different from most African societies. The reader should note a little nuance in the statement of the problem. In fact, I am not claiming that using concepts developed outside of Africa is a problem in itself. I am claiming that societies differ in their structure and that concepts are sensitive to this. Failure to take this into account has led to the production of representations of Africa, which appear to be a function of the analytical dimensions of the concepts deployed, rather than representations of African social reality in its full complexity.[31]

One consequence of this is the failure to treat European social reality in its proper historical context and, concomitantly, the failure to appreciate the extent to which concepts are tools for understanding, rather than empirical descriptions in themselves.[32] In fact, many scholars have drawn attention to the pitfalls of applying inadequate conceptual schemes to societies which resist the underlying analytical categories. Some scholars, such as Mudimbe (1988), Mbembe (2001), and Miller (1990), to name but a few, have explained these representations with a Western will to power over Africa. In other words, the criticism has borne on the extent to which knowledge production can be innocent of the political, economic, and historical context within which it becomes possible. As is immediately apparent, we are faced here with a massive claim that touches upon the very possibility of knowledge and raises issues concerning objectivity in the social sciences. These are issues that go far beyond my modest interest here, and yet they need to be raised.

My claim is, of course, less ambitious than the epistemological research programme suggested by the issues. I am setting off from the very trivial observation that the studies which I conducted into how individuals and communities cope with disasters and crises brought out into the open the fact that whatever the level of development of these communities they operate within a social world of their own making. They made and make their social world drawing from cultural values and ideas which structure the frameworks within which they go about their lives. Max Weber's invitation to sociologists to adopt an interpretive approach that assumes that social action is embued with meaning which, in turn, makes sense to the actors themselves within cultural frameworks that may help to explain individual motivation, is as relevant to these individuals and communities as it is to individuals and communities in technologically more advanced societies. In this sense, then, in this chapter I am not concerned about arguing against theoretical and analytical approaches that reveal a will to power on the grounds that they are inadequate. Nor do I want to raise suspicions on the quality of the knowledge about Africa produced so far.

Rather, I am concerned with engaging seriously with the practical implications of doing science with theoretical and analytical tools developed under different rationales in contexts which, at least on the surface, appear different. To put it differently, my aim is to argue that the difficulty of applying these approaches does not ensue from an intrinsically different nature of African reality, as some would readily suspect, but rather, and curiously enough, from the failure to see the extent to which social action in Africa responds to the same impulses that account for social reality elsewhere. A closer look at fundamental theoretical debates in sociology reveals that the problem is, in fact, a theoretical one that has to do with the claims of the social sciences concerning their ability to make sense of social reality. I will discuss this issue in the first three chapters by taking a look at the controversy over order and contingency within sociology, but also with the methodological suggestion to include the idea of contexts of action in the appreciation of social action. The purpose of this discussion is to draw attention to a theoretical debate, which in my view lays bare the oversight of which Africa has consistently been a victim. The unresolved dispute over whether social theory should be concerned with the problem of order or contingency is important for an understanding of the reasons why theoretical and analytical approaches to Africa have tended to misrepresent social reality. This unresolved dispute accompanied my own attempts at formulating my research interest concerning local responses to crises and disasters.

Therefore, revisiting this discussion will allow me to place emphasis on certain key notions such as uncertainty, but also trust, which appear to be constitutive of African social reality as much as they are constitutive of social reality elsewhere. These are two of the key issues that emerged from the empirical studies. The discussion of these notions will be preliminary in nature, as I hope to return to them in detail later in the book. For the purposes of introducing the subject it will suffice to articulate them with the much wider notion of modernity which I briefly discussed in the introduction and which seems to me central to any attempt at understanding current social phenomena in Africa. The idea will be to draw attention to the historically constituted precariousness of African social reality.

Modernity deserves attention because its constitutive features are central to the structural conditions underlying everyday life in most of Africa. My argument is that features of modernity enable us to sharpen our perspective on social action in Africa, thereby, bringing into bold relief the tension that makes the application of theoretical and analytical approaches in the social sciences such an uphill undertaking as far as the description of Africa is concerned. The notion of modernity is not one that can be alluded to in a light-hearted manner. In African studies, in particular, there is a general discomfort with the concept which stems largely from the normative and even political use to which it was put in the past, especially in the context of modernisation theories. Indeed, in the past, modernity tended to be used as shorthand for accounting for differences between Europe and Africa. Africa's perceived traditional nature became functional to colonial rule, to the grounding of certain intellectual pursuits, and, in our own days, to the legitimation of development intervention. This has led some scholars to reject the usefulness of the concept altogether, the most recent examples of which being James Ferguson (1999) and Frederick Cooper (1996). While the former seems to interpret the disappointment of Copperbelt miners' expectations as the failure of modernity and what it can achieve in Africa, the latter questions its analytical claims and argues that modernity only has a discursive value. These are strong reservations, which I hope to address in this book.

One aspect of modernity on which I wish to concentrate in particular, especially as it inheres in the structure of everyday life, is what I have called elsewhere its 'ambivalent nature' (Macamo 2005b). Indeed, the experience of modernity in Africa has been a highly ambiguous one, premised as it has been on the twin opposing forces of promise and denial. In an earlier analysis of the regulation of native labour in the Portuguese colony of Mozambique (see Macamo 2003c) I was struck by the profoundly ambivalent nature of official colonial discourse and practice. While, on the one hand, the declared aim of the regulation of native labour was to free the African from the bondage of his primitive life and frame of mind, thereby presenting itself as a promise, the colonial State's intervention into African social life by way of tutelage over the African meant in effect, on the other hand, that the very same liberating moment, that is, labour, was premised on the denial of individual fulfilment and emancipation. Indeed, regulation itself made necessary an idea of 'African society' that made it next to impossible for Africans to enjoy the fruits of emancipation expected to be brought about by labour.[33] In other words, modernity has promised emancipation from the forces of nature and the arbitrariness of human action while at the same bringing about structures which have tended to actually deny this promise. In taking up this ambivalence, I aim at articulating it with notions that are central to the sociology of risk, namely uncertainty and insecurity.

Before I delve further into these issues, I offer a brief historical background to the research terrain. A fuller presentation of the terrain will be given in chapter four within the framework of the discussion of Patrice Lumumba villagers' accounts of their own lifeworld.[34]

Studying Africa, Understanding Patrice Lumumba

Two years after independence, more precisely, in 1977, Mbalalen was transformed into a communal village to resettle victims of severe floods that had taken place earlier that year.[35] It was given the name 'Patrice Lumumba communal village'[36] by the authorities, but most people in the neighbouring city of Xai-Xai as well as members of the Mbalan clan continued to call it Mbalalen. Later still, in the year 2000, people rescued from the Limpopo valley, following even more severe floods in that year, were settled in Patrice Lumumba Communal Village. The extension made to the village for this purpose became known as 'Patrice Lumumba 2000 Communal Village' in reference to the original post-independence name. Some people still call it Mbalalen, others call it 'Patrice Lumumba', and still others call it 'Patrice Lumumba 2000'.

Sitting uneasily on dry sanddunes leading up to the Indian Ocean, the village offers its residents little to eke out an existence. Most of them have fields and cattle down in the Limpopo valley. This is particularly the case for those who were settled in the village following the 1977 floods. Since these fields are about five to seven kilometres away from the village, most have built small shacks in the valley where they spend the night during the farming and harvesting seasons. The cattle are looked after by young boys who, for this purpose, hardly ever come to the village. The villagers distinguish the valley and the upper part in terms of what they can get from the soil. The valley is 'Bilen' which in Tsonga, the local Bantu language, has come to be synonymous with the dark and fertile mud soil in the valley. In actual fact, the name refers originally to a clan by the name of 'Bila', which traditionally has ruled over most of the downstream valley of the Limpopo River.[37] 'Bilen', the soil, is associated with cash crops such as cotton, wheat, rice, and maize, but also with vegetables for market sale, namely cabbage, lettuce, carrots, tomatoes, peppers, etc.[38] 'Bilen' fields tend to be the preserve of men.

The upper part – where the village is located – is known as *nthlaven*, which means 'on the mountain'. There are, indeed, many hilltops in the area. They are part of the landscape, which consists of sanddunes blown together by winds from the nearby Indian Ocean. The soils host '… creeping species, some of them succulent, which help to compact the sand, diminish the effects of wind erosion and add nutrients to the soil' (Bandeira et al 2007: 39). These soils absorb large amounts of rainwater. The crops favoured by villagers, such as cassava, sweet potato, and, to some extent, peanuts tend to impoverish the soils and the growing demographic pressure on land does not help to minder the problem.

A study conducted to ascertain the quality of the soil found that maize, a staple in the region, was contributing a great deal towards hastening the degradation of the soils as it required considerable amounts of water and nutrients.[39] Most families have small gardens where they grow these crops for immediate family consumption. They are tended to by women. Some households have fruit trees – mangoes and cashewnuts. While those who have been living in the village for much longer – that is, since 1977 – have managed to build solid concrete houses with piped water and electricity, those who came later – that is, in the course of the 1980s and in 2000 – live in makeshift housing, always subject to dust swept in by the ocean breeze and to a scorching hot sun.

They are worse off, but the longer-term residents are only marginally better off.[40] Although they indeed have electricity and piped water, most of them cannot afford the electricity bills and, what is more, the water services are unable to bring the water to their taps. Nearly all villagers are dependent on boreholes for water. Women and children spend hours on end to fetch twenty litres of water. The boreholes are manually operated and are often out of order. There are six of them scattered across the village. Every time I was in the field there were only three, at most, in operation. Once I accompanied a team of engineers and technicians who had been asked by the authorities to repair broken boreholes and was confronted with a graphic example of one of the consequences of the presence of products of modernity. One borehole had been out of use for nearly one year and the villagers, including the man in charge of maintenance, thought that the ghost of a man who used to live in the place where the borehole was dug was preventing the water from flowing because the authorities had failed to ask for his permission to dig the well there. Alas, it turned out that the borehole pump was once broken and the man who repaired it had screwed back the filter the wrong way round. This led to the failure of the suction mechanism.

Traditionally, members of the Mbalan clan as well as those villagers who had come from the valley in 1977 had several sources of livelihood. Over the years, wage labour became central, as most people took up migrant labour in neighbouring South Africa and others sought paid employment in the nearby city of Xai-Xai or even in the distant capital city of Maputo. It was usually the men who took up paid employment. Women for the most part stayed at home and tended their *nthlaven* gardens. Differences in income are consistent with the type of paid employment that families take up. As a general rule, families with members working in South Africa tend to be better off – boasting better housing and, in theory, access to such amenities as electricity and piped water.

Patrice Lumumba Communal Village is by any account a rough place to live in. Its soil resists farming and the more fertile valley lands require technical inputs that are beyond the reach of the ordinary villager. Emplyoment opportunities in the nearby city of Xai-Xai as well as in South Africa have been dwindling for the past twenty years. The usual male biography of doing one's initial stint in the gold mines of South Africa at the age of eighteen, followed by two brief stints to accumulate enough money to start a family, and several further stints before settling down to a life of farming and cattle-breeding in one's forties has been radically disrupted by regional political and economic changes beyond any measure of individual local control. The South African mining industry reduced the number of Mozambican migrant workers, rendering most young men into the uncertain situation of illegal border crossing. At the time of research, those crossing the border illegally were locally known as *mafohlan*, that is, trespassers. The floods in 2000 washed an unknown type of fish bred in South African fish farms downstream into Xai-Xai; it was given the name *mafohlan*, thus establishing a parallel with what young men did.

There are several schools in Patrice Lumumba. Normal attendance allows pupils to leave school with basic secondary education (grade 9). There are not enough places to go round, so competition is stiff, almost always involving bribes to teachers and educational authorities. On completion young people face a life of uncertainty, as the available schools do not provide them with any useful skills. Those who do not make it to South Africa or to Maputo, the capital city 200 kilometres away, kill time cutting reeds for sale, selling drinks, biscuits, cigarettes, and basic foodstuffs at market stalls or apprenticing as carpenters or mechanics. In general, all these activities are highly precarious, for customers do not pay – because they cannot afford to. In the final analysis, people pursue trades for the sake of doing something, not because they can actually live off them.

There is a health post in the village and, in theory, villagers are lucky to have a big provincial hospital right next to them. They can go to this hospital when they have major ailments or even to the public clinic in the city of Xai-Xai – a mere three to four kilometres away. In practice, however, the village is experiencing a very dramatic health situation. HIV-AIDS has become a major killer, especially for young men engaged as migrant workers in South Africa. Number one killer, however, continues to be malaria, a disease that had been brought under some kind of control in the late seventies and early eighties through spraying, but then returned with a ferocious vengeance.

During a group discussion with a cross-section of villagers a traditional healer remarked significantly, while admitting that he was powerless and referred people to the hospital, that he was unable to understand why diseases which he had been able to cure in the past resisted treatment now. This puzzlement was brought home in a poignant manner by other participants in the discussion who wove a conspiracy theory around their community's vulnerability to disease. Indeed, they remarked that, in the past, they had been able to walk long distances, even as far as South Africa – more than 400 kilometres away – and queried why they could no longer do so today. Their answer was that vitamins given to women and babies in hospital weakened them on purpose so that when they grew up they would require, and hence be dependent on, cars, bicycles, and trains to cover long distances.

This is the everyday lifeworld that forms the backbone of my empirical and analytical work in southern Mozambique.[41] The 'local' agency I am concerned with here consists of the strivings of individuals to make sense of a world that continually threatens to escape them at the same time as, paradoxically, they seek to recover it through their perseverance and the manner in which they cling to life. I am attempting to retrieve the story of the life of the people of Patrice Lumumba. These are not people who are merely born, live, and die.[42] They are people who struggle on and, in facing up to the challenges of a life that insists on turning them into guests in their own world, they give us useful and important insights into the constitution of social action.

In the final analysis I propose to argue in this chapter that African social reality provides a fertile terrain for social theorising. In the course of the discussion, which will be further elaborated on in the chapters that follow, I wish to introduce the notion of 'contexts of action' as a guiding analytical framework towards studying and understanding Africa. I will argue that observing social action in Africa, and elsewhere for that matter, is about describing the manner in which social actors actually create the conditions that should enable them to act. In the following chapters, I will document my indebtedness to phenomenological approaches. By placing themselves on the side of contingency vis-à-vis order they have drawn attention to the extent to which social reality can be viewed as an emergent entity resting on the strivings of individual actors to make sense of their lifeworld.

The notion of 'contexts of action' is, as already indicated above, of central importance to me. My methodological options in the empirical research on which my case-studies rest have been strongly influenced and structured by this constructionist view, but I also draw from reconstructive methodologies in order to emphasise my assumption that there is a context for action, and that accounts yield emerging entities just as they are deeply influenced by structure. In analysing my empirical material I have relied largely on hermeneutical and phenomenological tools to elicit coherent accounts from the data. These accounts bear directly on the ways in which social actors act in order to be able to act. To put it differently, I look for instances of the manner in which individuals *achieve* social action.

In the next section, I wish to take a look at some elements of the epistemology of studying Africa. I intend to use sociology and its founding preoccupations as the starting point for developing some ideas concerning the elements which appear to structure representations of Africa while at the same preventing us from appreciating the fundamental intellectual value of studying Africa for the sake of pursuing sociology. This will enable me to start laying the groundwork for further elaboration on the notion of 'contexts of action'.

The Problem of Order

The popular understanding of sociology depicts it as the study of society. While this may seem obvious enough, the exact meaning of the study of society has been at the centre of heated debates over the soul of the discipline. Debates have centred on knowing just what is meant by society when it is identified as the object of sociology. Is it society as a structure acting upon individuals, or rather individuals producing structure through their action? The terms of the debate were already set out by Weber (1980) and Durkheim (1988) with their emphasis on social action and social facts respectively. Ever since, doing sociology has often meant siding with one or the other of these approaches. Talcott Parsons' monumental attempt to produce a synthesis with *The Structure of Social Action* (Parsons 1967; see also Parsons 1964) was able, for a time, to generate the impression that sociologists had reached a consensus over the object of their efforts.

The American sociologist Jeffrey Alexander once wrote that Parsons' *The Structure of Social Action* had established 'the base line vocabulary for modern sociology' (Alexander, 1988: 97). Alexander was referring to Parsons' reformulation of sociology's object as the study of order, that is, the question concerning what holds society together (Alexander, 1988: 97). This reformulation has come to be known as 'the problem of order'. Indeed, sociologists have seemed to puzzle over the possibility of order in a context within which individuals pursue their own goals and interests. Some have traced the puzzle back to Hobbes, adopting his nightmare vision of a war of all against all. It is not at all clear whether the Hobbesian genealogy is warranted, but for reasons of relevance I do not intend to pursue this issue further. Suffice it to say that the assumption according to which the absence of external constraint, where individuals pursue their interests, leads inevitably to chaos has informed much theorising and empirical work in sociology. This made functionalism inevitable as the theoretical mainstay of the discipline. Talcott Parsons had argued that social order was assured by the individual internalisation of norms and values, a solution to the problem of order, which required a functional view of society and its conceptualisation as a social system.[43] Even scholars as critical to this functionalist view as Anthony Giddens has been, have not been able to shake off the long shadow cast by Parsons' normative solution. I suspect that Giddens' belief that individuals look for 'ontological security' owes its coherence to the preoccupation with order as the central concern of sociology (Giddens 1995).

The pride of place which the problem of order has taken in sociology is of direct relevance to an understanding of the epistemology of African studies. While sociology as a discipline is one among many disciplines that have sought to describe and analyse African social reality, its theoretical inputs are unmistakable. The dominant assumption from the fifties through to the seventies and eighties with regard to the traditional nature of African society, is not wholly unrelated to the problem of order. The perception that sociology studies modern, industrial society implies the existence of an opposite, traditional society, contemporaneous but geographically distant. No sociological account of the emergence of sociology as an intellectual pursuit will be complete without reference to the conditions which called for it in the Europe of the nineteenth century in the first place. Indeed, the major social, political, and economic transformations associated with growing industrialisation and the need to find adequate solutions to the ensuing problems led to the development of a way of looking at social relations which basically constituted them as empirical realities.[44]

The bottom line for the emergence of sociology can be simply construed. In fact, it can be argued that the science of society did not emerge because there was something out there called 'society' and which was crying out for study. It took the intellectual work of producing concepts and methods through which 'society' could be made visible and, subsequently, a relevant object of human concern. To put it bluntly, the emergence of sociology was a response to a longing for the invention of society, that is, a coherent empirical entity that could be retrieved conceptually at the same time that it lent itself as the object of policy intervention. Sociology provided the tools for describing 'society' and, in the process, made it visible, not only for study but also for interventions of all sorts.

The sociology of Emile Durkheim is particularly enlightening in this respect. One of the most interesting, if not the greatest achievement of his sociology, was his attempt to define the object of a science of society. A careful reading of his methodological essays shows that the concepts he wanted sociologists to use to account for society were not only descriptive tools, but also building blocks through which he actually invented society. Durkheim's notion of 'social facts' is a case in point. For him the notion of a social fact refers to ways of behaving, doing things, and relating to other people which are not individually determined, but given, influenced from outside. Central to his definition of a social fact is the idea that the social is constituted via external constraints. From this understanding of the social flows the logical conclusion of a whole held together functionally. We act in certain ways because we are members of a family and have roles within it which are independent of our individual will and are determined by forces external to us. In other words, social facts refer us to the constitution of society by allowing us to see what it is made of, and where it starts and ends.[45]

Durkheim's methodological statements were not just claims for the scientific status of sociology, but also statements about social relations as a whole at a time when they were being threatened by rapid social change in Europe. Sociology helped to raise awareness for something larger than immediate and individual social relations. It contributed towards making visible something that was no longer taken for granted. With its analytical tools, it helped to actually constitute society as an empirical reality. Herein lies the genius of classical sociologists, who in the turbulence of rapid social change discerned something much larger with which individuals should engage. Sociology was in an important sense one response to the search for community in the face of rapid social change. It offered an idea of a radically different community, one no longer based on status and face-to-face interactions, but rather based on contract and functional interdependence, among other elements. Notwithstanding these remarks, or perhaps precisely because of them, it should actually seem clear that the idea according to which sociology studies industrial, modern society needs to be qualified in order to make sense at all and for the purpose of establishing the contribution of sociology's concern with the problem of order to the nature of social scientific knowledge on Africa[46].

Indeed, sociology studies modern industrial society to the extent that it represents it in contrast to an assumed opposite, namely 'traditional society'. Yet, it is important to stress that modern society and traditional society are ideal-types and, as such, they can be quite illuminating. However, in the further development of the social sciences the perception that these were just ideal types gave way to a belief that both traditional society and modern society were accurate descriptions of actually existing societies. This was an unfortunate development, for it was partly at the root of highly normative approaches to social reality to the extent that ideal-types ceased to be treated as background against which reality could be checked out. They became commensurate with European empirical reality at the same time as non-European empirical reality came to be viewed normatively as failing to live up to the ideal-types. It is in this sense that the problem of order rears its ugly head against a useful study of African social reality.

Durkheim had made a useful distinction between forms of solidarity identifying two basic types, namely those based on mechanic and those based on organic forms of social integration.[47] In making this distinction, however, he was not describing actually existing societies. Again, a society based on organic solidarity was what Durkheim saw as the most likely outcome of the process of change that was sweeping across Europe, even if in his most pessimistic mood he feared that *anomie* would end up reigning supreme. In any case, the distinction between mechanical and organic solidarity reflected both his epistemological as well as practical interests. As far as his epistemological interests were concerned, the distinction helped him to place the changes in an explanatory framework that, in a teleological sense, allowed him to account for the breakdown of forms of social integration. Rapid social change did not necessarily mean the end of social cohesion, but perhaps the beginning of an era in which social integration would be achieved in a different manner. As for the practical interest, this was tied in with sociology itself, since the distinction also allowed him to lend legitimacy to sociology as the science which would provide the means through which social order could be made possible.

This conceptual distinction between traditional and modern society has had quite devastating effects on the study of Africa. As already pointed out, understanding sociology as the science of modern, industrial society has had the effect of removing history from the concerns of sociology and of confining societies branded 'traditional' to the past and perceiving them, as Shalini Randeria (1999) has pointed out, as the past of Europe. In his *Time and the Other*, Johannes Fabian (1983) had argued pretty much along the same lines with his point to the effect that, in dealing with the non-European, anthropology regarded him and his institutions as Europe's past. It was J. F. McLennan who provided the justification for this understanding of anthropology, when he argued that non-European societies were not chronologically old, only old in structure, something which rendered them interesting for an understanding of the historical evolution of contemporary society.

The social conditions that led to the development of sociology in nineteenth-century Europe have increasingly come to dominate African social reality over the past hundred years. Colonialism, the emergence of a cash economy and wage labour, a degree of industrialisation, and urbanisation have also contributed to rapid social change on the continent. Along with this there emerged a new sense of integration, which often was made sense of in political terms through the language of the Enlightenment: progress, freedom, and rights. I draw from my own work here (Macamo 1999) to argue that, broadly speaking, colonial rule created conditions that made Africa as a modern construct possible. In responding to the challenges posed by foreign domination, Africans engaged themselves and their immediate external world in a discussion about their relationship to their historical trajectory. In so doing they made Africa visible as a community of fate and values.

The term 'Africans' should be understood as shorthand for those who thought up Africa as a community of fate and, in the process, re-invented themselves as such. African scholars have tended to favour two positions on the status of the continent. One position holds that there is an original African community which was thrown out of history by European colonialism. The challenge for this position lies in recovering this original community and using it to rehabilitate the continent. Diverse movements like *Négritude*, *African socialism*, and *African personality* seem to have been informed by this concern. The other position maintains that Africa is a European invention with the purpose of serving the European will to power. They see the continent irretrievably lost in the discursive power of Europe and maintain, as a consequence, that calls for a return to an original Africa are pointless.[48]

These positions come especially into view in the long-running debate concerning the question whether there is an African philosophy or not.[49] Those who argue in favour of its existence define it in terms of a unique African way of perceiving the world – *la philosophie bantoue* – whereas those who argue against hold that this unique African *Weltanschauung* reflects the ideological hold Europe has over Africans' imagination. As I have shown in earlier work[50] it is possible to trace these debates back to their origins in the middle of the nineteenth century, when former African slaves in the Americas (were) returned to Africa. Their calls for the emancipation of African peoples from political and economic constraints provided important avenues to subsequent intellectual debates on the condition of Africa and Africans. These debates appeared to be firmly grounded in the existential condition of Africans and the continent. This realisation led me to assume that the debate over whether there is an African philosophy could not simply be about that. Rather, it seemed to document important social dynamics that were in very important respects constitutive of Africa.

Returning slaves were the first to posit Africa as a *sui generis*[51] category, pretty much the same way sociology became the means through which industrial society began to be represented. Men like Edward Blyden, Samuel Crummel, and Africanus Horton, to name but a few of the most articulate returned slaves, interpreted the experience of slavery, colonialism, and lack of political rights as moments in the construction of an African community of fate and values. Where there had been no sense of belonging together, of Africa as it were, struggles for political rights, cultural recognition, and economic emancipation gave it reality and substance. It is likely that African intellectuals engaged in inventing Africa failed to see their intellectual activity as a crucial moment in that invention because of the conditions under which intellectual discourse in Africa emerged. These conditions were largely determined by European ideas about non-Europeans, wherein the conceptual distinction between traditional and modern society was central. Assured by intellectual debates at home which seemed to confirm their daily experience of life in the 'heart of darkness' – to use a famous literary description of Africa[52] – colonialists went about their work in Africa as if, indeed, they were dealing with traditional societies.

The native experience of modernity was perceived essentially in terms of a breakdown of norms and the concomitant disintegration of the traditional normative order. Colonial officers' response to this perception was no different from the general attitude that African studies have tended to adopt in their description and analysis of Africa. Just as colonial officers sought to preserve traditional society as the most appropriate vehicle to long term stability,[53] scholars studying Africa have also tended to favour approaches which depict African social reality as a deviation from a norm, the contours of which strangely resemble ideal representations of Western society. The modernisation paradigm that swept across several social scientific disciplines in the early sixties and continues to exercise its fascination over development policy makers was in important ways a response to this diagnosis. The study of Africa became almost imperceptibly the study of disorder as a recent, much discussed book would come to state in an open manner (Daloz and Chabal 1999). Any cursory look at books on Africa will invariably document this. Book after book on Africa has been concerned with showing the patterns of deviation. The popular complaint about the depiction of Africa as a continent of crisis and catastrophes is to be accounted for by this normative approach to its study.

What this discussion shows, however, is not so much that concepts developed in Europe are inappropriate to studying Africa as the much more fundamental issue of the definition of the object of sociology. Indeed, it is the preoccupation with the problem of order that should bear much of the blame for the shortcomings of African studies. This is all the more interesting as, early in the development of modern sociology, important reservations were made against functionalism and its interest in order. Almost at the same time as mainstream sociology was busy thrashing out the theoretical and analytical details of its functionalist paradigm, currents erupted within the discipline which sought to put the concern with the problem of order into the right perspective. These currents traced their genealogy to Max Weber's interest in action, but most of all it was the reception of European sociology by American Pragmatism (Mead and Dewey) and, in particular, Alfred Schütz's phenomenological reformulation of sociology that fanned the flames of dissent against functionalist hegemony.[54]

In subsequent chapters (chapters three and four) I will delve into the details of this dissent with more concrete suggestions of the analytical and methodological challenges implied by it. A much more pressing task for the time being is to draw attention to the general theoretical nature of the reservations, as they have significant methodological implications, a large part of which bears directly on the subject of this book. In actual fact, critics of the functionalist paradigm rejected the idea that sociology was concerned with the problem of order. The assumption that social order could be accounted for with reference to normative constraints on individuals assumed, in the view of the critics, precisely the kinds of things that needed to be accounted for.

During fieldwork there was a story doing the rounds in Patrice Lumumba village. The villagers believed that there was an animal up and about at night. They called it *xingoko?*, a word which in the Shangan original does not really refer to any living and known animal. Nobody has ever seen a *xingoko?*. However, everyone was sure of its existence. I heard the story from a considerable number of people. This was a strange story. In the course of conversations with the villagers, however, I came to understand the background and to make sense of it. It was often mentioned in connection with attempts to account for everything that was wrong with community life. It seemed to me a powerful commentary on the problem of contingency in everyday local life.

There are three aspects of the story that need to be known. First of all, the villagers were perfectly aware of the fact that this animal does not exist. Yet, they were equally aware of the fact that it was up and about in their village. It would seem, therefore, that there was a serious logical problem in the reasoning of the villagers concerning this phenomenon. I asked them to tell me why they believed that this non-existing animal was in their midst. Their reply was inductive. They said there were certain things that happened at night, which pointed to the presence of the *xingoko*. Dogs barked frenetically for no apparent reason and the death rate was very high in the village. In the local imagination dogs have the ability to see invisible beings. As some villagers told me, if a person rubs the tears of a dog on his own eyes he can see 'things', that is, beings which that ordinary people cannot see. As for the death rate the villagers believed that malaria and HIV-AIDS were insufficient as explanations, for disease is part of life and has been with them for as long as anyone can remember.

Secondly, these 'animals' are actually people who can turn themselves into animals. That is why *svingoko*[55] do not exist, and yet they do. The villagers were pretty sure who the person was who turned herself into a *xingoko*. It was an old lady who lived on her own. When I asked why anyone would turn herself into a *xingoko*, I was told that the purpose was to 'scare people'. The reasoning behind this reply is no different from the beliefs that sustained witch-hunts in medieval Europe[56]. Witchcraft seemed an end in itself. European witches killed babies in order to extract an ointment which they applied on their brooms in order to be able to fly so that they could snatch more babies to extract ointment in order to fly… and so on.[57] The old lady in Patrice Lumumba turned herself into a *xingoko* in order to scare people at night so that she could be able to turn herself into a *xingoko* and stalk the nights.

Thirdly, no villager seemed concerned about establishing for sure whether the suspected lady was actually the culprit. Interestingly enough, everyone knew how to establish the fact. As I was repeatedly told by villagers, people who turn themselves into *xingonko* leave a bucket full of water in their bathroom.[58] The reason why they do this is is that if anyone goes to check whether they are at home they can quickly turn themselves back into their own selves and pretend nothing had happened. When I asked them, puzzled yet again, why they did not simply empty the bucket and wait for the person in question to return and confront her with that fact, the villagers had a disarmingly logical answer: 'what if it is the wrong person?' they retorted.

There is much in this story that belongs to the realm of the irrational. But this is only if one subscribes to a very narrow Cartesian definition of rationality and is not prepared to give rhetorical reason a chance. Indeed, the belief in the existence of an animal that does not exist as well as the shaky rules of correspondence that should establish the validity of the claim do seem to render the whole story irrational. Beliefs such as these have led generations of anthropologists and philosophers of science to question Africans' hold on reality. Discerning anthropologists such as Evans-Pritchard (1976) and Behrend (1999) sought to save the honour of Africans by accounting for magical ideas in terms of their function in keeping communities together. Philosophers contributed to this noble task by attempting to show that magic and witchcraft could be rational in their own terms (Winch 1971, 1987) or, following Robin Horton (1960), they actually represented equally valid ways of pursuing knowledge and explaining the world.

Yet, the charge of irrationality is not one that can be easily countered. Cartesian epistemology has accustomed us to view the world of social life as one that is governed by the same rules that govern the world of natural objects. Many critics of this perspective have traced it back to the separation of body and mind,[59] which has placed upon knowledge production the onus of naturalism. In other words, knowledge is only valid if it describes the world of observable objects according to research rules that deny the mind any role in the production of knowledge. For the belief in the existence of an animal to be acceptable it must be possible to establish an empirical referent to the object of that belief, independent of the circumstances which structure such a belief. In this sense, then, the villagers' belief is irrational, for it is not objectively possible to establish the existence of the xingoko in the world of nature out there.

Since Tambiah (1990), though, we also know how problematic this epistemology is. Tambiah argued in a pragmatist manner against the idea that magic and ritual could be usefully studied as attempts to describe the world of natural objects. Magic and ritual were not 'bad science'. Rather, he held the view that they were 'rhetorical acts' which were performative in nature. They gave meaning to the world and in so doing they made that very world possible. This view gained wide recognition with the so-called linguistic turn in philosophy, to which Richard Rorty's work (1992) provided important insights. There is a considerable body of literature in qualitative research, particularly in conversational analysis (Denzin 2001; Gubrieum and Holstein 1998; for a good overview see Housley and Fitzgerald 2002), and even in social psychology (Billig 1994) which supports the claims made by this new epistemology. Indeed, what emerges with vigour from this literature is the idea that social life is governed by rules different from those that govern the objective world of nature. In order to account for social life it is not enough to describe its external manifestations. One has to understand it. And understanding is not simply projecting one's own conceptual categories onto a phenomena and how it is experienced by those for whom it is relevant in the constitution of lifeworlds. Rather, understanding means engaging with the conceptual resources which individuals retrieve in ascribing meaning to their experience of life.

To allay fears of relativism in this perspective, it should be noted that understanding does not imply accepting the version of the world that beliefs such as the one encountered in the Mozambican village. It only means that observers must make an effort to understand what the world means to the social actors they are dealing with, and just how they make sense of it. Such an attitude is not only warranted by the critique of Cartesian epistemology as applied to social life. Perhaps it is also the only legitimate way observers have to describe, and understand, the world inhabited by the object of their scientific interest in its own terms.

Now, long before the 'linguistic turn' sociology had reached similar conclusions. The 'historicism' debate in Germany in the early part of the twentieth century anticipated these conclusions in very important respects. Dilthey's grounding of the social sciences in ontological opposition to the natural sciences[60] represented, in a way, an early resistance to the universalistic claims of Cartesian rationality. Within the narrower bounds of sociology this resistance was taken up, and furthered, by Max Weber, whose interpretive approach prefigures much that is now taken for granted in the separation of social life from the world of natural objects. I am, of course, not claiming the 'linguistic turn' for sociology. Rather, I want to pursue the overriding concern of this theoretical part that consists in showing the extent to which social action is contingent.

In order to do this I need, first, to revisit Max Weber's theorisation of social action. The aim will be to argue for the view that Weber's notion of social action can be construed as a response to the contingency of social life. Secondly, the limitations of Weber's approach will be discussed. Here the goal will be to show that meaningful social action depends on contextualisation. Not the kind of contextualisation assumed by Parsons in his reinterpretation of Weber's action theory in terms of the internalisation of norms by individuals, a view which would take us back to the problem of order. Rather, what is meant here is the kind of contextualisation that arises from shared experience within local contexts that cohered historically. Finally, I will close with a brief discussion of the implications of such an understanding of social action for a discussion of the role of contingency in social life.

Contingency and Social Action

How would Weber have approached the villagers' story? His sociology of religion suggests that he was no friend of magic, but his apparently scornful comments on magic in his celebrated 'science as a vocation'[61] mask a deep appreciation of context and the need to take this context into account in any effort at understanding the rationality of what individuals do. The self-sufficient savage (sic) who believes in the existence of magical forces seeks to tame them in order to achieve whatever he has set himself to achieve and, in so doing, responds to the larger cultural and social context within which his action becomes intelligible and acquires meaning. A vulgar interpretation of Weber would probably fail to introduce this caveat and would draw the conclusion that the villagers' story about the *xingoko* is an instance of irrational belief.

Yet, to be true to Weber's own grounding of sociology such a verdict would not be at the start of his analysis.[62] Just as in the opening statement of his sociology of religion he warns that a definition of religion can only come at the end, it is fair to assume that in this case he might factor out an assessment of the story and, instead, reconstruct the meaning that underlies it. In so doing he would be responding to his own stricture to premise description of social phenomena on an understanding of the meaning social action has to social actors. In other words, in order to be able to understand what people do, and this includes what kinds of beliefs people entertain, how they perceive the world, and how they engage others, it is necessary to know why people do what they do.

In his discussion of the basic concepts of sociology Weber draws attention to what makes an action social. For an action to be social two conditions must be met. First, individuals must attach meaning to what they do. Secondly, they must seek to communicate this meaning to others. He illustrates this with two instructive examples. In the first one, two cyclists clash. In Weber's view such an accident does not constitute an instance of social action, for the two conditions that are necessary for it to obtain are not consciously present. He does concede, however, that the ensuing argument could be seen as an instance of social action, for both parties would be concerned to make the other aware of how they saw the situation. Simultaneity of meaning and communication is exactly what happens in his second example. Here two cyclists who have become aware of each other and endeavour to avoid a clash. This would be a classic example of social action in Weber's sense.

The analytical relevance of Weber's theorisation of social action is not limited to the distinction between behaviour and action. Social action has consequences.

One major consequence is that meaningful social action allows individuals to formulate expectations. In other words, individuals in society take into account the actions of others, that is, they adjust their own actions to the meanings they attach to what others do. Weber calls the ensuing context 'social relationship' to draw attention to the fact that social action takes place against a background that can offer it stability, regularity, and permanence. Significantly, for us, Weber does not make a social relationship dependent upon a correct interpretation of the intentions of others. He defines it as the 'likelihood' that individuals in a given situation act in a given manner. In other words, one's expectations may not be met.

Now, precisely this element of uncertainty, which Parsons conceptualised as 'double contingency' and sought to domesticate with reference to the force of norms over individual action, is what makes the object of the social sciences particularly difficult to grasp and use for description and explanation. Social life is indeed extremely contingent, and this reflects what Dilthey and subsequently Weber and others had argued for, namely the idea that the social sciences deal with an object that is historically constituted. To put it differently, social life is not subject to fixed rules that can be safely assumed to be valid across space and time. There is, indeed, a sense in which every social situation is unique. It is made possible by conscious individuals interpreting the actions of others against the background of cultural values, which they understand and interpret differently. While they may avail themselves of moral, institutional, and cultural resources to do this, their action is still structured by expectations that may turn out to be inadequate, wrong, or unwarranted.

In view of the aforesaid, it might be fair to draw the tentative conclusion that Weber's social action theory draws particular attention to the role of uncertainty in social life. Understanding social life in this sense might be premised on the acknowledgement of this fact. Talcott Parsons' ambitious attempt to cast Weber's action theory into a functionalist mould could be interpreted, in this connection, not so much as a disservice to Weber, as some have suggested, but rather as a well-intentioned, yet misguided service to social actors. Indeed, in defining action as the conscious fulfilment of social norms acquired in the process of socialisation, Parsons was not so much 'functionalising' Weber as he was attempting to bring certainty back into social life.[63] His approach was, therefore, normative on two counts. First, it was normative to the extent that it turned sociology into a science that described how individuals *should* act. The second count on which it was normative was the unspoken belief that accurate description of society in the manner suggested by Parsons himself would enable individuals to make their life more predictable.

Parsons' normative biases were, of course, problematic and for this reason they are still the subject of vigorous debate (Alexander 1988). For our present purpose, however, there is one important sense in which they are problematic. They sought to eliminate from social life precisely that which renders it different from the world of natural objects, namely its historicity. As Weber, following Dilthey, remarked, social life is historical in character. It is constituted by the action of individuals, which is, in its turn, also constitutive of action. The possibility of social life is intimately related to what Anthony Giddens and ethnomethodologists have referred to as a 'double constitution' and 'reflexivity' (see chapter three for a discussion of this perspective), respectively. It is contingent because the social action upon which it rests is also contingent. Individuals can never know for sure whether their expectations are warranted until others have acted. And while the action of others may give them the opportunity to correct their expectations, it is also the beginning of a new uncertainty which they must master.

One reason that possibly led Parsons to seek to reduce uncertainty might have been Weber's silence on the nature of meaning. In his basic concepts of sociology Weber does not elaborate on the notion of meaning. He seems quite content with identifying it as the element that turns behaviour into action. He assumes it without really explaining it, as Alfred Schütz remarked in his critique.[64] This comes out clearly in the suggestion that social action is intentional. Presumably, meaning would be what structures interaction between two or more individuals. In other words, if one understands social action as the combination of subjective meaning and its communication, then it could be argued that Weber sees meaning precisely as the context and substance of social action.

As a definition this seems quite unsatisfactory for several reasons, chief among them its circularity. To argue that meaning is the content and substance of social action amounts to the same as restating the idea that social action is meaningful action. This is still not really a definition of meaning. Max Weber seems to have been aware of this logical difficulty. He seems to have based his hopes of surmounting it in the emphasis he placed on the intentional character of social action. The immediate methodological implication of this insight was the inference that there are reasons behind every action. Uncovering them might help in making intentions visible, which in turn might settle the question of the nature of meaning. Put differently, meaning would, in this sense, be the intention that an actor associates with a given action as revealed in the set of motivations that impelled him to act.

Weber's social action types are in fact an elaboration on this issue. They do not describe what individuals do. Instead, they provide a heuristic device with which sociologists can try to understand why individuals do what they do. It is still not a convincing definition of meaning, but it has the merit of acknowledging the constitutive role patterned individual reasons play in social life. Such recognition is essential to the interpretive goal of understanding social life.

To return to the story that opened this section, it can be noted that this brief review of Weber's theorisation of social action clearly shows how limiting it would be to reduce analysis to whether the underlying beliefs are rational or not. Actually, much more interesting than this question is the interpretively informed query as to the reasons why the villagers believe what they believe, but also the conditions that must prevail for such beliefs and practices to be possible. In theory, of course, one could still answer that the villagers are ill informed. As a matter of fact, this is an answer that informs much theorising about Africa and Africans. It is, as discussed in the introduction, behind the inability of African studies to go beyond description of African social phenomena, to a consideration of their import to sociological theory in general. Once one moves away from a positivist account of social phenomena one is in a position to gain useful insights into the way in which social life makes itself possible. To be sure, it is not Niklas Luhmann's 'auto-poetic' constitution of social systems, for such a view would reduce the endless flux of history to a mechanical logic that appears to be absent. It is, rather, the spontaneous emergence of social situations against the background of patterned interactions and as a result of thinking individuals consciously anticipating the actions of others.

So Weber, in Patrice Lumumba village, might have found that belief in the existence of an animal that does not exist was constitutive of village social life. It was a creative moment that rested on the ability of the members of the village community to exchange meanings and, in so doing, establish social relationships that allow them to anticipate the behaviour of others. Weber might have found that villagers are not really interested in establishing once and for all whether the animal does, indeed, exist, or whether the suspected old lady is the person to blame. Rather, belief in the existence of the animal and in the culpability of the old lady would be communicating the villagers' anxieties about community life. Through this belief they stress the unpredictable nature of social relations in the village and they seek to create contexts of action within which they can be able to anticipate the actions of others with some degree of certainty. Such a belief is not *functional* to community life as such a view would be akin to suggesting that the community provides a normative canopy to the actions of individuals. It is *constitutive* of social life in the sense that it offers an interpretation of the world which others may accept, or reject. In the process of accepting or rejecting interpretations people engage with one another and, thereby, foster social relationships.

This approach to the villagers' belief allows an interpretive sociologist to understand social phenomena in the village. It may also allow him or her to pass judgement on the intellectual faculties of the villagers. However, what it will not allow him or her to do is to fail to acknowledge the extent to which social reality is produced by the actions of individuals in society. People who believe in the existence of an animal that does not exist will not go out at night. If they do they will pay special attention to the barking of dogs, always ready to retreat into the security of their homes. People who believe in the existence of an animal that does not exist will ask themselves why their village was befallen by such an evil phenomenon. They will seek answers from knowledgeable people. These might be village elders, experienced villagers, healers, or sorcerers. People who believe in the existence of an animal that does not exist will look at a certain type of people with suspicion and will deal with them in a particular way. They will also learn to make sense of events in village life with reference to those people and their evil intentions.

In so doing, they will be both responding to their awareness of the nature of social relations in their own midst at the same time as they are structuring their social reality. There is, of course, no guarantee that their responses to situations will always be adequate and will always produce the kinds of outcomes they expect. Individuals may assume frames of reference for what they do and say, but the final test of their rightness is the reaction of others and the kinds of situations that will ensue thereof. These rather general remarks point to aspects of social action to which Weber's conceptualisation has helped sharpen our gaze. In fact, his emphasis on the constitutive role of exchanged meanings in the conditions of possibility of social action does not establish, as it were, a stable framework within which routine action takes place and produces expected outcomes. Weber's conceptualisation draws our attention just as much to how social action is possible as to how it can go wrong.

In this section I have been concerned with working out some ideas on how things can go wrong. The central aspect in those ideas is that there is an element of uncertainty in social life which, however, does not necessarily mean that social action ceases to be possible; rather it draws our attention to the conditions under which social life is possible and the kinds of consequences flowing from social action. I have dwelt on these ideas to suggest that failure to regard the constitutive role of uncertainty in social life has led to an exaggerated concern with order which, in turn, has affected the manner in which African society has tended to be perceived in the social sciences. The concern with the problem of order is more normative than objective and, as such, less inclined to be sensitive to an interpretive approach to social phenomena, however distant they may be from familiar realities. With regard to the problem of order, uncertainty was translated as contingency, and the intellectual challenge ensuing thereof was seen as developing conceptual apparatuses that not only could tackle the underlying problem, but also give instructions to individuals concerning how best to go about their business. My claim is that a sociological research programme structured in this manner and drawing from this kind of assumptions was unlikely to predispose researchers to be open-minded about the logic of social action. However, worse than the failure to be open-minded was the oversight with regards to the fruitful insights revealed by a fuller understanding of Weber's notion of social action and what its application to African social reality might have contributed to social theory in general.

I will continue to explore Weber's position in the following section. This time, however, I will do it with reference to conceptual precisions introduced by Alfred Schütz, especially with regard to the sense in which social action produces social reality. The aim is to elaborate further on the underlying analytical elements in the notion of social action, but also to continue amassing evidence on the centrality of uncertainty to the very possibility of social action. This will enable me to stress once again the claim that the search for deviance in African life forms is less relevant to sociological understanding than confronting the analytical challenges posed by the way in which individuals in Africa deal with uncertainty. Therein lies an analytical treasure that has not been adequately tapped.

Social Action and Meaningfulness

The idea that individuals' actions produce social reality means that the latter is made of social relations in Weber's sense. In fact, social action is an aspect, or better still, an element of social relations. In this sense, arguing that social action produces social reality means that social relations mediate between the former and the latter. In socially acting individuals engage in relations, that is, a framework that is both cultural and structural at the same time as it enables individuals to formulate expectations concerning others. This is the sense in which Weber's understanding of sociology helps us to perceive social reality as the product of social action. It sharpens our senses to the extent to which action produces social reality because of the central role that meaning plays in its conditions of possibility. One sociologist who, after Weber, gave much thought to the role of meaning in the possibility of action was Alfred Schütz. Inspired by phenomenology Schütz developed his ideas in direct response to Weber. He set himself the task of making out the conditions under which meaning became possible. By answering the question he provided sociology with a powerful analytical framework to account for the social construction of reality, a task that Peter Berger and Thomas Luckmann (1991) would spell out in more detail in their path-breaking book under the same title.

What makes action meaningful? Schütz rejected Weber's idea that motives – that is Weber's action types – could adequately be construed as sources of meaning. Motives, as he made clear in his analysis, were temporal dimensions. They allowed observers and individual social actors to explain action. Hence his distinction between 'in-order-to-motives' (*um-zu*) and 'because-motives' (*weil*). The former refer to the reasoning that precedes action and can be evoked by the acting individual to set out what he or she intends to achieve with a given course of action. In other words, individuals attach objectives to what they are about to do. They want to achieve a given goal. The latter, in contrast, are referring to the account of the consummated action. To put it differently, once an action has been accomplished one can explain it with the benefit of hindsight with reference to the initial objectives before the action was initiated. These distinctions are not entirely absent from Weber's own work, but Schütz makes them more explicit and in so doing draws attention to the larger context within which social action takes place.

Such accounts of action, which have given symbolic interactionists and ethnomethodologists a considerable amount of food for thought, do not offer an adequate definition of meaning from a sociological perspective. As far as Schütz was concerned, and drawing from his phenomenological frame of reference, meaning pertained to the actual life experiences. To put it simply, the life-world with its structures of relevance is the place where meaning is constituted. According to Schütz, before individuals are able to perceive the life-world they must experience it. They experience pain, joy, hardship, and all sorts of natural phenomena, for instance, before they are compelled by that very experience to make sense of it.

Meaning arises from individuals' ability to relate one particular experience to another. As they relate such experiences individuals recognise those which are similar, different, and new. Meaning is the ability to make such distinctions. It acquires its relevance for action because it allows individuals to anticipate events, the actions of others, as well as their own actions. There is an important point to make out of Schütz' analysis of meaning, for it bears directly on the nature of action and contingeny discussed further below. We pointed out in passing that experience precedes perception. In actual fact, however, each is premised on the other.

To experience phenomena, whether natural, emotional, or social, is to perceive them; by the same token, to perceive phenomena is to experience them. This is so because, as Schütz suggests and Berger and Luckmann spell out in greater detail, in relating experiences much more happens than just establishing whether one has to do with the same thing again. Indeed, individuals group experiences, identify, and attribute roles to individuals and objects that perform tasks within them and, above all, store information on those same experiences. Against the background of such stored information recurrent and new experiences can be properly integrated into individuals' experience and perception of the life-world in their everyday life. Schütz describes this process as the sedimentation of experience.

Out of Schütz's and Berger and Luckmann's rich descriptive vocabulary I would like to select the notions of 'typification' and 'social distribution of the stock of knowledge' to pursue Schütz's discussion of Weber. Typification is the term that Schütz and Berger and Luckmann give to individuals' grouping and role identification and attribution. Experience is sedimented through the way in which its different manifestations are made to conform to socially recognisable types. Such types are socially recognisable for two main reasons. First, they can be classified as distinct categories of general phenomena. For example, patterned interactions between parents and children and husbands and wives can be understood as distinct types of social interaction within the larger context of family relationships. Weber's notion of social relation immediately comes to mind here. Secondly, individuals and objects have roles and functions within a given type of experience. For example, being a parent or offspring corresponds to a role or function that an individual has within the family. Through the process of typification such roles and functions, which are basically reducible to any kind of action within the fluid experience of the life-world, acquire a patterned, stable status, which allows other individuals within society to classify phenomena.

One may feel tempted to see in this account of typification a functionalist description of social reality. However, nothing could be farther from the intentions of interpretive sociology. In fact, Schütz and Parsons discussed this issue at length, until they agreed to disagree. While Schütz, and Weber before him, would not deny the usefulness of a functionalist account of social reality, he maintained that such an account was a preliminary to the much more interesting objective of reaching a descriptive understanding of the construction of social reality. Roles and functions were themselves the result of meaningful social action. Interpretive sociology was concerned with uncovering the structures underlying such social action. Typification was one such structure, as roles and functions could be shown to have arisen out of individuals' attempts at making sense of their life-world experience. Roles and functions gave social reality an institutional character. Through them the experience of the life-world could be apprehended by individuals as a distinct relevance structure.

Typification shows, therefore, the role that meaningful social action plays in the construction of social reality. Not only motivations, as Weber thought, help us retrieve meaning from social action, but also our reflexive experience of the life-world. As we experience the life-world we structure it and, in the process, allow it to structure our experience. Our relationship to the life-world is akin to what Giddens has referred to as 'double hermeneutics' (Giddens 1985) and ethnomethodologists have agreed to call 'reflexivity' (Garfinkel 1967). Experience is the pre-condition of perception, but perception constitutes itself as a pre-condition of experience.

This reflexive moment in the social construction of reality is particularly evident in Schütz's notion of the 'social distribution of the stock of knowledge'. Indeed, the process of typification implies that individuals are able to store information about the experiences they accumulate as they move through life. The more complex such typifications become, the greater is the amount of information which they have to process in order to be able to keep track of the meaning of phenomena in their life-world. While individuals share a common fund of information concerning such meanings, it would be fair to assume that such information is not evenly distributed among the members of a given community. There are those who have more information than others and, more importantly, command a greater ability to process such information.

The social distribution of the stock of knowledge refers to differences in access to information about the experience of the life-world as well as to differences in the ability to interpret such information. In every society with a common fund of experience of the life-world there are individuals who specialise in the processing of information. They are socially acknowledged as repositories of the collective memory of a society. Collective memory should be understood as a shorthand for the sedimented experience of a society as it is to be found in the degree of specialisation.

Schütz's phenomenological sociology set in motion a whole field of study concerned with the distribution of knowledge within a society. The central question the research programme of such a field of study seeks to answer can be stated simply as the following: who knows what?[65] Answers to this question take up issues related to the degree of complexity as well as to levels of social differentiation within a given society. It is a far-reaching enterprise, which is, however, intimately linked with basic processes of constructing social reality.

Berger and Luckmann (1991) have suggested that knowledge could be defined as the certainty individuals have that the social world exists. Drawing heavily on Schütz they sought to show the centrality of knowledge to social reality by leaning on processes of typification and the social distribution of the stock of knowledge to describe social reality as a social construction. Much in Schütz's line of reasoning they sought to go beyond Weber's understanding of meaningful social action and, by incorporating Durkheim's structural perspective, they were able to show the reflexive relationship which experience and perception entertain.

To briefly return to the villagers' belief in the existence of an animal that does not exist[66] we could refer to Schütz to argue that sociology's main interest should be to describe how the local community came to take for granted the meanings associated with the belief in the existence of an animal that does not exist. In more phenomenological language, what is the 'natural attitude' of the village community made of?

Such questions may lead to the findings we attributed to a Weberian perspective above. In other words, we may find that this belief documents the nature of social relationships within the village. Put differently, the villagers' social action is informed by the shared understanding of the implications that such a belief carries with it. This is how far a purely Weberian approach would take us. It would show us how functional a collective illusion can be to community relations. It would not show us, and this is the point of Schütz's critique of Weber, how such a collective illusion came into being and how it came to stand for the nature of local social reality. So, in a sense, a Schützian approach takes us a step further. First of all, on the basis of the notion of typification we could infer, for instance, that the belief represented the sedimentation of villagers' experience of the phenomenal world. We may assume that the villagers had compared experiences, classified them, and defined the role of various individuals within them. Secondly, and drawing on the notion of the social distribution of the stock of knowledge, we might argue that the production and reproduction of the belief rested on the acknowledged expertise of certain individuals to describe the phenomenal world in ways comprehensible to most villagers.

We may note, in passing, the difference between Schütz's phenomenological approach and an ordinary functionalist explanation of the belief. Indeed, while the latter might argue that the belief is functional to the production of the authority of magicians, witch-doctors, and religious prophets, the former simply describes the role which such authorities play in the production of an intersubjectively communicated social reality. More importantly, however, it does not purport to apportion blame. Its main drive is to uncover the meanings constitutive of the local social reality.

The relevance of this discussion of Schütz's phenomenological clarification of the implications of Weber's notion of social action to sociological inquiry should have now become apparent. Indeed, Schütz shows just how difficult it is to see social action in isolation from the wider context which makes it possible while at the same time producing it. Such phenomenological notions as typification and the social distribution of the stock of knowledge help us to see in social action much more than the incoherent and inarticulate activities of human beings and direct our attention to the underlying sense of everyday life. To be sure, this underlying sense is not a recipe for action, but rather a resource that individuals draw on to go about their lives. Engaging with social action, therefore, goes beyond simply identifying what is specific about human action; it brings to light a world that exists quite independently of the concepts we use to retrieve it.

Again, this is extremely relevant to the study of Africa. For one thing, we see in the clarification of this central sociological category of social action a general account of social life and the conditions of its visibility. For another, the plausibility of this account is not dependent on a prior definition of the type of society that a sociological observer may be concerned with. Rather, the account sets out to establish the criteria which social action must fulfil in order to be categorised as social action. In other words, what is at stake in sociological description is an account of the extent to which social action draws on a social reality that is both pre-condition and outcome, albeit not in a causal manner. The question we need to ask with respect to Africa, therefore, is whether social phenomena satisfy the criteria set out in the understanding of social action as presented here. This book answers this question in the affirmative, but in order to understand the nature of the challenge which both the question and the answer pose to us we need to set the issues, in moving towards the conclusion of this chapter, in a slightly different manner. The following section asks, therefore, what particular challenges are presented by an understanding of social reality informed by the analytical implications of the concept of social action as discussed here. This will lead us straight back to the notion of contingency that we started off with as a response to the problem of order.

The Nature of the (Social) World

So far, I have been arguing in favour of an interpretive approach to social life. Indeed, in the course of my discussion I have established that social action is the starting point both for identifying the object as well as for gaining access to its constitution. The question that should concern us now goes beyond this and asks whether an interpretive approach commits us to a view of the social world which foists a specific perspective on the world upon us. Related to this is, of course, the overriding question of this chapter concerns what it means to study Africa from a sociological point of view.

In fact, an interpretive approach raises an important issue related to the nature of the world. Does it really exist? How can it be retrieved for analysis? Most of the issues evolving from these questions have been taken up by the so-called constructionists and radical constructionists (Glasersfeld 1997). In sociology, they have found their most outspoken proponents in 'science studies' (Latour 1984, Knorr-Cetina 1981) and in the writings of the Edinburgh school of 'radical sociology of knowledge' around the sociologists Barry Barnes (1985) and David Bloor (1997). Constructionists and radical constructionists claim that reality is an artefact of human imagination. It is socially constructed. While constructionists are prepared to accept the realist idea that there is a reality independent of human imagination, radical constructionists reject the idea altogether. The former emphasise the analytical idea that reality only begins to matter when humans have engaged it. The latter, however, insist that reality is a property of our conceptual categories.

In the sociology of knowledge constructionism has been used to reject the claims of natural scientists, who say that they are describing the world as it really is. Bruno Latour and Knorr-Cetina have, each in their own way, provided evidence against this claim. The point they have emphasised in their work is the extent to which natural scientists produce in their laboratories the external world which they claim to describe. In the context of the debate over the question whether the social sciences are scientific enough, the findings of the sociology of knowledge are of great relevance.

They bring into relief two broad issues. The first concerns the nature of reality, the second deals with the most appropriate way to describe it. The Cartesian *res extensa* suggests the idea of an orderly natural world. Science, from this perspective, would be the development of appropriate measurement instruments, enabling mankind to uncover the laws that govern its orderliness. At its best, so the claim, science is causal in its attempt to explain the world. Positivist social scientists, such as a Durkheim, have sought to emulate this understanding by defining sociology as the attempt to uncover the laws that govern social life. Long after Durkheim this positivist orientation was revived by Talcott Parsons in his general action theory. Parsons believed to have come closer to this great nomological goal with his functionalist account of action as a response to normative constraints for the sake of reproducing the social system.

Against this positivist background, social scientists informed by historicism have had a hard time sustaining their claims of scientificity. An interpretive approach as expounded by Max Weber would seem to give up the search for the causal laws that account for social life. Indeed, it appears that once the goal of sociological inquiry is defined as understanding, there is no reasonable way in which one could lay a claim to providing the only valid description of social reality. To be sure, this is not a relativist position, yet there are important senses in which understanding can be construed, especially by positivist oriented social scientists, as an acceptance of the possibility that descriptions of the social could lay equally legitimate claims to validity. It may not be merely a matter of where one stands, but rather what meaning one uses to access a given reality.

This is the point at which matters concerning the appropriate ways of describing reality intervene. In fact, the issue is not so much what one describes, that is, takes as the reality to be accounted for, as how one goes about it. As we have seen, positivist sociologists, such as Durkheim and Parsons, would assume that there is an orderly world out there which can be described with recourse to causal language. The interpretive approach, however, raises serious misgivings about the assumption of an orderly world that sociologists could retrieve with causal language. Put differently, the interpretive assumption that social reality can be retrieved from intersubjectively produced meanings suggests that positivist accounts of social reality are normative. They are normative to the extent that they appear to provide instructions for individuals as to the appropriate ways in which they should act.

The interpretive approach can lay claim to objectivity by pointing out that it is merely interested in describing the world as rendered by individuals in their social actions and relationships. In other words, interpretive sociology does not claim that its search for meaning is consistent with the real nature of the external world.

In fact, the interpretive approach raises the issue whether an understanding of the external world can necessarily help to account for what individuals do in their everyday life.

Positivist sociologists seem to think that this is the case. As a matter of fact, the assumption of the orderliness of the external world is functional to the idea that individual action is structurally constrained. Parsons was the first to bring this issue to the fore of sociological debate. He saw his sociology as a contribution to the solution of what he called 'the double contingency problem'. Briefly, the double contingency problem describes a situation in which two individuals are unable to act because they cannot anticipate the actions of the other. In other words, Parsons believes that sociology should primarily provide an account of why individuals act in spite of the fact that they do not have any apparent reason to assume that others will behave in the way they expect them to behave. His answer to this question, and hence, his grounding of sociology, was that individuals are constrained by the social system to act. They have internalised norms which allow them to make assumptions about the reactions of other social actors. In this sense, then, society provides individuals with a normative canopy. They act in order to reproduce the social system.

Another important contribution to this issue was made by the German sociologist Niklas Luhmann. Drawing from Parsons he also labelled it 'the double contingency problem'. Unlike Parsons, however, Luhmann assumed that the problem was solved in a systemic way. In other words, Luhmann argued that double contingency could be understood as an instance of complexity. Within the framework of his theoretical approach Luhmann assumed that the solution to the problem of double contingency followed from the natural tendency of social systems to reduce complexity by self-producing themselves. To put it differently, the social system translated the insecurity characterised by the contingency problem into trust and, hence, predictability. Interestingly, Luhmann saw strong parallels between trust and risk and used a similar distinction to explain the latter as derived from hazard by opposing the former to the notion of confidence (Luhmann 1989).[67]

Both Parsons and Luhmann assumed, therefore, that social action should be explained with reference to the structural constraints individuals are subject to. It follows that social action as such is largely irrelevant as a guide to an understanding of social life. Whether one adopts a normative-functionalist position, as Parsons does, or a normative-systemic position, as Luhmann does, solving the double contingency problem does not really overcome a major analytical difficulty. This difficulty consists in providing an adequate account of what makes individuals act. Societal or systemic constraints merely state the same problem at different levels of abstraction. The strength of norms as well as the determinism of social systems does not really explain why individuals act. Why do they?

Interpretive sociology brackets out the question. It merely observes that individuals do act. It acknowledges that the context within which social action takes place is a delicate one. This is central to the epistemology of interpretive sociology. Individuals trade off meanings. This is by definition a precarious foundation for action. One can be misunderstood, not understood, ignored, shunned, etc. Fear of the reactions of others does not prevent individuals from acting. In fact, not acting out of the fear of the unknown is a form of action. Whatever the circumstances, individuals act and in so doing they construct the social context of their action.

In some important respects, contingency is essential to an interpretive approach. It is because individuals do not know, or at any rate, cannot take much for granted that their social constructions of reality become so important as a focus of sociological analysis. Berger and Luckmann made a brave attempt at reconciling the structure and agency camps within sociology. Drawing from Durkheim and Weber they argued that social action is both individual as well as structural. Individuals construct their own world, the result of which acts as a constraint upon their own as well as the actions of others.

Contingency, I would like to claim, defines social life. Weber as well as Schütz's critique of the former represent approaches to social life that acknowledge the role of contingency therein. While their interpretive approach goes a long way towards accepting the gauntlet which such an acknowledgement represents, I would like to contend that sociology has, so far, failed to formulate a research programme which fully engages with the issues that spring thenceforth. Economic sociology has come close to this with its focus on the conditions for cooperation in economic activity.[68] It has, however, fallen short of a full acknowledgement of this self-insinuating research programme because of its assumption of the embeddness of economic relations. Such an assumption commits economic sociology to the view that social relationships need no further clarification, as they provide the context within which economic activity takes place.

More recently, Jens Beckert (1996), a German sociologist, has come even closer to formulating such a programme. Beckert argues that uncertainty is at the heart of sociological theorisation. He spells out a research programme, which picks up Dewey's notion of 'ends-in-view', that is, the immediacy of horizons of action. His point is that uncertainty obtains because actions have consequences. Individuals are constantly changing and adjusting their goals as they interact with others. Sociology should be sensitive to this. It is my intention to show that the way in which Patrice Lumumba villagers perceive crises and disasters and try to prevent as well as cope with them can provide us with interesting empirical, but also theoretical insights into how this sensitivity should look like.

In fact, what has dogged the study of Africa all through the years has been sociology's lack of a vocabulary that made uncertainty, and contingency for that matter, central to its theorising and to its attempts at describing and analysing the world. So long as the contingency of action was seen as a problem to be surmounted by norms or overarching structures, it was unlikely that sociological accounts of African social phenomena could perceive them without the urge to either dismiss them as deviation or correct them. The discussion so far, however, should have offered grounds for assuming that there is nothing particularly extraordinary about African social phenomena except, perhaps, for the fact that uncertainty is heightened by the precarious material conditions that influence everyday life on the continent so heavily.

African Objects

This is, broadly speaking, the theoretical and analytical challenge that this book seeks to address. Africa as an object is not interesting because of the practical solutions research could produce with regard to the continent's problems. While this, of course, should be accorded importance in any piece of research – ultimately it is often on such grounds that funding is provided – there is a need to acknowledge the extent to which Africa's condition warrants greater attention from social theory. I intend to show in the following chapters, both in the theoretical and empirical ones, that how Africa's problems present themselves and come into view, makes them extremely relevant to some of the most perennial discussions in sociology. In fact, it is the unresolved nature of these discussions that appears, as I have tried to show in this chapter, to have influenced African studies in general and contributed, indirectly, to a less than satisfactory production of knowledge about the continent.

The challenge in the following chapters will be to spell out this problem in more concrete detail, in both theoretical-analytical and empirical terms. The immediately following chapters, that is, three and four, will dwell on the first part of the challenge, namely on the theoretical-analytical. I will try to show that long before economic sociology, and following hard on the beaten track of Schütz's phenomenological sociology, ethnomethodology had placed contingency and uncertainty at the centre of its sociological project. Its assumption was that the social was chaotic in nature. Consequently, sociology should be concerned with spelling out the ways in which individuals succeed in making sense out of chaos and lead healthy lives.

I will engage with ethnomethodology to pick up themes suggested by recent discussions in the sociology of risk which appear to me to be of enormous significance to the further discussion of the problem of order versus contingency. In doing this I will also clear some conceptual ground that will enable me to introduce the notion of 'contexts of action' which will guide me through the presentation of the empirical material. The case studies that form the backbone of the empirical challenge are a combination of methodological experiments, i.e., the systematic use of qualitative analytical methods to make empirical data speak, and an attempt to give substance to the suggestion that individuals act in order to be able to act. In other words, I am arguing that we should concern ourselves with the creation of contexts of action.

3

Risk and Social Reality

Engaging with Risk

When the German sociologist Ulrich Beck published his book *Risk Society* ([1992]1986) he struck two vital nerves. On the one hand, he rode on the wave of social unease about the risks of technology, especially of the nuclear kind. In Germany, where the issue was debated in a particularly hysterical way (see Pettenkoffer 2003, Viehöver 2003), Beck's book found an ideal terrain to make its way into sociological journals and departments as a respectable and legitimate sociological perspective. On the other hand, he linked up with a perennial sociological problem, namely the question concerning what holds modern societies together. Indeed, one can read most sociological classics, from Durkheim and Simmel all the way through to Weber, as attempts at answering this question just as we have seen in the previous chapter on the problem of order.

In this chapter I intend to trace these attempts to answer the question concerning what holds modern societies together. My aim is to go beyond the notions of order, contingency, and uncertainty as introduced in the previous chapter, and expand my reflection to include such analytical dimensions of risk as trust, predictability, and fragility, especially as they are inherent within the particular meaning that sociology attaches to modern society – by which technologically advanced societies are meant – and articulate this meaning with my immediate concerns in this book. In the process, I will pursue my efforts towards identifying the object of sociology in ways which are relevant to the attempts at understanding social phenomena in Africa, especially as they relate to the prominent role played by precariousness in everyday life.

My claim is that the sociology of risk is not only useful to describe and analyse a particular stage in the development of contemporary society. I will argue, instead, that the sociology of risk owes its relevance to how it potentially engages with basic social processes. The aspects of society dealt with by the sociology of risk deals with have a wider import than its proponents have been willing to consider. It touches, as we have seen, upon issues of order, uncertainty, and contingency, but also upon trust, predictability, and knowledge as we will see in this chapter. Furthermore, to the extent that the sociology of risk seeks to work out criteria for the description of certain forms of action, I would contend that such forms have a common denominator in the social nature of the action itself. In this sense, it is my assumption that social action under precarious conditions offers valuable insights into how this could be accomplished. I will elaborate on this particular point with reference to an already mentioned insight made by Niklas Luhmann concerning the distinction between hazard and risk. For reasons that are perfectly understandable, the sociology of risk has come to be conflated with the study of modern society[69] in ways which have foreclosed any useful interest in societies held to be non-modern for the immediate purposes of the research programme heralded by the discovery of the role of risk. In elaborating further on Luhmann's insight I will be concerned to suggest lines for rethinking the sociology of risk. In so doing I will be committed to revising the disregard of which societies held to have failed the test of modernity have been victims. Through this revision I will try to lay the ground for the analytical framework which I use in this book to integrate my empirical findings. Indeed, if my empirical findings are anything to go by, as indeed I think they are, then we can in all fairness argue, as I do, that the creation of contexts of action lies at the root of social action.

Sociologists, as we have seen, have wondered about what holds society together. The concept of risk appeared appropriate to provide an answer to this question for the simple reason that it identified an aspect of social reality which was thought to be specifically modern in nature. Anthony Giddens, who as a social theorist has been particularly sensitive to issues concerning modernity (see Giddens 1990), embraced the concept of risk and articulated it with his notion of *reflexivity*. In so doing he was able to define modern societies as risk societies to the extent that they were characterised by the ability to question themselves (Beck, Giddens, and Lash 1994).[70] Much like Beck, Giddens argued that the proliferation of technological risks led significant sections of the society to question not only science and its legitimating slogan of progress, but also the authority of scientists in assessing the risks of their own activities.[71]

When risk became a catchword in the eighties the issues it addressed in sociology were not really new. They had only been approached from different concepts. One such concept was insecurity. There are two German-speaking sociologists worth mentioning in this connection. In the seventies Franz-Xaver Kaufmann wrote quite extensively about how modern society dealt with insecurity. He identified social security systems as the mechanism through which this happened (Kaufmann 1973). Some of his insights were later developed in a much more critical way by the French disciple of Michel Foucault, François Ewald (1993)[72] who, in his work on the welfare state, moved away from the idea of dealing with insecurity to identifying state welfare with power, control, and discipline. In the eighties Helga Nowotny (1989) saw the rational appropriation of nature through science as the dominant modern strategy in coping with insecurity.

Let us acquaint ourselves with the literature on risk through a typology suggested by Deborah Lupton (1999) several years ago. As we move along the different approaches to risk we will come to appreciate both the diversity as well as the potential uses to which placing risk at the centre of sociological theorising can be put. My immediate concern will be to link up with the discussions in the previous chapter concerning both the centrality of social action to sociological description and analysis as well as the nature of social reality that emerges from of the concern with social action. I will then move in the direction of selecting aspects of the discussion on risk, which I think are crucial to my own undertaking in this book, to interrogate the sociology of risk in search of ways of engaging with the precarious nature of everyday life in Africa, in general, and in Patrice Lumumba Communal Village, in particular, in a manner that can contribute to furthering sociological research.

Deborah Lupton (1999) has identified three approaches to the study of risk which appear to cover scholarship on the subject at the moment. She calls them (a) realist, (b) weak constructionist, and (c) strong constructionist (Lupton, 1999: 35). These are epistemological approaches to the study of the nature of risk and how societies deal with it. While realist approaches assume risks to be objectively given in nature, constructionist approaches make their availability for analysis dependent on how societies perceive risks. Weak constructionist approaches accept, like realist approaches, that risks are objectively given, but argue that social and cultural debates and conflicts over the nature of hazards constitute them as objective realities and make them visible to the social scientist. Strong constructionist approaches, in contrast, argue that there is nothing objective about risks since they are a function of how societies articulate their anxieties and worries.

Constructionist approaches, whether weak or strong, have brought to light two aspects of risk which are of direct relevance to this book. The first aspect relates to the social constructedness of risk itself. What these approaches emphasise in this connection is the idea that risk is the objectification of threats to human livelihood which gain shape in societal debates. Niklas Luhmann (1993)[73] made this point forcefully with his analytically useful distinction between risk and hazard. In Luhmann's view there is a difference between these two concepts. This difference is related to the accountability of decisions. Hazard refers to phenomena which occur without conscious human agency, whereas risk envolves a decision on the part of social actors. In other words, risks are constructed to the extent that they are socially calculated hazards. Nuclear disasters, for instance, are in a technologically advanced society risks in Luhmann's sense because the decision to use nuclear energy takes the potential occurrence of such disasters into account and its awareness encourages actors to take measures which will keep the possibility of a disaster to a minimum.

The usefulness of Luhmann's distinction lies in the emphasis it places on social action. Indeed, he invites us to see risks in a dynamic perspective as actors' or society's intervention in nature to translate hazards. In other words, Luhmann is arguing for a positive understanding of risk as something people consciously produce in order to make life possible. As ethnomethodologists and symbolic interactionists have shown (see Garfinkel 1967, Blumer 1986) much of social life is produced in response to contingency, in the sense that individuals engage with others in an attempt to interpret and anticipate their actions. Such responses amount to the production of risk, since they draw from decisions, which are based on expectations that may prove to be misplaced.

The second relevant aspect brought to light by constructionist approaches is the idea that risk is specific to a particular type of society. While Mary Douglas, for instance, assumed that risk-taking was a general anthropological condition to be found in lesser or greater amounts in different cultures (see Douglas 1992, Douglas and Widavsky 1982), sociologists of risk have tended to identify risk with modern society. Wolfgang Bonss (1995), for example, holds the view that the recognition of risk depends on scientific knowledge. Where no such knowledge is available, there cannot be risk. Indeed, he distinguishes between insecurity and uncertainty and argues that risk responds to insecurity, whereas magic is a response to uncertainty.

Elements of this understanding of risk are present in the conceptual clarification introduced into the debate by Niklas Luhmann. Indeed, to the extent that Luhmann stresses the role of decision in the mere possibility of risk he seems to contemplate the idea that risk might be specific to a certain type of society. As a matter of fact, he argues quite pointedly that the growth in risks is related to the increase in decision possibilities, which, in turn, result from the increase in ways of protecting ourselves from hazards.[74] He does this by pointing out that hazards are present in any kind of society and in this sense we can hardly claim that life in modern society is less hazardous than in any other. Yet, he makes a point of claiming that what characterises modern society is the increase in the number of risks.[75] This point is taken up by other sociologists working on risk. We have already seen Wolfgang Bonß, for instance, whose distinction between uncertainty (*Ungewißheit*) and insecurity (*Unsicherheit*) emphasises precisely the different nature of modern society, in fact its unique nature that claims risk to be the constitutional condition of possibility.

Ulrich Beck and Anthony Giddens go down the same conceptual avenue. In their discussion of the globalisation of risks they posit developing societies as victims of risks produced in the developed world. They seem to reserve this concept to the social effects of a technological society while assuming that these effects can be felt across the globe. The view that risk is modern in nature has many advocates, especially in the disciplines that have traditionally dealt with the subject. Peter Bernstein's book *Against the Gods* (1996) is a case in point. Much like Bonss he lays a lot of emphasis on the availability of scientific knowledge for there to be risk calculation at all. A slightly different approach is taken by the philosopher Ian Hacking (1990), who in his history of probability identifies state-making and bureaucracy as important frameworks for the development of risk calculation and thereby echoes some of the things that critics of the so-called 'neo-liberal governmentality' say concerning the role of risk in society.

The point that should be brought to the attention of the reader in this section is crucial for the further development of the argument in this chapter. The sociology of risk arose in response to the challenge posed by technological disasters and the growing dependence on expert knowledge systems. As it established itself as a legitimate sub-field of sociology and developed its own research programme, the sociology of risk became increasingly concerned with justifying itself on the basis of the argument according to which it provided a more accurate and updated description of the nature of modern society. In the context of the search for what is unique about modern society, perspectives developed in other subfields of sociology and brought to bear on issues bearing on risk were claimed by the sociology of risk as foundational work. The American sociologist, Charles Perrow, who wrote a path-breaking book on the organisation structure of complex technological systems, was classed with the sociology of risk on the assumption that what he labelled 'normal accidents' fit well into the belief that the insecurity bred by risks was characteristic of modern society.[76]

While it is true that the sociology of risk was constituted on the back of an issue that is central to our current understanding of the nature of modern society, there is a sense in which such a truth fails to acknowledge an even more significant contribution that the sociology of risk could make to social theorising. Part of the reason why the sociology of risk failed to acknowledge its own potential is related to the focus on modern society. Indeed, the focus limited attention to risk as such without reference to its place in the general sociological scheme of things as far as accounting for social action is concerned. The existence of risk was simply assumed, but the question of how it could be accounted for in terms of action from an individual point of view has never really been asked. Matters were made worse by the assumption that risk was modern in nature and, therefore, irrelevant as an analytical category for societies seen not to meet the standards of being modern. With this assumption it became next to impossible to ground risk within social action.

This neglect needs urgent correction. The sociology of risk has much wider relevance than its ability to describe modern society. The question for which the sociology is in search of an answer is not the nature of modern society, but rather how action is possible in spite of everything else that may appear to make it impossible. It is the contingency question that I started formulating in the previous chapter and which we need to continue to pose. This requires revisiting Max Weber again, but also ethnomethodologists who bring more precision into Weber's highly illuminating thoughts on social relationships. We need to probe further into the structure of social action at the same time as we argue that extreme situations are extremely relevant to our ability to account for everyday life.

Social Relationships, Trust, and Predictability

In Max Weber's *Wirtschaft und Gesellschaft* (1972), risk is hardly mentioned. It does not belong to his fundamental concepts of sociology. Yet, I contend, much of what Weber writes in his grounding of sociology is of direct relevance to risk theory. Most critical commentaries of Weber's grounding of sociology have stressed his ideas on social action. Talcott Parsons' *General Action Theory* draws, as we heard in the previous chapter, directly from this and discusses the stability of action in normative terms, that is, in terms of the extent to which society constrains individual agency. In the following section I will seek to articulate Max Weber's notion of social relationships with trust and predictability as important residual categories that emerge from a closer look at social relationships. The idea is to make these two categories fruitful to a discussion of the usefulness of risk to the description of extreme situations.

In fact, I want to suggest that the operationally and analytically useful aspects of Weber's concept of social action are contained in one of its categories: *social relationship*. A social relationship is what action is made of, i.e., interaction which, by virtue of the subjective meaning attached to it by one or more individuals, takes account of the behaviour of others and is, thereby, oriented in its course (Weber 1972: 13). Social relationships decide whether action will be social or not, and in which way. Weber makes a distinction between two basic types of social relationships, both of which relate to his action types. Social relationships can be communal (*Vergemeinschaftung*) or associative (*Vergesellschaftung*).[77] This distinction is similar to Ferdinand Toennies' *Gemeinschaft* and *Gesellschaft*,[78] except that Weber does not thereby describe a given condition or state, but rather the processual character of action.

Action that takes account of subjectively felt common belonging is to be understood as geared towards the constitution of community. This is usually the case with such action types as traditional and affective. Conversely, action that refers to how conflicting interests are harmonised by way of the best means available is geared towards the constitution of society. Weber includes in this category instrumental and value-oriented action types. This distinction describes the reflexive context within which an action takes place because it is both the condition and the outcome of action. The concept of reflexivity as employed by ethnomethodologists (e.g. Garfinkel 1967) draws attention to the fact that individuals act on the basis of understandings of the frame within which they act, and, in the process, change that frame. Similarly, with social relationships the understandings that individuals bring to bear on their nature provide the context for actors to give meaning to what they do, at the same time as their quality is influenced by what individuals do.

In fact, it is no coincidence that the deeper meaning of Weber's concept of 'social relationship' was taken up by ethnomethodologists. The latter, as we saw in the previous chapter, trace their intellectual pedigree back to the work of Alfred Schütz, who brought his phenomenological understanding of society to bear on Weber's notion of meaning. In his critique of this notion Schütz showed[79] that Weber had simply assumed it without actually accounting for it in his grounding of sociology. Not reasons for action yield meaning, Schütz argued, but rather the sedimentation of experience. Meaning is the ability to relate different experiences and normalise them into a coherent and familiar structure. Such structures provide individuals the backdrop against which they go about their everyday lives. They are mainly routine and renewed continually by the active interpretation of new situations into the established pattern of action.

Schütz's structure of the life-world (Schütz and Luckmann 1979) is consistent with the analytical relevance Weber's social relationship has for an adequate understanding of social reality. Both illuminate the context within which individuals act. On the basis of how individuals understand this context, they can appreciate different courses of action and they can formulate expectations. Both the structures of the lifeworld as well as of social relationships are like decision structures[80] which function like Goffman's frames (Goffman 1979, Manning 1997) in contextualising action. Such frames have an enabling effect on individuals, for they allow individuals to deal with contingency.

Trust and predictability play a very important role in this. Traditionally, social theory has seen trust as a resource that individuals muster in order to deal with the difficulties of coordinating action in complex contexts. Luhmann (1989) in particular drew special attention to the function of trust; hereby it comes across as a functional equivalent of knowledge about how others will react to our own actions. This led Giddens (1994) to argue that trust is made necessary by lack of information, which under conditions of modernity is made available to us in a diffuse manner by abstract systems such as money and expert systems. Most of us have no other option but to place our trust on such systems and hope that our expectations about the actions of others are secure and reasonable as long as our ideas about the nature of their motives are consistent with our understanding of the nature of the social system within which we live. Trust is in this sense an important property of social action to the extent that it helps individuals to deal with contingency.[81]

Another important requirement for social action that emerges from a closer look at social relationships is predictability. In fact, social relationships are social action made durable.[82] Predictability refers to the ability of individuals to formulate more or less safe expectations concerning the action of others. While recognising the immanent contingency of social action, we can still argue that individuals look in social relationships for hints of what to expect. The nature of social rerlationships is crucial for the search, just as are historical experience, norms, and values. Predictability, as a property of social action, had already been emphasised by Weber, particularly in connection with increasing instrumental rationality. In fact, if we follow some of Weber's interpreters[83] who claim that his was a cultural sociology, it is not difficult to acknowledge the analytical role that predictability can play in his conceptual scheme. Indeed, it elicits values and norms into a consideration of social action without, thereby, and in contrast to the later Parsons, reducing it to culture.

Both trust and predictability are important properties, which require a further look into here. At the same time, however, trust and predictability pose methodological challenges for which there is no turnkey answer. The notion of risk may however be pushed into positing possible answers. Thus I propose to look more closely into the sense in which trust and predictability are properties of social action, with a discussion that bears particulary on the methodological challenges which such an understanding of social action places on social scientists, but also on the very notion of order in combination with fragility, which is the point of entry that ethnomethodologists chose to describe society.

Encounters and the Fragility of Social Relationships

The European encounter with Africa is full of misunderstandings. Early missionary and travellers' accounts describe them in a vivid manner. A particularly fascinating example is provided by Arthur Grandjean, a Swiss Missionary in late nineteenth-century Mozambique. Nicolas Monnier (1995), a Swiss scholar, analysed reports and letters written by this missionary during his work in southern Mozambique from 1888 to 1896. Grandjean is puzzled by many things in the lives of the natives. They do not like work, but they expect the missionary to give them food. He wants to save their souls by converting them to Christianity, but they are too primitive to understand the true scope of the story of Immaculate Conception. They are cunning and go through the motions of accepting his teachings, but all they are interested in is in his cloth and other material goods he has. It is a tale of two incommensurable worlds. Grandjean's experience was not unique. Colonial officials made similar experiences. The British District Officer in Wole Soyinka's celebrated play *Death and the King's Horseman*[84] bears witness to this. Thoroughly confounded by the natives' resolve to commit suicide for honour's sake he makes an emotional admission of his inability to understand the natives when he exclaims 'why do you people have to speak in such mysterious ways?' (Soyinka 1984).

Such misunderstandings are sociologically relevant and refer us to the constitutive role of social action as discussed by Weber. They bring into bold relief issues related to what makes social action possible, against which backgrounds, and for what purpose. In this they show, on the one hand, the extent to which social reality is dependent upon local contexts to be intelligible. To put it differently, social reality represents a systematic ordering of local experiences. As such, the phenomena that give it substance acquire their meaning within the bounds of underlying experiences, which in turn have been formed over time as part of individuals' negotiation of their own understandings of social reality with others. Individuals are able to participate in that reality and share the meanings ensuing thereof because, through their own experience of everyday life, they contributed towards the construction of the meanings giving such reality substance. Misunderstandings are, on the other hand, useful reminders of how much is taken for granted in social interaction, an area of social action properly taken care of by the notions of trust and predictability which I briefly discussed above. Taking things for granted confirms the phenomenological insight concerning the importance of the natural attitude to the possibility of social interaction. Individuals cannot afford to see everything as if it were the first time. Much social interaction is structured on the assumption that individuals perceive the same reality most of the time.

Now, what is particularly interesting about the misunderstandings described above is precisely the fact that neither of these assumptions works. Europeans neither shared the experience which would have made native social reality intelligible to them, nor was their natural attitude adequate for the local context. They could not take their own assumptions for granted. As a result of that they were unable to make immediate sense of what they saw. The real scope of these remarks comes into full view in chapters six and seven when I discuss conflicting interpretations of reality in my research area and where I seek to show the role of cultural norms and experience in making sense of extreme situations.

Of immediate theoretical and analytical interest is the fact that such misunderstandings do not necessarily announce the end of social interaction. Phenomenological approaches to social reality premise social interaction precisely on the potential ability of individuals to make interaction possible, in spite of all the odds. Conventional sociology might be unable to do so because of its methodological insistence on the ordered nature of social life as we saw in the introductory chapter. Its assumption that norms provide an action framework might place constraints upon the ability to envisage outcomes other than the total breakdown of interaction in the absence of a shared set of norms within which individuals were socialised. It is no accident that precisely this kind of sociology led to the eventually unenlightened concern with deviation at the height of functionalism within the discipline. Such a concern documented the pitfalls of normative definitions of social action as championed particularly by Talcott Parsons in his derivation of it from the internalisation of norms.

In contrast, phenomenological approaches turn the absence of a normative framework of action into a problem to be accounted for. This is an important methodological comment that can be drawn from the concern to find a definition of social action that can adequately take care of contingency. In turning this into a problem phenomenologists, and those inspired by it, are actually concerned with how individuals themselves overcome the problem. Schütz and his closest followers, Berger and Luckmann, assumed that individuals translated problematic situations of everyday life into non-problematic situations. Central to such translation processes was the ability of individuals to reflect upon their own experience through the typification of situations, roles, and functions. In a certain sense one could argue that individuals overcome the problem of the absence of a common normative action framework through a communicative taming of the unknown.[85] In other words, individuals seek to interpret novel situations in terms of the cultural resources available to them within the social reality which they can take for granted. Such cultural resources consist essentially of their existential experience as I hope to show in the empirical case studies, especially in connection with the categories of relevance and knowledge within the analytical framework I use here.

I shall return to the use of cultural resources shortly. In the meantime, I should draw attention to the relevance of this reflection to the problem of the contingency of social action. Problems of misunderstanding refer us in a forceful manner to the much more basic problem of the nature of social reality. It seems obvious that misunderstandings are particularly revealing in this respect. They not only allow us to cast doubts on the conventional sociological assumption of a normatively ordered social reality, but also help us to put into greater relief the uncertainty that inheres in social interaction. It would appear that there is much at stake in any given instance of social interaction. While the assumption that social interaction is normatively ordered may be useful to individuals, they make it at their own risk, as the European encounter with African social reality should make abundantly clear. In fact, in every instance of social interaction there is a basic element of uncertainty that lurks behind individuals' attempts to make sense of the world.

The idea that social interaction is uncertain means not more and not less than that no amount of orderliness which individuals bring to bear on to how they approach others and to contexts of actions will allow them to fully predict the outcomes of what they are about to do. Individuals experience social interaction interpretively. Put differently, to the extent that their actions are subject to the (mis)interpretation of other individuals, the construction of social reality can be usefully conceptualised as work in progress. Individuals are constantly engaged in the immanent task of making sense of their reality, where every form of ontological security (see Giddens 1994), which they may assume or achieve, is only safe until further notice. Further notice, in this instance, refers to the assumptions made by others.

I think that the sociology of risk can be pushed further in the direction of a discussion of the fragility of social interaction as an interesting instance of the contingency of social action. I want to do this by drawing from the insights of ethnomethodology to argue in two directions. Firstly, to insist that viewing social interaction and order as contingent makes good methodological sense, especially as it helps to account for the ways in which individuals repair problematic social encounters. As it will be shown in the course of this work, African social reality is fraught with such problematic social encounters. The African experience of modernity, as indicated in the introduction, is marked by pronounced social change. This prevents individuals in African social settings from taking their social reality for granted. They experience the contingency of social action as a constitutive part of everyday life. It would appear therefore that contingency should be the starting point for any description and analysis of African social reality. Secondly, to draw attention to analytical insights made by ethnomethodology. These concern the emphasis that sociologists of this persuasion place on the methods employed by individuals to create their own reality in the face of very little information as to the designs of others. In other words, to the extent that ethnomethodology is interested in the ways in which individuals in society produce order out of the chaos of social interaction it is a useful companion. It helps in uncovering the assumptions, which make social reality coherent and stable from the perspective of individuals. I explore these issues drawing further from empirical data in the following chapter. At present I am basically interested in stating the issues.

For a useful discussion of fragility in social encounters we need, to start with, a broad notion of action. In other words, we need an all-encompassing notion of action which takes into its fold both conscious direct responses to the actions of others as well as ignorance. Conscious direct responses are actions, which refer immediately to an individual's understanding of the action of others and his, or her, reaction to that understanding. A general category under which these responses could be subsumed is Weber's meaningful social action. Ignorance, in contrast, refers to the structural features of interaction and describes situations in which individuals fail to take notice of one another. Weber's broader notion of action would apply here, with a small qualification. While such actions may not be of immediate relevance to an interpretive approach, they may be useful in the long run. Indeed, they may be remembered as lived experience, which individuals retrieve for the purpose of making sense of a given situation in the future.

The recourse to this broader notion of action should help us set the scene for the discussion which will follow shortly. In the opening paragraphs of this chapter mention was made of misunderstandings that ensued from European encounters with African natives. As history has already taken care to assure us, such misunderstandings were not inconsequential. In other words, communication did not break down. Both Europeans and Africans set about repairing the encounter through a host of practices known to them. For our immediate purposes the exact nature of such practices is less interesting than the mere fact that interaction continued.

Interaction proceeded because, in the face of the unfamiliar, both Europeans as well as Africans resorted to interpretive techniques that allowed them to make sense of the ensuing situations. The unfamiliar presented itself to them in the form of a social situation enclosing roles and expectations unknown to them. Neither of them, that is, neither Europeans nor Africans, could make sense of the situation in terms of their traditional procedures for apprehending social reality. Their interpretive techniques had no import on the situation because they lacked the kind of experience on the basis of which the reality confronting them would have been an artefact of their own action.

The general lines along which Europeans sought to come to terms with the situation ensuing from the encounter correspond to what nowadays would be seen as the discursive power of Europe over the 'Other' (Said 1980, Mudimbe 1988). With the benefit of hindsight one can interpret European meta-narratives as instances of the attempt to come to terms with the unfamiliar. Science, religion, and politics played a crucial role. Indeed, by seeing African forms of life as manifestations of a pre-logical mentality, Europeans were able to integrate them into their own historical experience. Much early anthropological work can be read as an attempt at documenting the stages through which Western reason had to go until it reached its destination in the form of Western scientific thought. The work of Henry Sumner Morgan, Edward Tyler, as well as James Frazer bears witness to this. Their evolutionary frame of reference, which classified African thought as magical and Western thought as scientific, enabled them to make sense of the content of African *Weltanschauungen*. What was initially strange and unfamiliar could, in this way, be rendered normal and familiar.

Adam Kuper's discussion of the notion of 'primitive society' in anthropology (Kuper 1988) brings this point into relief. In fact, the transformations through which the notion went documented much more than just the anthropologist's classification of the 'Other'. It documented the process by which individuals made sense of the unfamiliar. Much in the same way as the evolutionary framework helped make sense of the *Weltanschauung* of native Africans, missionary work, too, could be understood much along the same lines. The idea of conversion to a single God reduced African difference to the Sameness of the West. In so doing missionary work made the lives of Africans intelligible to Europeans. The same applies to politics. Colonialism and its attendant idea of civilisation were not merely a gloss over Europeans' will to power. The power wielded by colonialism allowed Europeans to render African lives understandable.

African analyses of the encounter with Europeans have tended to privilege perspectives that emphasise its violent nature. Examples of such approaches abound. Mudimbe's *l'Odeur du Pére* (1982) as well as his *The Invention of Africa* (1988) are particularly good examples. In these approaches Africans deplore the manner in which, to say it with Mudimbe, 'African Weltanschauungen' are represented (1988). Not surprisingly, African reactions to the encounter are often seen as responses to European power politics. Africans critique modernity (Louise White 2000), resist capitalism (Comaroff and Comaroff 1993), instrumentalize their dependency (Bayart 2000) or disorder (Chabal and Daloz 1999). There have even been much larger explanatory frameworks seeking to make sense of the encounter from a perspective sympathetic to Africans. Such was the case with the so-called 'dependency school' or even 'world-systems theory'. They made sense of the encounter by arguing that European views of Africans were functional to a given political economy. Their immediate point of reference was, of course, modernisation theory, which could be interpreted, in its turn, as a European interpretive procedure to account for the unfamiliar in the encounter with African natives.

The point of this brief discussion of European and African reactions to the encounter is not to analyse the relative merits of each position, but rather to draw attention to important features of interaction. These are relevant to any discussion on the contingency of social action. There are two main features of interaction which this discussion brings to the fore. First of all, it shows that individuals need not share any common set of understandings in order to interact. Traditional sociology assumed that social order is made possible by such shared understandings. The examples, however, clearly show that even in the absence of such understandings individuals act, and in the process produce order.

The question, therefore, is how they are able to accomplish this. The answer to this question is perhaps to be found in the second feature of interaction that should be mentioned in this connection. In fact, by showing that interaction does not break down in the absence of shared understandings, the discussion draws attention to the strategies individuals bring to bear on their interaction. As we have seen in connection with European and African reactions to the unfamiliar, individuals use interactional constructions to this end. Europeans reduced African Otherness to the Sameness of the West, while Africans saw in European views of themselves the manifestation of a Western will to power. Such interactional constructions allow individuals to experience the world in a practical manner as an orderly and shared one.

This last point is of enormous importance to the discussion of the contingency of social action. Indeed, it is opposed to the idea that social order presents itself to individuals as a structured objective reality. Ethnomethodologists would argue that social reality is much less objective than that. In fact, so the argument would run, social order is fragile and malleable, for individuals do not necessarily have a shared sense of understanding and meaning. What individuals share are methods for making sense of what they see. In other words, Europeans and Africans were able to overcome the unfamiliar in their encounter by practically accomplishing a sense of order through their interactional constructions. This echoes Zimmerman's and Wider's understanding of order as '… a practical accomplishment of the everyday interactions of members of a group' (1970: 286–90).

It appears therefore that social order can be understood as fragile to the extent that it is based on interactional constructions. Put differently, it is because individuals have to interpret, typify, and negotiate meanings and situations that they cannot take social reality for granted. In order to do this, individuals make assumptions about the orderly nature of social reality. However, they do this at their own risk, for the expected background features of everyday life – social structure, roles and institutions, for example, – are not properties of social reality, but rather 'emerging properties of human interaction', as Garfinkel quite aptly argued. He goes on to state that,

> The firmer a societal member's grasp of what anyone like us necessarily knows the more severe should be his/her disturbance when the 'natural facts of life' are impugned for him as a depiction of the real circumstances. This is what the breeching experiments are intended to test. Individuals are presented with events that can only be understood by changing the objective structure of the familiar, they cannot be understood in terms of the understood background structure. Presumably, individuals will tend to try to normalize any incongruities (Garfinkel, 1967: 67).

Interaction and Emerging Properties

Schützian phenomenological sociology makes basic assumptions about the individual's perception of reality. These assumptions form the background against which individuals take social reality for granted while, at the same time, ignoring that they make it happen through their own actions. Ethnomethodology differs from other phenomenological approaches in that it brackets out the assumption that the socially constructed reality is apprehended as objective by individuals. Ethnomethodology treats such assumptions as problematic by focusing on the methods which individuals use to make the objective features of social reality available for observation.

There are two aspects which conceptually need to be distinguished from each other. The first aspect concerns the assumptions made by individuals, and the second aspect concerns the methods ethnomethodologists employ to reconstruct the way in which individuals come to have a perception of a shared understanding of reality. Both have important implications for the notions of fragility and order. The assumptions made by individuals, and beautifully summarized in the quote that introduces this section, concern what Garfinkel has labelled 'seen but unnoticed' expected background features of everyday life, while the methods refer to the emerging properties of human interaction.

Ethnomethodologists argue that social interactions consist of two elements. One element is made up of the actual action of individuals, that is, the practices through which individuals engage with one another. These practices are observable both to the acting individuals themselves as well as to the sociologist whose task it is to describe such interactions. They both observe actual behaviour at the same time as they apply interpretative grids to make sense of what they are seeing. The sociologist draws on his knowledge of social structure and assumes that the behaviour he is a witness to is consistent with the normative expectations elicited by that very same social structure. The acting individual may also make similar assumptions, but he must be prepared to adjust them to the ongoing interaction. In other words, as far as the individual is concerned social interaction cannot be reduced to rule following. Through his interpretive and typifying behaviour he helps to produce the structural context of the interaction. Individuals are, in Garfinkel's (1967: 67) fitting terminology, no 'judgemental dopes'[86] incapable of adjusting their actions to their perception of social reality and the actions of others.

The other element of social interaction is made up of what for lack of a better word we could call tacit knowledge. In the sense in which this notion should be understood, here tacit knowledge refers to the individual's share in the social stock of knowledge. This knowledge manifests itself through the expectations that individuals project upon a situation. For instance, whenever an individual acts on the assumption that others know what he means or is doing, he is, as a matter of fact, displaying his share of the sedimented experience of a given group. This might range from meanings left implicit in conversation, to the expectation that by virtue of one's position in the social structure one is entitled to certain forms of treatment. Tacit knowledge confirms the general phenomenological principles of reciprocity while at the same time stressing the local frameworks within which utterances and practices become intelligible.

Both practices as well as tacit knowledge lend substance to the background assumptions individuals make in social interaction. They are both necessary for social interaction to take place, while at the same time they have the potential to make it difficult. After all, individuals may have conflicting views as to the structural nature of their interaction. Garfinkel brought this point home with his so-called 'breeching experiments'. In these experiments he set about showing the extent to which social interaction hinges upon these 'seen but unnoticed' expected background features of everyday life.

While the experiments were able to demonstrate the role of background assumptions in the possibility of social interaction they also confirmed another finding of ethnomethodology. This finding was the idea that individuals repair failed interactions by normalising incongruities. They use their capacity of interpreting and typifying situations and individuals to negotiate their way into an interaction.

The process by which individuals make sense of social reality reveals the emerging properties of human interactions. Ethnomethodologists have identified three such properties, namely *reflexivity, indexicality, and the documentary mode of interpretation*. These properties give individuals a practical sense of an orderly and shared world by allowing them to account for the production of social reality. I want to look at each one of these properties in order to emphasise the constructed nature of social reality. This demonstration will help me to be more precise on the sense in which the fragility of social order should be understood.

Reflexivity

As we have seen, a major feature of social interaction consists of the background assumptions that individuals bring to bear on a given instance of interaction. Phenomenologically speaking such background assumptions are the result of the sedimentation of experience. When individuals typify situations and other individuals, they ascribe to them objective properties with reference to which they are able to structure their perception of reality.

Social roles such as 'father' or 'daughter' as well as social institutions such as 'the family' are given in the world as a result of individual typifications. They do not necessarily exist out there in the world. Individuals, however, assume their objective existence as a resource in their interpretation of reality. The notion of reflexivity refers precisely to the meaning that social phenomena have for individuals. This meaning changes as individuals engage with phenomena. As Pfohl aptly summed it up,

> ...*reflexivity* express(es) that paradoxical characteristic of human existence whereby objects only exist in relation to the interpretive meaning they have for the people who behold them. In other words, for all practical purposes, who you are is never independent of the way in which I construct and express my understanding of you. ...There is no pure objectivity, or for that matter pure subjectivity. ... Everything is in relation to everything else. (Pfohl, 1985: 294) (emphasis added)

Indexicality

While through the notion of reflexivity ehtnomethodologists are able to take account of the relationship individuals have with the social contexts of their action, they have another concept, which allows them to describe the way in which individuals retrieve the information that those same situations hold in store to them. Ethnomethodologists assume that everyone of us relates to the social context within which they act on the basis of their experience of everyday life. While the fate of lived experience is sedimented into a collective experience, individuals retain an individual capacity to make sense of the world. The objects that present themselves to them as social reality are structured according to the unique experiences that each individual makes in his biography. The individual perceives social reality against the background of such experiences. Objects, in this sense, have the quality of signposts which guide the individual through reality. They are indices, on the basis of which social reality can be made sense of.

Ethnomethodologists call this 'indexicality'. What they mean by the term is the property that objects and phenomena have to be retrieved by individuals as indicators of relevant properties of social reality. Again, Pfohl provides a useful summary,

> The term *indexicality* refers to the fact that all human interpretive work is bound to the context in which it occurs. The 'reality' of deviance will be conceived very differently, depending on whether it is viewed from a police patrol car or from the back seat of a vehicle full of partying teenagers. The importance of indexicality to the labeling of deviance is suggested by David Sudnow's study of public defenders. Sudnow describes an overcrowded court context in which public attorneys are pressured toward using commonsense stereotypes about who is and who isn't the 'normal' criminal and who should be provided with a certain type of defense or plea bargaining. The stereotypical identification of 'normal crimes' is linked to the practical demands of an overworked and understaffed public defenders office. Such contextual or indexical demands significantly influence the shape of societal reaction. (Pfohl 1985: 293)

In other words, individuals do not only construct reality socially. They also use it as a resource to make sense of reality itself. One could resort to the French sociologist Jean Baudrillard (1992) and argue that from an ethnomethodological perspective social reality functions as a kind of *simulacrum*, that is, it is a representation of something that does not exist. Of course, the objective existence of social reality is guaranteed by the reflexive process that firmly binds individuals to their own constructions.

Documentary Mode of Interpretation

Reflexivity and indexicality build an interactional and interpretive complex. Individuals produce social reality, relate to it, and are able to perceive it from different perspectives. In so doing they engage with it interpretively by ordering perceptions of it in a coherent manner. In order to do this they use what ethnomethodologists call the documentary method of interpretation. They draw from the sociology of knowledge of Karl Mannheim who suggested that sociology's hermeneutic orientation could be served properly by a method which sought to articulate observations of social phenomena about the social groups and contexts from within which they had been produced. The ethnomethodological form of documentary interpretation takes its cue from this idea and expands it to include the procedure according to which individuals use typifications to infer meaning and motivations in the behaviour of others.

In other words,

> Appearances are treated as documents of something deeper, as expressions of underlying patterns or structures. According to Garfinkel, 'Not only is the underlying pattern derived from its individual documentary evidences, but the individual documentary evidences, in their turn, are interpreted on the basis of 'what is known' about the underlying pattern. Each is used to elaborate the other.' ... The method of documentary interpretation is used by people to make sense of other people. ...Wiseman describes the manner in which such things as physical appearance, past performance, and social position are taken as indications of the kind of person a particular offender is and how his or her case should be handled. (Pfohl, 1985: 295–96)

Documentary interpretation is the method which individuals employ to make sense of the world. Making sense of the world means, in the main, to piece observed phenomena and objects together into a coherent account. We may note in passing the role that the individual's interpretive capacity plays in bringing about the reality of social order.

Reflexivity, indexicality, and the documentary method are aspects of the way in which individuals both construct their social reality while at the same time rendering it visible. This brief discussion offers two insights, which are relevant to an analysis of the contingency of social action. The first insight is related to the practices that are constitutive of reality. Indeed, reality is unthinkable outside of the things that individuals do. Reality has no ontological priority over and above action. Reality exists, and is available to us, because individuals do things and we can observe the things they do. From an ethnomethodological perspective the idea that reality is socially constructed acquires a radical meaning. Reality is, in fact, an artefact of action.

The second insight is of more direct relevance to the notion of contingency. Since reality as such is a construct, the notion of order owes its existence to action. It appears therefore that any consideration of social order should have as its starting point the things that individuals do. As a matter of fact,

> Ethnomethodology extends the phenomenological perspective to the study of everyday social interaction. It is concerned with the methods which people use to accomplish a reasonable account of what is happening in social interaction and to provide a structure for the interaction itself. Unlike symbolic interactionists [*Labeling Perspective*], ethnomethodologists do not assume that people actually share common symbolic meanings. What they do share is a ceaseless body of

> interpretive work which enables them to convince themselves and others that they share common meanings. (Pfohl, 1985: 292–93)

In this connection, individuals' ability to deal with the unfamiliar in their social environment rests largely on the relationship they establish with what they themselves and other individuals do. Thus it would appear that a methodologically sound approach to the conditions under which action takes place has to engage with individuals themselves. In other words, the problem of contingency can only be usefully approached from the things that individuals do, that is, from their action. It is actions that make actions possible. This should be understood in a double sense. Actions make actions possible in the sense that one action follows another. This is the first sense. The second sense refers to the idea that individuals must interpret an action in order to be able to act themselves. However, their interpretation may not be consistent with the interpretation of other individuals. Individuals may fail for a number of reasons to successfully predict the real intentions of other individuals, or they may positively wish to misinterpret them. And since social life is made possible by necessarily different experiences of life the potential for misunderstanding is quite considerable. This potential makes social order fragile.

The fragility of the social order builds a useful bridge between the sociology of risk, on the one hand, and its relevance to the description and analysis of African lifeworlds, on the other. Indeed, the concept of risk can be broadened, enough to encompass basic social processes of the constitution of meaning and sociality in local settings. As we have seen drawing on ethnomethodological discussions of reflexivity, indexicality, and the documentary method, the social worlds we are concerned with in sociology are such that risk appears to be central to their possibility at all. The very narrow definition of the notion of risk in the current sociology of risk serves the useful purpose of allowing for focused empirical research to be conducted, yet it may fail to make us aware of the role which central dimensions of risk are actually present in everyday life and everything that make the latter possible. The potential for fragility, typical of social order, calls for broadening our understanding of risk. We can achieve this by interrogating the concept with a view to eliciting aspects that enable us to account for social action in ways that acknowledge the constitutive role of contingency and uncertainty. The analytical implications of this interrogation are taken up in the following chapter where I present the analytical framework I use to make sense of the empirical data in the second part of this book.

Making Risk Relevant

My aim in this chapter has been to build a bridge between what I think to be the challenges faced by African studies, in general, and the particular tasks which African social reality sets the social sciences. The bridge consists of the current understanding of the object of the sociology of risk. As the brief discussion in the introduction to this chapter showed, the sociology of risk seeks an understanding of risk which helps it to describe the nature of modern society. In the idea of risk as a defining moment in the structural conditions of action in modernity, sociology believes to have found an appropriate tool to make this description possible. Luhmann's very useful distinction between hazard and risk, however, has wittingly, or unwittingly, toned down the enthusiasm with which the special affinity of risk within modern industrial society has been greeted by risk sociologists.

In fact, in emphasising the dynamic relationship between hazard and risk, Luhmann referred us to decision structures and, thereby, returned sociology to where it belongs, namely in the description and understanding of human action. In so doing, he reached out to perennial discussions concerning the precise status of social action in sociological theory and made it possible for sociologists to begin to ask analytically forward-looking questions about the meaning of contingency in accounting for human experience. In their discussion of these issues, especially their emphasis on the emergent properties of action, ethnomethodologists may have been ahead of their time. Seen from the vantage point of what the sociology of risk tells us about the nature of human action, the ethnomethodological perspective on society and social relations may yet come to be vindicated as a very shrewd move that inflates sociological theory with a renewed lease of life.

The challenge in sociological theorising has, since the days of Weber and Durkheim, boiled down to knowing what is to count as an appropriate account of human behaviour. While Weber stressed the subjective meaning that individuals attach to what they do, Durkheim insisted on the primacy of overarching factors. Alfred Schütz' introduction of a phenomenological perspective on this took the discussion to other planes, especially in terms of methodological approaches which allowed ethnomethodologists and symbolic interactionists to pay more attention to the dialectical relationship that structure and agency entertain. Risk, unpredictability, contingency, and uncertainty are concepts that allow us to raise this old sociological question and seek to answer it with fresh empirical data. To a large extent, this is the purpose of this book.

While risk may be a useful tool to describe the nature of modern society, there is a strong sense in which it is much more than that. Risk is about the conditions of possibility of social action and human behaviour. The ability to produce risk is an anthropological constant, as I hope to show in the following chapters. The recognition that risk is an anthropological constant has far-reaching consequences for our understanding of the perennial question of sociology, namely, how to account for social action. The idea closely follows ethnomethodological discussions of the emergent properties of action and posits action as intrinsically risky behaviour.

To put it simply, when individuals act, they risk something. They risk failure, being misunderstood, or exposing themselves to ridicule. Simply by acting they engage with other people and with their natural and social environment, exposing themselves to reactions they cannot necessarily foresee within the more limited individual frame of reference. It is in this sense that social action is risky behaviour. Individuals, however, are not necessarily aware of the risky nature of their behaviour. My point, then, is that this ostensive lack of awareness of the risky nature of social action can be accounted for with the help of the insights of the sociology of risk and ethnomethodological discussions of human behaviour. Indeed, I am claiming that the relationship between structure and agency has seemed to elude us because we appear to have failed to appreciate the circular nature of social action: individuals act in order to be able to act.

This circularity is at the heart of the empirical findings from Patrice Lumumba village in southern Mozambique. The description of how individuals and communities cope with disasters and crises suggests that the major concern is to ensure that whatever the circumstances, individuals and communities are in a position to do something. Everyday life boils down to making sure that social action takes place. To put it simply, the tension between structure and agency is resolved by individuals creating conditions for agency. To do this, they create contexts of action, a notion to which I now turn in the next chapter and which, with the help of interview material from the village where I carried out my research, I will attempt to discuss in the light of the theoretical implications of the notion of risk.

4

Methodological Issues: Contexts of Action

Introduction

This chapter is about the methodological centrepiece of this book, namely *contexts of action*. Drawing on the theoretical notes made in the previous two chapters, I am interested in showing that there is more to social action than just purposefully doing something, which either has a meaning or is meaningful. Furthermore, I will try to demonstrate that central aspects of risk sociology can be brought to bear on research designs that draw from the analysis of extreme situations to make informed comments about the general structure of everyday life. The claim I wish to make is that when individuals act socially they are simultaneously creating the context of their action. I draw a methodological implication from this observation, which can be spelt out simply along the following lines: *people act in order to be able to act*. This requires some explaining.

In fact, spelling out this methodological implication and explaining its import is the main object of this chapter. To this end, I will briefly dwell on the precise sense in which this implication should be understood as a prelude to working out the details of the analytical framework, which emerges from it. Indeed, while most of the chapter will be taken up by a description of the research terrain against the background of a general phenomenological approach to social life, it will nonetheless draw on a very specific methodology to provide a description, which is not simply empirical, but also inferential to the extent that it seeks to organise the empirical material in a certain meaningful way. The procedure which I hope to document in the process of making an inferential description will give us insight into what the analytical framework based on the idea of 'contexts of action' should look like.

Excursion: *What does it Mean to Say that People Act in order to Act?*

The question needs to be rephrased: what does it mean to say that the idea according to which people act in order to act has methodological implications? The answer to this question is crucial for the development and understanding of the analytical framework to be worked out in this chapter. I will answer the question with a look at a reality, which is geographically distant from the kinds of realities my studies focus on here. I do so because that distant reality is made available to us in a way that brings the methodological issues into a much broader relief. Indeed, I am drawing on the work of the German anthropologist Gerd Spittler on agency in the context of famine (Spittler 1989a), in which he describes, from first-hand experience, the social behaviour of Tuareg nomads during the 1984/85 Sahel drought. I come back to this work because it raises the issues that are central to the analytical framework that I am trying to construct in appropriate ways.

At one point in his graphic description of the reaction of the Tuareg to the drought, Spittler is puzzled by a decision female shepherds do not make, namely selling their goats in order to purchase millet. According to own account in other writings (Spittler 1989b), millet is central to the diet of the Tuareg and, given the fact that the drought placed a severe strain on their purse, it would only appear logical that they sought to acquire this grain to feed on. Instead, however, they fed on the unsavoury leaves of *agar* which one of Spittler's female informants described as tasting like the contents of a goat's stomach. The anthropologist is puzzled because he sees a number of reasons why the goats should be sold in exchange for millet. For this he lists the follwowing reasons:

- The women could purchase millet with the proceeds from the sale of goats;

- In the year in question (84/85) the goats would be of no use at all since they were not going to give any milk;

- In contrast, finding pastures and water for the goats had become more exacting than usual;

- On top of it all, it was not clear whether the goats would survive the coming warm season at all, given the fact that fodder had became even scarcer;

- Because of tending the goats the female shepherds were condemned to stay in one place. They stayed in the wild, in fact far away from the places where there was still some food. If they had sold their goats they could have actively pursued the search for food for themselves.

The question that arises here concerns how the story might proceed. What kinds of action or courses of action ensue from these questions for the researcher? Basically, there are at least two possible courses of action. In the good old tradition of interpretive sociology, a researcher might wish to question the subjectively intended meaning of the action of the female shepherds. In other words, what did the shepherdesses think they were doing when they decided not to sell their goats? The other course of action would be to assume the irrationality of the actor and thereby forego the opportunity to appreciate the rich social texture of the actor's decision. There is a general way in which the tension between the two courses of action can be stated. In fact, what seems to be at stake here is the question concerning the subject of the puzzle. Is the decision not to sell a puzzle for the actors themselves or, what is more likely, for the researchers? Any researcher who opts for the second course of action, that is, assumes the irrationality of the actors, actually transfers the puzzle to the actor himself and fails to consider that even in very mundane terms it is the researcher who is in search of understanding. Sociological thinking has benefitted enormously from the assumption that individuals know, that is, have good reasons for, what they are doing. These points deserve further attention.

We are faced with a methodological challenge that presents itself in the time-honoured form of the difficult relationship between concept and reality, but also in the form of how our analytical operations help us to structure the way in which we make sense of reality. Even if the jury still seems to be seeking the exact nature of the relationship between concepts and reality, there is a measure of consensus on the extent to which concepts help us to retrieve fundamental aspects of reality in the form of data. Our accounts of reality are based on what data tell us about that reality. Of course, there are problems with the assumption that data speak, and philosophers are still arguing over whether it is not we who make the data speak. Perhaps we can seize the significance of this issue by focusing on the notion of data itself.

Richard Rorty, the American Pragmatist philosopher, once argued that '[T]he world is out there, but descriptions of the world are not. Only descriptions of the world can be true or false. The world in its own — unaided by the describing activities of human beings — cannot' (Rorty, 1989: 5). In other words, Rorty was suggesting that the quality of being true or false was not a property of the world itself, but rather of the descriptive categories we employ to retrieve the world. Thus, translated into the language of the methodology of the social sciences, he seemed to be placing emphasis on the nature of data as consisting of our own decisions concerning what is to count as an accurate representation of reality.

I understand Rorty's relativism here as an invitation to scientists to be aware of, and sensitive to, the limits of their accounts of reality. Indeed, our data cannot claim to translate reality one-to-one into our concepts, and vice-versa, but precisely because this is so we need to guard ourselves against assuming our problems to be the problems either of the reality which we seek to describe or of the individuals whose action we want to understand. Rorty may be overstating his case when he goes on to argue that '... we do not discover the Truth; we make truths with our languages' (Rorty 1989: 6), but the point is well taken. Through our methodological decisions concerning the concepts, the measurements, and the analytical frameworks we employ in order to describe and analyse reality, we frame our own way of perceiving the world and, thereby, probably reduce the complexity inherent to it. It is no coincidence that some methodological schools of thought[87] argue in favour of an attitude that emphasises the assumption that our concepts and tools are mere vehicles that carry us into possible worlds.[88]

The world, says Rorty, is out there and can neither be wrong nor right. What we say about the world is decisive, for alongside the claim we make to the effect of actually describing the world, we are also claiming that it is possible to discover the world, or reality, in what we say. This is, of course, a commentary on the discursive nature of the relationship between the social sciences and their object, but it is also much more than that. In fact, it is about how data makes the world accessible to us without thereby bringing it any closer. We have a special relationship to data that allows us to assume that we are speaking truthfully about the world, when in reality all we are doing is to surrender to our own criteria of validity inhabiting the analytical operations we are carrying out. What we can truthfully say is what can be right or false, not the world we seek to render intelligible. By the same token, however, our ability to check the plausibility of our interpretation of our own data provides us with the contours of a framework of analysis that is worth thrashing out in a little more detail.

As a matter of fact, the idea that our data provides us with the contours of an analytical framework brings us back to the issue of the subjectively intendend meaning. Max Weber was of course the sociologist who brought this notion to the attention of his contemporaries and later generations of social scientists. In his famous distinction between value judgement and relation to value, he sought to make the point that we draw on our norms in order to select and perceive aspects of social reality. The choices we thereby make do not affect the substance of the reality we seek to account for, but we would render this reality a great disservice if we elevated our own normative positions to the status of relevant criteria in establishing the accuracy of our accounts.

This leads us straight to the exact meaning of a subjective meaning of social action as discussed by Weber. In his *Economy and Society* Weber defines sociology as an intellectual enterprise concerned with the interpretive understanding of social action and thus with what he terms the causal explanation of its course and consequences. Social action, therefore, is the object of sociology; this immediately warrants the question concerning the precise meaning of this central notion. Weber argues in this connection that sense, in which action is social, has to do with the extent to which the subjective meaning of action takes account of the behaviour of others and takes its cue from that behaviour.

Unfortunately, the way Weber states the issue, and as we saw in chapter one, does not provide us with a solution, but rather it posits a problem that needs solving before we can proceed. What does it mean to claim that social action must be understood interpretatively and thereby providing a causal explanation of its course and consequences? Is this what the anthropologist Spittler would be doing in his approach to the puzzle of the shepherdesses if he was to make it his own problem, not theirs? Why should social action take pride of place in this undertaking and, incidentally, what is the exact empirical meaning of social action? In the previous chapter we saw that there is no easy answer to this question.

Max Weber himself favoured an answer that drew on the tradition of historicim in German philosophy of science, arguing, along with Wilhelm Dilthey, that social action consists of what individuals do plus the reasons which they have for doing it. In so doing individuals may follow rules and norms as objectified in life orders, but such rules and norms are not the cause of the action of individuals. For this reason, Weber emphasised interpretation in the sense of understanding as opposed to explanation in a causal manner. This, however, did not foreclose the possibility of positing causal factors. In fact, as Alfred Schütz' further elaboration of Weber's understanding of social action to include motives clearly showed,[89] an adequate understanding of what individuals do is only possible after we have established the past and future of what they do in terms that do justice to individuals' intentions.

In a sense, therefore, the subjective meaning of social action consists of all the information that we require in order to be able to claim that what we see individuals doing is what we think that they are doing. This implies, again following Weber and Dilthey for that matter, that our data deliver information on two levels. The first level is that of the world as it is in terms of what, in a given society, could be taken as an appropriate description of an activity. Merely providing this appropriate description would, however, fall short of what an interpretive understanding of social action is, for another level should be considered. This is the level of the kinds of intentions an individual articulates through his or her action. In other words, this particular piece of writing can be readily recognised as a very specific form of scientific communication. To fully understand it as social action, however, one would also need to be aware of the context which makes it possible and perhaps motivates me to produce it, but also of all the reasons I may have, beyond the immediate context of professional academic life. The sheer quantity of such reasons is extremely daunting but cautions us against the scope of conclusions, which are not adequately informed by the full range of options individuals have to give meaning to their lives.

Social action, therefore, consists of actual practice and the reasons people have for engaging in such practice. Reasons do not explain practices, but together with them they are powerful instruments for researchers to appreciate the richness of social life. Interpreting social action in this sense goes beyond simply making causal attributions. It is in fact a very special way of describing the social world. Alfred Schütz' point to the effect that sociology has the task of describing typical actions by typical individuals is well taken to the extent that it enjoins us to seriously engage with the context within which social action takes place.

This brings me back to Gerd Spittler's puzzlement over the shepherdesses' decision not to sell their goats. The phenomenon to be described in this case is the behaviour of the shepherdesses, not their decision not to sell their goats. In other words, the one piece of knowledge that can help us understand their decision is a full description of the meaning of tending goats. An appropriate description of this activity will provide insight into the meaning which preference for goats over millet, the value of goats, the types and levels of importance of work, knowledge about animals and the weather, ideas about patience, initiative and creativity, and, finally, the relationship between humans and animals have. Put differently, a comprehensive description delivers answers to Spittler's 'why-question' and these answers are in fact properties of the activity of tending goats. All the while, the description takes the reasons given by the shepherdesses seriously into account, but does not reduce them to the level of explanations of why they act the way they act.

Generally speaking, therefore, my claim that individuals act in order to be able to act refers, firstly, to the nature of our relationship as researchers to social reality which is mediated by data, and, secondly, to the substantive requirements that data place upon us when we go about describing the world. We retrieve reality through our own data, but these data document our understanding of reality, not reality itself, although our understanding of reality is informed by the nature of reality itself. Data may bring us closer to reality and, in particular, to the kind of reality that concerns us as social scientists, if we are prepared to acknowledge that the concepts we use to retrieve reality are our own. The point that should be emphasised in this connection is not that there is no hope of knowing for sure what reality really is, rather, the point is that a more productive way to engage with our data and conceptual categories is to be sensitive to the inherent strangeness of what we wish to describe. Interpretive sociology's approach to social action is sensitive to this and owns up to it by inviting us to be empirical in the way we engage with the world.

When we follow these strictures, we soon realise that the objective world our data seek to report on, is also in the making. It is not given once and for all. It is a product of history and its appearance of permanence is simply subject to the proviso that it is until further notice. The idea that individuals act in order to be able to act has several meanings, all of which are standard knowledge in the social sciences. The first meaning is that, through their actions, individuals create the overarching political, economic, and social frameworks within which they can go about their business, i.e., doing things. Anthony Giddens has drawn particular attention to this in his attempts to reconcile structure and agency through his suggestion of the notion of 'structuration' (Giddens 1985). The second meaning expands on the structural dimension of action and draws attention to the fact that the frameworks produced by individual action provide the context within which such action becomes intelligible. Indeed, it is with reference to those frameworks that reasons and motives can be formulated and individuals can gain certainty about what they do. Phenomenological sociologists have given us valuable insights into this, particularly Alfred Schütz with his focus on the social stock of knowledge. Finally, a further meaning is to be found in the creative nature of action to the extent that it opens up possibilities for further action. In other words, every action brings historical potential to fruition. This idea has found a particularly vigorous proponent in Hans Joas (1996) and his pragmatism-inspired notion of 'ends-in-view'.

This is what is meant by the claim that individuals act in order to be able to act. An action is not an end in itself, it has a history and a future. Taking note of this may be useful in equipping our methodological approaches with the right kinds of tools to strengthen our assumptions concerning the relationship between our data and reality. In other words, I am claiming that when we observe social reality we are concerned with describing contexts of action and that we should do this by taking a particular interest in documenting reality in as comprehensive a manner as is required in order to be able to make claims concerning our ability to understand. Social action is process that we tactically stabilize in the form of contexts of action. Towards the end of the chapter I will come back to these issues and suggest an analytical framework for the empirical material at the root of this book. For the time being I will take up the more general theoretical issues by way of an introduction into the setting.

Warrants for Empirical Grounding

As I attempted to show in chapters one and two, the idea that individuals act in order to be able to act is not a novel idea in itself. Phenomenologically informed sociology has been concerned with clearing the conceptual ground to bring this idea to fruition. This kind of sociology has placed at the centre of its methodological and conceptual work the challenge of accounting for action both in terms of what it means to the individuals who are engaged in it, as well as, and more importantly, in terms of what social action means to its own conditions of possibility. Therefore, my concern here is to combine the discussion of my empirical material, drawing on discourse analytical tools bearing on the properties of social action with the more theoretical aim of contributing towards the empirically warranted grounding of this view of social action.

As I have tried to suggest in the brief excursion into the claim that individuals act in order to be able to act, there is a sense in which we could argue that social action entails its own conditions of possibility. Methodologically, we can tease these conditions out through forms of description, which are essentially inferential in nature. I am drawing here from King, Keohane, and Verba (1994) who claim that, while there may be differences between quantitative and qualitative approaches in social science research, a considerable part of qualitative research consists of descriptions which already assume a certain type of coherence of the object, that is, the social world. The empirical grounding of the entailment of the conditions of possibility of social action in social action itself means that, in appreciating empirical data, however it may have been collected, we are required to infer its meaning in terms of the kinds of assumptions that we make about the social world. In this sense, the challenge in this book in inferring the meaning of the empirical data consists in taking the precarious nature of the local lifeworlds of the research terrain seriously and assuming a subtext that posits the classical Simmelian question of knowing how society is possible in the first place.

As we will see further below this question is well taken up in ethnomethodological approaches. Its importance in the context of the data, and the lifeworld which the data seek to describe, lies in the fact that it allows us to focus on the mere possibility of social action in a precarious context. Given everything that we know about existential conditions in the research terrain, how is social life possible there? What sorts of resources do people draw from in order to be able to go about their lives? It is obvious that this sort of questions leads us to place the sociology of risk at the centre of our analytical endeavours and to seriously engage with Niklas Luhmann's seminal point concerning the translation of hazard into risk. Indeed, the precarious nature of the lifeworld of the research location is characterised by the efforts of the individuals making up the web of social relations within that context in actively engaging in risky behaviour.

Contrary to a widespread assumption in scholarly circles that practical and humanitarian considerations lend legitimacy to the study of African social phenomena, I argue, as indicated in chapters one and two, that Africa is interesting for social theory because it offers us phenomena that allow us to sharpen our conceptual and analytical tools. The region where I conducted my research has experienced rapid social change, ecological degradation, and political strife to an extent that poses huge challenges to the intentional content of our concepts. I think such conditions offer an ideal background against which we can honour our commitment to test the scope of our scientific tools, over and above any immediate practical gain that we tend to readily associate with the purpose of academic pursuit in Africa.

In the introduction to the book I gave a few hints concerning selected aspects of the everyday life of the village of Patrice Lumumba. I now want to focus on certain aspects of the village lifeworld; this will accomplish two tasks. The first task is to acquaint the reader with the natural and social environment within which I carried my empirical research. The second task, however, is to provide a description of the villagers' lifeworld with the purpose of drawing attention to the circular nature of social action. To put it simply, in this chapter I want to present the natural and social environment of the research area as an everyday accomplishment of the villagers themselves. Indeed, to remain true to the theoretical framework that informs much of the discussion in this book, the description offered here does not take the background reality for granted, rather it attempts to present it in a dynamic manner as the outcome of what individuals do when they go about their lives. I will seek to capture these accomplishments in the accounts villagers give and will aim at drawing the conclusion that what they are in fact doing is creating the context of their own social action.

Right at the outset a caveat should be noted. The approach favoured here is not constructionist in the ordinary sense in which the notion of constructionism is often understood.[90] In other words, I am not making the claim that the facts of nature as well as the very real social constraints that act upon the individual either do not exist or that they are just figments of the imagination of those who lead their social lives within the context where such constraints operate. While the theoretical perspective adopted here, particularly through Berger and Luckmann's interpretation of Alfred Schutz' work, may seem to suggest a constructionist approach to reality, the point that should be borne in mind is already contained in the path-breaking work of the former. This refers specifically to their definition of knowledge as the certainty that individuals have that reality exists (Berger and Luckmann 1991). It is obvious, therefore, that neither Berger and Luckmann nor Schütz suggested that the idea of the socially constructed nature of reality had anything to do with the rejection of the essential quality of the natural world. As a matter of fact, the idea that social reality is constructed was derived from notions of how individuals perceive reality and come to terms with it.

These ideas chime in quite well with central aspects of the sociology of risk at the heart of the theoretical framework favoured in this book. In fact, coping with uncertainty is social action deeply ingrained in individual and collective perceptions of reality as well as in the manner in which such perceptions become the currency through which individuals engage with one another. Just as the sociology of knowledge seeks to know what makes people sure about the actual existence of reality, the sociology of risk should cast a look at social interaction in order to find out the extent to which it reflects the manner in which individuals perceive threats to their idea of a stable social world. To put it more simply, the description of the social and natural environment of the empirical research is in actual fact the description of the ideas individuals have of social reality as well as of the interactional strategies which they deploy to sustain that reality. The phenomenological concept that comes closest to this intention is the idea of a world taken for granted. Indeed, describing the social and natural environment of the research context is about uncovering the reasons for and the ways by which individuals take their world for granted.

Mundane Reasoning

A useful methodological and analytical suggestion that I would like to pursue in this chapter was made by ethnomethodologists, who actually saw themselves as working in the long and fruitful sociological tradition established by the work of Alfred Schutz. I wish in particular to use Melvin Pollner's notion of 'mundane reasoning' (1987). In an initial statement of the problem Pollner (1974) had drawn attention to the need for sociology to remain true to the ethnomethodological injunction to treat social facts as accomplishments. Furthermore, he emphasized that '[W]here others might see "things", "givens" or "facts of life", the ethnomethodologist sees (or attempts to see) process: the process through which the perceivedly stable features of socially organized environments are continually created and sustained' (Pollner 1974: 27). These reservations allowed Pollner to develop his notion of mundane reason. He defined mundane reason as the assumed nature of the objectivity and intersubjectivity of everyday life. In other words, Pollner argued that such an assumption of objectivity and intersubjectivity is intricately related with the manner in which individuals seek to sustain, assert, or even call the reality it conjures up into question. This is mundane reason, the taken for granted world of everyday life to which individuals refer.

The description offered in this chapter of the natural and social environment within which the empirical material informing this book was collected draws directly from Melvin Pollner's notion of mundane reason. He developed a set of analytical concepts, which I have found extremely useful for analysing the empirical material in a systematic way. According to Pollner mundane reason has an idiom upon which the assumption rests concerning the objective existence of the features of the social world. This idiom is underscored by three basic interactional features.

On the one hand, the idiom is sustained by so-called 'authorisation practices', that is, the manner in which individuals in society make claims about the validity of their perception of reality and, on the other hand, reasoning practices, meaning, the devices which they deploy in order to make sense of their perception of reality. The final interactional feature consists of 'secondary elaborations', which refers to the basic beliefs that individuals bring to bear in order to forestall doubts about the objective nature of reality. As I hope to demonstrate further below these analytical concepts are useful, not only because they allow me to provide a description of the social and natural environment of the research as an accomplishment of villagers themselves, but also because, as it will become obvious as the argument

Methodological Issues 89

unfolds, they refer us to the precarious nature of this environment and, thereby, force us to engage with the issues of risk, certainty, and insecurity.

Indeed, in opting for ethnomethodological analytical tools in this chapter, I intend to bring into bold relief what I hold to be the main impulse behind social action, namely the translation of hazard into risk. The accomplishment of social reality is the outcome of this translation process as individuals respond to their perception of a precarious environment and endeavour to create a context of action. Furthermore, I attach particular importance to the fact that the description of the research terrain on which my analysis is based draws from villagers' own accounts. This is important in order to be consistent with the theoretical and methodological remarks made earlier concerning the relationship between data and researchers, on the one hand, and the social world and its actors, on the other.

I draw from general literature on the region where I carried out my research, but more importantly from observations made *in situ* as well as interviews I conducted in the course of the research. For the analysis of mundane reasoning in the research area I will mainly rely on recorded interviews. All in all, I conducted thirty recorded interviews, five unrecorded interviews, as well as several informal conversations. I had all of the interviews transcribed into Portuguese by a native speaker of both Tsonga and Portuguese. The analysis of mundane reason draws specifically from a pool of seventeen interviews. I coded them with reference to Melvin Pollner's discussion of the features of mundane reason. In other words, I searched for instances of the idiom, which individuals use to account for the local social reality and I subdivided these instances into (a) definitions, (b) authorisation procedures, and (c) reasoning practices. I also coded and searched for instances of what Pollner calls 'secondary elaborations'. I used the computer software MaxQdata version 2 to code and analyse the data. Before I present my data in more detail, I wish to make a few general remarks about the research area.

Patrice Lumumba Communal Village

This is a sprawling village sitting uncomfortably on sand dunes that separate the city of Xai-Xai in southern Mozambique from the Indian Ocean, about ten kilometres away. Actually, it is not appropriate to call the place a village. According to information provided by the local authorities[91] there are about 18,000 people living in what is officially known as Patrice Lumumba Communal Village. The sheer numbers make mockery of the notion of village.[92] At any rate, they are not consistent with the predominant idea of 'village' that people have in Mozambique. In the traditional sense of the word, a village is the home of a lineage or clan and usually does not have more than thirty to fifty people. Originally, that is, up to the end of the colonial period in 1975, the area now known as Patrice Lumumba Communal Village was indeed a village in the traditional sense of the word. There lived a lineage by the name of Mbalan. Down in the Limpopo valley, there were major floods in 1977, which provided state authorities with an opportunity to create a communal village on Mbalan territory through resettling the victims. In the course of the 1980s further people found their way to the village. They were refugees, fleeing from the war in the countryside. In the year 2000 they were joined by yet more flood victims in the wake of the so-called 'great 2000 floods' (Hanlon and Christie 2001).

With each wave of new settlers the village lost more of its contours, bursting at its seams and overflowing across a wide expanse of sand dunes. In a certain sense, population influxes seem to punctuate the history of the area. Three periods can be clearly distinguished, all of which document social change of a very specific kind. Indeed, one could say that the village and its diverse populations have been experiencing successive waves of modernisation brought on by the state, claiming increasing chunks of their everyday life. The first period is not well remembered in the village. It is only older members of the original Mbalan lineage who can recall key features of the past. They remember to have been under the rule of the Gaza-Nguni[93] until they were overthrown by the Portuguese in 1897. The Mbalan lineage seems to have entertained very good relations with the Gaza-Nguni, but the defeat of the latter does not seem to have affected its position in any significant way. In fact, the Mbalan continued to hold political power through the system of traditional chieftainship which the Portuguese installed in the wake of their military victory. In other words, the Mbalan had the right to install a *régulo*[94] who served as an intermediary between the Portuguese colonial state and the local indigenous population within the Mbalan confines.

State colonial rule brought the modern state and its artefacts – hospitals, schools, police, army, and wage labour – into the lives of the villagers. The fact that political power was bestowed upon the Mbalan by the colonial state weakened, without necessarily completely undermining, traditional forms of political legitimacy, which rested in the main on religious and traditional justifications. On several occasions during fieldwork I could sense a fundamental unease with the artefacts of modern political power, which were not only confined to forms of authority, but also included, as mentioned above, health, education, and employment. It was as if villagers had been forced to live in an alien world, a world which they found very hard to understand. In informal conversations, for instance, they would often speak about the new times as if they represented a conspiracy against them. They compared the times before the arrival of motorised vehicles, hospitals, and schools, that is, the time when they could still walk long distances, be healed by their own healers, and children were expected to look after the cattle or join in in farming activities, with present times. They suspected, for example, that vitamins given intravenously to pregnant women in hospital were actually substances designed to weaken the babies, so that later, as grown-ups, they would prefer the new institutions to the older ones. During a group discussion, most participants claimed that the real purpose of the vitamins was to weaken the people so that they were no longer able to walk long distances and, as a result, became dependant on motorised vehicles.

When Mozambique achieved independence in 1975, major changes swept across Mbalan territory. The Marxist oriented new government did away with the system of political authority installed by the Portuguese. It introduced its own system based on so-called 'dynamising groups' which were basically party structures consistent with the one-party system that held sway in Mozambique until the adoption of a new, multi-party constitution in 1990. Mozambique's Marxist regime was officially declared in 1977. This coincided with the single most important factor that was going to change the face of Mbalan territory for good. Indeed, in 1977 there were major floods, which the authorities took advantage of to resettle people living in the valley to Mbalan territory. At the same time, the new settlement area was transformed into a communal village and named after Patrice Lumumba, a Congolese nationalist, who had led his country to independence from Belgium. The new political structures that came to replace the Portuguese invention of a traditional system of authority placed political power in the hands of the new arrivals. These, not members of the Mbalan lineage, became the new rulers of Mbalan territory. Given deeply ingrained ideas on the source of political legitimacy, this transfer of power was later to become a central element in the attempts of villagers to make sense of their world.[95]

The third significant period in the history of the area comprised a mixture of events. During the eighties a civil war that had started in the centre of the country spread to the south, engulfing most of the countryside. As the situation worsened, there was a steady influx of refugees over the second half of the eighties, later exacerbated by the resettlement of victims of the 2000 floods, which hit the Limpopo valley severely. This placed major strains on the village's resource basis. While there had still been enough land for the 1977 flood victims, with each wave of new settlers this extremely important resource dwindled. Furthermore, the increase in population led to a proliferation of normative frames of reference. As far as religion was concerned, Pentecostal churches became a major reference to many, competing with prophetic and more mainstream confessions (Presbiterian and Catholic) for space in the market of means of salvation. Traditional forms of religiosity continued to hold sway, and often a silent but bitter war raged beneath the surface between traditional healers and prophetic cults. These religious developments played a major role in the manner in which villagers sought to account for their life-world.[96]

It is against the background of a village that had ceased to be a village, a community that had ceased to be a community, and a natural and social environment that had seemed to have lost its contours that the inhabitants of

Patrice Lumumba Communal Village sought to make sense of their world. I will now focus on villagers' own and direct descriptions of their livelihood, relying, as indicated at the outset, on the analytical framework of mundane reasoning as suggested by Melvin Pollner. My aim in so doing is to pursue the claim that social action is about the creation of a context of action. Furthermore, I want to prepare the descriptive ground for the more empirical discussion over the next four chapters concerning the question of how people cope with uncertainty. While bringing much of the analytical focus to bear on the uncovering of the mundane reason from which the inhabitants of Patrice Lumumba village drew, I will also work towards showing the extent to which the village lifeworld was strongly influenced by factors, which seem to bring into sharp focus the ways in which individuals create contexts of action.

The Reality of Uncertainty in Patrice Lumumba

The idiom of mundane reasoning in Patrice Lumumba refers to a social and natural environment, which, over the years, has become hostile to the inhabitants. More specifically, in drawing from this idiom to make sense of their environment the inhabitants of Patrice Lumumba appear to refer to a problematic reality which they retrieve not only through the manner in which it affects their livelihood, but also on the basis of the knowledge claims which they make towards it. In what follows, I want to discuss the problematic nature of this environment by focusing on the definitions that mundane reasoning offers of reality as well as on the authorisation procedures and reasoning practices which help the inhabitants to sustain their idea of a stable social reality.

Definitions

The social and natural environment of Patrice Lumumba is apprehended in two different, but related ways. There are objective and subjective dimensions. As far as the former is concerned, it refers to the criteria that the inhabitants use in order to determine whether they are faced with a problematic situation, whereas the latter engages with how they articulate the existence of a problem with their own values. These dimensions are brought to bear on the facts of nature that are of immediate relevance to the people's livelihood. In this sense, floods play a major role just as much as do droughts, for villagers are mainly dependent on farming for subsistence. It is true that in their repertoire of actions there are further sources of livelihood, such as migrant labour, wage labour in the nearby city of Xai-Xai, or even farther afield, networks of solidarity that stretch across kinship ties over long distances, as well as petty trade.

The process of defining a problematic situation in their livelihood in an objective manner proceeds in two steps, which can be illustrated on the basis of responses to floods. These are normal occurrences in the region and because of that there is no obvious reason why floods in themselves should be seen as problematic.[97] Usually, the immediate response to a flood is to check whether water levels are likely to rise to a point where people will be forced to leave. If this is found to be the likely scenario, people move out to higher places, as the following interview excerpts show:

Text: Definitions\Interview7
Code: Mundane Reason\Idiom\Definition

There are places on the banks of the Limpopo which people could use as refuge. These were higher located areas. That is where we stayed until the water levels lowered. I remember that people living in the interior of the country would come to the banks of the river in search of food. Since we knew the area very well we would accompany them in boats to help them carry whatever they had found back to their places of origin.

Text: Definitions\Interview5
Code: Mundane Reason\Idiom\Definition

It was in 77 that people were resettled for the first time. During the floods of 55 there was no need to rescue anyone. In those days the people just sought refuge in higher located areas. As soon as the water receded they just went back to their places in order to continue cultivating maize and other things. In those days we just went down and up, down and up, all the time.

This is the routine response to floods. The bounds of normality are determined by the extent to which people can react to the presence of water without having to introduce substantial changes to their routine. This is also the major criterion for the severity of floods, as the following excerpt clearly shows:

Text: Definitions\Interview5
Code: Mundane Reason\Idiom\Definition

Interviewee: Those from 77 were much bigger than those from 55

Interviewer: Is that so?

Interviewee: yes. In 55 we could move about. The roads were not blocked like in 77. We could move, even coaches could.

Moving to higher places is not the only response. In fact, not everyone moves. Inside the mud huts and cement houses that people have down in the valley, they build a makeshift attic where they put their most precious belongings, seed and food. Usually, one of them stays behind to control the water levels as well as to ward off thieves. Sometimes, however, they have strange bedfellows:

Text: Definitions\Interview3
Code: Mundane Reason\Idiom\Definition

Yes, a snake was on my bed. You see, I had asked my wives to seek refuge in town.

The situation was better there. So when I got back to my house and climbed the ladder to my bed up there I cleaned my feet and lay down. I could not leave because I had to watch over our belongings from people who took advantage of our absence to steal our things.

And he went on:

Text: Definitions\Interview3
Code: Mundane Reason\Idiom\Definition

@Yes@. It [the snake] did not move. You see, when there are floods snakes also have a problem. They also look for ways to survive even @if that means that they seek the help of people@. They do not do anything to you.

As long as routine responses are an option, floods are not a problem. They begin to be a problem when people's experience is no longer a guide to action. This is usually the case when the water masses are so violent that some people do not even make it to the safer places and there is loss of cattle and the fields are completely destroyed. The following excerpts illustrate this:

Text: Definitions\Interview11
Code: Mundane Reason\Idiom\Definition

This is what brought me big trouble. You see, I had cattle, but today I do not (??) have any more. I lost my cattle during the floods. I have no fields, nothing.

Text: Definitions\Interview9
Code: Mundane Reason\Idiom\Definition

We were badly hit by the floods because our fields were hit. We had fields down in the valley. We lost everything that we had sowed, we lost our tools. We have been left poor because our life depends on agriculture.

Text: Definitions\Interview9
Code: Mundane Reason\Idiom\Definition

We lost our fields. We are hungry. We cannot do any farm work. Even if the authorities help us I don't think that we will recover. Look, we don't even have ways of raising cattle, we don't have seeds and other basic stuff. Clothing and other petty things, that is no problem.

Text: Definitions\Interview13
Code: Mundane Reason\Idiom\Definition

There is no single tractor that could help us. Sadly, many things have changed. Even here where we live, we feel like strangers. We are dependent on the help of others. We lost everything.

Methodological Issues

The taken-for-granted world is one in which people respond to floods by seeking safety in higher places, making sure that their belongings are safe and hoping to take up farming as soon as possible. Everything that happens within the bounds of a routine world such as the one mapped out in this repertoire of actions defines a familiar world. It is only if none of these assumptions hold that people begin to gain a sense of having a problem. In particular, it is through the inability to go about their normal activity, that is, farming, that the sense of a problem is heightened. The single most important indicator of a problematic situation is hunger, which happens as a consequence of people's inability to till the land. It is interesting to note, in this connection, that most people I spoke with used the word hunger (*ndhlala* in Tsonga) as a synonym for drought and severe crisis. While floods prevent people from farming only temporarily, droughts have a longer span and lead almost always to starvation. It is fair to suggest that when people talk about hunger they are not only indexing a mere breakdown in their routine. Indeed, they seem just as well to be defining the point at which we can properly talk of a crisis or disaster.

This is in line with current sociological definitions of disasters (see Geenen 2004 and Spittler 1984), which link their occurrence to the collapse of coping mechanisms. Hunger marks precisely this collapse. Major disasters in the region are always remembered in connection with hunger. Their names always refer to hunger. In 1917–18 there was a severe drought in the south of Mozambique which, among other things, led to the emergence of millennial cults, the most famous of which was that of 'Murimi'.[98] This cult was based on the belief that the drought was God's punishment. He was inflicting this punishment on the people because of their love for witchcraft and sorcery. The only salvation, the leader of the cult claimed, was conversion to Christianity and a return to farming. The word *murimi* translates as 'farmer' and significantly enough members of the cult greeted one another with the word *mpfula*, meaning 'rain'. In Patrice Lumumba this drought is remembered as 'Murimi's hunger' (*ndhlala ya murimi*). Another major disaster occurred in 1955, following severe floods that left most people in the valley homeless and dependent on outside assistance. The colonial authorities at the time distributed food packs which inspired the people to name that particular disaster the 'food packs hunger' (*ndhlala ya maphaki*).

The definition of a problematic situation is only one aspect of the description of the social and natural environment that forms the lifeworld of the research area. There is nothing automatic about the procedure. It is not like people wait for the precise moment at which they will find it appropriate to see a given situation in one way or another. In fact, the definition of a problematic situation is a reflexive attitude, which forces people to engage with one another, but also with their own perception of reality. In the next section I want to discuss this process with reference to authorisation procedures, that is, the manner in which people feel entitled to make authoritative claims about reality.

Authorisation Procedures

Authorisation procedures refer to the knowledge claims that individuals make when they reflect about social reality. Social reality itself, as phenomenology would argue, consists of a socially distributed stock of knowledge. Mundane reason can be said to draw from the certainties of this stock of knowledge to make assumptions about the nature of the social world. In chapter seven I discuss at length the way in which the social distribution of the stock of knowledge inheres in the way in which individuals look for the causes of a disaster. Authorisation procedures, therefore, provide the reasons why people should trust the wisdom claimed by individuals. In other words, what reasons are there to share the assumption that the definition of the problematic nature of the floods, for instance, should proceed in a gradual manner, that is, first rising water levels and safety in higher places and, secondly, return to the fields or failure to return?

The interviews yield two types of responses to this query, both of which have the function of strengthening trust in the definition of the problematic situation. Respondents ground their definitions on past experience and knowledge. Past experience consists in the claim that, formerly, the assumptions currently made about the behaviour of nature always applied. In other words, the inhabitants of Patrice Lumumba argue that anything that experience has not proven wrong is worth trusting. A few excerpts illustrate the manner in which past experience is summoned up in defence of definitions:

> **Text:** Definitions\Interview12
> **Code:** **Mundane Reason\Idiom\Authorisation procedures**
>
> Initially we refused to leave because we assumed that it was one of those normal rises of the river current, which we had known since the times of our parents. Yes, in those days it was not necessary for people to leave their homes for good. However, in that year the rise in the water levels was not normal, that is why we had to leave our homes and fields.
>
> **Text:** Definitions\Interview17
> **Code:** **Mundane Reason\Idiom\Authorisation procedures**
>
> Yes, of course, fish does not leave its habitat just like that. Those places where we used to live, there also lived our grandparents.

Essentially, then, past experience is not the problem. Everything being equal, past experience can be of great help. Of course, past experience must be based on people's ability to make use of it. They do this by articulating certain observations of the behaviour of nature with the standard repertoire of actions that past experience teaches them to apply. This is their knowledge base, as the following excerpts document:

Methodological Issues 97

> **Text:** Definitions\Interview7
> **Code:** Mundane Reason\Idiom\Authorisation procedures
>
> In December, for instance, the river current rises and the water changes its colour.
>
> **Text:** Definitions\Interview3
> **Code:** Mundane Reason\Idiom\Authorisation procedures
>
> Look, in the past we measured the water levels with reeds. But in 2000 the situation was different. It was just abnormal.

In other words, neither past experience, nor the knowledge base was inadequate. The problem was the natural occurrence itself, which did not correspond to what people took for granted. It was abnormal. It would be interesting to draw a parallel here with Weber's notion of traditional action. The manner in which respondents used past experience and knowledge would suggest that theirs was a typical traditional form of action. We reacted to the floods the way we did because we have always reacted in that way and people before us also reacted in the same way. Traditional action does not, of course, mean that people act in an unreflective way, nor does Weber suggest this. Traditional action is action seasoned by experience. In taking decisions as to how to respond to a given situation, reference to the way people have always done things is mediated by conscious choices that people make. Past experience itself is not an essential quality of things, but rather the trust individuals think they can place on what other individuals did at a given time and place. Past experience is indeed an accomplishment and it is in this sense that reliance on it should be understood. In a nutshell, this is traditional action only to the extent that people assume that they can take the world for granted.

This assumption, of course, derives much of its force from the nature of everyday life. Indeed, so long as individuals can rely on assumptions concerning past experience and knowledge of the behaviour of the natural world, there is no reason why they should see their trust shaken. Knowledge is sedimented experience, which yields reliable recipes for mastering everyday life. When such knowledge ceases to be reliable, people no longer have a reason to take the world for granted. Then they have a problem. I now want to turn to a final feature of mundane reasoning, which takes us even deeper into the reasoning structure of people in Patrice Lumumba.

Reasoning Practices

Whereas authorisation procedures appeal to the authority of the knowledge claims which individuals make about their everyday life, reasoning practices show the kinds of articulations that people make between what they know and the social and natural environment in which they go about their lives. There are three elements that structure reasoning practices: the search for the causes of an occurrence, the relevance of response mechanisms, and, finally, the meaning that should be attributed to whatever happened. Reasoning about an event is structured around the failure of past experience and knowledge. As the following excerpt shows the process is set in motion by an oddity in people's perception of the way things are:

>   **Text:**   **Definitions\Interview2**
>   **Code:**   **Mundane Reason\Secondary elaborations**
>
> Well, we don't know how things happened. Even the older people told us that what happened this time was strange. They said that these floods [2000] were different from those which they had experienced in the past.

The perception of an oddity invites people to take a serious look at the cause of an event. As far as floods were concerned, several causes could be pinpointed.[99] Here I will just draw attention to the official explanation, which many people found convenient to repeat, even if it is to be doubted whether they were really prepared to go along with it:

>   **Text:**   **Definitions\Interview11**
>   **Code:**   **Mundane Reason\Idiom\Reasoning practices**
>
> I think the cause were the rains. I believe that everything started in South Africa or in one of those neighbouring countries. I hear that that they opened their dams and we ended up with the problem here. We live in a lower region, you see.

During the floods the mass media, of course, offered explanations that insistently levelled responsibility for the floods at the doorstep of neighbouring South Africa. In the colonial period, there had been arrangements between the countries to control water flows. The Portuguese colonial government had sought to build dams upstream on the Limpopo River in response to Mozambique's geographically vulnerable location. All along the course of the Limpopo stations for the control of water levels had been installed which enabled the colonial government to respond immediately to the threat of flooding. The idea that there might be a culprit behind the floods held very strong appeal to Patrice Lumumba inhabitants, for it allowed them to place their own understanding of the occurrence into the right perspective. Once again, it was not their reliance on past experience that had failed, but rather the radically different nature of the occurrence:

>   **Text:**   **Definitions\Interview2**
>   **Code:**   **Mundane Reason\Idiom\Reasoning practices**
>
> That's it. We were just told that there were going to be big floods. It was not a normal situation. These were not ordinary rains. With normal floods all you have to do is to seek safety on a tree or something like that. In fact, there are people

who escaped thanks to their own cattle. They just held on to it. Others lost their houses, that is what happened to me.

Again and again, they muster the whole weight of experience to confirm to themselves that they acted in a perfectly rational way in trusting experience:

>**Text:** Definitions\Interview17
>**Code:** Mundane Reason\Idiom\Reasoning practices
>
>You can compare floods to a guest. They don't come to stay. They come and go. That's why in 55 and 77 it was not difficult to go back to the fields. All you had to do was to throw the seed and in no time you would see it catching. But this time it is different. We tried to sow our seed, but that was to no avail.

Interestingly enough, it appears that the search for causes is not an engagement with the natural event itself. In actual fact, from the perspective of Patrice Lumumba inhabitants, searching for causes means accounting for the failure of local responses. In other words, people are not primarily concerned about knowing what causes water levels to rise. Their attention is geared towards the failure of their own response, and, in this sense, any explanation that gives them the feeling that the event itself was not like anything people had ever experienced in their lives will satisfy them. Again and again, people come back to the same idea in order to strengthen their faith in their own response mechanisms:

>**Text:** Definitions\Interview1
>**Code:** Mundane Reason\Idiom\Reasoning practices
>
>Well, we could really not know whether floods were going to be big or not. Our house in the Bila chieftaincy was very close to the river. The place where we got water gave us the information we needed. We could see from the strength of the water whether there were going to be floods. This time we were not able to do this because the floods were not normal.

>**Text:** Definitions\Interview2
>**Code:** Mundane Reason\Idiom\Reasoning practices
>
>You see, the water changed its colour and we started moving out to higher places. After the floods we came back down to the valley and carried on farming. This was always like that. When floods came we moved up, and when the water lowered we would come back. People with more solid houses had no problem rebuilding.

A final element in the reasoning practices is the search for the meaning of the whole occurrence. The search for a meaning is, again, different from the search for the causes of an occurrence. It is a search for the ultimate reason behind what they have gone through, with the purpose of restoring confidence in their stock of knowledge. The search for meaning tends to be metaphysical. This is not surprising because the search for the causes is also less concerned with the event itself. The dominant meaning suggested by respondents was religious in nature:

Text: Definitions\Interview11
Code: Mundane Reason\Idiom\Reasoning practices

There are people who talk about Noah's Ark, for instance, which was built because of floods at that time. According to the scriptures God said 'Noah, build an Ark and take a pair of each living thing, men or domestic pets and wild beasts because there is going to be a big flood'. Well, in 77 and 2000 I was taken aback by the floods. That's when I saw how violent water can be and that it can kill. That's why our church makes a comparison with Noah's story. Now, if there are people who don't want to believe that these things have existed for many years, well, that's their problem.

Text: Definitions\Interview8
Code: Mundane Reason\Idiom\Reasoning practices

Well, it's like the Bible says: The day of the floods will arrive. That'll be the end of the world and there will be a lot of suffering on earth.

Text: Definitions\Interview7
Code: Mundane Reason\Idiom\Reasoning practices

I don't know how to explain this, but since I'm an adult and believer I think that sacred scripture can explain this. The history of peoples older than our own, people who lived at the time of our own grandparents, teaches us that there used to be droughts and floods. That was in Egypt, Canaan, and so on. There were people who moved from one place to another because of those things.

A further meaning people indicate relates to their own cultural traditions. Several respondents spoke about traditional ceremonies carried out in order to appeal to the spirits of the ancestors. The assumption, of course, was that the failure of their own responses was somehow directly related to how these spirits felt about the way they conducted their life. While this may be the case, it is important not to exaggerate the importance of reference to the spirit world. In 2003, during fieldwork, I followed the lead on the importance of ceremonies and asked my interview partners to take me to the place where they claimed to carry out such ceremonies. On the way there we stopped to talk to a blind witchdoctor who was said, and claimed himself, to have officiated at the most recent such ceremony. In two long hours of (recorded) conversation he told me about the importance of the ceremony, how it was carried out and what one could expect from it. He claimed, confirming what other interview partners had already told me, that the ceremony was held at a sacred bush called *gandzelu*. It was guarded by a 'huge snake'; everyday somebody renewed water in a vessel placed in the sacred bush for the snake. The place was so sacred that nothing else could be done there. People who attempted to destroy the bush and turn it into farmland would just be frustrated, for the next day everything would be back in its place again. After three hours of driving in a four-wheel-drive vehicle and walking up and down sand dunes we arrived at the sacred bush, only to find that it was gone. No trace of anything even remotely resembling a place where ritual ceremonies took place. No snake, no vessel with water, no trees; instead, someone had planted his or her cassava stems and they seemed to be thriving. Still, such meanings are interesting not so much for their face value, but rather for the kinds of means they provide individuals to produce coherent accounts of their social reality:

> **Text:** Definitions\Interview6
> **Code:** Mundane Reason\Idiom\Reasoning practices

If no rain fell, there was drought. That's why some people met at the homestead of the big chiefs to prepare traditional ceremonies. These were useful in helping us to do away with everything that prevented us from having good harvests.

> **Text:** Definitions\Interview4
> **Code:** Mundane Reason\Idiom\Reasoning practices

Well, rain and traditional principles that's something for the elders. They and other important people are in charge of making sure that our customs and mores are respected. They choose (?) one another and are chosen. Even now if we were to choose someone to do that we would see rain falling. The trouble is that we are not doing that anymore. That's why I can not say whether the thing works or not. You see, this year [2002] there was no rain. Even if we till the soil there will be no outcome.

> **Text:** Definitions\Interview3
> **Code:** Mundane Reason\Idiom\Reasoning practices

The elders used to meet. After checking up with the sorcerer somebody was picked up to lead us all. We went to the place of the ceremony with animals and drinks. When we got there we sang, danced and prayed to the ancestor spirits. At the end, rain fell. But nowadays that is not done anymore. Nobody follows customs, nobody respects the elders. That's why we have all these problems. We must respect our traditions because it is like a family. If there is no respect for the elders, nothing can work in that family.

The next excerpt sums up the search for the meaning of occurrences quite well:

> **Text:** Definitions\Interview3
> **Code:** Mundane Reason\Idiom\Reasoning practices

Wherever there is loss of life people try to find out the reason.[100] I remember that some people said something was going to happen in the year 2000. In church people were talking about the diluvium. So when I saw those floods [2000] I thought that was the end of the world. I can't imagine anyone having caused that. I know some people here say there are people who can control water. When they see that the current is not normal, they discharge the water which flows our way. Well, since our homes are on the flood plains of many rivers here, we suffer from floods. This is how it was in 2000. It will be hard to forget those floods. In fact, our suffering today is caused by our own lack of respect for traditional principles and God's commandments. We don't have traditional ceremonies anymore. The only people who still respect these things are church ministers. But there are others who instead of making us pray are only concerned with the tenth of the income of poor people. I mean, they are violating the principles. If we respected traditional principles and traditional customs, maybe our life would improve.

Secondary Elaborations

I will end my description of the social and natural environment of the research area with a brief discussion of what Melvin Pollner calls 'secondary elaborations', that is, the discursive resources individuals use in order to strengthen their basic beliefs. As we have seen in the presentation of the local definition of the problematic situation, as well as in the authorisation procedures and reasoning practices, natural events such as floods are perceived as problematic, not so much because of their essential qualities, but rather because of the way in which they challenge local assumptions about the world. In other words, what is at stake in the local idiom about the social and natural environment is the way in which individuals try to make sense of the world.

In what follows I want to focus on the kinds of strategies adopted by Patrice Lumumba inhabitants to forestall doubts about the objective nature of the world they inhabit. These strategies are not different from the reasoning practices which they employ as they seek to come to terms with the failure of their responses. However, what is different is the intention. Whereas, as suggested, reasoning practices try to account for the failure of responses to natural occurrences, secondary elaborations seek to strengthen trust in the basic beliefs about the inhabited world. They do this in two basic ways. The first way consists in arguing that even if they had been able to predict the scale of the occurrence other factors would have prevented them from doing the right thing:

Text: Definitions\Interview15
Code: **Mundane Reason\Secondary elaborations**

Of course we were aware of what was going to happen. There (were) rumours around about the rise in water levels and that we should leave. But as you can imagine it was very difficult for us, who had been living there, to just leave, leaving behind our belongings – just like that. In our case, for example, we still spent the night at the village in the hope of carrying a few things with us. But the following morning everything was flooded. Everyone was left to his devices…

The second mode is less sanguine. In fact, they ask themselves if everything they do is altogether appropriate. In other words, they do not seek for explanations outside of the events proper, but rather consider whether their way of life as such not might be the main culprit:

Methodological Issues   103

Text: Definitions\Interview14
Code: Mundane Reason\Secondary elaborations

> In fact, we declared war on nature. We don't observe the principles of nature and for that reason God punished us. That is the reason why we are suffering.

Note that it is not the same argument as in the reasoning practices. They are not saying that their failure to respect the ancestor spirits or even the will of God rendered them vulnerable to nature. What they are saying is something fundamentally different, namely that there might be something wrong with the way they intervene in nature:

Text: Definitions\Interview14
Code: Mundane Reason\Secondary elaborations

> What I wanted to say was that we can influence nature to the extent of undermining our own livelihood. The destruction of the environment, the deaths, the lack of respect for the law and all those things could well be the cause of all these calamities. I don't think that traditional ceremonies will be of any help here.

Text: Definitions\Interview13
Code: Mundane Reason\Secondary elaborations

> Nowadays, there are many women in our region who try to observe customs. However, with new forms of behaviour and new principles, rituals cannot be successful.

This is a significant admission, especially because we can detect an attempt to recover a holistic view of social life in the village as the precondition for harmony. The last excerpt claims that it is not just the rituals that are missing from village life, important as they may be. Rather, it is the overall background encompassing the local way of life that is central to the success of any attempt at restoring local values. There is a subtle critique of change, which does not simply imply a rejection of modernity and its artefacts, but merely seeks to protect the integrity of the local lifeworld. At the same time, however, there is recognition that, as the context changes, their ways of doing things might be becoming increasingly inadequate. There is an almost fatalistic resignation to circumstances, as documented by the following two excerpts, which are replies to the question why they think phenomena such as floods occur and whether there are local specialists who are knowledgeable about such things, respectively:

Text: Definitions\Interview1
Code: Mundane Reason\Secondary elaborations

> Well, it is hard to say because in our times there were no such phenomena. We are bewildered by what has been taking place here. Maybe it is a change in times.

Text: Definitions\Interview1
Code: Mundane Reason\Secondary elaborations

> In our region there (are??) no people like that. Even the older people are bewildered by these phenomena. Formerly, there were seasons for rain. Nowadays, it is very hard to know for sure. If anyone says 'I can make it rain' he will be lying. All we do is wait for the rain. Formerly, people carried out traditional ceremonies or rain rituals where people would dance and sing to ask for rain. Today, that is not done.

It appears obvious that villagers have rhetorical resources, which allow them, in the process of making sense of their livelihood, to shield their worldview from outside attacks. They use these resources to explain away inconsistencies in their own worldviews, for instance, when they insist on the idea of changing times and idealise the past. In explaining away they preserve the integrity of their ways of perceiving reality by an act of admission of its irrelevance to their present condition.

The Lifeworld of Patrice Lumumba

The mundane reason of Patrice Lumumba villagers brings to the fore what is at stake in the process of constructing social worlds. Indeed, this mundane reason shows the extent to which individuals engage with their physical and cultural environment. They do this by drawing on the cultural and material resources which their world makes available to them. The use of such resources allows them to take matters into their own hands by enabling them to actively intervene in the world. What we see in operation in the way in which villagers account for their own world is social action made durable through social relationships, which, in turn, branch out into trust and predictability as a response to the fragility of social action. The latter point will become more evident in subsequent chapters when attention is focused precisely on action. In this chapter I was concerned to show the extent to which we are dealing with a terrain characterised by extreme situations, which, in spite of that, require the same methodological steps and decisions we apply to any other situation of interest in sociological analysis. It is not an essential notion of the culture of Patrice Lumumba villagers that is crucial to understanding them and their context, but rather the structure of social action. This theme will run through the remainder of this book.

In a way, we are dealing with the tale of how a community tames its fate. There is nothing particularly spectacular about how it does this. Nonetheless, we need to elaborate on this methodologically by way of an analytical framework that brings together the insights gained in chapters one and four. I will use a specific framework in order to integrate the central findings of the case studies presented in the second part of this book. In the following section I offer a description of the main features of this framework, the mainstay of which is Luhmann's key distinction between hazards and risks.

An Analytical Framework: Translating Hazards into Risks

The interview excerpts I discussed in this chapter give a good sense of the precarious nature of the local environment. At the same time, however, the interviews do much more than providing mere descriptions of this environment. Indeed, what they do is document how the world in which the villagers live is their own world. This is a world under massive attack from outside forces, forces that increasingly escape their conceptual schemes and resist integration into established ways of perceiving the world. Yet, by the very act of accounting for this world Patrice Lumumba inhabitants are claiming a role in it by writing themselves into whatever scripts nature and politics impose on them.

The question for villagers is not whether they should give up. The question for them is how they can provide accounts of the world that make it intelligible to them and whether criteria of intelligibility can help them to find a way through everyday life. The villagers are involved in an uphill struggle to create a context within which they can live as individuals with a history, a memory, and expectations. They retrieve their history by arguing for the relevance of their past ways of life as a referential world. They use memory as the intelligent selection of past experience with relevance to the challenges of the present and, more significantly, they 'do' talk as a way of documenting their agency and their ability to act meaningfully.

An Analytical Framework for Descriptive Inference

With this description of the research terrain, drawing on Pollner's notion of mundane reason, we have now established the context to which the data refer. It is certainly a precarious context, yet the manner in which villagers report on it brings elements of the analytical framework which I now propose into focus. The framework consists of three pillars that stand in a dynamic relationship to one another. All of them draw on Luhmann's definition of risk as calculated hazard. To put it differently, in approaching the data and the lifeworld to which it refers, I focus attention on elements of social action, which provide clues as to how villagers translate hazards into risk. The general idea is that the data report on villagers' perception of their environment and the people with whom they live, how they come to terms with both, and, most importantly, how they cooperatively create their lifeworlds. In suggesting that they create their lifeworlds cooperatively I do not wish to claim that the whole social process is free of conflict and tension. Villagers lead normal lives to the extent that they argue, fight, differ on important and fundamental values, and seek their place within their village in competition with others. The larger view of an emerging lifeworld is at the centre of the message which the data are expected to elicit. This lifeworld is born of local experience, that is, an experience that builds on what villagers went through in the past, retained in their individual and collective memories, and, generally, through everyday interaction, have pasted into their understanding of the texture and fabric of social relations.

There are three analytical elements in the process of translating hazards into risks that should structure the reading of the data: (a) **Relevance**; (b) **Knowledge** and (c) **Certainty**. In this analytical framework they are understood as dimensions of the process of translating hazards into risks. The relevance dimension refers to the properties of the object on which the data report. In other words, the data are understood to be reporting on aspects of the physical and social world of the village as well as on the individuals who inhabit it.

Relevance

The notion of relevance is drawn from the phenomenological sociology of Alfred Schütz and refers, in a broad sense, to individuals' perception of the social environment within which their lives unfold. This is to emphasise the importance of reality as a phenomenon that is deeply grounded in the consciousness thereof, which social actors themselves have. The relevance dimension, therefore, breaks down into two *categories*, namely the *natural* and the *social* worlds. The natural world category is related to the clues given by the data on the natural world, and the social world category on the social relations of the worlds inhabited by the villagers. In our particular empirical case studies we will see that natural hazards such as droughts and floods are important properties of the natural world, while forms of social, political, and economic organisation provide useful hints about the nature of the social world.

Knowledge

The knowledge dimension is entirely based on Alfred Schütz and his central tenet concerning the role and place of knowledge in society. Indeed, Schütz argues that a distinguishing mark of lifeworlds is their social stock of knowledge, namely the distribution of expertise, skills, as well as the availability of an appropriate vocabulary to describe facts. Following this we can identify two central *categories* within the dimension of knowledge, meaning, the *distribution of the social stock of knowledge* and the *status* that types of knowledge have within the village. The distribution of the social stock of knowledge speaks directly to the social division of labour in the form of roles that individuals acquire on the nexus of the stock of knowledge, and the types of knowledge which gain relevance within a particular lifeworld. Chapter eight explores aspects of this phenomenological distinction in some detail, with the slight difference that here we are concerned with teasing out the general descriptive relevance that roles in connection with the distribution of the stock of knowledge play in helping us draw conclusions on the context of action. Indeed, the knowledge dimension occupies an axial role between the relevance dimension and the certainty dimension presented below. This is all the more so since the second category of the knowledge dimension, namely status of types of knowledge, relates to villagers' own valuations of knowledge forms and provide, therefore, further clues to the kinds of expectations that individuals formulate with regard to their natural and social worlds.

Certainty

The final dimension is that of certainty. The opposite of certainty, uncertainty, plays a central role in the sociology of risk as we saw in chapter three. It is often used to describe the general condition of those who are thought to lack the knowledge that would enable them to engage actively with their natural and social environment. In such accounts, uncertainty describes non-technological societies and the general helplessness of their members in the face of nature and its caprices. In considering the notion of certainty as a dimension of the process of translating hazards into risk, I take up the conceptual reservations detailed in the respective chapter and engage with them in an analytical way. In other words, I take the problem of contingency seriously and, instead of dealing with it in an evolutionary way by consigning it to history, I place it firmly at the centre of social action. In this respect, I argue that individuals invariably act under conditions of uncertainty, given the contingency problem. In attempting to describe action under uncertainty we should, however, focus on *trust* and *repair strategies*. Both are *categories* of certainty. Although there is a considerable body of literature on trust which gives useful insights into the role of trust in reducing contingency, I will be using the notion here in the sense used by phenomenologists when referring to the natural attitude to the world, namely the taking for granted of reality. In other words, I understand trust to be made up of assumptions individuals make concerning the correspondence between their knowledge of the nature of the physical and social world and their expectations concerning the actions of others. Repair strategies in turn pertain to the array of actions that individuals resort to in the event that what they took for granted proves to be wrong.

The Operational Dimension of the Framework

These three dimensions and their pairs of categories make up the analytical framework, which will inform the interpretation of data in the studies to be presented in the following chapters. The interpretation procedure is abductive, that is, it organises the data into sets of hypotheses, allowing me to infer the best possible explanation for the relationships observed in the data. Abduction appears better suited than deduction and induction for two main reasons. First of all, given the epistemological reservations made at the opening of this chapter concerning the relationship between data and reality, it does not seem wise to insist on the idea that we can derive safe knowledge about the world on the basis of the deductive validity of our data. Secondly, for the same reasons, the cogency of any inductive operation performed on the data depends less on the reality we seek to account for and more on what we think we know about the world. Hence abduction as a method of inference is in line with the descriptive tasks addressed to the data and is consistent with the more general theoretical orientation to making contexts of action visible.

	Translating hazards into risks		
Dimensions	**Relevance**	**Knowledge**	**Certainty**
Categories	• *Natural/ social* • *Individual*	• *Roles* • *Status*	• *Trust* • *Repair strategies*

Figure 4.1: A graphic representation of the analytical framework

The Claim of the Analytical Framework

The general statement this analytical framework is making is quite simple. It argues that the process of translating hazards into risks provides an accurate description of how individuals, acting in order to be able to act, create contexts of action. The translation process itself can be plotted along three dimensions, namely relevance, knowledge, and certainty, each one of which consists of a pair of categories, which yield empirical indicators for a descriptive inference following the principles of abduction. This analytical framework will be used throughout the studies making up this book as a complement to the case-study-specific methodology applied to bring order into the collected data.

The Explanatory Framework

The claim the analytical framework makes is, in a sense, explanatory. By arguing that the translation of hazards into risks describes how individuals create contexts of action, the analytical framework offers an explanation of the emergence of social reality understood as context of action. This explanation is not causal in the established sense of this notion.[101] If, as Hempel (1970) forcefully argues, scientific explanation is an argument involving a law which offers a reason as the cause of an event or phenomenon, then my analytical framework falls short of this definition. Indeed, while it seeks to offer an explanation by way of a conclusion based on premises, there is no sense in which the rule of inference connecting premises and conclusion could be construed as a law, let alone as a cause of the phenomenon under study.

The sense in which this analytical framework offers an explanation is more in line with the discussion of the nature of social reality pursued so far. Two essential elements came to the fore in the course of the discussion. The first element concerned the role of meaning in the possibility of individual action, while the second element related to action itself. Each of these elements yields a scheme of intelligibility[102] that allows me to make sense of the data structured by my analytical framework.

The first scheme of intelligibility could be called interpretive. It holds that social phenomena are expressive in nature, which means, they document a meaningful context. In this sense, the explanatory claim that the analytical framework makes is, simply, that observed phenomena (how individuals cope with crises and disasters) refer us to a context that needs to be made visible and accounted for. The formula looks like this:

$$C\Sigma R / C(-)P$$

where C stands for how individuals cope with crises and disasters, R for social reality, and P for the phenomenon under study. The full statement is to the effect that the way in which individuals cope with disasters and crises (which includes their interpretations as well as activities) is part of a social reality $(C\Sigma R)$, which in turn can be retrieved through the assumption that coping expresses the underlying phenomenon $(C(-)P)$, which in turn yields social reality as construed by the individuals themselves. As will be shown in the subsequent case studies, this explanatory claim forms the backbone of the approach favoured in this book and bears heavily on fieldwork decisions concerning what to ask, and how to collect and register data.

The second scheme of intelligibility is based on an action perspective and holds that social phenomena are part of a reality, which consists of individuals purposefully doing things. The formula looks like this:

$$C\Sigma R, R\Sigma i \Sigma \rangle \Sigma o$$

where C stands, as above, for how individuals cope with crises and disasters, R for social reality, which in turn consists of the sum of (i) individuals acting and producing (o) outcomes, so that the phenomenon under analysis can be conceptualised as the outcome of the subjectively meaningful action of individuals. The full statement that this formula makes in the context of the analytical framework is that coping with crises and disasters is based on individuals' actions and that these have outcomes that help us properly understand the way human communities deal with adversity, since such outcomes are, more often than not, the result of purposeful social action.

In other words, the explanatory framework is descriptive in nature, for it simply makes the terms under which I describe local coping mechanisms more precise and firmly grounded in an understanding of sociology that seriously engages with individuals as authors of their own lifeworlds and narratives. In the concluding chapter I will come back to these two schemes of intelligibility to further explore the implications of the analytical framework against the background of what has, so far, been my main theoretical concern, namely making risk sociology relevant to social theory, and using the travails of a local African community as the empirical basis thereof. This concern will also prove useful in helping me to tie up the loose ends of the claim according to which individuals act in order to be able to act.

The Methodological Tool-box

I will round up my discussion in this chapter with a brief presentation of the methodological toolbox. In fact, no single methodological tool will be favoured in the presentation and discussion of data. While the bulk of the data was collected on the basis of interviews, observation, archival work, and informal conversation, it is mainly the material recorded from interviews that provides the backbone of the empirical basis. Instead of using a single method of data presentation and discussion, I opted for a mixture of methods.

There were mainly two reasons for doing this. The first reason was to adjust the tool to the nature of the object. The case studies making up the book deal with issues relating to uncertainty, risk, and disaster. Data collection was carried out in the same setting. The analytical framework was developed after data had been collected and preliminary analyses based on different methodologies had been undertaken. At the outset, the general orientation of the research was to collect data on aspects of how local communities perceive crises and deal with disasters. The assumptions underlying the original conception of the research made heuristic methods central to the whole undertaking.

The original conception, for instance, assumed the unity of the local lifeworld and the uniformity of local responses to crises and disasters. The first field trip and the results it yielded put this assumption into the right context by suggesting a very complex local setting that resisted the original unifying and homogenising conceptual categories. Another set of assumptions was with respect to the phenomena that were the object of study. Right from the start a decision was taken to be heuristic in approach, that is, not to depart from an established definition of the central concepts, namely crises and disasters, but, instead, derive their intensional and extensional meaning from local communicative strategies. Here again it became obvious that the research was not only up against an extremely complex and heterogeneous setting, but also faced different ways of accounting for reality. Owing to both of these sets of assumptions it became necessary to focus attention on particular aspects of the local lifeworld, that is, accounting for floods, dealing with floods, accounting for civil war, producing self in the context of religious movements.

This necessity became the mother of the eclectic methodological approach adopted for this book. The original idea of research was one large study, but the experience of research itself broke it down into smaller case studies, each suggesting a specific methodology to yield the most information for the purpose of making a descriptive inference that would tie the loose strings together again into one big coherent study. This tying of the strings is accomplished through the reference to the analytical framework designed to show the relevance of contexts of action and how they emerge.

This is, therefore, the background against which the structure of presentation should be understood. The next section of the book consists of four case studies dwelling on four separate, but organically linked phenomena. These are, first, biography and the creation of locality, secondly conflicting interpretations of natural phenomena, thirdly, the problem-solving apparatuses they bring forth, and, finally, memories of war and how they practically accomplish disasters. Each case study draws on what may appear to be an ephemeral moment, but it weaves the underlying script into the general theme of translating hazards into risks in order to check on the constitution of contexts of action.

Chapter five on conflicting interpretations of disaster takes as a starting point two group discussions organised in the village with the intention of confronting villagers with the researchers' own understanding of local interpretations. The ensuing lively discussions lent themselves to a reconstruction of underlying notions of causality and perceptions of the local lifeworld with reference to the methodology developed by the German sociologist Ralf Bohnsack. The analysis of the transcripts of the discussions brings the communicative resources into view which villagers use to retrieve their own lifeworld. Such resources reveal themselves to be documents of social reality creatively combining past experience with future expectations and unfolding crucial aspects of the process of producing contexts of action. Translating hazards into risks appears to be intimately linked to the ability of individuals to produce interpretations of disaster that enable action.

The theme of conflicting interpretations is the subject of the following chapter. In contrast to the preceding chapter, however, attention in chapter six does not focus on the interpretation itself. Rather, attention is focused on the groups which are carriers of types of interpretations. A deeper understanding of this required a methodological approach that allowed for a description of the emergence of patterned and stable responses to disaster. Hence, the focus on Walter Sprondel's notion of a problem-solving apparatus was meant to bring to the fore the distribution and attribution of expertise within the local community, but also to focus on a very specific instance of institutionalisation. Translating hazard into risk in these circumstances takes place against the background of the emergence, maintenance, and predictability of local institutions. There are interesting elements here for an analysis inspired by the sociology of organisations, as local problem-solving apparatuses prove to be truly indigenous offsprings in stark contrast to official state institutions, which simply add to the problems of local communities. I also make use of Alain Blanchet's and Rodolphe Ghiglione's contrastive analytical instrument in order to bring into bold relief the major differences in local and external discourses.

Chapter seven discusses the experiences of refugees during the civil war that ravaged the country throughout the eighties. These are chilling accounts of human suffering and capacity for brutality. In approaching the interview material I was faced with the problem of finding ways of letting it bespeak the violence and apparent senselessness of the people's experiences of war. I opted for the membership categorisation devices suggested by ethnomethodology because their focus on actors' categories and actors' own efforts at documenting the way they accomplished social reality seemed to provide the right kind of descriptive resources to make sense of experiences that otherwise did not seem to make much sense. Here the question about how society is possible became essential to the extent that the overall perilous context of everyday life under conditions of war placed an enormous strain on people's ability to lead a normal life. In this sense, it became extremely interesting to document the ways in which individuals made life possible in spite of the circumstances. As later analysis in the corresponding chapter will show, the translation of hazards into risks requires a skilful and persistent hold on the reality of everyday life.

Finally, chapter eight on the creation of locality through the appropriation of a biography draws specifically from an intensive intercourse with members of a Pentecostal sect. It was during the services that I realised that membership was not simply about being a part of something. It was also, and most importantly, an opportunity that individuals had to create a coherent biography for themselves and, in this way, define their lifeworld. In order to be able to describe this I felt that it was necessary to go back to ethnomethodological and symbolic interactionist discussions in search of resources on how knowledge is constitutive of identity and how the latter, ultimately, is responsible for the social realities that are relevant to people in their everyday life. We will see when we come to discuss this material that the creation of locality is a central element in the process of translating hazards into risks.

The general conclusion of this book ties up the individual instances of the production of contexts of action against the background of the process of translating hazards into risks. The main thrust of the argument, one that bears directly on social theory and its potential for describing and accounting for social phenomena in Africa, rests on the idea that social change is fate challenging individuals to assert themselves. Translating hazards into risks and thereby producing contexts of action is not only an Africans way of taming fate, but also a document of the conditions of possibility of social action in very broad terms. The conclusion shows that these insights, which can be directly articulated with the sociology of risk, cannot be limited to this special area. They have a much broader import that makes the particular conditions of African social life extremely relevant for sociological theorising.

Part Two

Studies in Coping with Disasters and Crises

5

When Disaster Strikes[103]

Introduction

This chapter attempts to analyse local interpretations of disaster as presented to me during two visualised group discussions. These were conducted in 2002 in Patrice Lumumba Village and had two main objectives. The first objective was to invite villagers to talk freely about disasters, drawing their associative inspiration from an image depicting two contrasting views of the same phenomenon of floods. The second objective was to test my own understanding of what villagers had been telling me during informal and formal conversations on their idea of what a disaster is. Since a recurrent theme in those conversations was the floods of 2000, I limited the test of my understanding to these.

The 2000 floods were devastating. They swept through the southern part of Mozambique (see Christie and Hanlon, 2001) and hit the research region in the Limpopo river valley hard. According to the official account, the floods claimed the lives of about 700 people. 544,500 lost their homes and more than 700,000 became dependent on food aid straight off. The floods destroyed ten per cent of the cultivated land and nearly ninety percent of the irrigation infrastructure, according to UN figures. More than 600 primary schools were either destroyed or severely damaged. The World Bank estimated the direct economic losses at US$273 million and the indirect ones at US$247 million. All in all the losses were higher than Mozambique's export earnings for the year 1999.

My analytical framework is the so-called reconstructive methodology, which, without reference to any pre-established theoretical framework, seeks to provide a description of the lifeworld of the interview partners. More specifically, I will draw on Ralf Bohnsack's documentary method of interpretation, which, in turn, is derived from Karl Mannheim's documentary method (Bohnsack 1993, Mannheim 1995, see also Wagner 1999). The documentary method of interpretation looks for information on the obvious nature of the experience of everyday life and also for how taken-for-granted things are produced in daily interaction. Bohnsack describes this task as the search for an appropriate access to the 'indexicality of alien fields of experience' (Bohnsack 1993: 35, author's translation).

I will start by discussing the immediate theoretical context of the group discussion. I will skip a presentation of the region where I conducted research, since this has already been done.[104] Then I will introduce some of the central ideas of Bohnsack's reconstructive method. In this discussion I will argue for the relevance of this method not only as a social scientific tool, but also as an important strategy to approach the social experience of an extreme event and the conditions for its construction as a disaster in the context of everyday life. Afterwards, I will take a closer look at my empirical material. I will aim at interpreting the local refusal to consider the floods a disaster.

Documenting a Disaster

When I first took up research in Patrice Lumumba village I was not quite sure whether the conceptual and methodological scheme with which I had equipped myself was adequate to elicit the kinds of response that would help me understand local perceptions and interpretations of disasters in the village. I had two research instruments. The first one was the documentation of disasters and crisis drawing from the historical experience of the villagers. In order to do this, however, I needed to arrive at a common understanding of what a disaster – and, for that matter, a crisis – is for the villagers. To this end, I availed myself of my second research instrument consisting of a narrative interview schedule.

This schedule opened with the very general question whether anything extraordinary had happened in the village in recent times. While this question already pointed to some sort of definition, as it grounded on the assumption that disasters are rather extraordinary events, the main idea behind such a formulation was to challenge my interview partners to share with me their own ideas of what they thought to be normal or abnormal in their own lives. A year earlier a whale had been stranded on the beach, barely eight kilometres away from the village, and many villagers had gone to see it and help themselves to its meat. Not surprisingly, the whale was the most extraordinary thing that had happened to the villagers in recent times!

Further probing as to other extraordinary events yielded the floods of 2000. Some interview partners had immediately spoken of the floods, but most had not. Those who did speak of the floods were mainly village officials who in recent months had grown accustomed to talk to outsiders about the floods. Most of these outsiders were university researchers, members of non-governmental organisations, and state officials dealing with the resettlement of flood victims. I was puzzled by the apparent lack of interest on the part of the ordinary members of the community to draw my attention to the floods. In fact, in the course of my research, those who came to talk about the floods with any degree of enthusiasm did so at the insistence of the village secretary who always accompanied me on my rounds through the village. He would 'prepare' my interview partners by saying to them, half-jokingly, that they should just tell me that they were hungry and that their lives had been disturbed by the floods. Since my narrative interview schedules had a much wider brief than just such experiences, I was able to place their 'official' answers into the right perspective by asking them to reflect on the significance of such disturbing events for their own livelihood and biography.

These interviews as well as several informal conversations and exchanges with villagers seemed to point to a very ambivalent local attitude towards floods. On the one hand, villagers seemed to hold floods in awe, especially those that had occurred in the year 2000, but, on the other, they played down the significance of their occurrence by insisting that they were part and parcel of their life. What notions of security informed their attitude towards such natural events? What place did social organisation occupy in villagers' understanding of the occurrence of such natural events? If the floods themselves were not a problem, what was the problem? These were the immediate analytical challenges I faced when I conducted the group interviews. I expected these group discussions to bring conflicting views into the open, show lines of demarcation, and generally give me useful leads into local conceptual schemes for making sense of disasters and crises.

Sociology offers many ways of approaching disasters as social phenomena. Jerry Stallings (2003), for instance, suggests that we understand disasters as the sudden interruption of normality. Elke Geenen (2003) gives this view more precision with her idea that disasters should be seen as part of a larger phenomenon, namely 'collective crisis', and that they occur when all prevention and coping mechanisms fail. Geenen compares disasters with processes of social change. In a certain sense, both Stallings and Geenen understand disasters from a phenomenological-constructivist perspective and place great emphasis on the conditions under which the routine of everyday life is constituted.

In other words, disasters are not only about external events, but rather about the interpretation of reality, which manifests itself in social action. Like Geenen, Wolf Dombrowski (1996: 70) defined disasters as the outcome of society's inability 'to solve problems adequately, i.e. in such a way that those counterproductive effects which inhere in all action remain manageable.' In his opinion, international disaster relief fails because its policies offer solutions to problems defined elsewhere which cannot be transferred. Action in the context of a disaster is based on a definition marked by uncertainty (see Clausen and Dombrowsky 1993).

The emphasis these perspectives place on the entanglement of interpretation and action is consistent with the approach favoured by the reconstructive method. The routine of everyday life, which is interrupted by extreme events, includes the twin aspects of problematic and non-problematic areas of social life as identified by Berger and Luckmann (1991). The non-problematic area of everyday life refers to the world of routine, that is, to what is taken for granted. In this area, no one asks for the meaning, aim, and appropriateness of an action. One is sure of one's action. This certainty, which is based on the strong belief that the world is the way one perceives it, is constitutive of the social nature of reality. Sometimes, however, some actions fall out of what one might consider routine. The meaning, aim, and appropriateness of an action need to be explained beforehand. This explication takes place in the context of social interaction. It aims at integrating the problematic areas into the non-problematic world of everyday routine.

In dealing with uncertainty societies use a repertory of actions that allows them to routinise extraordinary situations. The construction of a given situation as a disaster depends on this mechanism. In his inquiry into a famine crisis among the Tuareg, Gerd Spittler identified three moments which lead to the social construction of disasters, namely, stress, crisis, and catastrophe. In a stress situation people apply measures that have proven themselves effective in the past. If these measures are not successful, then the situation evolves into a crisis. Society attempts to establish normality through discursive means. To this end, the community exchanges experiences, engages in intensive discussion, and everyone gets ready to die in dignity. A disaster is the total breakdown (Spittler 1989). If we were to translate Spittler's terminology into our own language we would reduce the three moments in the construction of a disaster to a process of translating the problematic into the non-problematic. To a certain extent, social action in stress situations corresponds to the use of a repertory of actions which have proven effective and can help to re-establish normality. The discursive process that takes place during the crisis situation corresponds to the attempt by society to achieve a definition of reality that provides a common basis for action.

The documentary method draws on this basic phenomenological structure of society. It assumes the existence of two forms of experience: a conjunctive experience and a communicative experience; these are based on the fundamental difference between 'Verstehen' and interpretation (Bohnsack 1997: 194).[105] 'Verstehen' relates to the direct nature of the meaning of an action in the context of social relations, whereas interpretation refers to comprehension and negotiation of the meaning of an action. The similarities with the phenomenological view of everyday life are quite striking.

Even more important than these formal similarities is Mannheim's remark (1995) that conjunctive realms of experience make up meaning wholes, which result from social interaction. This remark is important because it draws attention to a property that interpretation features: the functional nature of concepts is embedded in everyday experience. The way in which people perceive reality is related to human existence. It follows that an interpretation can only be complete if the embeddedness of an interpretation in an existential situation can be proven.[106]

In its reconstructive interpretation of reality, the documentary method seeks to prove the social determination of interpretation.[107] In order to achieve this Bohnsack suggests a multi-layered approach. The first layer is what he calls formulating interpretation. It consists of the formulation of an overview of the perceived interpretative moment. This layer is concerned with the identification of the indexicality of a text, that is, the elaboration of the thematic structure of a text that points to the background social structures. The next layer refers to the reconstruction and explication of the way in which interview partners deal with a problem. Bohnsack calls this layer the reflexive interpretation which he places within the tension of positive and negative opposing horizons. Interview partners make statements with which they agree or disagree. A positive horizon obtains when there is agreement; the converse is true for a negative horizon. This tension constitutes a framework within which realms of experience are constituted. A further layer suggested by Bohnsack includes the description of discourse and the constitution of types.

The Group Interviews

The conversations in the appendices were recorded in the summer of 2002. They followed an intensive research phase (summer 2001 and spring 2002) in which narrative interviews and focus group and individual discussions had suggested that the local community placed the exact time of the occurrence of disaster not where the representatives of the international relief apparatus had identified it, but rather afterwards. A statement that came up again and again was 'floods are a guest who comes for a visit, stays for a few days, and then goes.' In order to establish the exact meaning of this statement we asked a Mozambican student to try and depict these contradictory views of the disaster (see figure 1) and then asked our interview partners to comment on the drawing.[108] We carried out two group interviews on different days; the composition of the groups was mixed and reflected the most important social groups within the village. In the first group interview we had internally displaced people, members of the local lineage, religious groups, etc. In the second group we had leading members of the village. The discussion was in the local language, Tsonga. We recorded it and prepared transcripts, which we render here literally in English.[109] The excerpts reproduced here refer to matters of direct relevance to ur topic.

The Process of Socially Constructing Disaster

In this part of my presentation I would like to work out the thematic-structural aspects of the discussion. Both group interviews contain three thematic fields. The first field relates to the attempt to establish what happened. In this respect, the first thing is to describe floods from a practical point of view. One cannot till the land; one does routine work, such as sticking poles in the ground to measure water levels so as to know when to move back. Preparing oneself for the time afterwards is also part of the practical way of dealing with disasters. If one has reason to believe that the floods are going to be ordinary, one has to get ready to till the land once the waters have receded, in full expectation of a good harvest.

The second thematic field refers to the conclusion that the floods were not at all normal. The criterion to establish this is the failure of the floods to conform to normal expectations. Again, routine work plays an important role in this field. The old strategy of forecasting the extent of the floods fails: measurement of water levels and retreat to the hills at the edge of the valley are not adequate responses to the event. People have to flee, often very quickly, and lose their belongings. Moreover, the time afterwards, that is, after the floods, is problematic. Routine tasks such as as cultivation, the main occupation of the local community and their main criterion to establish whether an event was extraordinary or ordinary, become futile. Against all expectations the soils are dry and hard and, furthermore, the tools normally used for tillage are rendered useless.

The third thematic field is the definition of what, under the circumstances, should be done. The community cannot cope on the strength of its own means. It is reliant on aid. However, the assistance the community requires should aim at bringing events back to their normal course. People want to cultivate and need tractors which, however, they cannot afford. If they can till the land and achieve a good harvest, they have managed to come to terms with the floods. Things get back to 'normal'.

These three thematic fields correspond to the process of socially constructing a disaster. First, there is a discussion about whether the event is normal. The criterion for this is the possibility of using old and tried coping methods. If these fail, then the question has to be asked as to what is not normal in the event. Here the same criterion applies: do old and tried coping strategies work? People then look for ways of enforcing normality. The criterion here lies in challenging the event successfully: even if the soil is hard and dry, one must go on working.

In this part of the presentation of the empirical material I would like to show how contexts of meaning 'develop processually in the course of discourse' (Bohnsack 1993: 41). In other words, I am interested in the structure of the interpretive model against the background of which the social construction of the event as a disaster takes place. The documentary method suggests an approach that contemplates a contrast between opposing horizons. In the case at hand I am interested in the local position vis-à-vis the external appreciation of the floods as a disaster. Do the interview partners agree with this appreciation or not? What is important here is not just agreement or disagreement, but rather the contours that contexts of meaning take and and how they present themselves as positive or negative opposing horizons. These contexts of meaning are very important as

When Disaster Strikes
123

far as reconstruction of the realm of experience of the local population from the perspective of the sociology of knowledge is concerned.

In both group discussions there are positive and negative opposing horizons. Positive horizons are present in the following statements:

> 'during floods you cannot do anything at all' (VGD1-Bf/002); 'these [floods] from 2000 showed us that they are not a guest'; 'these floods are not like before' (VGD1-Cm/005); 'these floods (2000) surpassed everything' (VGD2-Bm/004); 'floods are a big disaster', 'both the floods and the drought, these are big disasters' (VGD2-Cm/005); 'I don't mean to say that people from abroad shouldn't help us because there is no disaster in Mozambique, quite the contrary, in fact there is a disaster because people died, there is also a disaster in the water' (VGD2-Dm/018); 'floods are like when you have a guest who then dies while at your place, he must be buried, your neighbours cannot refuse to help you only because he was your guest, you have death at home you must do something ' (VGD2-Em/019); 'a disaster is there where the water is ' (VGD2-Fm/020).

Negative opposing horizons can be found in the following statements:

> 'they [the floods] tricked us' (VGD1-Bf/004); 'our main worry is the next drawing[110], the water is there, everything is flooded but now the water is gone and now we want the other drawing we want to cultivate' (VGD1-Cm/009); 'I just wish to insist on cultivation' (VGD1-Ef/011); 'that's why we keep repeating ourselves, we're asking for assistance with this other disaster' (VGD1-Cm/014); 'your drawing is correct, our ancestors used to say that floods are like a son-in-law, he comes to you to take the bride and then goes back to his own place, the floods are gone we have less strength but have to cultivate' (VGD1-Dm/015); 'what is on this side [floods] is part of everyday life, the disaster is here [drought] this is a big disaster water just comes and goes' (VGD2-Bm/002); 'do we want to starve in beautiful houses?' (VGD2-Em/019); 'in fact floods have their own rules they come and go and we must follow the water'; 'what troubles us what makes us cry is our stomach, with our fingers we cannot till this dry soil' (VGD2-Gm/021).

The local position in relation to the opposing horizon does not come out clearly in the statements:

> 'well floods are in fact a guest who causes trouble'; 'in my opinion the floods used to be a guest in the past but these from 2000 (.) showed us that they are a guest they showed us death' (VGD1-Cm/005); 'if the floods take everything that we have then we have a disaster, we need a granary, we could work down in the valley' (VGD2-Cm/005); 'you are right the floods which are our guest come and kill and take away our maize but how do we get it back?' (VGD2-Am/008); 'I don't mean that the floods are the only disaster, when the water is gone we must till the soil but if the soil is hard how can we do it?' (VGD2-Dm/018); 'I want to support what has already been said here, a disaster is there where the water is but previous floods made us insensitive until these floods overtook us'; 'that's why we are saying that there the second disaster is ' (VGD2-Fm/020).

In the agreement and disagreement over the opposing horizon a confrontation takes place with the local interpretive model. This confrontation takes place alongside the social construction of the disaster which I had occasion to establish with the formulating interpretation. To put it differently, agreement or disagreement are embedded within a discursive process which defines the exact location of the realm of experience of the local community. Both the agreement and the disagreement are bound to criteria, which are relevant to answering the question concerning the normality of the event. In both cases the answer to the question whether the floods are a disaster or not depends on whether reasons can be given that meet the criteria set out in the formulating interpretation.

In this sense, the floods are defined as a disaster because coping strategies failed. They are also seen as a normal event because the floods would be hardly worthy notice if coping strategies had not failed (tilling the soil). In VGD2 Bm says something very interesting: 'people find refuge up here, that people died that has nothing to do with the floods, people simply reacted too late to the news, they are used to previous floods, they thought it would just like before...' (004). What is happening in the discussion is an attempt to place the event firmly within the boundaries of the normality of everyday life. How did they react to such events in the past? How effective was that reaction? What should be done in order to reestablish normality again?

The discussion reveals a very complex world consisting of routines and strategies that seek to habituate extraordinary events. These routines and strategies contain socialised expectations. When the water comes we have to check the water levels; at the same time, however, we must prepare places of retreat; we must also be ready to 'follow the water' when it begins to retreat; if we cannot do this, that is, till the soil, then the situation is indeed bad; possibly we have to define the event as a disaster.

Analytical Integration

Let us now organise the data discussed so far against the background of the analytical framework that should inform our reading of the individual case studies. My analytical framework seeks to show how contexts of action are created through the translation of hazards into risk. In this respect, the process of translating hazards into risks is understood as consisting of three dimensions, namely relevance, knowledge, and certainty; each one entails two categories and several indicators. I will briefly organise the data along this scheme and then discuss the insights it yields as far as the relationship between the translation process and the creation of contexts of action is concerned.

The Object of Discourse

The group discussions that form the basis of this case study bring to the fore the awareness of an object of discourse and action that is independent of the individuals engaged in discussion. This object is the natural and social world that provides context to the individual. The natural world has an objective existence beyond the individuals and their volition. It acts upon them, but they can also act upon it. It is the world of nature particularly as perceived through phenomena. Rain and its absence, drought and its effects, the soils and their fertility, the implements and their suitability to human design, they all cohere into the people's awareness to form the background against which individuals can organise themselves to come to terms with everyday life. The natural world challenges individuals to take it into account in their dealings through the havoc it can wreak on them when it does the things it should do in order to be itself.

In this respect, rain provides a very good case at hand. No rain is a problem. Too much rain is also a problem. Average rain is also a problem to the extent that only those who have done their homework, namely prepared the fields for sowing, can actually profit from it. Individuals have no control over when it will rain. However, this does not mean that they are helpless in the face of nature. As we shall see later as we work our way through the analytical framework, the functioning of nature is a central part of everyday life, especially as far as rain is concerned, and individuals refer specifically to this in organising their livelihood. This is an important point to make, for lack of scientific knowledge on nature is often taken to mean helplessness before nature. What people know about nature and how they use that knowledge is actually irrelevant to their own sense of ontological security. Their awareness of the natural world forms the basis of the decisions they take concerning how they should structure their lifeworld.

These remarks suggest the other side of the relevance coin, meaning the social world. The natural world produces hazards for individuals. The latter respond to the hazards through forms of social organisation. These forms are not explicitly put forward in the discussions, but references to biological needs (especially food and shelter) as well as to activities designed to secure livelihoods strongly suggest a close relationship between the two worlds. The social world comes into view in remarks about structured collective responses to natural hazards (for example, measuring rainfall and water levels, retreating, building away from the valley, ensuring food production, securing assistance). In so doing, individuals underline the importance the natural world has for them; at the same time they seem to be suggesting the extent to which their social world is organically linked to their awareness of the natural world.

The relevance dimension in the group discussions points, indeed, to an organic relationship between the two worlds. It is important to point out here that in bringing these worlds into relief, the aim, from a phenomenological point of view, is not to identify possible natural constraints on human agency. Rather, the purpose is to bring the world into full view, forming the basis of the individuals' discourse. The narrative sequence identified in the group discussions refers to individuals' consciousness of something that emerges as a natural world with very specific behavioural patterns and a social world that is made coherent through the kinds of responses it has to the natural world. The visualisation of contrasting accounts of disaster presented to the participants in the group discussions merely triggers the individuals' consciousness, rendering visible what is relevant to their lifes.

The second dimension of the process of translating hazards into risks is knowledge and ties in quite well with the preceding remarks concerning the relevance dimension and the role of consciousness. In fact, to the extent that knowledge is the certainty that individuals have with regard to the existence of the world, a case can be made stating that skills, expertise, and appropriate vocabularies to talk about phenomena (Davidson 1984) are good indicators of the existence of the world. These factors are part and parcel of social relations and can be retrieved by anyone who is socially competent enough. It is useful to see these factors as part of a stock of knowledge, which is socially distributed in the form of a labour division concerning who knows what and what individuals know about where to acquire specific knowledge about the workings of the world. Moreover, individuals not only have to know where to acquire knowledge, they also need to have trust in the nature of the knowledge transmitted to them. This point draws our attention to the importance of knowledge status, that is, to the tacit hierarchies that people employ in the valuation of skills, expertise, and vocabularies.

The group discussions give a few hints about the distribution of the social stock of knowledge. We learn through them that the relationship of the social world to the natural world is mediated by the reactions of the former to the hazards emanating from the latter. We learn, more specifically, that individuals acquire certain routines, which they have to apply in certain circumstances. This is the case with the measurement of rainfall, water levels, retreat, flight, and the usual repertoire of actions that become relevant in the event of floods. The same would apply to other natural phenomena such as drought. The issue here is, indeed, how these routines are acquired, and the simple answer is that they are acquired through reliance on individuals deemed to possess the right kind of knowledge about the behaviour of the natural world, but also about the constitution of the social world. It is obvious that participants in the group discussions refer to the authority of tradition as a legitimate source of knowledge by pointing out, for instance, that reacting to floods according to established patterns of action is deeply ingrained in their experience. It is fair to speculate that this recourse to tradition reveals the status that local experience as passed on through traditional channels (elders, wise individuals) enjoys under certain conditions. Simultaneously, it is important to note that such recourse to tradition, which amounts to a recognition of the validity of certain forms of knowledge, is not one that is given once and for all. As the protocols of the group discussions further show, when conditions change people acknowledge that their sources of knowledge become less relevant. This is particularly the case in the discussion on the drought, especially the recognition of the inadequacy of local means to deal with the situation. In this instance we see a stronger emphasis on external expertise, which comes across as a further knowledge resource that individuals are aware of in their relationship with the natural world.

The picture that emerges from of the description of the properties of the lifeworld of villagers as documented in the group discussions is one of individuals who actively engage with their world. They are aware of the natural world and they respond to it through their social organisation, the perception of which is deeply related to the distribution of the social stock of knowledge. Knowledge, however, is based on what real individuals make of their own experience, that is, the interpretation they make of past events and present circumstances. This reliance on some individuals raises the issue of the grounds upon which many other individuals can legitimately build expectations. To put it differently, reliance on other people's expertise and skills raises the issue of certainty. How much certainty is required in order for people to build expectations on the natural world and social relations? Now, certainty is a key issue in social relations as I tried to show in chapter three. It is in fact an issue that has not yet been adequately addressed in sociology even though much progress has been made in recent years thanks to the work of systems theory and the sociology of risk. This work has in fact drawn our attention to the central place occupied by uncertainty in social action owing to the larger problem of contingency upon which Niklas Luhmann has dwelt quite considerably.

For present analytical purposes it is sufficient to draw attention to two categories that can be built into the dimension of certainty. These are trust and repair strategies. While the former refers to the reasons individuals muster in order to act in spite of uncertainty concerning what might happen afterwards, the latter refers to how the same individuals seek to react, in deeds and words, to outcomes contrary to their expectations. In the group discussions the overriding trust category in the certainty dimension is local experience. The natural world is experienced as an entity that can be relied upon to behave in expected ways, allowing the local community to respond to it in patterned ways. The rains come, the water leaves the riverbed, people retreat or, if the water volumes are massive, they are rescued and, when the floodwaters recede, people can expect a good harvest. Not surprisingly, when things turn out differently, individuals relate their repair strategies to the failure of local experience. Interestingly enough, they simply point out that things turned out differently, that is, the natural world behaved in an unusual way. In this manner, they appear to be seeking to protect their own experience from criticism, but it is equally probable that with time – and recurring betrayals by nature – they may come to revise their experience.

The general analytical argument, as far as the interpretation of the protocols of the group discussions is concerned, is that the local community is faced with a natural world that behaves in ways which are beyond its control. Individuals respond socially to the natural world by adapting to its whims. To this end, they develop forms of knowledge which reassure them of the real existence of this natural world and of the things it does to them. On the basis of this knowledge they take decisions concerning the structure of their everyday life and use the grounds upon which they take decisions as the background against which they judge the usefulness of their knowledge. In the general conclusion I will come back to these issues. For the time being I should note that this simple analytical framework allows us to appreciate the extent to which even in the face of great adversity and apparent helplessness social action is derived from individuals' active awareness of the constraints within which they move. They may not quite understand how nature 'really' works as far as received wisdom in science is concerned. Nonetheless, they use their own understanding to steer a course through the minefield of life in precarious circumstances. Their ideas about relevance, knowledge, and certainty reveal the kinds of operations they make in order to turn hazards into risks and, in so doing, create contexts of action. Deep down, we are, therefore, in the presence of what phenomenological sociology would describe as the translation of problematic events into non-problematic ones. I will close this chapter with a closer look into this process by way of summarising the results of the group discussion and their immediate meaning.

The Drought as the Cause of the Disaster

I drew attention to the dialectics present in the constitution of everyday life and experience in the process of translating problematic events into non-problematic ones. This translation takes place within the framework of the social construction of the floods as a disaster as well as in integration of this special event in the realm of the community's experience. In the process of socially constructing a disaster, my informants use discursive strategies, which enable them to reach a consensus over the assertion that the events were really not normal. The extraordinary elements in the event are not to be found in the event itself, but rather in the irrelevance of local coping means. Even though the local everyday experience places floods within the non-problematic area, the objective situation the local community faces places a big question mark over the local assertion that floods are just guests. In retrospect, the guest was no guest, after all. He forces the community to rethink his position within its realm of experience.

The integration occurs in the form of developing adequate strategies against drought. What at first is only hinted at discursively is in fact a set of instructions for action. In the course of the group discussion different measures are discussed which transform the strategies brought about by the emergency into routine tasks. These, in turn, will be used to fight future emergencies. It is striking that the reflection does not relate to the prevention of floods. No word is lost on early warning systems or on how to improve protection mechanisms. All the local community talks about is how to tame the consequences. These consequences have to do with how the local community can recover its normal everyday life (till the soil). One needs better implements, for example, tractors, in order to prevent disaster.

The local community agrees with the international relief apparatus that the floods are a disaster. This agreement, however, depends on the fulfilment of a condition, namely that these floods behaved very much unlike normal floods. To put it differently, even if people die or flee and fields are destroyed, floods by themselves are not a disaster as long as the community can 'follow the water'. When fields cannot be tilled any longer because, contrary to the taken-for-granted expectations they are dry, then the floods, but especially the time afterwards, become problematic. '... *that people died, that has nothing to do with the floods*' (VGD2-Bm/004). This quote demonstrates the local perspective on disaster which does not take its cue from the event itself, but rather from social action.

Whether or not an extreme event is perceived as such is an issue that depends on whether a society construes it as a disaster. In the case of the 2000 floods in Mozambique they were declared a disaster in retrospect when the community was forced to acknowledge that it was unable to cope with the drought on its own. After the disaster (as defined by the international relief apparatus) came the disaster for Patrice Lumumba Communal Village.

The drawing: *When is/was the disaster?*

The perspective of the external relief apparatus	The perspective of the local community

Figure 5.1: Perspectives on the disaster in Patrice Lumumba Communal Village

The interviews

Text: Group-Interviews\Interview1-disaster
Code: Reconstructive method\Transcript-VGD1

Am: He has spoken now we have to give him an answer @(5)@

Bf: Well floods are in fact a guest (.) who causes trouble (.) during floods you cannot do anything at all and now it does not rain (5) a lot what worries us are the floods; when a lot of water comes we must move but then we follow the water but the last floods °from°[

Am: from 2000

Bf: Yes, 2000 (.) they tricked us we were indeed told that the water is coming but we thought that we new knew enough floods it will be like in the past the water will not come that far and the whites do not have to rescue us but only because we thought about the previous floods but these were different (.) we thought we could follow the water after its retreat but it is hard the soil is very hard you know the soil in the valley is not like this one up here as soon as the water recedes if you don't make haste to till the land you will not be able to till it with your own hands you cannot help your own household anymore (5) that is all I wanted to say

Cm: In my opinion the floods used to be a guest in the past but these from 2000 (.) showed us that they are a guest they showed us death they took everything we had and after the water was gone the only thing that was left was ( ) there are two types of soil there is soil for food plants and soil which is only waiting to be carted away (3) after the floods the soil for food plants dried up if you till the soil with the hoe this soil does not ripen and for that reason nothing can grow at any rate not immediately as for me it's only now in 2002 that I was able to harvest something but I had started in 2000 with a plough and then a tractor and now I can something something like before the floods this is the extent of my suffering these floods are not like before before water came and after it had been gone you could easily till the land this didn't happen now (.) people tried to follow the water but then a lot of rain came and now everything is a forest this was all farmland from here to

Am: To town

Cm: Everything was farmland which we cultivated

But now nobody works here if you want to do something here you must pay 500.000 Mts for 1,5 ha where do you want to find so much money? These are our problems but previous floods when the water recedes you plant sweet potatoes that was wealth we harvested anything we wanted these floods were not like the ones of 77 then afterwards we were at least able to till the land but now everything is dry we thought now that there is so much water we will be able to feed the family well afterwards but it is like (pointing at the drawing) it's dry when the water goes we have to be able to work but this time there was no assistance the only projects that we saw were for the roads the roads destroyed by the floods this is our problem when the water goes we must follow it this time the water was so fast we couldn't run to safety quickly enough

Am: Maybe we should come to the second point for each one of us will just say the same thing we can see the water on the board everything is under water but our main worry is the next drawing the water is there everything is flooded but now the water is gone and now we want the other drawing we want to cultivate (.) we can't we want to be assisted with the cultivation of our fields we don't have implements with our bare hands we can't till this soil even if these people were here during the floods and built houses what do you do when you go home and you have nothing to eat? Can you fall asleep? What do you need? We want to go down the way of assistance with cultivation this is the drawing where we are now the floods are long gone those of us who stayed behind want to be assisted with cultivation ( )

Dm: Our plea for assistance with cultivation is not over (.) here we are up here there are no floods we have two problems even when it rains there are no floods but what worries us is cultivation if we had implements we would be eating pumpkins now but without mealie-meal there isn't much one can do we need assistance if the people from abroad help us and God helps them we will be able to harvest maize ( ) we only eat what we harvest ourselves we don't buy food that is not our way of life

Ef: I just wish to insist on cultivation we came here during the floods of:::::

Am: '77

Ef: '77 not now in 2000 that year as soon as the water was gone we went back to the valley and followed the water even this time we did it like that but it looks just like that (drawing) in '77 we sowed maize beans pumpkins sweet potato and we reaped everything but now you can sow anything you wish and nothing will be harvested I don't know what is in this water you must first knead the soil preferably with a tractor then you can try with a plough ( ) those who did it that way harvested maize but the soil is hard hard it is we are people from the valley up here is not our home here not much grows

Cm: Yes the reason why our fields are dry that's something that has to do with the sea (6) the sea closed itself off during the floods the dirt could not flow into the sea there was a lot of dirt from far away was brought here by the floodwaters but the sea just spat the dirt out so this dirt accumulated on our fields the sea was closed we don't know where the dirt came from perhaps from Chokwé this dirt accumulated and now if you want to cultivate you must dig very deep indeed with your bare hands it is hard a tractor costs 1 million since with the hands you can't cultivate that's why we keep repeating ourselves we're asking for assistance with this other disaster (drawing)

Dm: Your drawing is correct our ancestors used to say that floods are like a son in law he comes to you to take the bride and then goes back to his own place the floods are gone we have less strength but have to cultivate we are starving the soil in the valley cannot be cultivated with the hands if only we could get assistance with cultivation the floods burnt the vegetation in 2001 the rains destroyed everything again there are no cultivated fields anywhere here the only assistance we have got are our own hands we have nothing to cultivate the land

Dm: Even cattle we can't feed the grass is burnt

Am: You don't have to give us a tractor just money for petro is enough it is better than paying 1 million

Text: **Group-Interviews\Interview2-disaster**
Code: **Reconstructive method\Transcript-VGD2**

Am: (introduces participants and asks them to take the floor)

Bm: Thank you I would like to say that what is on this side (floods) is part of everyday life the disaster is here (drought) this is a big disaster water just comes and goes and we can till the soil and harvest our life is here (tilling) this is very important because this is where we organize our life we can satiate ourselves

Y1: Do you mean to say that you don't need any assistance when there are floods?

Bm: People find refuge up here that people died that has nothing to do with the floods people simply reacted too late to the news they are used to previous floods they thought it would just like before usually we stick a pole on the ground and check the water level in the valley there are a few hills where we can run to even in 1955 many stayed there they didn't go away but this time the floods were different 1977 many stayed in the valley these floods (2000) surpassed everything sticking poles on the ground was of no use there were not ordinary floods

Cm: I would like to say something each one of us has his own opinion many think that we all have the same opinion only because two people say the same thing people down in the valley have their opinion us up here have our own (.) floods are a big disaster both the floods and the drought these are big disasters our problem is that we don't have room to keep our belongings down in the valley we were able to till the fields and bring the harvest up here then we could all have the same opinion if the floods take everything that we have then we have a disaster we need a granary we could work down in the valley and live up here all I want to say is that I for one see the disaster in the floods they are a problem to all of us and for the people down there

Am: Where do you see then the biggest disaster? In the water or in the tilling of the fields? Here we are in the water it is our guest (.) our maize was washed away what should we do in order to have our things back? We must stand up again here where we till the fields

Cm: Did I mix up things?

Am: You are right the floods which are our guest come and kill and take away our maize but how do we get it back?

Cm: That's what I mean maybe I did not speak clearly enough we must indeed work our life depends on that we must eat that's what life is about but we must be able to keep our harvest in a safe place just in case the water comes then the harvest can help us

Am: Here and there (drawing) what do you like best?

Cm: What I like best is to till the fields @.@

Am: That's why we are saying the guests destroyed everything they re now gone what do we do next? Now we want to

Cm: But that's what I'm saying too we want to till our fields

Dm: But there was a question from our guest here (Y1) he asked if we shouldn't be assisted when floods come

@10@

Cm: Bisaster

Am: <u>No, now it's my turn</u>

Dm: I just agreed with what he said it sounded like he was mixing up everything he said the floods are a disaster because they become a disaster when we leave the things we harvest down in the valley and the guest comes and takes away everything what is it that we need? We must I mean if we work down in the valley we need room up here to store our harvest I don't mean that the floods are the only disaster when the water is gone we must till the soil but if the soil is hard how can we do it? I don't mean to say that people from abroad shouldn't help us because there is no disaster in Mozambique quite the contrary in fact there is a disaster (pointing at the drawing) because people died there is also a disaster in the water (.) that's what I wanted to say

Em: Floods are like when you have a guest who then dies while at your place he must be buried your neighbours cannot refuse to help you only because he was your guest you have death at home you must do something we need assistance we need it in tilling the fields if people from abroad build houses for us what are we going to eat? Do we want to starve in beautiful houses? We must work you can get food from abroad but how long for? How many kilometres will this food walk? How many days will we be able to eat for? Look we are nurturing forests in our own farmland (.) this is a big disaster a disaster notwithstanding it is a disaster just like when people say somebody died in this house the first thing you do is helping we start with tilling the fields that's where we help because only cultivation can help bring us forward

Fm: Now the others should listen to me I want to support what has already been said here a disaster is there where the water is but previous floods made us insensitive until these floods overtook us but while the disaster was there we saw how people from abroad cried with us (.) we saw how people from other countries cried with us because of those floods (pointing at the drawing) they helped us took care of us fed us built houses for us (.) and then they went away and now disaster is here it stayed it is a drought we don't have the strength to wake up the earth the soil is hard the water there was strong enough to dry the soil (.) that's why we are saying that there (pointing at the drawing) the second disaster is and we are asking for help from the people from abroad since if they abandon us we will die they have the strength to wake up the earth they must help us with tilling the fields with all their strength if they they abandon us we will face the second disaster ( ) these are the words I wanted to say (.) I don't want to exaggerate what we see there (pointing at the drawing) is the second disaster which destroys our existence the people from abroad can help us we know this with tilling the fields

Gm: We keep repeating ourselves but when somebody starts working the first thing he wants is eating when somebody works and harvests nothing that is nothing in fact floods have their own rules they come and go and we must follow the water but these floods and the previous ones °that was too much° when we hit the soil with our hoes it does nde-nde-nde-rere nothing but the people from abroad heard us crying and they came they built houses for us but what troubles us what makes us cry is our stomach with our fingers we cannot till this dry soil we are all affected in the same way us up here and those down in the valley our stomach is where we till the land[

Bm: There is something I would like to add here where we live in times of drought like the drought in 1983 there are small ponds which helped us in the past when it did not rain our ancestors when everything was dry in the valley and up here they sew near these ponds in 1983 they were able to survive this is all I wanted to say

Y1: Do you go to these ponds now?

Cm: It's not possible now because everything is full of water and where there is no water everything is dry

Bm: We try to teach our children these things but there are things[

Am: The floods are gone now we want to talk about tilling the fields]

Bm: We are doing our best but the soil is hard we must go down to the valley what we must do is till the land.

6

Conflicting Interpretations of Reality[111]

Interpreting Reality

In studying social phenomena the question as to whose reality counts appears unavoidable. Epistemological and methodological requirements encourage social scientists often to assume that the question about reality poses few problems. The major assumption is that there is a single reality, which can be accessed in several different ways. More often than not, these several different ways are reduced to two major perspectives, namely a scientific-rational way and a magical-transcendental way. Most social scientists draw from the former to structure their work and their attempts to describe and understand the world. Those who are the object of social scientific study, however, may not always share the scientific-rational perspective on the world. In Africa, in particular, the latter, that is, the magical-transcendental perspective, competes, often successfully, with the former to give individuals their bearings in the world.

Under such circumstances carrying out research in Africa is not only about describing the world and understanding social action, but also analysing the role that approaches to reality play in structuring social action and the nature of reality. In other words, a major challenge faced by social research in Africa is answering the question concerning the perception of reality which should be taken into account in a manner that allows researchers to remain faithful to the rich texture of social relations while, at the same time, pursuing their principal goal of making the world intelligible or, less ambitiously, finding out the criteria which individuals use in order to make the world intelligible to themselves. In fact, there is a sense in which such criteria of intelligibility are not only relevant to individuals as far as they are able to make sense of reality. More importantly, it seems, making the world intelligible appears to be tantamount to making it predictable in the sense of allowing individuals to build stable contexts of actions.

The purpose of this chapter is to discuss the manner in which approaches to reality are constitutive of social action. In order to do this I am going to describe two different approaches to the causes of the 2000 floods in the Limpopo valley with emphasis, on the one hand, on the views of external actors as represented by the emergency relief apparatus and, on the other, on the views of local actors as represented by villagers in Patrice Lumumba. The discussion will draw from interview material collected in the summer of 2001 as well as in spring 2002. I had over sixty interviews with Patrice Lumumba Communal Village's inhabitants of different backgrounds and origins and in different official positions within the village's administrative hierarchy. The interviews were carried out by students from Eduardo Mondlane University, Maputo, who accompanied me to the field for this purpose. We had a week of preparation during which I coached the students on the objectives of the research and practised with them how to conduct interviews in the local vernacular of Patrice Lumumba Communal Village. In the appendix I attach a brief report of our arrival in the field together with two sample reports of the sessions we had every evening after a day's work. Also in the appendix are two interview reports with members of what I call the 'external problem solving apparatus' to give the reader an idea of the issues that emerged during the conversations and how they were approached.[112] While the general and immediate interest of the research was to ascertain local perceptions of crises and disasters as well as to describe the way they are prevented or coped with, the nature of the responses in the interviews made it necessary to look more closely into local worldviews.

Indeed, the initial and standard reaction to questions concerning the causes of the 2000 floods consisted in the repetition of the official explanation given by the emergency assistance apparatus,[113] namely: too much rain, storms, opening of dams in South Africa, and the destruction of dykes along the Limpopo valley. Since a working hypothesis of the study was the idea that there is a reference system that forms a background on which local knowledge constitutes itself in the interpretation of the reality of everyday life, I was puzzled by this response and probed further. Eventually, and as local informants became more confident and comfortable with my presence, they put forward other explanations, which contradicted the official view and, more importantly, seemed to draw on a more locally grounded worldview consisting of an interplay of social, natural, and transcendental forces.

In analysing the different nature of explanations presented by peasants and the emergency assistance apparatus in Patrice Lumumba, I want to show that both types of explanation refer to differing fundamental reference systems which, in turn, lend legitimacy to everyday accounts and social action. At the same time, I am interested in bringing to the fore the extent to which these explanations are not only different, but potentially, or as a matter of course, (can) clash in local contexts. My claim is, therefore, that the difference between local explanations and the explanations of the emergency assistance apparatus is made possible by the social determination of the underlying knowledge.

The confrontation between these two approaches to reality takes place within the framework of socially interpreting an event. Only one explanation can become a guide to action in an effective manner. Where there are two explanations a decision has to be taken between the different explanations. In an earlier attempt at making sense of such clashes I used the notion 'interpretive hegemony'.[114] My understanding of this notion was based on the assumption that the structure of social action is informed by decisions that individuals take to perceive reality in a given manner and, moreover, that such decisions are taken against the background of a tension between interpretive frameworks, which compete for dominance in apprehending reality.

Interpretive Hegemony

In the very special case of Patrice Lumumba village in southern Mozambique the struggle over interpretive hegemony is fought out by the already mentioned opposition between a scientific-rational and a magical-transcendental approach to reality. Of particular relevance in this case is the empirical assumption that Patrice Lumumba village displays forms of everyday life that are less impregnated with technical-scientific knowledge. This empirical assumption adds analytical specificities to the attempt to describe and understand the texture of social relations.

In fact, the predominance of a scientific worldview in a given social context does not mean that every individual thinks at all times in ways that are consistent with science, nor is it legitimate to assume that those who seek to apprehend the world through science necessarily believe that this is the right way to reach the truth. The predominance of science only means that the ways of thinking fostered by science are hegemonic, which is another way of saying that the structural configuration of society encourages those patterns of thought that are consistent with a scientific worldview, independently of what individuals consider more convincing on a personal level.

Phenomenological approaches to social reality, some strands of which I intend to explore further in this chapter, draw our attention to the fact that much social action is based on individuals taking aspects of reality for granted. What people take for granted is not necessarily scientific in nature. Rather, people take for granted what is not problematic, in other words, that which does not contradict their existential experience and the kinds of expectations which they can legitimately formulate with regard to other people's actions.

Nonetheless, when situations become problematic and individuals are faced with the challenge of making sense of them, one may become interested in accounting for them. Basically, there are two kinds of questions individuals may ask in order to make sense of problematic situations. They can ask how a situation arose, but they can also inquire why it arose. Here I want to use these questions to draw a distinction between types of society with different degrees of scientific penetration.

I want to suggest that 'how' questions are typical of a scientific orientation. In other words, a 'how' question assumes, and quite legitimately so, that reality consists of elements that are known and, therefore, are accessible to anyone who approaches them with the right kind of knowledge and tools. The 'how' question refers to the constitution of reality and makes claims concerning the nomological framework within which reality becomes possible at all. As far as the behaviour of nature is concerned, the 'how' question seeks precisely to describe this assumption in terms of the posited ontology and asks, for instance, what natural factors known to science account for natural events such as floods. Inquiry leads one to ask, among other questions, how the floods happened, how they could have been avoided, and how people should react in order to prevent such a dramatic destruction of livelihood.

In contrast to this 'why' questions are typical of an attitude of mind that does not claim any profound knowledge of the inner workings of nature.[115] Instead of seeking to know what aspects of a reality that can be ontologically grasped can be made to account for natural events, the 'why' question tries to understand the reasons that explain that something happened to certain people. This difference in focus may be related not only to a different understanding of the natural world, but also to the realisation that a focus on social relations, which is what a 'why' question elicits, may enable individuals to recover agency in the face of the brute facts of nature.

Descriptive Itinerary

These more theoretical points should be borne in mind as we delve into the material. After a brief account of the empirical starting point I will discuss a few general points concerning the general conceptual scheme which I intend to apply here, drawing from phenomenological sociology of knowledge, particularly Hans-Georg Soeffner's insightful remarks on the structure of problem-solving apparatuses (Soeffner 1987). I will use this central notion to attempt a descriptive reconstruction of the empirical material, on the assumption that this allows us to bring into focus conflicting interpretations of reality. Ultimately, these provide the basis upon which I will seek to rest my case on the role of worldviews in structuring social action and, by extension, in enabling individuals to make their everyday life more predictable. I intend to illustrate my discussion with a brief analysis of two interview excerpts, which are representative of a local and an external viewpoint.

Peasants in the Limpopo Valley

The part of the valley where I carried out my research is located near the coast. The fertile valley is surrounded by savannah in a tropical environment. Rainfall allows for rain-fed agriculture, even though the rains themselves are erratic most of the time. Since 1951 there have been official and standardised measurements of rainfall in Mozambique (See Table 6.1). These reveal an extreme variability that makes livelihood precarious.[116] Long periods of drought are interrupted by floods, but the local population seems to have adjusted itself to this highly unstable ecological pattern. Only rarely do such natural events take a heavy toll on the population, as was the case most recently during the great floods of 2000. The best remembered floods amongst those who have lived in the region for a longer period of time are those of 1977 and 1955. Official statistics confirm that these were years of unusual rainfall, especially as far as December is concerned. Indeed, the measurements for December 1954, 1976, and 1999 are 317.3, 332.0, and 211.4 millimetres[117] respectively (see Figure 6.1). To gauge the significance of these values it might be useful to note that out of forty-five measurements for the month of December between 1951 and 1999 (there are no figures for 1961 and 1987) rainfall was below 100 millimetres in twenty-two instances; eight times it was even below forty millimetres (see Figure 6.2). Given that most inhabitants of the village live off farming, extreme variability constitutes a serious problem. Perhaps I should add that rainfall alone does not account for the magnitude of floods as these depend on several other factors, including how much water is released by dams upstream in Mozambique and South Africa.

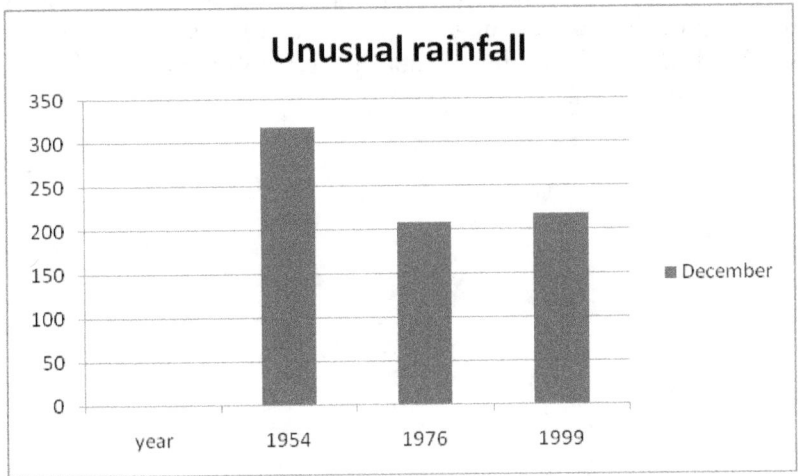

Figure 6.1: Unusual rainfall in years preceding great floods

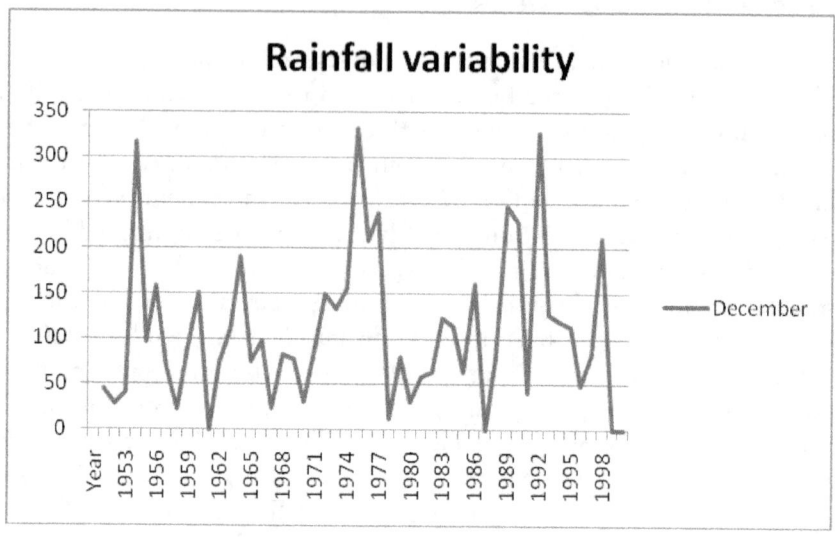

Figure 6.2: Rainfall variation for the month of December between 1951 and 1999 (No data for the years 1961, 1987, and 1999)

Table 6.2 presents the typical agricultural year for the villagers living away from the valley. Their dependence on rainfed agriculture makes their livelihood precarious. The most critical months are always those between planting and harvesting, that is, April to June and September to December. If rain does not fall adequately in the months preceding these, hunger almost certainly sets in. For most villagers life is about bridging these hunger months, something that is only possible if there is adequate rainfall.

Table 6.1: Rainfall data (1951 – 2000)

Station : XAI - XAI

Time Frame: 1951 - 2000

Entry: Total monthly rainfall (from 9 am to 9 pm, in mm)

YEAR	JAN	FEB	MAR	APR	MAY	JUN	JUL	AUG	SEP	OCT	NOV	DEC
1951	67,9	9,1	114,1	114,4	49,2	35,0	95,3	46,0	83,9	134,2	10,1	45,3
1952	28,0	205,4	176,1	57,7	118,0	0,0	55,4	4,3	25,6	30,8	152,6	28,4
1953	68,4	189,2	99,9	101,4	56,2	39,6	22,2	23,9	80,8	9,3	74,6	41,4
1954	100,5	223,1	92,8	70,2	92,0	61,3	19,8	11,0	9,9	34,0	211,6	317,3
1955	261,9	144,8	162,6	164,2	116,5	46,8	8,6	51,6	14,8	67,7	222,2	97,0
1956	51,8	280,0	69,0	38,7	111,2	129,8	5,0	37,8	48,5	12,2	30,7	158,6
1957	53,6	214,3	70,2	64,7	110,1	28,3	43,3	51,8	7,3	74,3	55,4	68,1
1958	91,2	345,6	31,0	57,9	0,0	64,3	17,4	43,1	60,2	34,3	130,7	231,8
1959	116,6	148,8	179,0	49,4	53,7	36,1	44,3	93,4	98,5	59,0	19,4	87,9
1960	61,8	216,9	91,3	186,0	24,0	17,6	38,7	18,6	78,1	77,4	103,1	150,4
1961	49,1	175,2	49,1	15,8	6,0	92,6	106,5	104,5	4,1	60,1	---	---
1962	177,1	67,5	65,3	167,6	66,0	12,2	8,4	79,1	0,5	82,9	254,2	73,5
1963	49,1	77,4	79,1	155,5	48,9	117,4	12,7	1,1	6,8	30,0	29,1	109,8

1964	159,5	105,3	49,9	75,6	12,4	19,2	56,8	37,8	3,6	86,8	47,6	191,2
1965	47,1	48,7	66,9	67,0	45,0	52,3	2,9	58,9	69,5	98,3	116,6	74,7
1966	290,4	176,7	15,8	78,4	14,2	52,4	23,3	49,9	15,8	52,6	42,0	97,6
1967	158,9	487,0	128,7	385,1	186,2	49,0	92,5	13,5	8,1	178,8	33,6	22,9
1968	82,7	124,9	34,9	51,2	93,8	97,9	18,6	8,1	29,4	5,5	58,5	82,1
1969	17,6	13,0	137,2	274,8	96,0	21,9	46,5	18,2	18,7	234,4	23,8	77,0
1970	15,7	50,4	55,2	74,1	8,6	30,7	21,3	2,2	1,4	39,5	25,2	30,8
1971	179,7	77,9	126,5	32,3	135,4	169,2	35,3	3,6	11,2	69,0	37,3	91,7
1972	270,1	332,0	167,5	21,0	529,5	108,1	15,8	11,9	11,4	14,4	37,0	149,4
1973	41,3	228,9	73,3	216,7	29,8	75,5	98,7	7,6	45,0	51,9	102,6	133,0
1974	96,8	174,1	125,6	249,0	163,5	22,3	53,2	6,8	21,0	28,2	125,8	155,4
1975	110,4	164,4	191,2	95,2	27,8	37,7	25,2	12,1	0,7	19,7	63,8	332,0
1976	386,5	60,5	240,3	77,7	108,8	71,8	56,0	60,3	20,7	32,5	20,2	208,2
1977	142,4	340,9	313,5	29,5	38,6	24,0	46,3	90,8	71,8	33,0	27,3	239,1
1978	303,4	152,7	134,3	186,2	27,1	140,4	161,9	3,1	34,9	71,0	130,3	132,6
1979	81,2	30,0	98,4	45,5	145,6	45,5	70,9	37,8	20,5	69,4	37,0	79,5
1980	34,7	100,0	68,9	101,0	31,2	52,8	34,1	26,0	72,3	130,6	93,6	30,8
1981	119,8	195,6	59,9	58,4	198,7	49,3	11,5	41,5	299,8	64,6	114,0	58,4
1982	70,5	82,7	21,6	60,2	81,4	23,3	60,8	9,7	40,3	45,6	9,9	63,9
1983	56,3	29,8	31,2	20,9	66,3	35,1	29,5	52,0	3,8	43,0	100,8	122,5
1984	294,8	62,3	152,2	107,0	82,9	121,0	73,8	9,7	51,0	49,5	107,3	114,3
1985	221,6	114,7	133,8	55,0	196,6	73,9	97,3	8,1	22,1	124,1	---	63,0
1986	224,0	52,9	67,8	32,7	48,1	78,2	14,1	7,3	16,6	69,5	103,6	160,3
1987	60,3	31,0	138,8	34,5	39,6	74,2	83,0	106,1	58,0	22,6	31,8	---

1988	55,4	25,7	135,2	93,1	44,1	53,9	51,7	34,4	7,6	82,5	14,3	79,8
1989	39,3	129,9	50,4	80,7	79,5	50,9	62,3	48,7	13,0	33,9	146,1	246,7
1990	206,3	243,8	122,9	28,0	17,8	--	18,1	--	28,0	--	56,5	228,8
1991	51,4	191,7	111,4	183,3	38,2	55,6	33,9	2,5	30,8	3,9	26,5	40,8
1992	118,4	23,0	29,3	2,2	12,5	71,1	15,6	49,1	12,1	20,1	186,1	326,5
1993	23,6	140,0	168,6	72,4	78,8	11,9	87,4	78,1	9,3	29,3	300,3	126,1
1994	253,4	48,7	41,6	61,0	46,2	45,2	167,5	43,0	32,8	68,9	18,2	119,0
1995	5,5	65,6	70,9	149,6	104,5	32,6	12,0	22,3	7,5	82,4	52,2	113,0
1996	147,0	123,1	181,0	221,3	131,8	68,7	66,0	65,6	1,9	6,5	5,3	48,7
1997	139,2	70,4	163,8	19,6	123,0	9,3	56,1	5,0	26,9	55,2	89,7	82,2
1998	232,9	58,8	--	16,2	20,7	3,8	16,9	109,9	54,1	85,3	103,0	211,4
1999	234,6	401,1	81,9	63,8	12,0	21,1	10,6	26,1	14,5	56,2	218,1	--
2000	--	--	--	--	--	--	--	--	--	--	--	--

Source: National Meteorological Bureau, Maputo

Table 6.2: Farming activities and main crops

Activities (A)	Months January	February	March	April	May	June	July	August	September	October	November	December	Crops (C)
Cultivation	A,C	A,C	A,C				C	A,C	A,C	A,C	A,C	A	Sweet potato
Sowing	A		C	A,C	A,C	A	A		C	A,C	A,C	A	Cassava
Clearing		C	C	C	A,C	A	C			C	C	C	Maize
Harvesting		A,C	A,C	C	C	C	C	A,C	C				Beans
													Vegetables
											C	C	Peanuts

The typical biography of a man in the region includes a stint as a migrant worker in South Africa, while the typical biography of a woman has historically been reduced to marrying a migrant worker. Migrant labour is a central feature of the economy of southern Mozambique. Scholars have often studied this phenomenon against the background of an expanding mining capital defined by a political economy based on the principle of denying the migrant labourer the full status of a proletarian.[118] Farming is done primarily for domestic consumption. Only a small part of the harvest is sold on the local market or bartered off to neighbours. Peasants especially sell vegetables and fruit on the main road that links the city of Xai-Xai to Maputo in the south and Inhambane in the north. The produce is also sold at informal markets in Xai-Xai itself. The main source of income of most of the families consists of remittances from migrant workers as well as seasonal wage labour earned in private and state agricultural enterprises.

Patrice Lumumba is, as we have already seen in the introductory chapter and also in chapter one, by all accounts a hard place to live in. There is a very specific repertoire of action that defines the manner in which people cope. This repertoire comprises an external and a local dimension. The local one includes everything in the livelihood of the local community that contributes to the reduction of insecurity. An important element of this repertoire is the aforementioned migrant labour. But there is more, especially strategies adopted to diversify income sources. These include wage labour and informal trade, both of which ensure subsistence beyond the vagaries of farming, appropriate farming methods, and a shrewd engineering of kinship relationships into social security networks.

The external action repertoire consists of the state relief work apparatus[119] as well as foreign governmental and non-governmental organisations. The most important ones include Save the Children Fund, Caritas, Red Cross, World Vision, and UNICEF, a multilateral organisation. They are all involved in project work encompassing aid in agriculture, education, and health provision. I subsume the state relief apparatus as well as International NGOs under the label 'external' for the simple reason that they are structured and work according to strictures informed by a worldview drawing specifically, and exclusively, on a technical-scientific rationality. Even denominational NGOs such as World Vision, which place much emphasis on faith as the guiding principle of their work, also draw on this type of rationality, as an informant from that organization made clear during an interview. When I confronted him with local transcendental views on the causes of disasters he pointed out that it was also their duty to teach people about the true nature of the world.

Standard Peasant Reactions

Reaction to floods depends on the interpretation that is made of the phenomenon. Normally, the local population relies on its own methods of forecasting impending disaster. It checks water levels in three ways. Firstly, the people use sticks to measure the progress of the water, secondly, they check the colour of the water. There is a belief that if the water turns progressively brown it could be a sign of increasing volumes of water. This is said to happen when, as they believe, the sea refuses to take more water from the river. When this is the case, the water accumulates in the rivers and changes its colour. Thirdly, the presence of a very special type of blossom in January indicates to local connoisseurs impending floods. Most people with whom I spoke about the relevance of these methods before the Great 2000 Floods agreed that the signs had been rather confusing. One possible reason why people insisted that the signs had been confusing was the locals' concern with preserving the integrity of their methods or, perhaps, the need to explain their failure to leave the valley in time.

Indeed, the peasants asserted that the water neither changed its colour to brown, nor did it swell as it should have done prior to a flood. For this reason, members of the community reacted belatedly to the warnings of the authorities. To a certain extent, one reason for ignoring the warnings of the authorities was the locals' lack of confidence in the civil servants. In fact, most people thought that the warnings, which were issued asking them to leave the valley, were just a ploy by civil servants to give them the chance to seize the peasants' livestock. A further reason may have been the sheer extent of the floods, which truly overwhelmed local experience. '*The floods cheated us*', they said repeatedly.[120] The last time they were visited upon by similarly terrible floods, namely in 1955 and 1977, they had saved their lives by simply moving to higher ground, which often was then surrounded by water. This time they did want to do this. They clung to their belief that floods are just 'a guest who bids farewell after three days'. Contrary to expectations, floodwaters 'covered everything'[121] and stayed for four weeks.

The official emergency authority, by contrast, invested in the interpretation of weather data, the carrying capacity of dams, the solidity of ditches, and the intensity of flood waves.[122] This enabled the authorities to issue warnings to people living in the valley to leave. Some officials I spoke with admitted, however, that warnings may not have been dramatic enough to impress upon the people the magnitude of the threat. Whatever the case, it is obvious that these different dimensions of the repertoires of action play a major role in the explanation of the Great 2000 Floods.

Local and External Explanations of the Floods

A general assumption that informs this study draws on the sociology of knowledge as expounded by Berger and Luckmann. Knowledge is the certainty about the actual existence of reality. This assumption reaches back to the phenomenological foundation of the social sciences set out particularly by Alfred Schütz (Schütz and Luckmann 1975, Schütz und Luckmann 1984). Schütz holds the view that social reality constitutes an intersubjectively experienced life-world, which is both the condition and outcome of social action. Knowledge plays a very important role in this respect for reasons that appear obvious.

On the one hand, the taken-for-granted nature of social reality – the so-called natural attitude – resides in the knowledge that some things in society are just the way they are. They are not doubted, for if they were life would appear impossible. On the other hand, the process of "typification", roles, and legitimation allow for the objectification of knowledge through the constitution and construction of reality (Berger and Luckmann 1991). Social reality consists of the experience that individuals carry in them. Experience draws from the social stock of knowledge, that is, the context within which individuals think and act in their everyday life. Hans-Georg Soeffner, a German sociologist, puts it as follows:

"… the subjective origin of social knowledge and the a priori of society – that is, the empirical priority of the social stock of knowledge over the knowledge available subjectively – together constitute in a process of appropriation the network of the structures of the lifeworld. What appears to the subject in the natural attitude as lifeworld, that is, what the subject goes through and experiences also comes across as socially constructed, as the result of social action and socialized experiences (Soeffner 1987: 807) (translation by the author).[123]

In its description of society, a phenomenologically informed sociology of knowledge attaches a lot of importance to uncovering, describing, and analysing the social stock of knowledge, which reveals itself in what we take for granted. One essential question in this undertaking concerns, of course, the issue of knowing who knows what.[124] Indeed, it is in the social distribution of knowledge, as Schütz pointed out, that we find important clues concerning what a society takes for granted. In other words, such clues tell us what individuals within a society consider problematic and to whom they turn when problematic situations arise in order to reestablish the normalcy of everyday life.

Social Distribution of Knowledge

The normalcy of everyday life refers to and describes a situation in which social reality is taken for granted, that is, is not seen as being problematic. In his article on the informed citizen Alfred Schütz (1964) pointed out that the social distribution of the stock of knowledge is constitutive of the experience of everyday life. Knowledge in a society is not evenly distributed. There are some individuals who know more about particular areas than others. The relevance of this extra knowledge depends on the recognition that other members of society give to those who have it. Incidentally, this is the reason why Schütz (1964: 134) argues that experts are acknowledged as such by way of social recognition of their skills.

Walter Sprondel (1979: 147), in turn, makes a distinction between everyday knowledge and special knowledge. He rightly points out that the difference between the two rests on the fact that the former describes the objectification of subjective experience. The constitution of expert systems (Hitzler, Honer, and Maeder 1994; Lachenmann 1994) is primarily a social process. Certain individuals distinguish themselves from the rest on the basis of the size of their take in the relevant social stock of knowledge. The relevance of this knowledge rests on its ability to normalise everday life experience. Sprondel emphasises the fact that social forces are at work whenever expert systems come into being (Sprondel 1979: 149). According to him, this process can be sociologically described as the institutionalisation of a structure for the resolution of a problem. To put it differently, special knowledge within the context of the sociology of knowledge is always an indication of the definition of a problem and its corresponding solutions.

Special knowledge is to be distinguished from the general everyday life knowledge on the basis of its particular ability to handle problematic situations. It comes into fruition when the majority of the members of society are overwhelmed by a given situation. In another discussion I argued, together with Dieter Neubert (see Macamo and Neubert 2003c), that society can be viewed as a structure of knowledge. We defined this structure analytically as local knowledge. In societies such as those we find in most developing African countries, that is, societies which do not present a structure of everyday life impregnated with science, the distribution of knowledge consists in a very simple emancipation of special knowledge from everyday life knowledge.

In such societies there are, to simplify the matter, two types of actors: first, there are those who have the necessary knowledge, which enables them to master routine situations, in other words, everyday life, in a competent manner. These are the majority. Secondly, there are those who over and above such common sense knowledge are in possession of special knowledge, which enables them to master problematic situations. This special knowledge acquires its legitimacy by way of religion, magic, or tradition in a very general sense. Increasingly, however, this second group is being joined by practical experts, that is, individuals who benefit from the presence of modern institutions to acquire technical-scientific knowledge enabling them to master problems posed by the presence of modern artefacts. Their legitimacy comes from science. In the initial stages, their skills as well as knowledge tend to be viewed by local communities as less effective and less useful than the locally available special knowledge.

Practical experts must submit their knowledge to local scrutiny and acceptance before they can hope to establish themselves as relevant social actors. It should however be pointed out that the maintenance of knowledge and the resulting social action as well as its forceful assertion (Latour 1984) impact differently on the distribution of the stock of knowledge. It is fair to assume that the successful assertion of the type of knowledge that is legitimated by science leads to the relegation of locally legitimated special knowledge to the condition of knowledge with limited influence within society.

The presence of different forms of knowledge in everyday life can be described with reference to the institutionalisation of a structure for the solution of problems as suggested by Sprondel. In order to do this, I will now look into competing accounts of the Great 2000 Floods in Patrice Lumumba Communal Village in southern Mozambique.

The External Problem-solving Structure

The floods posed a problem in Patrice Lumumba Communal village. While the state relief apparatus saw the problem as a technical one that required a rational-scientific solution, the local community held ready several interpretations. There are three important differences in the way the local community and the state relief apparatus perceived the problem. First of all, the local community did not perceive the floods in themselves as problematic. Rather, the problem for the local community was what came after the floods, that is, when the water had receded. Secondly, because of this no great deal of attention was paid to technical solutions as far as water control was concerned; the main concern of most people was to rescue as much of their belongings as possible and be ready to make the best of the situation once the waters had receded.[125] Finally, the community began its attempts at defining the problem after the event itself.

The data for my discussion consists of interview material[126] and press releases issued by the provincial flood commission.[127] The commission was set up immediately after initial signs of imminent floods. The commission consisted of the heads of provincial directorates in charge of technical and administrative tasks.[128] The press releases are very useful sources, as they document a very strong reference to a scientific interpretation of the floods. They show the extent to which the apparatus acted on the basis of natural scientific norms and, consequently, favoured technical solutions consistent with the underlying worldview.

The apparatus drew from an expert type of knowledge based on what development cooperation and international relief work know. This expert knowledge makes assumptions about the ecological, political, and economic conditions that influence the livelihood of local communites. The practices that characterise this expert knowledge are scientific in nature. Using the means at their disposal, practical experts seek to establish the normality of everyday life of the local community disrupted by floods. The state agencies represented on the provincial floods commission seek to assert the legitimacy of the state locally. They sit between the state and the people and take up the role of mediators between local communities and the international development aid, as it is connected to the state. The main grounds for legitimacy are, of course, their special type of knowledge, which they consider far more superior to that of the people.

The press releases document, as indicated above, the scientific orientation of the work of the commission. The structure of these press releases is thoroughly consistent: first, they inform about the general situation, then about the state of technical devices including the progress of preparations for coping with the floods. Secondly, they provide a list of the needs of the state relief apparatus and, finally, they warn the population against the imminent disaster and call upon law and order institutions to evacuate the population from the areas in danger.

Information on the general situation consists of data on water volumes. This data is drawn from different measuring stations located along the Limpopo River. On the basis of these measurements, which have been collected since 1955, data is produced which allow the authorities in the provincial capital to gauge how serious the situation is. The data collected in January and February 2000 was serious enough to require the activation of the provincial disaster management services. Furthermore, weather forecasts were made in these press releases. Already in January the provincial floods commission feared that both dams on the Limpopo might have to be opened to release the water, leading to a situation in which the dykes protecting the provincial capital would not be able to withstand. For this reason the press releases included an inventory of available rescue means: how many boats and helicopters were there? Is there enough food for the people? Would it be possible to build alternative roads and bridges swiftly? Simultaneously, a list of all needs was drawn up and appeals were made to the international community for assistance. In the case of the Great 2000 Floods the main weekly papers and state television were invited to the provincial capital to report on the imminent disaster, in the hope of reaching a wider public.

Only after describing the situation and verifying the current state of technical preparations attention was turned to the population. Interestingly enough, almost invariably the population is described as 'stubborn'. The reasons accounting for the 'stubbornness' of the population are related to the fact that the latter would rather rely on its own experience than trusting what it is told by the authorities. The 'stubborn' population is requested to leave the valley and it is the job of the police to enforce this. In practice, however, most of the warnings were not heeded for the reasons already mentioned concerning people's reliance on their own judgement and mistrust towards officials.

As far as the state relief apparatus is concerned, the floods constitute a problem that originates from natural processes that can be apprehended scientifically and, accordingly, demand technical-scientific solutions. In order to do this technical measures are called for, which are superintended by the practical experts represented on the commission. This is, in fact, the way in which a problem-solving apparatus is institutionalised and which then reserves the right to competent intervention for the state relief apparatus. This apparatus makes claims about being in possession of expert knowledge to which the population has no direct access. Equipped with this knowledge the state relief apparatus believes to have the right to normalise the life of local communities. The problem, however, is that in order for the expert knowledge claimed by the apparatus to be locally seen as legitimate knowledge it must be locally accepted and, furthermore, it must flow into the local stock of knowledge. Yet, this process is not obvious at all, as local accounts of the floods differ fundamentally from those espoused by the experts from the state relief apparatus.

The Local Interpretive Diversity

The structure of local interpretations of the floods is much more complex than that of the state relief apparatus. Before dealing with the local accounts it is necessary to draw attention to three relevance areas which are constitutive of local accounts. The population of Patrice Lumumba 2000 Communal Village is quite heterogeneous. There are basically three groups, namely, first, the local Mbalan clan, secondly, people internally displaced by war and drought and who came from the interior of the province and, thirdly, flood victims from 1977 and 2000. Each group draws from an existential experience, which makes up a clearly defined lifeworld and which is expressed in the natural attitude through which each group perceives village social reality. A powerful new element is the growing influence of religious communities in the form of Pentecostal and prophetic churches which reach large parts of the local population.

The social stock of knowledge feeds on this diverse existential experience. Each existential experience constitutes a relevance area with the help of which each member of the community goes about lending meaning to everyday life. The way each community member experiences social reality is determined by the knowledge that belongs to each relevance area. This is valid for the interpretation of the floods which takes its cue from the corresponding relevance area. An important point to bear in mind in reading local accounts is the insight from the sociology of knowledge according to which interpretations of reality are really descriptions of relevance areas in their reference to everyday life knowledge and special knowledge. While the former refers to the strategies available to every community member to get along in his or her everyday life as well as knowledge about where to get competent assistance, the latter, by contrast, refers to the kind of knowledge, which is only available to a minority of people who, by virtue of training, talent, or esoteric powers, have ways of normalising everyday life which go beyond the ability of ordinary members of the community.

The Traditional Lifeworld

The traditional lifeworld is sustained by the original Mbalan clan. This clan, much like the rest of the people in Patrice Lumumba, lives off agriculture and migrant labour.[129] The clan has been living in the area for nearly 200 years. Interviews with older members of the clan revealed that their historical memory reaches back to the time of the Zulu wars[130] in the nineteenth century. In their historical accounts members of the clan establish a link with the Gaza-Nguni (see Liesegang 1967) with whom they claim to be related. The historical memory of the clan consists of three periods: the time of the Gaza-Nguni, Portuguese colonial rule, and, finally, the post-colonial, socialist development of the country. The most important moments in these periods were the Zulu wars, forced labour and forced cultivation of cereals and cotton during the colonial period, as well as the policy of communal villagisation after independence. Most people in the village still remember the policy of villagisation as if it had been yesterday, but even more recent are the memories of the civil war that ravaged Mozambique from 1979 to 1992.

Communal villages and the civil war changed the life of the Mbalan clan in a very radical manner. Indeed, communal villages introduced new administrative structures and brought the relative political autonomy of the Mbalan clan to an end, which in the colonial period still enjoyed the recognition of the colonial authorities. In the aftermath of independence, especially after the 1977 floods, the Mbalan had to adapt to new political structures, which were often in conflict with the clan's notions of political legitimacy. The state, in fact, used the 1977 floods to pursue its villagisation policy by compelling those living in the valley to move and settle on Mbalan land. The whole was officially named 'Patrice Lumumba Communal Village'. Those who were settled in the village after the 1977 floods seized political power, since they were in the majority. The later influx of people fleeing the war in the eighties corroded the position of the clan even further, as it became an insignificant minority in its own territory.

According to traditional views the well-being of a community depends by and large on the benevolence of ancestor spirits towards the living. Well-being is when a community can till its land and reap good harvests, when young men can sign up for work in South Africa, and, more importantly, when nature behaves in a normal way, that is, when droughts, cyclones, and floods do not reach proportions beyond the local coping capacity. To make sure that the land can be tilled, migrant labour is available, and the environment is good, the ancestor spirits of the clan do everything in their power. Indeed, they have the power to influence the natural and social environments.

In the course of the interviews carried out during fieldwork in 2001 and 2002 it became obvious that the Mbalan clan played a central role in the accounts of the floods of 2000. The accounts had a systematic structure. First of all, floods were seen as normal natural events, which are useful to the community because they make the soils fertile, eliminate rodents, and promise a good harvest. Normal natural events are a gift of the ancestors and for this reason they do not transcend local coping capacities. They are part of everyday life. Secondly, attention is drawn to the Great 2000 Floods. Because they transcended local coping capacities they are classified as problematic. Their problematic nature, however, is not due to the damage they caused. Rather, this problematic nature owes to the possible meaning that floods beyond local coping capacity may have with regard to the relationship between the community of the living and the dead. In fact, to the extent that it is the job of the ancestors to ensure the well-being of the community, they have no interest in seeing the community suffer. The only reason why they would let the community suffer would be if they were, for some reason, angry with their own people. The problematic natural event, therefore, must be accounted for through the anger of the ancestors.

The most important moment in the traditional account of the floods is the interpretation of the action of ancestor spirits. Not everyone in the community is in a position to do this. Within the community there are magic specialists who command the knowledge required to make sense of the signs issued by the ancestors. Very much like the practical experts of the state relief agency, these specialists define a problem and the corrresponding solution. As far as they were concerned, the floods were a sign of the anger of ancestor spirits. These were not happy. Ordinary informants in the village suspected that villagers had failed to pay due respect to the ancestors. This was confirmed by leading members of the Mbalan clan as well as the most important village sorcerer, who presides over important ritual events. The lack of respect manifested itself in the failure of the community to carry out regular rituals.[131] The ancestors had no way of communicating with their community other than by denying it their support. The informants drew attention to the fact that one reason why the ancestors were angry had to do with the presence of people in the village who were not originally from there. They just neither knew, nor were they prepared to accept the local norms.

In the view of local specialists the only solution to the problem as defined consisted in strengthening the position of the Mbalan clan within the village. This would mean that state institutions should listen to the clan more closely, especially in matters pertaining to decisions on new settlements or the distribution of plots for construction or cultivation. An important element of the position of the clan is the acknowledgment that the well-being of the community depends on the will of the ancestor spirits. Consequently, it is imperative that the clan is allowed to reintroduce traditional rituals which should be attended by the whole village.

The traditional account constitutes a very specific problem-solving apparatus. The definition of the problem depends on the acknowledgement of the magical knowledge of specialists. In their interpretation these specialists attempt to normalise the experience of the floods. This normalisation occurs through the firm integration of the event in everyday life with reference to the structure of social relations. The central element in these relations is the clan with its web of authority and obedience on the basis of its transcendental legimitimation.

The Religious Lifeworld

In the village there are many religious, especially Christian, groups. Pentecostal and prophetic churches have a slight numerical advantage over the others and are quite instrumental in formulating the religious interpretation of the floods. These churches hold the view that it is in God's power to influence life on earth in a direct manner. Natural phenomena are caused by God. When they are benign and cause no harm it is because people behave and follow God's commandments. When natural phenomena are adverse and cause harm it is because evil forces are attempting to undermine God's work. Pentecostal as well as prophetic churches call upon their members to behave according to God's will.

Pentecostal churches attach a lot of importance to prayers (see chapter eight), as they believe that only prayers can heal individuals and communities. Prophetic churches, by contrast, hold the view that healing is only possible if believers are ready to follow their prophet, namely the church leader. Prophets speak on behalf of God and they pass on His orders to the faithful. As a matter of fact, the theology upon which these churches are based does not make any difference between this-worldly and other-wordly spheres (Macamo 2002). Both worlds form a single entity. In the other world, that is, in heaven, God lives in the company of angels, including ancestor spirits, and ensures the believers' wellbeing. In the worldview to which these churches subscribe, witchcraft presents the major danger to the livelihood of the community of believers.[132] Witchcraft conjures up evil spirits. These are understood to be fallen angels, chased out of heaven after a failed attempt to topple God. Here on earth they create unrest as a way of pursuing their struggle against God.

Because God is benevolent by nature, disasters cannot be levelled at his door. For this reason, Pentecostal and prophetic churches interpret disasters as manifestations of the presence of evil forces amidst the community. In the religious interpretation of the floods witchcraft plays a prominent role. This interpretation is based on a problem structure that makes a sharp separation between those in the know and those who are not in the know. The main knowledge, which only priests and prophets command, lies in the ability to relate natural phenomena to religious action.

In accounting for the floods, three moments were central. First of all, it was established that the proportions reached by the floods were by far greater than anything in memory. At first, when I asked people about the meaning of the floods, many referred back to an eschatological interpretation and pointed out that the Old Testament had predicted abnormal events for the year 2000. Later, however, this interpretation was abandoned on the grounds that the floods hit everyone in the same manner, just as much as the following drought and the general precarious economic situation had done, whether they were believers or not. No one was spared. As far as the priests and the prophets were concerned, there could only be one explanation: evil spirits were at work. [133] This was the only way one could account for the fact that even those who worshipped God were not spared the harsh fate. The floods were, on this account, no natural disaster, but the diluvium itself sent by evil powers to wreak havoc on mankind's faith in God.

Neither God nor nature can be made responsible for the problem. Rather, it is witchcraft that should be blamed; in other words, social action within the community. Consequently, the solution to the problem consists in appealing to the community to defend itself against the onslaught of witchcraft. Pentecostal priests call upon their followers to concentrate even more on prayer. The "prophetics", on their part, appeal to their followers to destroy the external symbols of witchcraft, that is, sorcerers, ritual shrines, and the like. During the second fieldwork trip to the region, in the spring of 2000, a lady was accused of witchcraft and was threatened with expulsion from the village if she did not 'stop' it. Many deaths resulting from a combination of malaria and AIDS, which are rampant in the village, were accounted for in this way. Even a well, which had stopped delivering water due, as it turned out later, to the incorrect installation of the filter after repair work was thought to have been deliberately stopped by evil spirits.

Just like the traditional lifeworld the religious account constitutes a problem-solving apparatus. It defines a problem, that is, loss of faith due to the evil influence of witchcraft, and offers a solution, which consists in recovering faith and turning one's back on witchcraft. The abnormal natural phenomena is brought firmly back into everyday life, a process which confirms everyday life experience and, therefore, normalises the disaster by conferring upon religious leaders the authority to diagnose the community's problems, place blame, and suggest cures.

The Community Lifeworld

The social lifeword takes its cue from the heterogeneous origins of the inhabitants of the village. The first to come from outside the village were the victims of the 1977 floods. In the course of the 1980s an increasing number of people came to the village from the countryside, fleeing the civil war, drought, and the precarious economic situation. The 2000 floods brought even more people to the village. This incredibly high influx created dauntig problems for the village. The first people to settle in the wake of the 1977 floods were still able to acquire plots of land for subsistence agriculture. Even those who came after them, during the civil war, managed to acquire plots of land, both for building their houses and farming. The third wave of immigrants, however, overstretched the village's resources. While they still were able to obtain land to build houses, there was no more land available for agriculture.

A profitable, illegal business got off the ground, with people selling and buying land that, legally, belonged to the state. Protected ritual areas were occupied by people. A particularly instructive example of this was the destruction of a very important Mbalan shrine by immigrants who were not aware of its significance.[134] They were later accused of having put the well-being of the community in jeopardy.

The village accommodates different lineages with diverse normative ideas concerning how a community should be organised. While the village has official administrative institutions representing the Mozambican central state, there are many other institutions which lay leadership claims over parts of the community: these are the churches, the Mbalan clan, and traditional authorities which, fleeing from the civil war, were brought to the village by the refugees and continued to enjoy authority over their own people. As one informant put it, the problem with immigrants is that they are no longer 'greeted'.[135] This comment refers to the widespread traditional practice in southern Mozambique of bringing strangers before the village head in order to find out where they came from as well as to introduce them to the laws and customs of the village. During this occasion they were also asked about their needs. Since this practice has been abandoned in Patrice Lumumba 2000, people no longer have the feeling of being a community. As far as they are concerned, the village is just a place where people happen to live, but it has no binding rules.

Particularly older members of the community, but also local representatives of the ruling party, complained about the lack of social cohesion within the village. In their interpretation of disasters they pointed out that it is not the extent of the event itself that matters, but rather the ability of the community to cope. In this sense they defined the problem posed by the floods as one that was related to the inability of the village to successfully apply its coping strategies, due to general lawlessness. Both older members of the community and local party members agreed that the vulnerability of the village could be accounted for on the grounds of the general lack of respect towards postulated norms. Interestingly enough, they all appealed to the Mbalan clan to use its position within the village to advocate order.[136] The appeal was based on the assumption that all village dwellers would accept the authority bestowed upon the clan by the ancestors.

In this social account of the floods the problem-solving apparatus is based on the idea that a community needs shared norms in order to withstand hazards. People with a long life experience are acknowledged as experts, as they are seen as the repository of these norms. The way they interpret the floods strengthens their position and encourages the community to behave in ways which, in turn, will also strengthen traditionally legitimated behaviour.

Making Life Predictable

These accounts of the floods are firmly grounded in existential relevance areas. Their plausibility is derived from the intersubjective experience of everyday life. What they seek to achieve is not control over nature, but a discursive taming of the consequences of abnormal natural events, such as the 2000 floods. Local accounts aim at strengthening social relations and, in this way, equipping people with the necessary means in their everyday struggle for existence. Each and every account appears to be closely intertwined with the social construction of reality.

In all three accounts dangers perceived to have an other-wordly origin are explained in terms of wrong behaviour in the community, causing ancestor spirits or God to be angry. This anger can only be dealt with successfully if individuals behave correctly in accordance with local norms. The greatest challenge posed by disaster is to re-establish the normative order implied by every one of the interpretations. In fact, abnormal natural events are the irrefutable proof of the significance of the normative order. They draw attention to the need to preserve it. It is a circular argument, but one which in the village context provides for predictability.

The very special nature of this type of accounts can be best explained with reference to Max Weber's reflection on the concept of social relationship. In his reflection, he distinguishes communal orientation (*Vergemeinschaftung*) from associational orientation (*Vergesellschaftung*),[137] a distinction that is reminiscent of Ferdinand Tönnies' own distinction between society and community (Tönnies 1957). Very much like Tönnies, Weber defines 'association' as the orientation of social action towards subjectively felt notions of belonging (Weber 1980: 21). In other words, social action, in this sense, is neither value rational, nor is it based on a means-end rationality. It is oriented towards strengthening the community as well as the community spirit. 'Socialisation', in contrast, is the opposite of 'association'; it is value-rational and instrumental (ibid. p. 21). To put it differently, the ends are at the forefront of everything people do. In a certain sense, the differences between local and external accounts of the floods correspond to Weber's distinction.

As far as local accounts are concerned, the definition of the floods as well as the suggested reaction to them depends on the opportunities it opens up for the promotion of a sense of communal belonging. In contrast, the accounts of the state relief agencies give pride of place to the (instrumental) rational control of nature. In order to put this into effect society must be restructured, even if this means ignoring old traditions of social organisation. This, of course, does not commit us to the view that local accounts are illogical or naïve. All they do is to draw from other types of justification. In actual fact, the distinction made by Weber between association and socialisation can be reduced to his famous formula on the 'disenchantment of the world'. In his Munich lecture of 1919, 'Science as a vocation', Weber defines disenchantment as the fundamental recognition that 'no mysterious unpredictable forces' shape the world, but rather '… that in principle all things can be brought under control through calculation' (Weber 1991: 250). The accounts of the state relief agencies use technical means and calculations in order to '… control and persuade the spirits' (ibid. p.251). Local accounts, by contrast, seek to do the same with transcendental interpretative models.

An Empirical Illustration

In this section I turn attention to the analysis of two interview excerpts to illustrate my argument. I conducted both interviews in the summer of 2001; my interview partners were the representative of an international NGO operating in the city of Xai-Xai, a middle-aged male Mozambican, and a male villager in his early fifties. The excerpts I selected for discussion concern the views of my interview partners as to the causes of the floods. Methodologically, my discussion will draw on the so-called propositional analysis suggested by Ghiglione and Blanchet (1991). This method argues that every piece of discourse constructs a referential world which imposes a structure on the different objects that make up the world. To put it differently, this referential structure articulates different objects into a coherent whole. These objects are the central references; the relationships established between them are represented in speech by verbs which can report, assert, or even indicate status.

This method is highly appropriate to this exercise because it allows us to check the statements of my informants against the general working hypothesis of this chapter that maintains that worldviews are central to the constitution of social action. By drawing our attention to the way in which my informants' statements make this referential world visible, the method provides useful insights into the empirical relationship between worldviews and social reality. Immediately below I reproduce the two interview excerpts, followed by a brief discussion of the codes I use. Thereupon, I present central passages of the interviews with their respective coding and discuss their significance.

The Interview Excerpts

> Villager:
>
> **Why is nature so unpredictable?**
>
> (…) Well, such things are like this, we don't know them because they did not exist when we were growing up. We are also just surprised and wonder what it is that makes the times change in this way.

Conflicting Interpretations of Reality

Amongst us there is no one who knows these things, even those who claim otherwise are simply surprised ... in the past we knew that there were times for such things, but now, well, there is nobody who knows, if anyone says that he knows, he is just lying. We are just wondering because we have lost control of the times. You see, in the past people would sing, dance and do all sorts of things, our forefathers, so when they danced a lot there would be rain. But now there is nothing you can do ... even if people do these things, nothing happens ... while we were growing up such things were done, people would check the divinatory bones, come together like in a 'meeting', they would reach an agreement and then they would go to check the divinatory bones and find out something, take oxen and goats to the forest, these are forests chosen by them, slaughter the animals and then on their return, well, it is already raining...

Nowadays, even if you do it, there is no effect. Nobody observes the law ... in the past after this kind of ceremony people would know what the cause of these things is. You see, where people carry out this ceremony, at the 'gandzelweni', it is not just anybody who does it, people must find the right one ... to do that they had to check the divinatory bones, witchdoctors in the past were discerning ... they chose the person who belonged to the land. It was not just any chief, no chief could give them orders, these people just did their ceremonies in accordance with their own traditions (...)

NGO representative

Causes?

(...) Well, I can't say anything because there is a lot of politics behind the causes. Generally speaking everybody knows that it was too much rain, but the dam ... the suggestion concerning the dams I am not technically prepared, not even concerning the consequences of such assertions. But it seemed very clear that the problem of managing dams, I don't know why, but the case of Chokwe the biggest wave was on 28th and the information did not arrive on time and with the right magnitude for the people to understand that what was coming was a wave. People were even surprised at dawn in Chokwe, so that shows that some dams in South Africa and even the Massingir dam must have failed, you see. This is an area that nobody, ... well, I don't want to make assertions, but it is clear that there is a problem with the management of dams. So, that counts, I think those are decisive factors. And for them to have that impact that means there was a lot of resistance for people to understand that there were big floods because they had the 77 floods as their reference which they considered the biggest ever, they would say that the 77 floods reached this point, so these cannot go beyond here, but unfortunately the water went farther.

Other (local) criteria?

Well, I think the main problem was the perception of the magnitude of the floods. I think the type of information which ... like I am saying, in terms of the magnitude it surprised everyone because apparently the dams, they saw that they were simply ... if they don not open them, they will be destroyed. So, they opened them and the water came the way it did and it went on raining, so, nobody could really understand ... nobody was giving information on the magnitude and also, well, there could not be, if the information is wrong the perception will also be wrong, therefore, that is the first thing, and, but also the people had in fact other references and around here people spoke about the 77 floods, so people did not think that the water would reach such heights. Therefore, in terms of priorities it was noted that even with the water many were reluctant to go because they did not want to lose their belongings including cattle and houses, but in some cases they ended up losing them. There were some who were able to rescue some heads of cattle, but it was very clear that most of these people ... they are very attached to the land where they live and to the cattle and to their fields and to the goods which they accumulated over the years ... it became very clear, so much so that in the critical moments they left, but came back to check whether the water levels were lowering, what was left, that kind of thing.

Interpretation (local)

Well, I don't think the question is well stated. Whatever, if it is a crisis it is a big crisis, people can die in a matter of seconds and people did die. They lost property. Therefore, there were human losses and material losses. Now, in that moment when people lose shelter, they don't have food, they don't have ... they lose everything and are reduced to the condition of displaced people and become automatically vulnerable, they don't have anything when the water is there. That is the moment of crisis and a lot of people come because it is sensitive because it is clear that it is necessary to save lives precisely because people may die within an hour or less as a result of the water, it is usually dirty water, flood water, people need to eat, they don't have food, they need to drink water, such things belong to basic and minimum needs, there is no clean water to drink and many drink dirty water under such circumstances which means that illnesses resulting from the consumption of inappropriate water emerge immediately, there are very serious problems of bad sanity when there are floods, therefore, it is a big crisis which is there at that moment. Now, I agree when they say that there should a longer post-emergency programme, but they cannot say that it is not a crisis at that moment, but there should be continuity, a greater amount of support, now, it is necessary to see that in strategic terms most of these families are peasants and there was a distribution of farming tools to nearly everyone, or at least to nearly everyone. There was the distribution of seeds to nearly everyone. There was a distribution of sweet potato stems to nearly everyone, what I was saying, simply the season was not favourable, it did not rain sufficiently because in fact it was noted that the soils must have suffered from some contamination. That is not a problem that an NGO can solve. That requires another type of work to correct the soils which is not really the work of an NGO. Therefore, I don't think that one can say ... the idea that there is, of supporting a new start in life, if you see on your way from Maputo, you must have noted many houses from Palmeiras up to here in Xai-Xai which resulted from assistance, therefore, support and shelter were given, many had, there was a redistribution of plots, distribution of seeds, there was a distribution of food until April, May 2001, that is twelve months afterwards. Well, it is true that not everyone could be satisfied, but there was assistance. And it is necessary to see that the city of Xai-Xai and even Chokwe saw a lot of destruction, there was a lot of rehabilitation, reconstruction, school classes were rebuilt with a lot of work. But it is a matter of perception, like you say, when people say that others don't understand that one is suffering at that precise moment. That is an ordinary human feeling, but like I was saying some of the answers to such things are not the answer given by emergency, only with development. Therefore, it is necessary to encourage development in order to solve many of these problems, it is necessary that people at last see that it should be them looking for the answers for their situation, each person must think: am I living in the right place? Can I not live elsewhere, can I not do something else? Because there is a lot of insistence in living in the same place, there is a lot of insistence in doing the same things which at times don't lead anywhere. No. It is not people from outside who must solve this, it is a mentality problem which must also be solved. There are faults in the process of strategies, in the process of implementing post-emergency and development programmes, but I think that people should not have the attitude of poor souls, people must have the attitude that they must solve their own problems (...)

The Code System

The central references in these excerpts, as indeed in the interviews as such, are clearly the floods and drought as threatening natural phenomena, local and external actors, property, especially that belonging to local actors, namely cattle and housing, rain and water, technical artefacts such as dams and dykes, transcendental and natural forces, and, of course, death, which is viewed differently by local and external actors. I include coping and prevention strategies as well as the overall political and economic context to contextualise the account in the excerpts, but these are not central to an understanding of the import of the statements to my working hypothesis. The codes include signs, which I use to represent the statements semantically. There are six in all. The first one is what I call linkage and refers to the manner in which the informant connects his statements. These linkages can be causal, explanatory, temporal, or additive in the sense of elaboration. We will notice that the NGO representative avails himself of causal and explanatory linkages to produce meaning, a strategy which is not innocent with regard to my assumption that he is speaking within a technical-scientific frame of reference. The second sign refers to the subject of the sentence which, in this particular case, can be a local or external actor. In some situations technical artefacts or transcendental forces are accorded agency by the informants. The third sign represents the predicate. Here there are three options, namely statement of fact, report, and status. Interestingly enough, the local informant merely reports, whereas the NGO representative moves comfortably between statements of fact and status and reporting, especially on the action of local actors. The fourth sign stands for the qualifier, that is, the normative emphasis that a speaker lends to his propositions. These can be causal or deontological in the sense of saying what must be. A further sign, the fifth one, refers to the object of the sentence. Finally, the sixth sign stands for circumstances that contextualise whatever is being said.

Table 6.3: The Code System

Code Key	
	Central references
F/D	Floods / Droughts
Ea	External actors
La	Local actors
P	Property
Tf	Transcendental forces
R/W	Rain / Water
Nf	Natural forces
Ta	Technical artefacts
⚰	Death
Pr.	Prevention
Cp.	Coping
Ct.	Context
X	Non-referenced subject
Y	Non-referenced object
Z	Non-referenced circumstance
+	Additional
⋲	Causal
:	Explanatory
⏳	Temporal
!	Deontological
F	Fact
S	Status
R	Report
Ø	Empty
_	Negative value

Analysis

Here, then, the propositions broken down into the analytical elements suggested by the method of propositional analysis. Note that I do not reproduce all the propositions that the excerpts contain. The main reason for doing this is that it is not necessary in order to drive home the point I wish to make.

Conflicting Interpretations of Reality

Table 6.4: External Actor

Number	Linkage	Actor	Predicate	Qualifier	Object	Circumstance	Interview
1	Ø	Ea	_R	ð	Ø	Ct.	Well, I can't say anything because there is a lot of politics behind the causes
2	Ø	X	R	Ø	R	Ø	Generally speaking everybody knows that it was too much rain
3	Ø	Ea	_R	Ø	Ta	Ø	the suggestion concerning the dams I am not technically prepared
4	:	Ø	S	Ø	Ta	Ø	But it seemed very clear that the problem of managing dams
5	Ø	X	S	Ø	Y	Ø	the information [on the floods] did not arrive on time and with the right magnitude
6	Ø	La	S	Ø	Y	Ø	for the people to understand that what was coming was a wave
7	Ø	La	R	Ø	Y	Z	People were even surprised at dawn in Chokwe
8	:	Ta	S	Ø	Ø	Z	so that shows that some dams in South Africa and even the Massingir dam must have failed
9	:	Ø	S	Ø	Ta	Ø	but it is clear that there is a problem with the management of dams
10	:	Ea	S	Ø	Ø	Ct.	So, that counts, I think those are decisive factors
11	ð	La	S	Ø	F	Z	And for them to have that impact that means there was a lot of resistance for people to understand that there were big floods
12	ð	La	R	Ø	F	Ø	because they had the 77 floods as their reference which they considered the biggest ever
13	Ø	Ø	R	Ø	F	Ø	Well, I think the main problem was the perception of the magnitude of the floods

14	Ø	Y	R	Ø	Ta	Ct.	in terms of the magnitude it surprised everyone because apparently the dams, they saw that they were simply… if they don't not open them, they will be destroyed
15	ð	Ea	F		Ta	Z	So, they opened them and the water came the way it did and it went on raining
16	Ø	Ø	F	Ø	Y	Ø	nobody was giving information on the magnitude [of the floods]
17	:	Ø	S	Ø	Y	Ø	and also, well, there could not be [information on the magnitude of the floods], if the information is wrong the perception will also be wrong
18	:	Ø	S	Ø	Ø	Ø	therefore, that is the first thing [one needs to know]
19	+	La	R	Ø	Y	Z	but also the people had in fact other references and around here people spoke about the 77 floods
20	:	La	R	Ø	F	Ø	so people did not think that the water would reach such heights
21	Ø	Ø	R	Ø	P	Ø	in terms of priorities it was noted that even with the water many were reluctant to go because they did not want to lose their belongings including cattle and houses
22	+	La	F	Ø	P	Z	but in some cases they ended up losing them [their goods]
23	Ø	La	F	Ø	P	Ø	There were some who were able to rescue some heads of cattle
24	Ø	La	S	Ø	P	Z	they are very attached to the land where they live and to the cattle and to their fields and to the goods which they accumulated over the years
25	Ø	La	S	Ø	Ø	Ø	Whatever, if it is a crisis it is a big crisis, people can die in a matter of seconds and people did die
26	Ø	La	F	Ø	P	Ø	They lost property
27	:	Ø	F	Ø	P	Ø	Therefore, there were human losses and material losses

28	:	La	F	Ø	P/Y	Z	Now, in that moment when people lose shelter, they don't have food, they don't have
29	Ø	La	F	Ø	P	Ø	they lose everything
30	+	La	F	Ø	Ø	Z	and are reduced to the condition of displaced people and become automatically vulnerable
31	Ø	La	F	Ø	P	W	they don't have anything when the water is there
32	Ø	Ø	S	Ø	Ø	Z	That is the moment of crisis
33		Ea	R	Ø	Ø	Ø	and a lot of people come because it is sensitive
34	ð	La	S	!	Y	W	because it is clear that it is necessary to save lives precisely because people may die within an hour or less as a result of the water
35	Ø	Ø	F	Ø	W	Ø	it is usually dirty water
36	Ø	La	F	Ø	Y	Ø	people need to eat, they don't have food, they need to drink water, such things belong to basic and minimum needs
37	Ø	Ø	F	Ø	W	Ø	there is no clean water to drink
38	Ø	La	F	Ø	W	Ø	and many drink dirty water under such circumstances
39		Y	F	Ø	W	W	which means that illnesses resulting from the consumption of inappropriate water emerge
40	Ø	Y	F	Ø	Y	F	there are very serious problems of bad sanity when there are floods
41	:	Y	S	Ø	Ø	Ø	therefore, it is a big crisis which is there at that moment
42	Ø	La	S	Ø	Cp.	Ø	I agree when they say that there should be a longer post-emergency programme
43	:	La	_R	!	Ø	Ø	but they cannot say that it is not a crisis at that moment
44	+	Ø	S	!	Y	Ø	but there should be continuity, a greater amount of support

45	Ø	La	F	Ø	Ta	Ø	now, it is necessary to see that in strategic terms most of these families are peasants and there was a distribution of farming tools to nearly everyone, or at least to nearly everyone
46	Ø	Ø	F	Ø	Y	Ø	it did not rain sufficiently
47		Ø	S	Ø	Y	Z	because in fact it was noted that the soils must have suffered from some contamination
48	Ø	Ea	S	Ø	Y	Ø	That is not a problem that an NGO can solve
49	Ø	Ø	S	Ø	Cp.	Z	There are faults in the process of strategies, in the process of implementing post-emergency and development programmes
50	+	La	S	!	Ø	Ø	but I think that people should not have the attitude of poor souls
51	Ø	La	S	!	Y	Ø	people must have the attitude that they must solve their own problems.

Conflicting Interpretations of Reality

Table 6.5: Local Actor

Number	Linkage	Actor	Predicate	Evaluation	Object	Circumstance	Interview
1	Ø	Y	S	Ø	Ø	Ø	Well, such things [natural forces] are like this
2	Ø	La	R	Ø	Ø	Ø	we don't know them [natural forces]
3	:	La	R	Ø	Ø	Ø	because they did not exist when we were growing up
4	Ø	La	R	Ø	Ø	Ø	We are also just surprised
5	Ø	La	R	Ø	Y	Z	and [we] wonder what it is that makes the times change in this way
6	Ø	La	R	Ø	Ø	Ø	Amongst us there is no one who knows these things
7	+	La	R	Ø	Ø	Ø	even those who claim otherwise are simply surprised
8	Ø	La	R	▬	Ø	Ø	in the past we knew that there were times for such things
9	Ø	La	R	▬	Ø	Ø	but now, well, there is nobody who knows
10	Ø	La	R	Ø	Ø	Ø	if anyone says that he knows he is just lying
11	Ø	La	R	Ø	Ø	Ø	We are just wondering
12	:	La	S	Ø	Y	Z	because we have lost control of the times
13	+	La	R	▬	Y	Ø	You see, in the past people would sing, dance and do all sorts of things
14	Ø	La	R	▬	Y/R	Tf	our forefathers, so when they danced a lot there would be rain
15	Ø	La	R	▬	Ø	Ø	But now there is nothing you can do
16	+	La	R	Ø	Ø	Ø	even if people do these things, nothing happens
17	Ø	La	R	▬	Ø	Ø	while we were growing up such things were done

18	∅	La	R	∅	Y	Tf	people would check the divinatory bones, come together like in a 'meeting', they would reach an agreement and then they would go to check the divinatory bones
19	∅	La	R	∅	∅	∅	and find out something
20	∅	La	R	∅	P	Tf	take oxen and goats to the forest
21	∅	La	R	∅	Tf	∅	these are forests chosen by them
22	∅	La	R	∅	P	∅	slaughter the animals
23	∅	La	R	⌒	R	∅	and then on their return, well, it is already raining
24	∅	La	R	⌒	∅	∅	Nowadays, even if you do it, there is no effect
25	∅	La	R	∅	Y	Ct.	Nobody observes the law
26	∅	La	R	⌒	Tf	Tf	in the past after this kind of ceremony people would know what the cause of these things is
27	:	La	R	∅	Tf	Tf	You see, where people carry out this ceremony, at the 'gandzelweni', it is not just anybody who does it
28	∅	La	R	!	Y	∅	people must find the right one [person to officiate]
29	:	La	R	∅	Tf	Tf	to do that they had to check the divinatory bones
30	:	La	R	⌒	∅	∅	witchdoctors in the past were discerning
31	∅	La	R	∅	La	∅	they chose the person who belonged to the land
32	∅	La	R	∅	La	∅	It was not just any chief
33	∅	La	R	∅	La	∅	no chief could give them orders
34	∅	La	R	∅	La	∅	these people just did their ceremonies in accordance with their own traditions

Co-occurrence

My analysis will focus on two aspects, namely the co-occurrence of local and external actors with certain grammatical objects, and the most frequent predicates in the accounts of the informants. Tables 6.6a and 6.6b summarise the statements of each of the informants with regards to the first aspect of my analysis, that is, co-occurrence, while table 6.7 summarises the frequency of predicates in the statements of both informants. A very striking finding in table 6.6a is that the local informant is totally oblivious of the external actor. The external actor is not brought into any relationship with any of the grammatical objects. The local actor, in contrast, is mentioned in connection with floods and droughts, but also in connection with transcendental forces and other local actors as grammatical objects. Compare this with the statement of the NGO representative, who mentions the local actor in connection with floods and drought, technical artefacts, and coping strategies. He also mentions external actors in connection with technical artefacts and coping strategies.

We can read the propositional structure of the statements of our informants as reflecting both the world which they seek to retrieve and their own relationship to the other relevant actor. The world of the local actor is concerned with natural events and how they relate to transcendental forces and other local actors. The way that the local informant ignores external actors and their artefacts appears to document the relative irrelevance of the world represented by these external actors. This lends weight to the importance that local actors accord to their own interpretation of the floods. In fact, we see in this propositional structure the identification of the local problem solving apparatus, which is built around the central axis of transcendental forces and local actors as they bear on the main hazards afflicting the community.

Table 6.6a: Local problem solving apparatus

Actors	Objects						
	F/D	Ta	Tf	La	Ea	Pr.	Cp.
Local actors	2	0	4	4	0	0	0
External actors	0	0	0	0	0	0	0

Table 6.6b: External problem solving apparatus

Actors	Objects						
	F/D	Ta	Tf	La	Ea	Pr.	Cp.
Local actors	2	1	0	0	0	0	2
External actors	0	2	0	0	0	0	2

Predicates

When we turn our attention to the most frequent predicate we realise that our local informant basically reports, whereas our external informant reports, albeit less frequently, states facts, and issues his opinion concerning the status of the world. All in all, the external informant's opinion of the world accounts for 41% of his predicates as against 35 per cent of statements of facts and 21.5 per cent reports. It is fair to assume that this propositional structure not only documents a complex worldview but, more significantly, represents hegemonic claims made by the external actors on the coherence of the world. A useful indication of these claims is the relative poverty of the propositional articulation of the local informant when compared to the generous use of causal and explanatory linkages in the discourse of the external informant. The latter's world is one which can be accounted for, made sense of, and described in ways that render it intelligible to others.

Table 6.7: Most frequent predicate

Actors	Predicates					
	F/D	Ta	Tf	Pr./Cp.	P	Mfp
Local actors	0	0	R(4)	0	R(2)	R (32), 94%
	R(3)	R(2)	0	S(2)	F(6)	S(21), 41%
External actors		S(2)				F(18), 35%
						R(11), 21.5%

Analytical Integration

The presentation of the properties of the context of action documented in the foregoing discussion is more straightforward than in the preceding chapter. This is mainly due to two reasons. The first reason is the content of the materials discussed here. Indeed, given that I was interested in bringing into view conflicting interpretations of disaster, I had to rely mainly on descriptive categories that are part and parcel of the analytical framework. Those who interpret disaster (a natural phenomenon) do so drawing from knowledge that clears space for their social action. In other words, they approach natural phenomena in ways which reflect their worldviews and, in so doing, document in the most direct way possible their certainty concerning the independent existence of the world. In this sense, we can describe straightforward the dimensions and their categories as documented in the accounts brought to light here. The second reason for our ability to present the properties of the context of action documented in the interpretations under discussion in this chapter is the fact that they actually build on the descriptive work with which we started in the previous chapter. What we are about to see here is the complexity of local lifeworlds being brought to light against the background of our analytical framework. I will come back to this point in the concluding section of this chapter.

The different interpretations of disaster bring into view a world that is much more complex and richer in texture than the one suggested by the visualised group discussions of the previous chapter. In fact, here we begin to see that the dimension of relevance in the process of translating hazards into risks is even more differentiated. Much depends on the perspective that is taken by individuals in their everyday life. Thus, while the natural world is generally perceived through its extreme manifestations that is, floods and droughts, it becomes less clear whether the hazards it produces precede or follow the structure of the social world. In other words, the exact relationship between the natural world and the social world, the categories of the relevance dimension in the process of translating hazards into risks, actually depends on the nature of the knowledge that is required to be sure about the existence of the natural world.

Worldviews

The social world breaks down into groups of individuals sharing a common worldview. In the particular instances under discussion, we were able to make out three main worldviews, namely the traditional, the religious, and the one based on communal life. Unlike in the previous chapter with the emphasis of participants in the group discussions on biological needs, here the relationship between the social world and the natural world is mediated by what the respective worldview deems important for the reproduction of the group. The religious worldview, especially in its Pentecostal version, sees the behaviour of the natural world as a punishment for the wrongs of mankind, particularly the wrongs connected with the practice of witchcraft. The traditional worldview, in its turn, stresses the rights of the original settlers in the form of claims to spiritual leadership in the village. The behaviour of the natural world is, therefore, seen as punishment for the villagers' lack of respect for the ancestor spirits. Finally, the community worldview deplores the absence of a stronger sense of community and overarching norms and rules, but unlike the former, does not see floods or droughts as preceding the social world. Rather, it argues that the absence of community weakens the ability of individuals to respond adequately to hazards.

The notion of worldview strongly suggests the role that knowledge plays in structuring the lifeworld of the proponents of different interpretations of disaster. Indeed, and again in contrast to the much simpler account of the previous chapter, the distribution of the social stock of knowledge respects boundaries that run along the limits of worldviews, while the status that knowledge has is a function of the commitment to a given worldview. Within the religious worldview prophets and preachers take pride of place in relaying to their followers God's perspective on the world. What they know is what the Bible says the world is. And the Bible, in their reading, says that people should worship God, follow their preachers and prophets, and reject any other being that claims birthright over them. Within the traditional worldview elders and sorcerers are the acknowledged experts on the world, and what they know is what lineage politics says the world is. And lineage politics say that the land belongs to the Mbalan clan and the wellbeing of all who live on it depends on the benevolence of the ancestor spirits of the Mbalan. Finally, the community worldview relies on the expertise of wise men and women who are knowledgeable about general social norms of etiquette and decorum and can pass judgement on what the appropriate kind of behaviour in given circumstances is. The status of each type of knowledge heavily depends on the contribution it makes towards ensuring the coherence of the worldview. Any other piece of knowledge brought into a worldview is subordinated to the primary authority of the piece of knowledge that renders the worldview coherent. To give an example, newcomers in the village who, according to the community worldview, must be inducted into local norms and rules are expected, by the religious worldview, to subordinate the respect they owe to elders and local norms to the much higher principle of respect for Creation.

Worldviews provide frames of reference for individuals to go about their daily business. The coherence of worldviews provides the backdrop against which individuals reassure themselves about the correspondence between what they know and the world that is external to them. Those operating within the religious worldview assume patterns of action that correspond, or not, to what they consider to be in line with the teachings of their prophets and preachers. This assumption will also inform their repair strategies, for if either nature or individuals behave in ways that contradict expectations, the explanation will be sought in deviation from right forms of conduct. The same logic operates within the other two worldviews. Whereas in the traditional worldview trust refers to the authority of local experience as made coherent by reference to the supremacy of local metaphysical accounts, in the community worldview trust is purveyed by belief in the importance of strong moral rules. Thus, repair strategies refer, in the case of the traditional worldview, to failure to respect the moral claims of the Mbalan clan over the village. In the case of the community worldview repair strategies also refer to failure to conform to community strictures.

Fact and Truth

This brief presentation of the descriptive properties of the interpretations of disaster brings to light an even more significant aspect of the social life of villagers in Patrice Lumumba. What they have in common is what, for lack of a better expression, one could call a logical fallacy in the way they account for the world. Indeed, their knowledge is premised on a question-begging conclusion, which consists in the idea that the world is as it is because of a condition which is actually an assumption they make. To put it differently, they assume that their social world is a consequence of the way it is. The proof is what the natural world does to them. Now, before anyone is tempted to see in this a document of intellectual failure it should hastily be pointed out that this apparent logical fallacy is the result of the supremacy of rhetorics over logic in the local lifeworlds. Michael Billig (1996), a British social psychologist working in a completely different context, put this idea forward in a forceful manner in his discussion of everyday communication. He argued, echoing Habermas and his theory of communicative action as well as Stephen Toulmin's (1990) enlightening discussion of the plural nature of epistemology in modernity, that logic is too rigid a system to provide guidance to individuals who have to relate to one another on a daily basis. Propositions about the world gain their coherence not with reference to the nature of the world, but with reference to ideas about the world that are functional to what people need to do in order to account for their social worlds and their position in it.

A small anecdote might illustrate this point. During fieldwork in 2004 I got involved in a conversation with a group of villagers on the issue of whether they make a distinction between fact and truth. My attention had been brought to these concepts by the realisation that the Shangaan language seemed to use the same word for both concepts, namely *ntyisu*[138]. The first attempt to start us off in the discussion failed because they replied to my question 'when is something true?' with 'when it is not false'. I insisted by asking on what grounds they would accept or believe a statement made by someone. They replied that it depended on who said it. The grounds for their belief or acceptance were whether the person was credible or not. Thereupon, I asked them how they would establish the credibility of someone they did not know, to which they answered that they would ask other people to vouch for that particular person's credibility. I then pressed them with a concrete example by asking them on what grounds they would believe or accept any credible person who told them that he or she had seen someone flying like a bird. I resorted to this extremely implausible example in order to see whether I could force them to make a distinction between truth and fact. Their answer was as disarming as it was charming. They simply pointed out that only two weeks previously a woman had been found early in the morning lying naked in a tree after having been on a nocturnal flight.[139]

I concluded from this exchange that 'bearing witness' is important to establishing the facticity, therefore truth, of a statement. Hence the conflation of truth and fact, for facts are not independent of the social context which requires them, and truth is simply the rule that yields an acceptable fact. This rule is a rhetorical one, that is, it draws its cogency from the communicative needs of a social group. The perceptive reader will notice here how communication is central to the operation of the translation that takes place within different and conflicting worldviews. In fact, what the worldviews are doing when they provide individuals with reasons which they avail themselves of in order to be sure about the existence of the natural world is actually enabling them to act. They are creating room for individuals to risk symbolic communication in the expectation that they will be understood by others, and, if not, they will be able to account for failure. Here again we are faced with individuals creating contexts of action for themselves through the translation of hazards into risks.

Struggles over Interpretive Hegemony

My aim in this chapter was to show the extent to which worldviews structure social action. It is in reference to worldviews that people place themselves in a position to make sense of what they do, why they do it, and with what kinds of expectations on the others and surrounding environment. The discussion of local and external views of the causes of the Great 2000 Floods showed that these are, indeed, informed by different worldviews. While external actors draw on a technical-scientific worldview, local actors refer to the articulation of transcendental forces and human beings in the world of social relations. Both approaches to reality enable the relevant actors to structure their intervention into the world. While external actors give pride of place to an objectification of the world and the people who live within it, local actors emphasise the importance of social relations for the constitution of reality.

The differences in themselves are not as significant as the empirical finding that they are fundamentally so. Purportedly, both types of actors are concerned with the same phenomena, that is, preventing and coping with natural hazards. However, it is obvious from the accounts of the causes of the floods that the actors are not really talking about quite the same thing. They are, in fact, talking past each other, laying claims, especially in the case of external actors, on the definition of how the world should be perceived. The discussion in the introductory chapter showed the precarious nature of local modernity. Local actors' attempts to define the situation in their own terms are, partly, highly critical comments on the nature of modernity in their midst. They are commenting on the unreliable and uncontrollable presence of technical artefacts in their midst, which combine to make their life precarious and unpredictable.

In a sense, therefore, transcendental accounts of the floods are the local actors' best bet on reclaiming local agency. The world of transcendental forces is not attractive simply because this is the only world they know. It is attractive because it helps them not only to make sense of what is happening to them, but also to do something about it. One can strengthen traditional authority, encourage faith, or foster social cohesion. Each one of these accounts places individuals in a position to do something, whereas the external accounts pits them against technical artefacts, which are unreliable and uncontrollable at the same time as they turn them into the object of external intervention.

7

War Refugees[140]

The Mozambican Civil War as seen by Refugees

On 4 October 1992 a civil war came to an end in Mozambique following peace negotiations brokered by the Italian Christian lay community of Santo Eggidio (de la Rocca 1997, Hume 1994). It was a terrible war, almost always described in superlatives. An American writer, William Finnegann (1992), saw it as the 'harrowing' of the country. Robert Gersony, in a commissioned report for the American State Department, described the main actors involved in the war, particularly on the rebel side, as 'Africa's Khmer Rouge' (Gersony 1988). A spate of books dwelt at length on the brutal nature of the war, invariably levelling much of the responsibility for it on the rebels (Hall and Young 1997, Magaia 1988, Minter 1994, Vines 1991, 1996). More recently, however, a more distanced look has been taken which places the horrors of the war into a political perspective that seemed lacking in previous analyses (Geffray 1990, Cabrita 2000, Chan and Venâncio 1998, Cahen 2004).

The war was waged against the Marxist government of Mozambique, led by Frelimo, an armed and political movement which, from 1964 to 1974, fought a liberation war against Portugal's colonial rule, by Renamo, the Mozambique National Resistance, a right-wing rebel army supported initially by Rhodesia's UDI government and later by the South African Defence Forces during white minority rule. Estimates indicate that the war, which lasted from 1978 to 1992, claimed the lives of two million Mozambicans. These figures do not necessarily reflect the real toll of the war, as they often include deaths from the consequences of natural disasters. During most of the eighties Southern Africa went through one of the worst droughts in recorded history. It hit Mozambique in a particularly bad way, especially against the background of the war, making aid lending to affected people in the rural areas impossible.

This chapter is based on interviews I carried out among war refugees in the village of Patrice Lumumba, on the periphery of the city of Xai-Xai in southern

Mozambique. They had sought refuge in the village during the 1980s. After the end of the war, most of them stayed on. My main concern in this paper is methodological. Indeed, I am interested in gaining insight into the notion of disaster through an engagement with refugee recollections of their experience of war. In a moment I will briefly set out the terms of my methodological approach. For the time being I wish to draw the reader's attention to the definition of disaster that ensues from refugee accounts. Indeed, while disaster can be described in terms of the physical hardship and material vulnerability it entails for the individuals concerned, it is mostly experienced as the inability of individuals to take their physical and social environment for granted. This insight has far-reaching implications for a sociological analysis of disaster, chief among which is the opportunity it offers us to document individuals' perception of the nature of their social world and, more substantially, the manner in which they go about restoring their confidence in reality. In war situations such as those experienced during the Mozambican civil strife, established normative frameworks came under considerable strain. Structures of authority and obedience either held no more or only under very limited circumstances. Yet life went on. Documenting the conditions of possibility of life under such circumstances seems a worthwhile sociological task.

I interviewed thirty-one war refugees. Most of them were women (19), which, to a large extent, reflected a very important fact of the experience of the war. Men experienced it either as combatants on either side of the hostilities or as migrant mineworkers who, for most of the war, were away in South Africa. All the interviews were carried out in Tsonga and were transcribed by a highly competent native speaker.[141] For the purposes of the discussion in this paper, I randomly selected fourteen interviews, the content of which I analysed using the computer programme MaxQdata (version 2) for qualitative research.

Membership Categorisation Devices

The methodological approach draws from the notion of 'membership categorisation devices' (MDC). This notion stems from ethnomethodology and, in particular, from Harvey Sacks (1974).[142] MDCs are the naming references which individuals use in order to account for social reality. In their crudest form MDCs comprise so-called 'membership categories', that is, the personal and non-personal individual elements that make up social reality. Personal membership categories include typical social roles and functions in society, such as father/mother, teacher, politician, as well as, of course, simply named individuals, for example, John and Mary. Non-personal membership categories, in contrast, refer to objects and states of affairs that act on, or are acted upon, by individuals in everyday life. These could be anything from household objects to normative notions, such as charity or hospitality.

Membership categories are central features of reality as perceived by individual members of society. They correspond to the general notion of "typifications", which is the subject of extensive treatment by Berger and Luckmann (1991). Membership categories are aggregates of roles and functions sedimented in individual consciousness by the experience of the lifeworld. As such, they enable individual members of society to make sense of social reality at the same as they go about producing it through the kinds of understandings they project on them. In the discussion to follow, we shall see how important the personal and non-personal membership categorisation devices identified in the accounts of interview partners are for their ability to document what they experienced and, in that way, provide important clues to their take on reality.

Apart from MDCs there are also 'category collections' (Sacks 1974: 218), that is, categorisation devices, which condense features of social reality into meaningful interaction units. Such is the case with 'standardised relational pairs', meaning, typical interactional dyads like husband-wife, doctor-patient, or teacher-pupil. 'Standardised relational pairs' provide individual members of society as well as second degree observers, such as sociologists, useful insights into patterned social behaviour. Now, while the notion of a patterned social behaviour suggests structural constraints upon the interacting individuals, ethnomethodology does not assume that such constraints set unchangeable courses of action. Indeed, just as with personal and non-personal membership categorisation devices, category collections are resources that individuals use to make the world and their interaction with it accountable. Here too we shall see how category collections are brought to bear on accounts of the war experience.

One final feature of MDCs is what Sacks (1974: 219) terms 'category predicates'. These are best understood as the active properties of membership categories. One particularly useful instance of them is the so-called category bound activities, that is, activities whose execution is expected of persons who are associated with certain categories drawn from certain category collections. Category bound activities are useful features in that they allow for the systematic reconstruction of life-worlds on the basis of what different social actors actually do, or not do, in everyday life. In the refugee accounts under analysis, close attention to these features brings into bold relief the main point of this paper. Indeed, the war context by itself was not necessarily a matter of uncertainty. It became uncertain as individuals pieced together personal and non-personal membership categorisation devices, category collections and, more crucially, category bound activities. Wanton brutality, a persistent feature in the refugee accounts, was not necessarily the typical behaviour of actors. As I hope to show, brutality was not the cause of, but rather the outcome of the interaction between groups of actors.

In line with ethnomethodological assumptions about the nature of social reality, Harvey Sacks suggested three analytical steps which I will also follow.

The first one refers to identifying a description in an account. This description is the material on the basis of which the sociologist should seek to make sense of what happened. The second step should then consist in recording the common sense meaning of the description. This task is accomplished by the identifier of the description. Finally, one should ask which membership categorisation devices made it possible to make sense of the description. The first step has already been made. The interviews which were collected provide the descriptions from which I will draw. The second and third steps still need taking. It is the second step that I wish to turn to now.

Common-sense Meanings of War

Several stories emerge from the accounts of the refugees. They speak of wanton brutality, suffering, flight, insecurity, uncertainty, despair, personal tragedy, poverty, arbitrariness, misery, hospitality, solidarity, hunger, hope, and fate. Every account is punctuated by references to several, or all, of these themes. They appear in connection with situations and actors, without necessarily reflecting a conscious attempt by the interviewees to give coherence to their accounts. In fact, nearly all of them just spoke with me apparently unconcerned with sticking to a storyline that would predispose me to see their experience in a certain way. In other words, they did not set out to tell me about their suffering, plight, or personal tragedy. They basically told me how they came to be in Patrice Lumumba Communal Village. Often, at the end of the conversation, when I asked them for the meaning of what they had just told me, they seemed genuinely taken aback. Here are a few examples:[143]

> **Text:** Refugees\Refugees-Hm
> **Code:** Appreciation

papayi[144] I ask myself even now when *titiya*[145] came and said we were wante:d I slept with my spirits upset when I try to understand I ask myself why this happened to me my undoing was migrant labour what did my child do this is how I saw it *papayi* I slept with no strength in me can you imagine my own child's blood poured completely on my back and I wondered why how and I said to myself it was the wa:::r I didn't blame anyone else for my predicament it was the war I must just live it was the wa:::r (..) that is it *papayi*

> **Text:** Refugees\Refugees-Gf
> **Code:** Appreciation

@oh ha@ I don't know what to say my opinion I think if we could rest just like now we are being spared like we are when nothing happens that would be good but merely seeing them[146] is already a problem because they left us in poverty[147] we don't have parents we have nothing we just live

Text:	Refugees\Refugees-Ef
Code:	Appreciation

> it was difficult my son we suffered a lot we suffered a lot we suffer:::d suffering there are people who say that they suffered and there are those who say they suffered I am like them but I suffered I suffered they cau::::ght us mostly I suffered from carry::ing °from carry::ing° you get somewhere on the way and they slaughter two oxen and then cut up the meat weave mats on which they place the meat and then put everything on top of everything else you are carrying my son (.) your clothes get wet from the bloo::d **he**

The structure of the account was simple and included three basic moments: the start of the war in their village; their experience of the war in the village and the flight. The start of the war is reported as the 'arrival' of the war. This might be related to the word *nyimpi* which is used in Tsonga to describe war. It is in fact a Zulu loan word and describes groups of warriors. The arrival of the war was actually the arrival of Renamo guerrillas. It is the first encounter with Renamo fighters. The most common account of this encounter tells of the arrival of *matsanga*[148] at their homestead. They are looking for food and they abduct people to carry the loot. Other accounts are of fighting between Renamo and the government army. Still others tell of compulsory resettlement in communal villages near the army barracks. The first encounter also indicates the way in which the war is going to run. Renamo fighters will come again and again. The war is not the fighting between Renamo and Frelimo; it is these encounters with Renamo fighters, the looting, the kidnapping, and the exemplary killings. It is a war without any frontline and clear rules of engagement. One knows that the war has arrived not because young men are conscripted and turned into soldiers, nor because people and resources are mobilised to defend the country. One knows that the war has arrived because the everyday routine is broken; from the first encounter on people have to learn to expect more encounters and must therefore integrate the new elements into their daily lives.

Experiencing the War

This is also how the war is experienced. The encounters with Renamo fighters structure the day. Normality has ceased. People do not wake up early in the morning to go to their fields and till the soil until mid-morning, come back home, heat up food from the previous evening, eat, go back to the fields, and fetch whatever they have grown to take home and cook in the evening, eat their evening meal, sit together for an hour or two, before going to sleep in their dwellings. The arrival of the *nyimpi* has changed this routine. Now people no longer sleep at home. They sleep in the bush, come back in the morning when they know it is safe to come home. They check whether their houses are still standing – they may have been burnt down by the rebels the previous night. They quickly go to the fields, get whatever they can get to cook, cook it at home, dig holes to hide their most precious belongings, and leave the village before sunset. As a female refugee put it:

> **Text:** Refugees\Refugees-Ff
>
> **Code:** Membership categorisation devices\category predicates\category bound activities
>
> We go in the afternoon and we get there and hoe-hoe-hoe-hoe and all the while you know that now that you are cooking you will eat a bit while listening if you hear anything you cook the food and give it to the children at about 5pm you pack up your things you go to the place which you cleared in order to lie down with your children then rain comes lightening thunder but you are there under the bushes

The importance of this routine can be measured from the following statement made by a female refugee reflecting on her current routine in Patrice Lumumba village:

> **Text:** Refugees\Refugees-Ef
>
> **Code:** Membership categorisation devices\category predicates\category bound activities
>
> well now we can relax we can rest because our living conditions are fine you can go to your fields you come back you lie down even if you have pain of some sort the next day you can go to hospital to be healed if you know someone who can knows healing plants they can find them for you

The bush becomes the villagers' social space. It has its own rules and norms. Women with small children must find a place to hide away from the rest of the villagers, lest the crying of the children gives them away to the rebels. Anyone with a cough must also find a place away from the others. Nobody should make a noise and everyone should just lie low and hope their hiding place is not discovered. Two interview excerpts, one by a woman, the other by a man, document this:

> **Text:** Refugees\Refugees-Gf
>
> **Code:** Membership categorisation devices\category predicates\category bound activities
>
> If you have a small child you just stick your breast into its mouth if it is still breast-fed if it is not breast-fed you just give it food but other people hiding with you without children will desert you

> **Text:** Refugees\Refugees-Dm
>
> **Code:** Membership categorisation devices\category predicates\category bound activities
>
> If she has a small child she must sleep elsewhere with her child if the child makes noise wherever they are it is their problem because if she gives her the breast and

the child doesn't want it that is their problem if they catch them they caught them on their own (..) you see

Sometimes the storyline may change. The rebels may, contrary to normal practice, come during the day. As soon as word goes round that they are on the way, people have to interrupt whatever they are doing. If they were cooking, they have to stop immediately, throw away the food, put out the fire, and try as best as possible to get rid of all traces of human presence, and run for their lives.[149] They either run to their hiding place in the bush, to the army barracks, if there are any in the vicinity, or to the next village. Sometimes it is too late. The rebels have already encircled the village. They assemble everyone, kill those known to be, or suspected of, being officials (party or state), plunder the village, and force the villagers to carry the loot. At this point the experience of war can take a radically different turn. Those who are forced to accompany the Renamo fighters may never come back. They walk for days, carrying heavy loads on their heads, always in fear of their lives.

It is a totally new social situation with its own rules and norms. There are clear hierarchies; the Renamo fighters have the say and, most importantly, they can decide over the life and death of those they have kidnapped. Those who are too feeble to eundure the forced march are beaten to death, summarily shot, or simply left to die. No one may speak on behalf of anyone else, and those who break this rule risk losing their life in a most bestial manner.

Text: Refugees\Refugees-Kfm

Code: Membership categorisation devices\category predicates\category bound activities

she has a child on her back well they asked her whatever they asked her and then they took the child on her back and hit it against the tree and the child died right there and afterwards they killed her and then they left[150]

Some are lucky and told to return home; others manage to flee. For most, however, abduction is the beginning of a new life.[151]

The experience of war comes to an end when people decide to leave their village and seek refuge elsewhere, mostly in Xai-Xai. The crucial aspect to bear in mind is what makes people take the decision. The single most important factor is the total unpredictability of the Renamo fighters. They are unpredictable because they can come at any time of the day. People are no longer able to keep a semblance of routine if they can only briefly visit their fields, have to cook hastily, and then run off to the bush. They have become an even easier prey for the Renamo rebels. This is the moment when people decide to leave. Interestingly enough, not the loss of their cattle, for those who owned cattle, nor even the burning down of their houses appears in the accounts as the immediate cause why people decided to leave. The loss of their belongings is built into the account of the routine occasioned by the arrival of the *nyimpi*. It becomes a major explanatory factor in retrospect, once people have found refuge and reflect on their experience. Others do not actually take the decision; their flight happens as a matter of course, especially if they happen to have escaped from captivity. Then they just keep running.

These three moments, namely (i) arrival of the *nyimpi*, (ii) new routine, and (iii) flight are the elements that come together to produce a coherent account of the experience refugees went through. While each individual story may suggest a very specific tale, such as suffering, ordeal, luck, or personal tragedy, there is nothing in the texture of the accounts that would warrant a normatively shared coherent account of the experience of war. Yet this normatively coherent account lurks beneath the narrative surface of the interviews, structures individual ability to remember what happened, and ultimately provides the clue to the way in which refugees came to terms with uncertainty. I now wish to turn my attention to this normatively coherent account by way of taking the third step in the analytical procedure suggested by Harvey Sacks. In other words, I try to recover the common-sense meaning of what the refugees told me by taking a closer look at the membership categorisation devices they employed.

Retrieving Social Reality

MCDs are the resources employed by individuals to account for social action. They entertain an indexical relationship with social reality to the extent that they provide markers of the points at which interacting individuals come into contact with social reality as an emergent entity. In the discussion that follows, I will pay attention to these markers and at the same time amass evidence that will allow me to show that the 'war' was not the cause of insecurity. Rather, the war was the outcome of social interaction, which ultimately, in a reflexive manner, made the 'war' the cause of insecurity. I will start by discussing the frequency of personal and non-personal membership categorisation devices as well as point to certain significant collective categories. Secondly, I will document typical category-bound activities and relate them to the personal and non-personal categories. Finally, I will draw analytical implications from the empirical observations.

Personal and Non-personal MDCs

There are basically six personal membership categorisation devices that structure refugee accounts: *Renamo fighters (50)*,[152] *soldiers (30), Frelimo (29), people (19), neighbour (8) and commander (7)*. There are also significant references to family members (father, mother, husband, wife, grandparents, daughter, son, uncle, and aunt), but since these are obvious enough I did not think it particularly important to mention them. They are more relevant as far as standardised relational pairs are concerned. Given the nature of the interviews (on the subject of war) and the interviewees themselves (refugees) it is actually not surprising that these particular devices play a prominent role in the accounts. They provide the first indication of the context within which the reported experiences took place. The relatively high frequency of references to violence actors is proof of this. Moreover, the score of Renamo fighters underlines the centrality of their role in the life-world that refugee accounts seek to make sense of. The warring parties – Frelimo and Renamo – can be considered 'external actors' who interact with 'local actors', that is, the refugees at the time of the reported occurrences. There are two other actor sets mentioned in the accounts. The first one is 'people' and the second is 'neighbour'. These references require some explanation.

The events reported in the interviews refer to experiences lived through by the interview partners themselves. As such, they use personal pronouns. References to the 'people', however, indicate a different perspective from the one that structures the narrative. In fact, interview partners use an interactional device described by Goffman as 'footing', that is, taking different perspectives in the course of a description. The 'people' are the refugees at the time of the reported occurrences, seen by the external actors. While the word 'people' gained wider currency in Mozambique in the context of Frelimo's socialist rhetoric, it is used in the accounts less as a politically laden notion than as a distancing mechanism to bring into relief the perception of victimhood. The 'people' are therefore those who are caught up between two warring factions. Ultimately, the notion describes a collective fate, that is, the fate of those who just happened to be there when the *nyimpi* arrived.

The 'neighbour' is also indexical. A somewhat strange aspect of the refugee accounts is the total absence of references to membership categories relating to the wider community. In fact, there is no community in the accounts. Kinship is important and there are enough references to that. However, references to family are just about as far as accounts go to recover a sense of a wider social context of interaction. The reference to 'neighbour' is already a clear indication that a village contains more than only family members. Furthermore, as we shall see below, most people had been compulsorily assembled into communal villages where they lived in spatial proximity of non-family members. The more likely explanation for the absence of community references seems to be suggested by the substantive content of the reference to the 'neighbour'. Most references to neighbours are about denunciation. The standard story reports the arrival of Renamo fighters who are tipped off by a 'neighbour' about the material possessions of those living next door. Here are two interesting examples:

Text: **Refugees\Refugees-Hm**
Code: **Membership categorisation devices\category predicates\category bound activities**

Here at the *neighbour's*[153] they are hitting hard and so they say:: you should not arrest us don't you want cattle and they said well there at the next homestead

Text: Refugees\Refugees-Hm

Code: Membership categorisation devices\category predicates\category bound activities

> and then they sai::d you are only arresting us but there are migrant workers who have just returned and even my husband sent things through them the day before yesterday there is one migrant worker who returned yester::day the day before yesterday well one of them a lorry just stopped and unloaded huge quantities

There is almost no reference to the 'neighbour' in connection with solidarity and assistance.

Non-personal membership categorisation devices are also interesting in their own right. The most frequent ones are: *homestead/village (50), communal village (21), bush (24), hiding place (9), Renamo base (14), army barracks (13), firearm (23), dwelling (13) and cattle (16)*. There are also references to clothing, household utensils, lorries, and hens, but these do not appear to be central to the accounts. The main non-personal MCDs document the settings where the action took place. Not surprisingly, they refer mainly to the war context and, in particular, to the experience of war. These settings were the home and the communal village, the barracks and the base, as well as the bush and the hiding place.

One way to characterise these settings is to see them with reference to the agency of refugees at the time of the reported occurrences. The home was their turf par excellence before the arrival of the *nyimpi*. After that the home became a transitional space, a place where they could stay only on borrowed time, that is, so long the *nyimpi* did not come. Their proper home became the bush/hiding place, where the only external constraints which they had to observe were those ensuing from the need to share space with others facing a similar fate. The communal village was not better than the home. In fact, it represented a double loss of agency. The first loss occurred when the Frelimo army came to bring them to 'safety'.

Text: Refugees\Refugees-Ef

Code: Membership categorisation devices\category predicates\category bound activities

> they said let's go, let's go to the village, let's go take your mat take your blanket take your mat take your blanket

The second loss occurred with the arrival of the *nyimpi* at the communal village itself. The rebel base and the army barracks were off limits to the refugees at the time of the reported occurrences, but these were the places of total agency loss. Whereas at home, communal village, bush, and hiding place they could still take the initiative on matters concerning their own life, at the army barracks and the rebel base they became mere objects of an external will to power.

Central non-personal MCDs also include references to *dwellings, firearms*, and *cattle*. Dwellings and cattle play an important role in the accounts. The former are ransacked and burnt down, while the latter are slaughtered or herded away to distant rebel bases. Dwellings and cattle are the villagers' livelihood, without them they lose everything. While never the immediate reason for taking flight, the loss of dwellings and cattle appears to be a good reason in retrospect. The firearm and its sound is the ultimate sign of power. Curiously enough, very few villagers saw people being killed by firearms. Most people were beaten to death with sticks or chopped up with axes and bayonets:

Text: Refugees\Refugees-Gf

Code: **Membership categorisation devices\category predicates\category bound activities**

> they put your child in a mortar and tell you to pound and you do it then they take your child and put it in a cooking pot and they tell you to put it on the hearth you refuse they kill you so that is how it was then they set the houses on fire they did this to two of our houses then they left that is why we run away till we arrived here.

Yet the firearm is the main symbol of the power that rules over the lives of the villagers. They speak in awe of the firearm and of the roaring sound it makes as it is used against other combatants. The onomatopoeic impression some of them gave can be ascertained from the following excerpt:

Text: Refugees\Refugees-Ef

Code: **Membership categorisation devices\category predicates\category bound activities**

We started hearing behind us *kadum-gitchigitchigitchi ha*

Category collections refer mainly to family relationships. These break down into a few standardised relational pairs: *husband/wife, mother/child, and grandparents/grandchildren*. The forms of interaction they engage in are entirely informed by the context of war. The husband/wife standardised relational pair is less frequent in the accounts. This is due to the fact that most men are migrant workers, spending long stretches of time – up to eighteen months – away in South Africa. Significantly, the standard interaction between husband and wife is the discussion over when to flee. Often the women are unwilling to leave, and it is the men who insist on it in letters and messages they give to colleagues and friends going home on leave. A migrant labourer's return home on leave might also precipitate the flight because someone tips off the rebels about the fresh arrival of someone with goods purchased in South Africa. More often than not, however, the decision to leave is taken by the woman. Once in the safe haven of Xai-Xai, husbands will ensure that their wives settle down smoothly in the new environment.

The most frequent and significant standardised relational pair is the mother/child one. The experience of the war actually revolves around this relationship.

It is the mothers who have to make sure their children have enough to eat, find a hiding place, and not put the lives of other villagers at risk at the hiding place; mothers and their children are kidnapped and mothers lose sight of their daughters taken away to become the wives of rebel fighters. One feels almost like saying that, without this standardised relational pair, much of the experience of war would be hard to sustain as a coherent narrative. It is an overarching relationship which, in the end, places the woman (wife, aunt, daughter, mother, grandmother) at the centre of crucial family interactions. A particularly chilling account of this was provided by a mother caught in a cross-fire at an army compound under Renamo attack:

> **Text:** **Refugees\Refugees-Hm**
> **Code:** **Membership categorisation devices\category predicates\category bound activities**
>
> there came a bullet and I turned the child away and the bullet just did *pha* and *whee* past me and hit the child when I turned around to see the child I found that I am bathed in blood the child is not crying anymore and I looked and saw that I lost the child so I left and saw that the bullet shot through the child and ended on the wall and I walked unsteadily and threw myself into the bathtub and slept there.

Category-bound Activities

I now turn to a crucial element of the analysis of refugee accounts. Ethnomethodology claims that talk is action.[154] Indeed, through talk individuals produce social reality by reproducing the assumptions that inform their perception of the world. We have seen that categories play an important role in this enterprise, to the extent that they document the criteria according to which individuals seek to sustain a sense of social reality. Categories are not enough by themselves. They may tell us a lot about the kinds of "typifications" that individuals make, but the sense in which such "typifications" are articulated with the experience of the life-world can only be recovered through the qualifications made with regard to categories as well as the ascription of activities to such categories. The MCD approach recovers this articulation through what it calls category predicates and category-bound activities. The former are precisely the kinds of normative descriptions made about categories, whereas the latter are simply the activities associated with categories. In analysing my data, I paid particular attention to category-bound activities in order to elicit these normative descriptions and, in that way, get to the heart of the assumptions that refugees at the time of the reported occurrences were making about their social world.

As can be seen in table 3/CBA, six activities dominate refugee accounts: *running (37), fleeing (27), killing (26), sleeping in the bush (13), carrying loads (6),* and *beating (5).* They all refer to the war context and, in particular, to the position of the interview partners within that context. I should note in passing that none of the activities recovers any sense of orderly rural life. These are activities that draw attention to an abnormal situation. To put it differently, they do not describe the routine world of villagers. Rather, they provide elements for the description of the manner in which villagers sought to re-establish a sense of normality in a world, which they could no longer take for granted. The activities listed below draw attention to the position of villagers in relation to external actors. For ease of analysis we could classify the activities according to two basic interactional types: local agency and external constraint. Of course, given the context within which individuals go about their lives this typology can be misleading. In fact, even what I propose to classify as 'local agency' takes place in reaction to external constraint. Still, this typology can be used to distinguish the normative assumptions made about each type of actor.

The activities that fall under 'external constraint' are beating, killing, and carrying loads. It is the villagers who are at the receiving end. In other words, external actors inflict these on local actors. The activities define clear power relations, whose main function appears to be the redefinition of roles. Indeed, the main function of beating, killing, and making people carry heavy loads was to produce difference, that is, to show who the external actors are, and who the local actors. External actors beat, they are not beaten; external actors kill, they are not killed (at least not by villagers); external actors tell others to carry heavy loads, they are not told by anyone to carry. More than showing wanton brutality, therefore, the category-bound activities interview partners used to document their perception of the social world in which they found themselves were functional to the new definition of roles. The beatings, killings, and the carrying of heavy loads did not take place arbitrarily. An almost pedagogical intention could be discerned behind them. Beatings using bizarre means were inflicted precisely for this pedagogical reason:

Text: **Refugees\Refugees-If**

Code: **Membership categorisation devices\category predicates\category-bound activities**

they took the hand of a dead person who died long ago and they used it to hit him here

Local agency was reduced to a mere response to external constraint. Villagers ran away, fled, and went to sleep in the bush. Their everyday life became a way of coming to terms with the arrival of the *nyimpi*. The ordinary activities that belonged to their everyday routine, such as farming, looking after their cattle, and tending to household chores was replaced by the need to respond to the presence of an external, powerful new element in their midst. This element had no discernible face, it made itself present through the arbitrary and brutal nature of its encounter with villagers. Some villagers report that the first time the *nyimpi* arrived, they just asked for 'something to add to the sauce'. The villagers understood that they were neither asking, nor did they mean just anything 'to add to the sauce'. This was a request that villagers could not turn down. The *nyimpi*'s firearms made sure that the villagers understood that much. Locally, things one adds to the sauce range from cassava, pumpkin, bitter leaves, to fish and meat. Fish and meat enjoy higher status than vegetables. To the villagers it was also clear what 'to add to the sauce' meant: meat. The villagers had to slaughter their cattle and what the *nyimpi* could not consume right away would be packed and carried by villagers selected to that end by the *nyimpi*. Interaction with the external actors became, strangely enough, a very pregnant, fleeting encounter. Most of it took place without any co-presence at all. One heard them coming; one ran for one's life; one took flight; one slept in the bush. If it was too late and it came to co-presence, then the encounter became an occasion to define the respective positions; the encounter became pedagogically charged.

Text: Refugees\Refugees-Jm
Code: Membership categorisation devices\category predicates\category-bound activities

I don't want to see anything related with this type of person I don't want to see him in my heart I don't want to see matsanga[155] he killed my people he just too::k people and to::re them apart tore bellies of pregnant women open and said he wants to see josina[156] and if the baby is male he said it is samora[157] then just left the mother lying on the ground and went to the bush he found a person and killed him then put a stake on the ground and placed the head of the dead person and said it is samora smiling at the people

Text: Refugees\Refugees-Jm
Code: Membership categorisation devices\category predicates\category-bound activities

my grandmother had her neck chopped they just took her ne::ck and cut it my own grandmother who gave birth to my mother I just found her head playing on its own her body was also playing on its own

Text: Refugees\Refugees-Jm
Code: Membership categorisation devices\category predicates\category-bound activities

my grandson was a leader with frelimo (.) they chopped off his hand and said take it with you to greet samora with but he later died

Text: Refugees\Refugees-Kfm
Code: Membership categorisation devices\category predicates\category bound-activities

They lit up a match and set him on fire eh: he burnt his body the ropes tying him gave in so he stood up and tried to walk when he did this they beat him beat him up and he fell down so they put straw on his body and he burnt even more if he tried to crawl they beat him up until he died now they did this because he worked for frelimo he was a local judge[158] that is how my father was killed

Brutality became a means of defining the situation and the respective roles to be taken by each party. It became a function of the process of socially constructing the reality of war. In other words, the war could not be reduced to violence; rather, violence became the defining moment of war, the mechanism through which both violence actors, that is, Renamo rebels and Frelimo soldiers, and civilians made war accountable. War became much worse than mere violence. It meant the loss of a sense of humanity, as the following interview excerpt documents:

Text: **Refugees\Refugees-Cf**
Code: **Membership categorisation devices\category predicates\category-bound activities**

in those days we were like wild beasts do you know wild beasts (.) that is how we lived we did not lead the lives of people we lived like wild beasts yes we lived like beasts

Life became totally unpredictable and this was, in the end, what turned the whole experience of war into a disaster:

Text: **Refugees\Refugees-Af**
Code: **Membership categorisation devices\category predicates\category-bound activities**

we were even scared of our own soldiers because if they found you they took you to the communal village and they killed you there they asked why you run away from them

Analytical Integration

Accounting for Disaster

Membership categorisation devices in themselves provide important clues to the properties of the context of action. To the extent that they draw directly from those aspects and categories of social life that are of direct relevance to individuals and the structure of their relationship to one another, they are, indeed, documents of the process of translating hazards into risks. Unlike in the previous two chapters on the definition and interpretation of (natural) disasters, in this chapter we are confronted with a different matter. While the category of the natural world is still central to the dimension of relevance, it is not in itself the immediate source of hazards to the community. The natural world, especially in the form of the forest, is evoked in the accounts of refugees as a place of refuge.

Yet, the natural world category as opposed to the social world category is still relevant, for there is a level of awareness in refugee accounts, which is distinct from their social world and actually stands in opposition to it. The natural world takes the form of a diffuse environment, that is, a civil war, which does not fall under the control of the local population. The natural world category in these accounts describes the war as a constraining factor on the life of the members of the community and forces them to organise their lives with respect to it. The social world acquires meaning and structure as a response to what this constraining environment does to its members. People are forced to change their routines and daily activities, they even question basic social relations (husband/wife, neighbours, grandchildren/grandparents) and move their spaces of sociality, away from physical villages to forests.

The knowledge that becomes relevant in the context of war is the kind of knowledge that enables people to restructure their lives accordingly. Its social distribution alters established hierarchies, skills, and specialisations. Authority figures, such as male heads of families, local political leaders, and local sages lose their importance in favour of those who know what to do when 'the war comes', where to hide, how to do it, which course to steer to stay away from the fighting, and which routes to take once the decision to flee has been taken. Farming skills are of course important, but basically irrelevant in the context of war. They become subsidiary to the much more pressing need of avoiding being caught up in the fighting. Women, in particular, become central actors in the local predicament. They are the ones who have to change everyday routines, such as farming, cooking times and, above all, how to hide family belongings (by digging them away and covering them up) and, basically, wipe out fresh traces of human existence. It falls upon them to know how to protect the weaker members of the community (elders and children) and, when necessary, to sacrifice themselves for the sake of the rest (as when women with small children have to hide far away from where the rest of the village, including their husbands, is hiding). The decision to flee falls upon them; then everyday routine is built around their activities and they are the ones who know when normality is no longer possible.

The context of war is an uncertain one. Yet, people go about their lives in the best way they can. They do this by relying on patterns in the way the war 'comes' to them, but also on their hope that the recognition of patterns will enable them to structure their daily lives in line with them. They know more or less when the 'war comes': especially in the early evening or the early hours of the morning. In other words, they know that during the day they can go about their daily chores and quickly retire to the safety of the forest. They place trust in the statistical validity of their observations of the patterns taken by the war. Most of the time trust functions quite well. When it does not function, such as when marauding gangs come unexpectedly and kill, ransack, and abduct, people level the failure either on the inaccuracy of their observations or assume that things are changing. The latter option was crucial for the decision to flee. In fact, it was only after realising that no semblance of normality was ever going to be established once the 'arrival' of the war had become unpredictable that people saw the need to seek refuge elsewhere.

'Doing' Disaster

This chapter is about a hazard that is different in nature from floods or drought. It is not a natural phenomenon as such. Yet, there is an elective affinity between natural phenomena that produce hazards to individuals and their communities, and social or political phenomena that do the same. Both challenge individuals to seek room for individual and collective initiative. My point, which will be fully developed in the final chapter, is that what such phenomena have in common is the opportunity they provide human communities to create the conditions of their own action. A war situation does not place an individual before the decision to flee or be killed. Rather, it opens up possibilities for individuals to recognise and use in the best way they can. In fact, human action seems to be directed precisely at that, at least at first instance. Refugee accounts seem to suggest that this is just how they responded to the war, namely by seeking to identify ways of establishing normality in the context of physical insecurity. And it was precisely these attempts to establish normality and the resulting routines that, in this particular case, constituted a context for action.

In this chapter I tried to define disasters as practical accomplishments of interacting individuals. While not denying the essential qualities disasters may have, I chose a methodological approach that allowed me to identify situations to be construed as such as properties of action by individuals. Refugee accounts of their war experience describe worlds of everyday life disrupted by events, which resist integration into the routine of everyday life. The war makes its presence felt through arbitrary violence and the violent negotiation of social relationships, yet this experience, by itself, is not enough to justify the description of war as a disaster. In fact, as long as villagers are able to produce new routines and bring a sense of predictability into their lives, the war remains a mere challenge confronting villagers in their attempts to lead normal lives. Disaster strikes when this is no longer possible. The accounts discussed here show this clearly. Indeed, the moment of flight to safer places – such as Patrice Lumumba village on the periphery of the city of Xai-Xai – is the crucial moment in the local definition of disaster: one takes flight when life becomes unpredictable and there is no way of upholding routine.

Talk is not only action, but also memory in a very basic sense. It is through talk that people recover their lived experience – in the phenomenological sense of *Erlebnis* – and, in this way, seek to make sense of their lifeworld. In doing so, they are not only reporting on their lived experience, but accomplishing the world they live in. It is not surprising, therefore, that my interview partners seemed to be taken aback by my questions concerning the meaning of what they went through. This is a question to which they had paid little attention, precisely because they take for granted much that structures their everyday lives. The inability to do this creates disruptions in the accounts and offers sociology insight into the manner in which social reality is a practical accomplishment of interacting individuals.

8

African Christian Converts and the Creation of Locality[159]

Introduction

She placed her hands on my head and started praying for me. Her voice was loud and I could feel the energy of its vibrations on her vigorous black arms glistening with perspiration. I do not know how to describe the sensations that rippled through my body and my soul. The trouble was that, on the one hand, I found the whole situation ridiculous. However, on the other, the conviction, earnestness, and vigour with which this woman, who was the head of a small Pentecostal community in a rural area in southern Mozambique, prayed to God on my behalf did not fail to move me, and, above all, to make me part of this small religious community in a very special emotional way.

There were ten of us, adults and children, men and women. We were in a tiny room measuring about seven square metres made even smaller by the number of people and the furniture scattered about: a table, three chairs, a stool, a few boxes with kitchen utensils on them. The woman leading the group insisted that I sit on a chair. She herself and all the others sat on mats spread on the earthen floor. There were two men sitting on the stool.

I did not understand some of the recitations she was proffering. I could just make out a few single terms from the unintelligible flow of words supposed to bring me God's blessing. *Mademoni* (demons) was one of them, and I thought she pronounced it very emphatically and with gusto. She was asking God to protect me, prevent evil spirits from approaching me, and make sure my research on the influence of a Swiss protestant mission on the work ethic of its African converts in southern Mozambique went well. In exchange for God's blessing, she offered the strength of her belief and faith, which translated into a wholesale commitment to prayer.

We had been praying for three hours. They called it a 'fasting prayer', a shorter version of their 'vigil prayer'. The former lasts for twenty-four hours whereas the latter takes seventy-two. The *Kanana 1 cell* of the Church of the Assembly of God was approaching the end of its fasting prayer. The members had been there since midnight, and all through the day they had fasted. They had abstained from food and, instead, had prayed in a show of faith and belief in the redeeming power of prayer.

I was in the region doing research on a Swiss Protestant mission. I had been led to this Pentecostal community by the ubiquitous presence of several religious outbursts that often translated into communities that were competing directly with the mission I was studying. In the course of several informal interviews with the woman leading *Kanana 1* cell I had slowly began to gain a more sophisticated understanding of the social reality of the region as well as of the types of social identities and belongings it produced, and vice-versa. What for me initially had seemed a homogeneous rural community began to lose its uniform appearance and, instead, acquire the mantle of a social reality held together by knots through which individuals sought to produce their own biographies.

The fasting prayer was being held at my request. Or rather, in one of the informal interviews with the leader of the group I had mentioned my wish to attend and observe a similar session. Her reaction was to summon one without delay. The beginning of a fasting prayer is not spectacular at all. The members just gather in the prayer room, which in its profane moments is used as a living and dining room. One by one they all confess. This procedure has a standard format. A member steps forward – or is indicated by the female leader, who also officiates like an informal priestess because in formal terms the group does not have any leader – and starts to sing a church hymn from a book of songs published by the Church of the Assembly of God.[160] These are simple hymns in terms of musical structure and religious content. The rhythm is fast and is an invitation for dancing. All the members know the hymns by heart and sing joyfully. After the hymn the member confesses his or her sins committed since the last prayer (which may have been a mere five hours before) or simply reports what he or she has done since then. After this confession the community sings another hymn and the whole thing is repeated again as another member steps forward.

After all have confessed, the whole group prays together, or better still, they all pray individually at the same time. Each member recites his or her own prayer. Some do it with their arms raised up and eyes gazing at the ceiling made of corrugated iron, which tenaciously keeps the stifling air in the room from escaping into the freshness of the night. Others lie prostrate on the floor and still others just stand in a humble position with their hands folded in their lap, the head almost resting on the chest. They all literally shout out their prayers, producing a cacophony that makes a unique impression on the observer. At the beginning, sitting in my corner and watching the proceedings, it all seems undisciplined and disorderly. As the crescendo of voices rises and ecstasy takes hold of the members, this impression gives way to a coherent reality. And suddenly they stop. Not all at once. It looks more like a negotiated end. They lower their voices and reduce their prayers to mere whispers and work their way to a full stop, with the exception of one or two, one of which is the female leader, who raise their voices again only to stop immediately, visibly exhausted by the exercise and seemingly enjoying the exhilaration. Then they are all quiet, but it is hard to know how long for because of the impressive stagecraft of the whole performance.

The next step is a reading from the bible. This time they read Jonas 2:9-11.[161] The leader reads and then they all sing a hymn, followed by the interpretation of the reading. This interpretation consists of a 'testimonial' that each member has to give. In other words, members have to say in which way they think the biblical passage just read to them is relevant to their lives. And then, once more, they sing. After the hymn, they pray again with the same vigour, enthusiasm, devotion, and faith, only, this time, they adopt a common posture (all standing, hands folded and eyes shut). This prayer is dedicated to someone indicated by the leader. It can be a member with health, family, or professional problems. This evening, however, they chose to pray for the sociologist, for his health and success of his research. That is why the leader placed her hands on my head.

The World According to Kanana 1

I argue in this chapter that we can think of social cohesion not only as the process through which community ties are forged, but also as the sum of individual biographies. The production of an individual biography is a social process that occurs in two moments. First, individuals interpret social reality in a specific way, and, secondly, they seek to create a social environment within which they will find recognition for an identity based on their view of the world. In other words, what comes across to us social observers as community is often the success or failure to make sense of reality through the individual production of selves. I wish to call this interpretative effort the production of biographies; it ultimately allows community to emerge as a series of biographical knots featuring at the core of social cohesion. The religious ritual I described above, which ended right after the prayers on my behalf and a meal consisting of boiled cassava and tea, is a piece of evidence I want to use in support of my argument.

In order to this I will start with a sociological characterisation of the observed social dynamics. This will consist in a sketchy hermeneutic reconstruction,[162] which basically entails the presentation of the social identity of this dynamics through an interpretation of the actions characteristic of it. This reconstruction will lead me to make a few micro sociological remarks concerning the role of knowledge in the constitution of everyday life. Drawing from a French sociologist, Michel

Maffesoli (1996), and established phenomenological approaches such as symbolic interactionism and ethnomethodology, I will describe the production of biographies as both a social activity that is intrinsically part of the structure of ordinary knowledge as well as an interpretative endeavour that seeks to make sense of reality.

The hermeneutic reconstruction suggested here hinges on three pillars: discursive, phenomenological, and sociological. The discursive element refers to the semantic and syntactic features that are distinctive of the group; the phenomenological elements, on their part, concern the life world and the horizon of the group, whereas the sociological elements draw on the forms of social action that are characteristic of the group. All three elements are constitutive of a social reality, which draws from a common vocabulary and worldview on the basis of a very specific type of social action.

The rural area where I undertook the research upon which this particular case study is based is not Patrice Lumumba village, but Chicumbane, on the other side of the Limpopo River. I collected the data at the end of the 1990s in the framework of the research I was carrying out on the influence of a Swiss protestant mission on the work ethic of an African community.[163] I include this case study here because I want to show the relevance of risk and social action to the analysis of extreme situations on a more individual level. While the focus is on biography, the analysis suggests that the operation is basically the same, namely the translation of hazard into risk.

The village has quite specific features. It boasts about 6,000 inhabitants. Contrary to what seems to be a common pattern in rural Mozambique, the dwellings are not spread out over a wide area, but stand quite close together in an almost urban structure. There are several wide intersecting roads made of hard soil, rather like avenues. There is a hospital, which was built by Swiss missionaries in the early part of the twentieth century and seems to be one explanation behind the demographic growth of the village. Apart from the hospital there is also an educational complex consisting of a nurse training school, a high school, a secondary school, and a hostel for pupils coming from farther afield. There are also two churches, one catholic, the other protestant, the latter being the Swiss mission church, and several religious denominations, ranging from Pentecostal to prophetic sects which hold their services in ramshackle buildings, often the homes of their respective leaders.

The main source of livelihood is subsistence agriculture, which is the province of women. As a rule they cultivate two fields, one big one down in the valley on the margins of the Limpopo river, with an irrigation system built by the Portuguese during the colonial period, and another one, closer to home, and which is mainly rain-fed. Men migrate to South Africa in search of work, but there are also many who work in a nearby town. Still others find work as nurses and waiters at the rural hospital.

During the civil war, which wreaked havoc in the country between the end of the seventies and the early nineties, the population of the village rose considerably. While before that and, especially during the colonial period, the local identity of the village was marked by the Swiss missionary church, this specificity has been lost as a result of the settlement of people displaced by the civil war and administrative measures taken by the government of Mozambique in its socialist drive to modernise the country in the first fifteen years immediately after independence from Portugal in 1975. While the traditional authorities, deposed by the post-colonial government, are claiming back their authority, the heterogeneity of the population as well as the growing influence of new religious denominations and new consumption patterns have considerably undermined the basis upon which this authority rested.

The village is a huge canvas teeming with social orders negotiating a common social reality. The high number of religious beliefs and practices, traditional and modern, play an important role in this process. They are the knots where identities and communities are constructed and, above all, they function like lenses through which reality is perceived. They produce social reality and, at the same time, they are produced by it in a dialectical relationship that seems to try to protect the social from social analysis.

Kanana 1 cell is a religious group and a member of the Church of the Assembly of God, a Pentecostal denomination on the rise in Mozambique and elsewhere in Africa. The group, as we saw above, is led by a middle-aged woman, to whose story we shall come back later. For the moment let us briefly attempt a hermeneutic reconstruction of the group. Let us start with the worldview that structures the perception of reality by the group. This worldview, common to nearly all Pentecostal movements, is based on the belief that the world is the outcome of God's work. God created nature and the people who live in it, to whom He gave free will. He also created spirits. These are central to the worldview of the members of *Kanana 1*. According to them God initially created angels, who lived in heaven with Him. One day one of the angels, Lucifer, disobeyed God and, seconded by a third of the angels, rebelled and subsequently lost the ensuing war against God and the angels loyal to Him. Lucifer and his followers were forced to abandon Heaven and settle on earth where the former became the devil, and the latter demons. The devil and his demons have ever since been the main cause of illness, misfortune, natural disasters, hatred, jealousy, and all the other evils that befall mankind. Central to the lifeworld of this community is, therefore, the presence of these *mademoni* (demons) in their midst.

The discursive element follows from the ubiquitous presence of demons in the life of these people. The structure of everyday discourse is dominated by references to 'spirits' to explain misfortune, to 'the Lord' and the 'Word' to seek help, to the literal interpretation of the Bible to show one's faith, to belief in God as the only one who gives meaning to life, and to His 'blessing' to indicate the final objective all members strive for in their efforts to give meaning to their lives. It is in the context of this discursive structure that other words acquire the specific meanings they have as identity markers for the group. Members are all 'brothers and sisters', they refer to the 'word' which carries 'fire' that will 'devour' the 'evil spirits'. This discursive element establishes a code much in the sense argued for by Wieder (1974), which not only describes the worldview of this community, but is also part of its internal life.[164]

The third, and final, element, social action, is the outcome of the reflexive character of the discursive structure of the members' everyday life, to the extent that the latter is only coherent in the moment it is enunciated. Their everyday life is shaped by the need, and obligation, to fight evil spirits. Hence the importance of prayer, the complexity of which reflects the level of Weberian rationalisation it has achieved. The virtuoso are those who can pray for hours on end; the vigour, energy, and conviction with which one prays are the criteria that pass judgement on whether one will attain salvation or not. Prayers structure the relationship to God, and it is for this reason why they are so important. Accordingly, there are several types of prayer, each of which punctuates the life of the community. There is, as seen above, the vigil and the fasting prayer. The former lasts for two days, while the latter lasts for one day. During both members do nothing but pray and abstain from food.

They seek all opportunities to pray. They visit each other in illness, for family gatherings, private celebrations, and other social occasions. And, each time, they seize these moments for prayer. Living is about fighting evil spirits. It is therefore about prayer, hard and long. These three elements, the phenomenological, the discursive, and the sociological, form a hermeneutic circle, which gives meaning to the social identity that the group constructs at the same time as it reproduces the conditions of its own possibility. The interpretation and construction of social reality are one and the same moment.

Producing a Biography

The story of this woman can be told in a few words. She is the daughter of an African Presbyterian minister. This means she grew up in a family environment marked, on the one hand, by total rejection of the magical worldview and, on the other, by the search for spiritual salvation through an ethical life conduct. In short, she grew up in a protestant environment characterised by a methodical and rational way of life.[165]

She learned a profession as a bank clerk, got married, and had children. Towards the end of the seventies she began to have health problems. She would often, as she told me, faint or become numb all over her body. During pregnancy and birth she began losing her teeth. She went to see several doctors who prescribed a treatment which did not seem to help. Later, her health problems were compounded by marital ones which culminated in separation from her husband, including the loss of custody for her children.

After having consulted many doctors, including one of the most famous Swiss doctors in Mozambique,[166] who diagnosed low blood pressure and recommended rest in a 'quiet and beautiful place', and seeing that her problems were not diminishing, she became receptive to suggestions made by her colleagues at work, who were members of the Church of the Assembly of God, to the effect that she was possessed by spirits trying to 'come out'.[167] They advised her to fight the spirits through devotion to God. Meanwhile, she lost her job because of her constant absences from work as a result of her ill health. Her father, the Presbyterian minister, having just about lost faith in bio-medicine, also begun to find the spiritualist argument convincing and, consequently, asked a Pentecostalism preacher to help his daughter.

This is how the leader of *Kanana 1* came to seek salvation through prayer. She began attending Pentecostal services where she learned to pray hard and long. Indeed, prayer and devotion to God became the hub of her existence. And her health improved, she maintained. She stopped fainting and her body no felt longer numb. As she told me, 'God's blessing, through his Word, devoured the evil spirits with its fire.' She found physical health in spiritual peace with God. My concern here is not with the medical facts of this story. Following W. I. Thomas' assertion that situations defined as real by actors become real in their consequences (quoted in Plumer 1996: 228) I would like to draw attention to two crucial moments in the life of the leader of *Kanana 1*. The first moment coincides with the medical definition of her ailment. The logical solution to her problem, which consists in seeing a doctor, brings no betterment. The second moment is marked by the spiritual definition of the problem. The solution, namely, praying, solves the problem, again from her point of view.

What seems worth retaining from these two moments is how both are constitutive of her biography. What she has become today is the outcome of two strategies. The first strategy consisted in interpreting the world in a certain way and reading her own condition into that order. The second strategy consisted in practices ranging from learning to pray, praying, and tuning her everyday life to serving God. Her biography, in other words, is premised on perceiving the world in a very specific way through a repertoire of actions that effectively produced an individual social space for her new personality. Let us submit the ritual prayer described above to a frame analysis along the lines suggested by Goffman (1974), that is, as a moment in the production of social reality.

Centre stage in this story is occupied by the leader of the group. Let us start with the name: *Kanana 1*. The leader herself gave this name to the group. It is a biblical reference (Canaan), which means destination in a figurative sense. This tiny community, which she herself created and within which she finds room to assert her new identity, marks the end of her suffering. It is the final destination of a long trip during which she patiently constructed a biography by not only acquiring a new identity but also by creating a social space within which her new identity could find social recognition. *Kanana 1* is she herself to the extent that it exists because she exists. The members of her community have other trajectories and will almost certainly create their own groups in the course of time.

The ritual prayer I attended took place at my request, as I explained above. All it took for the leader of *Kanana 1* to call one immediately was a hint from me that I would like to see such a session. As we saw in the hermeneutic reconstruction of this group, its worldview is structured mainly on prayer. Prayer is indeed the one element in the life-world of the members that gives substance to the way they perceive reality. In it the group distances itself from the rest of society while at the same time forging an identity that is specific to itself. Any opportunity is welcome to assert that identity. For the members, and particularly for the leader, ritual prayers are not only used to manipulate social distances, but also to produce dramatic effects in their individual lives. It is through prayer that she revisits her path to salvation while, at the same time, confirming her calling.

Even though ritual prayer is part and parcel of the everyday life of the community, its form is not fixed. This seemed deliberate, as far as I could ascertain. Before the start of the prayer the leader admonished some of the members for not being properly dressed to meet the Lord, as she put it. 'Praying', she explained to me, 'is a celebration before God. We must be clean and well dressed.' During the prayer she would step in to instruct members who did not seem to be praying with as much energy as she wanted them to show. She would stop the prayer and tell a member to pray properly, or not to smile.

These and similar interventions gave the whole occasion a negotiated character. A particularly instructive instance was the individual prayer right after the reading from the bible. In principle there seems to be no limit as to how long these prayers should last, and nobody says when they are over. Yet, after half an hour of individual praying there follows a quarter of an hour in which everyone seems to be adjusting the level of their voice to that of the others. They gradually lower it to a whisper, which is interrupted by sudden outbursts or the continued vigorous prayer by one or the other. The leader is the last person to lower her voice and end the prayer.

I interpret this negotiation of the structure of the prayer as part of the process of constituting a community. To pray from beginning to end is always an accomplishment, since, in principle, there is nothing to prevent the ritual from going on indefinitely. Bringing it to an end, moreover, strengthens the sense of belonging and the identity of the group. It establishes an unspoken pattern that, in the course of time, becomes ordinary knowledge necessary to the construction of the ritual prayer.

The prayer is also a show. The public are the members themselves, but also those who are not. As a show it consists of three elements. The first one is marked by the arrival of the members at the house of the leader and the ensuing small talk. The second element is the ritual itself consisting of the hymns and loud prayers. The last element, often very late at night, is when the members say farewell to each other and go home. All this takes place before the eyes of non-members. The group stages its own difference and, through the very act of distancing and marginalising itself, it fosters group consciousness.

This is, in a nutshell, the world of the leader of *Kanana 1*, a world she herself has created and within which she finds social recognition for her biography. Through it she gives a social identity to her biography. The production of her individual biography is a knot in the wide canvas of social relations that make up social reality in this rural outback. It is a knot made possible by her ability to perceive the world in a certain way and to act according to her understanding of it.

Different Biographies

In the previous section I looked at the constitution of biography as a central resource in coping with personal crises. In this section I wish to pursue the matter from a different perspective. The constitution of biography continues to be the subject matter but, in contrast to *Kanana 1*, the main issue here is not coming to terms with personal crisis, but rather integrating new experiences into one's biography in the course of life. I will continue to use membership categorisation devices as a methodological instrument to present, analyse, and make sense of accounts made by two elderly women I interviewed in 1998 in the course of the same research project that led me to *Kanana 1*. In fact, when the women concerned talk about themselves they are not simply reporting their lives. They are also accounting for the way in which their communities negotiate social change. These are women who in the course of their lives became housewives, Christian housewives and African Christian housewives. As I argued in the theoretical part of this book, such processes should not simply be taken for granted. Rather, they should be placed at the centre of the analysis.

Two Women

The first biography is that of a woman by the name of Masinge. She was born on 19th August 1928. Her father, a 'Zion'[168] minister, handed her over to a Swiss missionary school on 12 February 1938 where she spent the next seven years. Her father was not only a church minister; he had also worked as a migrant labourer in South Africa. In fact, it was in South Africa that he converted to Swiss mission Christianity. On his return he sent his daughter to school which she attended up to 1943, making it to the third grade of primary school. In 1944 she learnt 'how to work', for, as she put it, the Swiss had told her that she might suffer in her married life.

Two themes immediately emerge in the constitution of this particular biography. First of all, there is an insistence upon the domestic role of the woman and, secondly, as a result thereof, her preparation for such a kind of life. In 1943 the woman asked to be christened, but, in effect, this only occurred in 1945 after spending some years at her parents' home 'learning how to work'. In 1946 she married and in 1948 she became the leader of the Christian women's group. In the sixties she suspended her mandate in order to take care of her children, and only returned in 1980.

Here is the excerpt:[169]

> *As for being different well we are, as for being being different yes we are because when you are in church ... teaching another person how to forgive when they do you wrong they teach you how to control yourself when you meet with difficult things and that's different because someone who has not joined church there are things he can do without fear even insulting he can insult yes insult shamelessly actually he doesn't see anyone else, well he has no regard for others in church they teach you that when someone arrives you have to welcome them yes welcome them because tomorrow it could be you walking around yes if you walk around you may even arrive at that person's place and if you did not treat that person well he can also treat you badly and do you evil but if you are nice to that person he will also do a lot for you tomorrow, so that is the difference ... now it's not like in the past anymore now we have different times even locals can be better than people who are Christian because everyone has got his own heart yes everyone has his way of being in the church they just go but it is not because they like it they don't even accept the church they don't understand it is different yes it is very different.*

The excerpt is on the differences between members of the church (Presbyterian Church of Mozambique) and non-members. Not surprisingly, these differences boil down to the good manners taught by the church to its members and the lack thereof by non-members. These differences are important to the extent that the church teaches its members a way of being in the world that is consistent with the kinds of changes taking place all around them. There is also a temporal distinction in the excerpt which bears on the religious socialisation and takes as its cue the colonial and the post-colonial period. The interviewee eliminates the differences that emerged in the process of socialisation in the colonial period and suggests, thereby, that there are no differences between Christians and non-Christians. What she means is, of course, Christian decadence, an idea I will return to below.

The excerpt is a valuable commentary on the properties of the interviewee's social reality. I will apply membership categorisation devices to make this clear. The most important membership categorisation devices are the following: *you* (Christian), *person, church member, local, Christian*. There exists, therefore, an opposition between

Christian and *non-Christian* which is as much a result of the interview question as it is a central element of the way in which the interviewee's *Weltanschauung* unfolds. In fact, in the area where I carried out the interviews church members make a clear distinction between the perimeter of the church and what they call 'land'. Within the perimeter of the church there live those who are chosen, that is, those who lead lives that are compatible with changing times. Colonialism, as it were, challenged people to justify their existence, and these reacted by redefining their identities. This redefinition involved the appropriation of a Christian way of life. In this sense, the opposition between the membership categories 'Christians' and 'locals' acquires a new meaning as an attempt at redefining society itself.

This new meaning can be properly appreciated when we look at the category predicates. In the excerpt the following predicates are mentioned: *to forgive, do evil, teach, individual control, fear of, to insult, respect for, be welcoming, be generous, join the church, converting, be different, learn how to work, learn*. What comes to light are the differences between Christians and non-Christians; these manifest themselves through the qualities that distinguish each. These qualities are positive as far as the Christian is concerned and negative as far as the non-Christian is concerned. Things are positive when they embue the individual with the kinds of skills they require to face changes in the circumstances of their lives. Alongside religious qualities we also find studying and learning how to work as qualities to be acquired by the new member. These are strongly linked to the changing social environment, which requires individuals to develop skills and resources that will enable them to face the challenges of life.

The second biography is of a woman born in 1930. Her name is Bila. Her father was a local teacher. At one point in the interview the woman exclaims that her father needed nobody to write letters for him, a very interesting comment about the underlying social world. Indeed, and drawing from the work of Patrick Harries (1994) and Gesine Krüger (2002), it shows that letters were a very important artifact of the new ways of being in the world. According to Gesine Krüger (2002) letters were an important element in the the process of individualisation and the migrant labourer's focusing on his own nuclear family to the detriment of his extended family. Bila was born into a Christian family and attended the Swiss mission school. Her teachers were all Swiss missionaries from who taught her to read and write. She also learnt how to look after her family. Here is the relevant excerpt:

> *that means that we were born in the church we grew up knowing things of the church and not of outside and nothing from outside we knew little we accepted the church and we were christened and we grew up in the church we attended children's mass we joined the youth groups and got to know people like Bila and we were taken in marriage growing up in church means that we did not convert we were born there, we were born, attended children's mass and were taken in marriage...*

This excerpt is on what it means 'to be born in the church', a statement that members of the Presbyterian Church of Mozambique frequently use to distinguish themselves from those who were converted. 'To be born in the church' means to be the child of someone who is already a member of the church. It also implies being the carrier of certain values and having been socialised in a particular way which includes having been a member of youth clubs.[170] These youth clubs were important as contexts for living out new forms of sociability within constraints marked by the need to redefine identities.

It is in this sense that the main category collections are: *us, church, outside, children's mass, youth groups*, and *Bila*. Again we see the idea of a fundamental difference between the Christian and non-Christian strengthened and brought to fruition in the idea that one 'is born within the church'. When the interviewee uses 'us' it becomes clear that she is not only using a pragmatic resource to talk about a community. 'Us' is, in fact, metonymic in the sense that it stands for a whole *Weltanschauung* that constitutes itself in a very specific social and historical context. This specificity is marked by the assertion of an identity that is different, but which seeks to establish lines of continuity with forms of identity from which it seeks to distance itself. Thus, the interviewee is Tsonga, but she is a different kind of Tsonga because she was 'born in the church'. The predicates which distinguish her are those which assert her identity as a Christian Tsonga woman, namely having been christened, accepting Christianity, attending children's mass, being a member of a youth group, and enjoying a Christian education.

The interviewee sums up the whole trajectory of a Mozambican Christian woman who belongs to the Presbyterian Church of Mozambique in a very graphic, but concise manner with the following statement: *we were born, attended children's mass, and were taken in marriage*. This is a marvelous summary, which brings into the fore a tension between the individual and the collective which the construction of biography never quite manages to overcome. Joining the church was a conscious decision of many in order to attain access to resources denied to them by colonial rule[171] under the conditions of growing individualisation. However, the description offered by the interviewee in this wonderful sentence shows that women continue to be the object of somebody elses's will. How does one account for this?

Redefining Identities

The Swiss Mission arrived in Mozambique in the second half of the nineteenth century, brought by Mozambicans living in South Africa at the time (van Butselaar 1984). It became popular immediately and an important institution in the south of the country. One curious fact, however, and drawing from an excellent analysis of the diaries of a missionary, Arthur Grandjean, undertaken by Nicholas Monnier (1995), is that it was not easy to reach the Africans with the religious message. These seemed simply to go through the motion of conversion, while for the most part they seemed content to avail themselves of everything the mission was willing to give them. In this sense, and to repeat an already formulated hypothesis, it appears reasonable to assume that Africans 'accepted' the mission as a way of redefining their identity in a Portuguese colonial context of African labour regulation (see Macamo 2003c); this forced them to define themselves in terms of notions of tradition and primordial identities which were more in line with Portuguese colonial policy. In other words, by 'accepting' the church, Africans may have been attempting to circumvent the denial of modernity, which was so much part of the colonial experience.

The colonial economic and political structure had placed serious constraints on the social reproduction of African societies and communities. These constraints took on various forms, four of which deserve special attention. The first one relates to the way in which the Swiss Mission itself had come to Mozambique. It was a Mozambican, Yossefa, who, together with his wife and daughter and twelve other men and women, set up the first Swiss Mission in Mozambique (Linder 1998, van Butselaar 1984). This group caught the attention of people in the region because of the way and how often its members prayed.[172] The women in particular showed a high degree of fervour in praying, a fact that may be interpreted as a manifestation of the crisis of African societies at the time. Women actually experienced the crisis more directly. Men migrated and it fell to the women to fend for their families[173] and, even worse, in the absence of their husbands, they were left to pay the colonial taxes.[174] Failure to pay meant that they could also be conscripted to do public work. Some women left their families, moved to urban areas, and went down the road of prostitution. In a way, therefore, the fervour with which they prayed was also a manifestation of the greater psychological tension they were facing.

The third constraint regards the position of women themselves. Generally speaking, colonial authorities assumed that traditional African society oppressed women.[175] In this sense, the introduction of wage labour was seen by the colonial authorities as a way of improving the position of women[176] and forcing men to redefine their role in the context of their own society. The Swiss missionaries, in contrast, held that colonial rule had contributed significantly to the worsening of the position of women (Biber 1987) by strengthening the position of men and effectively turning women into slaves of their own men and communities. Finally, the fourth constraint resulted from the dependence of the colonial system, but also of the missionaries, on women as the touchstones of their respective societal projects. The colonial system sought to reconstitute 'African traditional society' on the backs of women and drawing on ideas about the role of kinship solidarity which, ultimately, only served, as pointed out by Ruth First (1983), to free the colonial state from its social security responsibility towards the growing number of Africans joining wage labour. The missionaries, for their part, depended on women for the construction of their own idea of a 'traditional African society', which was in actual fact the revival of a Swiss Calvinist family ideal.[177]

Two interesting phenomena need mentioning in order to emphasise the importance of these constraints for the construction of biographies. We may call them, following Foucault (1991) and Dean (1997), rationality and truth regimes. These regimes represented the way in which the Swiss Mission insinuated itself within local African cultures. The regime of truth involved a simple way of justifying missionary work. The Swiss Mission convinced itself that it had a mission to fulfill in Mozambique and explained its presence in the southern part of the country as an act of providence (Grandjean 1888). To this end, the Mission resorted to the problems in Portuguese colonial rule as a background against which to project its own identity as the carrier of appropriate forms of change. The Mission reduced Portuguese colonial problems to moral issues, essentially boiling down to the moral degeneration of Europeans in Africa (Berthoud 1888).

In order to reverse this, the missionaries made use of three tools. The first one was the integration of African culture and religiosity into the Christian religious framework. The missionaries interpreted African culture and religiosity as part of a divine plan and assumed that implementing that plan was part of their mission. Thus, they insisted that Africans were aware of God, even though their own evolutionary stage prevented them from knowing with certainty that it was the same God that the Swiss worshipped. Patrick Harries (1994) does a good job of showing the extent to which Henri-Alexandre Junod's great monograph (1913) on the Tsonga was an attempt to prove this point. Junod saw the rules and norms that structured the life of the Tsonga as deriving from God and regarded the Swiss Mission as the legitimate interpreter of God's teachings who, on the basis of this virtue, was in a position to establish the criteria of intelligibility of the local lifeworlds.

The seccond tool was intimately linked to Protestantism itself, especially its very strong ties with scientific programme of the Enlightenement.[178] Overall, the missionaries were solidly trained in the natural sciences. They firmly believed that the natural sciences provided an important resource to uncover God's revelation. This provided them with a rationale for fighting magic and witchcraft,[179] which they equated with undesirable African forms of life. They insisted, therefore, on medicine and education, which they held to be practical demonstrations of the superiority of Christianity. Wherever they set up a mission station they built schools and hospitals. Finally, the third tool they availed themselves of was the idea that acknowledging the value of community amounted to the best proof of divine election. In this sense, the missionaries regarded local African communities as spaces of intervention simply waiting to be transformed and organised into communities of faith. The missionary André Grandjean, for instance, saw the social havoc wreaked by Portuguese colonial rule on local communities as divine work that had merely paved the way of the missionaries.

Together these three tools sought to lend legitimacy to the presence of the Swiss mission while, at the same time, they created a regime of truth within which African religiosity, European rationality, and missionary work blended into a common frame of reference that made social phenomena intelligble. Applying such a view it is actually possible to see the accounts by the two women as being coherent and distinct from that which they do not want to be identified with. The accounts drew on a regime of truth that placed women and their communities and in their quality as Christians on a different level. This level was different because it was correct and more in line with the times.

This regime of truth drew heavily on a regime of rationality, which was also established by the missionaries. Given the kind of world described by their regime of truth, the question was one of knowing which rules and procedures provided the appropriate forms of action. The answer was obvious, at least as far as women were concerned. Their task was to build community, change their way of life, and adopt modern medicine and education. Building community was the keystone of the whole undertaking. The missionaries assumed, as already pointed out, that Portuguese rule had led to widespread moral degeneration. Thus, the challenge for the missionaries consisted in achieving moral regeneration and, for this purpose, they believed it was important to rehabilitate women. This meant saving women from urban perdition (prostitution) as well as freeing them from such forms of traditional oppression as the payment of bride price, and polygamy. Women were to be placed at the centre of their families as housewives and mothers and, thus, as the mainstay of new family units that would be the bearers of a new African society.

Van Butselaar (1984), for example, reports on a man called Jim Ximungana who had done a lot for the church when it was being set up, but who was refused church membership because he was polygamous. He was used as an example in order to stress the importance the mission attached to the adoption of new values and practices. Alongside this, the missionaries placed great emphasis on personal hygiene and cleanliness. An example of this is a small book with the title *Mahlayisele ya miri* (how to take care of the body).[180] The main message of the book is borne by the African Christian woman, who takes care of her home and community. Another important aspect worth mentioning is the role of education in the emancipation of women and their communities.

The regime of rationality not only gave substance to the regime of truth. It also had the important role of normalising life through the transformation of individuals, especially women, into human beings who could act correctly, that is, in line with the norms established by the missionaries. The excerpts presented above certainly carry elements of this regime of rationality in the way they emphasise such category predicates as education, good manners, and the importance of 'learning how to work'. In this respect, by including these aspects in their description of the differences between Christians and non-Christians, the two women were also stressing the properties of a world built on predicates of recent origin.

In fact, what we see, on the one hand, in this account is the way that the mission saw women. Women were a threat to the normative stability of the African lifeworld, but they also represented the potential for the reconstitution of that same world. The vulnerability of women under the structural conditions of colonial rule had given the Swiss Mission an entry point in its own moral discourse of regeneration, which implied the domestication of women in the interest of a redefinition of the native community. On the other hand, however, the mission was broadly used by Africans themselves in their attempt to gain control over their lives. The Africans who joined the Mission did so in response to their own interpretation of their history and of what they had to do in order to continue to be themselves. Hence the emphasis which the women placed in their interviews on the differences between Christians and non-Christians. In fact, differences are not simply religious. They are also differences between Africans who recognised the signs of the times, and Africans who did not.

Analytical Integration

The construction of individual biographies is a fine document of how individuals seek to create contexts of action. In this particular case study there is no extreme event lurking in the background. Instead, there is a general social situation marked by the apparent breakdown of frameworks of reference. The immediate relevance dimension here is best described with reference to the social category which presents itself as a social world with diverse frameworks of reference that compete amongst each other as social canopies for individuals. The general background upon which the social category projects itself is one of a rural community that can no longer be reduced to a single framework of reference. Traditional norms compete with new ones brought about by different religious denominations to provide individuals with several options regarding what to take into account in their everyday lives. The social world, therefore, is perceived by individuals as an extremely heterogeneus entity which calls upon everyone to choose for oneself the framework of reference that is relevant to individual existential challenges.

The decisive element, therefore, is heterogeneity. It becomes relevant for individual perception of reality when individuals must make existential decisions. In the particular cases under study the decisions are forced upon individuals by disease or by the general feeling of inadequacy with reference to the larger community. No extreme natural event forces itself upon individuals as an immediate reality; it is their own position within their communities, which they perceive as inadequate or inappropriate. This makes it hard for them to take the reality of their community for granted and, consequently, to be confident with regard to what they do in their everyday lives. This creates a situation in which social action becomes extremely uncertain, ultimately rendering their condition ripe for the process of translation.

The starting point for the process of translation is the knowledge dimension which, as we have seen, breaks down into two categories, namely the distribution of the social stock of knowledge, and its status. The individuals making up the group under study in this case draw on a Pentecostal worldview which renders them dependent on the leaders of their cult. In this case the immediate leader is the head of their cult, the lady who, like them, finds it hard to accommodate to the lifeworld of the village. Drawing on the general Pentecostal framework of reference, which sees the world under the throes of evil forces, the leader describes the social unease of her followers in terms of their election. The plausibility of her account is judged against the background of the followers' ability to make sense of their own predicament within their immediate individual social settings. The leader's descriptions, particularly the recipes she offers her followers in terms of channelling energy into building new identities, must go through the test of individual experience. The rituals that make up the biographical construction prove, ultimately, to be self-fulfilling prophecies, for everyone is concerned about putting on a good show.

The translation process is completed not through the solution of the individual problems that brought the members of the cult together, but the creation of a group identity, which provides every member with a context within which everyone can engage meaningfully with everyone else. This is the stage at which certainty returns in the form of trust, but also in the guise of repair strategies. Trust manifests itself in the ability to take shared meanings for granted. The members of the cult develop a common vocabulary, which describes a world that is familiar to them because it documents their own Pentecostal worldview. They also develop routine activities, which confirm their identity and belonging to the group. Whatever happens outside of their immediate group is made intelligible with reference to the worldview, so much that an important part of their repair strategies consists in attempting to make their perception of the world at large consistent with the underlying Pentecostal worldview.

We see in this case study the creation of a context of action through the translation of hazards into risk. In this case the hazard may be conceptualised as the social unease of certain individuals within their original community. This community becomes problematic to them because it is heterogeneous and offers no firm framework of reference. These individuals interpret their unease, often in connection with physical ailments, as a problem of inadequacy and go on to foster strong ties amongst themselves. These ties are ultimately responsible for creating a context within which their action becomes meaningful to them to the extent that they can formulate safe expectations with regard to the actions of others as well as make sense of them against the background of the worldview they entertain. The construction of an individual biography goes hand in hand with the translation of their personal predicament into a group predicament which, in the process, becomes its own framework of reference.

This, I wish to submit, is part of the stuff social cohesion is made of. It is fundamentally about interpreting the world and acting according to that interpretation. It is about producing a biography, that is, re-inventing oneself and creating the social context within which the re-invented self will find social recognition.

Social reality on the periphery of the Western world consists largely of knots located at the intersection of several biographies, which, more often than not, are reactions to processes of modernisation larger than themselves. They may be critical commentaries on modernity by its malcontents, as Commarof and Commarof (1993) would argue, or forms of resistance by the weak, as James Scott would put it, but deep down they are more than just artefacts of modernity. They are the illogical, ephemeral, and contradictory aspects of social life which Maffesoli identifies as troublemakers for social theorists who dream of forcing social reality into submission to their theoretical schemes. They are ties that bind in the sense in which they are produced by individuals as they go about making sense of the world around them and knitting it into a pattern only their everyday practices can unravel.

Part Three

Conclusion

9

The Taming of Fate

Struggles over Meaning

During fieldwork in Patrice Lumumba Village I was often confronted with the question: why are you asking us all those questions? There was hardly a day on which one of my informants or friends I made in the course of fieldwork over all the years did not ask me this question. The standard answer I gave them was that I wanted to understand how they perceived crises and disasters, in order to be able to understand how they seek to prevent and cope with them. This answer was consistent with the overall objective of the research project for which I was doing fieldwork. Indeed, as already mentioned in the introduction, the immediate context was the Humanities Collaborative Research Project of the University of Bayreuth, which was looking into 'Local Agency in Africa in the Context of Global Influences'. In aiming at understanding local perceptions of crises and disasters the project was also seeking a******* how agency in Africa was influenced by global forces and, conversely, how local agency shaped those forces.

My answer was good enough for the immediate purpose of justifying fieldwork and eliciting responses from my informants. Villagers may not quite understand why their perceptions, their prevention mechanisms, as well as their coping strategies are of interest to social scientists. They may not even care about whether researchers really mean what they say. Yet, they gave me their time, often bemused, but patient. They showed me around, drew others out of their reservation, and cajoled them into talking to me. They showed me their dwellings, their fields, and, as the years went by, shared with me their hopes and worries about the present and the future. They bracketed out their own curiosity and adopted the pragmatic attitude of simply telling me what they thought I wanted to hear from them. Sometimes, in fact many times, they engaged me strategically. They did not simply answer my questions, as one is taught to expect in handbooks on methods. Rather, they set out to tell me what they wanted me to know about them.

The village secretary, a jovial, intelligent, and perspicacious old man who always came with me when I did my rounds,[181] would at times preface his introduction with the words, '*so, this is Mr. Macamo, who is our own son, but lives with the white people in Europe, wants you to tell him how much you suffer from hunger; if he asks you how you are, tell him you are hungry.*'[182] We would all laugh – I did so nervously, of course – but it became clear to us all that the questions I asked and the answers they gave me were no longer simply 'questions' and 'answers'. They lost their innocence. His poisoned introduction became an opening gambit for moves that transformed the research encounter into a difficult negotiation, or even a struggle over meaning. In fact, the whole research became a struggle over meaning. The question, however, was which meaning? Or, even more pointedly, whose meaning? Were villagers shrewd enough to circumvent my questions and tell me something functional as to their own needs and interests? Were my research instruments robust enough to withstand such veiled attacks? Were we perhaps all engaged in a game of simply producing plausible stories?[183]

Whose Meaning?

The question was, indeed, which and whose meaning? It was in the process of reflecting on the word-game into which my interviews had transformed themselves that I began to see that my research interest went far beyond simply describing and analysing local perceptions of crises and disasters and their prevention mechanisms and coping strategies. As I collected biographies of men and women who had been born to what seemed to me – from the vantage point of a researcher funded by a university in Europe – a life of deprivation and insecurity, I became aware that there was much more at stake than the opposition between local agency and global contexts. During the preparation of the research tools I – together with Dieter Neubert, the research project leader – had become aware that our own conceptual categories concerning crises and disasters would not do as avenues into local practices and worldviews. Hence, our initial investment in narrative interviews from which we hoped to obtain a sense of the abnormal in local life.

As a matter of fact, we had decided after a long weighing-up of the pros and cons that we would not ask anyone directly about crises and disasters. We decided that we would simply ask if anything abnormal had happened in recent years. Our hope and bet was that our informants would mention the 2000 floods and, with a bit of luck, the civil war that had ravaged Mozambique for so many years. They did not. Almost unanimously the first forty people I interviewed during my first sojourn in the field answered the question by telling me about a whale that had been stranded on the beach, a mere eight kilometres away a year before which had provided huge quantities of meat for the whole city of Xai-Xai. Those who did mention the 2000 floods as an abnormal event, named it in connection with an unknown type of fish that came with floodwater. Significantly, the villagers called it *mafohlan*, which loosely translates as 'illegal alien'. It turned out that *mafohlan* is the name by which young men who illegally cross the South African border in search of work are known. Just like these young men, who risked their lives and security and ventured into unknown and probably hostile territory, the fish also arrived unannounced and provided much needed succour to people whose livelihoods had been placed under enormous strain by the floods. Strangely enough, people talked about this fish with a sense of disgust, and described it in mysterious ways. They almost wove a web of conspiracy around it, describing it as a fish with a lot of meat, but unsavoury, and bones that looked like human bones. Some wondered whether what had brought the fish was the same thing that had caused the floods.

I did not pursue the fish matter any further. Nonetheless, I found their conjectures as well as their immediate responses to my query concerning abnormal events quite revealing in terms of a way of being in the world that deserved more sociological attention beyond the usual background information to contextualise whatever research question one has. What is it like to live a life of material uncertainty and insecurity? Are the concepts uncertainty and insecurity themselves appropriate to describe such a life? What insights do the basic concepts of sociology, namely social action and social relations, offer to comprehend such modes of life? Is their intention and extension comprehensive enough to cover the range of experience that such lives imply? What is the precise meaning of a search for an understanding of local perceptions of crises and disasters? What are the preconditions for understanding that informants are talking about crises and disasters when they indeed start talking about crises and disasters? Will I spot it? Is my research question sensitive enough with regard to the possible worlds suggested by all that it does not ask and does not seek to know?

The Challenge of Intelligibility

As I puzzled over such questions, it became increasingly clear to me that my research on local perceptions of crises and disasters was also a personal search for the relevance of social theory to the lives of people in far-off places. And lest I be misunderstood, the issue of relevance does not concern the practical utility of research results in the usual generally approved manner of contributing to the welfare of whomsoever on the periphery of the world. The issue of relevance concerns the ability of social theory to make all possible worlds intelligible. Of course, this raises the subsequent question of knowing what is meant by intelligibility. Is it not the purpose of the social sciences to describe the social world and, thereby, render it intelligible, whatever this may mean, to anyone who cares to look at it? Are social scientific concepts, methods, and theoretical frameworks not ways of giving visibility to the social world? And if so, in which sense can the question become meaningful at all as far as intelligibility is concerned?

These questions pushed me in several directions. I felt challenged to make sense of the relationship between social theory and the study of Africa. My purpose in doing this was not to question the proprieties of such an enterprise, nor even to join the sceptical voices of those who take the principled stand that Western social science cannot make sense of African social reality. Rather, my purpose was to find an answer to my discomfort as regards the question asked by villagers on what I was searching for. As I delved into debates about African studies and began to realise, in a belated understanding of warnings issued by manuals on methods, that the questions we ask can reduce the ranges of experience and possibilities that the world is potentially made of, I also came to think that my discomfort may result from the wholly inappropriate, and naïve, belief that what is of interest to social theory is also of general interest. The sentence is written in a much stronger way than it is intended to be read. I will try again: why would villagers in distant Patrice Lumumba bother about helping me to acquire knowledge of their perceptions of crises and disasters? Would they do this in order to give me insights into the precarious nature of their livelihood? Would they do it in order to further the advance of science? In order to improve the understanding of what is at stake when relief operations are set in motion? And why should they care about these outcomes? Why would they have a stake in satisfying such curiosity?

Another direction I was pushed into was one which led me to the sociology of risk and some of its findings concerning how the notion of risk can be used to describe modern society. As I read my way through the fine distinctions drawn by proponents of this arm of sociology, and found out that non-modern societies, or to put it in more politically correct parlance, technologically challenged societies, are not covered by the intensional dimension of the notion of risk, I wondered what to make of the life of deprivation, struggle with the elements, and civil strife described over and over again by my informants? Is the notion of uncertainty with its implication of ignorance and despondency all that social theory has on offer to bring into relief the experience of the people of Patrice Lumumba? Could it really be possible that individuals live in society, interact, and develop ideas about the constitution of the world without the notion of risk playing any role whatsoever in their lives? How was their lifeworld possible? Was it, to borrow a fitting metaphor from Marshall Sahlins (1995), a life reduced to a simple narrative that read: 'they were born, they lived and then they died?' Was it, as one of my female interview partners (see chapter eight) said, a life reduced to being born, attending children's mass, and being taken in marriage? How did they come to terms with the fundamental indeterminacy of social action and social relations? How did they account for their own social relations? And how did they account for the failure of their accounts? And, most importantly, why should I care?

Ethnomethodology and, generally speaking, phenomenological approaches in sociology have given much thought and attention to these issues. In their attempts to go beyond the perennial problem of structure and agency in sociological theorising, these schools of thought asked the much more fundamental question – resonating through and through with Georg Simmel – of knowing how society was at all possible. Therefore, they placed at the centre of their attention the challenge posed by the consequences of individual action on structure, and vice-versa. However, they did not ask the egg and hen question. Rather, they looked for ways of describing the extent to which individual action is constitutive of the context that makes individual action possible. My readings of the relevant literature as well as my efforts to bring its insights to bear on the findings of the sociology of risk propelled me towards the idea that the structure-agency dichotomy can be usefully reduced to an account of the conditions of possibility of contexts of action.

Perhaps, I concluded, I was not concerned with really describing and analysing local perceptions of crises and disasters and their prevention mechanisms and coping strategies. Rather, my job as a social scientist trying to make sense of the lifeworld of villagers boiled down to seeking to describe the possibility of human behaviour on the basis of villagers' accounts. To put it differently, my interest in their lifeworld was not born out of the concern of improving the conditions of their livelihood, but simply fed off a genuine interest in human behaviour in general. The more I listened to accounts of their ordeal at nature's mercy and at the behest of fellow human beings, I realised that their life described in a very dramatic fashion the existence of human beings facing adversity and documented the ways in which humans respond to it. In a nutshell, the search for local perceptions of crises and disasters turned into a search for how humans tame fate.

It is important to mention in this connection that the background against which this search should be pursued is not an arbitrary one. Local African communities are not pursuing their lives in contexts of their own making. As a matter of fact, the general background against which life takes its course in these communities is one that contains local as well as external elements. The everyday life of individuals in Africa is increasingly dominated by technological artefacts, ideas, and ways of looking at the world which are not necessarily homegrown. Moreover, these artefacts, ideas, and perspectives on the world are very demanding on individuals and whole communities. They intensify processes of social differentiation and, through the havoc they wreak on the social division of labour, challenge individuals and communities to constantly define their place and role in the general local scheme of things. In other words, alongside theoretical concerns which may take us in the direction of seeking answers to general sociological questions regarding the exact nature of social action we need to ask questions about processes of change under conditions largely influenced by modernity. In other words, even if we have misgivings concerning the usefulness of the notion of modernity we need to address the practical challenges it is posing to individuals and local communities through its artefacts, ideas, and perspectives on the world.

The Taming of Fate: Relevance, Knowledge and Certainty

Humans tame fate in several ways. Central to all of them is the analytically critical insight that people act in order to be able to act. I now want to discuss this insight with reference to the analytical framework presented in chapter four and used in subsequent empirical chapters to integrate the findings of the case studies. The starting point for the analysis is Niklas Luhmann's distinction between hazards and risks. I introduce process into this distinction to argue that social worlds constitute themselves against the background of the translation of hazards into risks. In other words, the transformation of hazards into risks is a fundamental condition of being human, but the way this is done takes into account the larger cultural and material world that frames human life in specific circumstances. My analytical framework seeks to take account of this by identifying *relevance, knowledge, and certainty* as crucial dimensions of the process of translation. The background against which individuals transform hazards into risks consists precisely of these three dimensions. They not only inform the action of individuals, but are also constitutive of it.

The Social and Natural Areas of Relevance of Patrice Lumumba Village

In Patrice Lumumba the immediate reference for individuals in their everyday life is provided by the natural environment. Drought and floods are essential elements of this natural environment. In fact, the history of the people who live in the village is a history of the struggle against nature, as, hopefully, the brief account in the introductory chapter showed. What is sociologically significant about this struggle is the fact that the manifestations of the natural world pose dangers and threats to the livelihood of the individual members of the community. Too much rain may lead to floods and too little rain may lead to droughts. Droughts are, in fact, more frequent than floods, but the latter are more dramatic in their immediate effects. This element of danger to livelihoods makes it legitimate to include in the category of the natural world other external factors outside the immediate control of the community. This is the case with politically motivated violence, which, in this instance, became manifest in a civil war that forced individuals to seek refuge away from their original homes.

The social world, that is, the second category within the dimension of relevance, is intrinsically linked to the natural world category. The social world is a response to the natural world and represents the order that individuals call into being in their attempts to come to terms with the natural world. Indeed, much that makes up the social world of Patrice Lumumba village is only understandable against the background of the perception of the hazards and threats which the natural world casts upon villagers. The repertory of actions that describes local livelihoods as well as the typical biographies of villagers sum up the role which the natural world of drought and floods plays in structuring local everyday life.

Here then, we see a first element of a conscious response of human beings to the natural environment within which they have to go about their lives. In fact, it is even extremely difficult to pinpoint the exact moment at which the natural world dissolves into a social world that is sensitive to the vagaries of nature. It is true that there are circumstances under which individuals have no choice but to endure the vagaries of nature. Most local livelihoods in Africa today can indeed be described in terms of the vulnerability of individuals to forces beyond their own control. Yet, even under such circumstances living with an arbitrary natural world challenges individuals to structure their livelihoods in full awareness of what might happen to them. The question here is what goes into this conscious response to the natural world.

The Knowledge of Patrice Lumumba Village

The answer refers us to the second dimension of the process of translating hazards into risks. This second dimension is knowledge, that is, the certainty that individuals have that reality exists independently of them. Knowledge in Patrice Lumumba takes on very complex forms, which reflect the complex nature of social relations in the village. Knowledge breaks down into two categories, namely the distribution of the social stock of knowledge, and the status that different forms of knowledge possession has. In this sense, the data brought to light different worldviews, each with its own specific local bearer. This refers to certain people within the village to the extent that following them, that is, listening to their counsel becomes an instance of conferring status on the authority of their knowledge. Preachers and prophets, in the case of religious communities, elders and experienced individuals, in the case of the general community environment, and traditional healers and members of the local lineage, in the case of the traditional worldview, are the individuals who render authoritative accounts of the world and, in so doing, grant their followers elements with which they can go about structuring their social relations.

However, the lines separating these worldviews are not impenetrable. To put it differently, following one authoritative knowledge bearer does not commit anyone to persist, even when such knowledge becomes irrelevant to one's own life. In fact, precisely because individuals have this freedom, we can safely assume that they are not simply innocent victims of circumstances. Rather, they actively engage with the circumstances and avail themselves of their cultural references and value systems to make sense of the factors that put constraints on their livelihood. In this sense, the idea that action in traditional contexts is traditional, that is, unconsciously repetitive, may be one that needs radical revision, for nothing could be farther from the truth. It is true that custom does provide a framework within which the cost of deviating may indeed be high but this does not mean that individuals are bound forever by such frameworks.

The Certainty of Patrice Lumumba Village

We see this particularly in the third dimension of the process of translating hazards into risks. The dimension of certainty, which rests on the two categories of trust and repair strategies, refers to the assumptions that individuals make in the direction of what might follow action. Trust is particularly important in this regard, for it informs the expectations by individuals that a given course of action will yield given sets of outcomes or, with reference to social action, that it will elicit certain patterned responses from other individuals. These expectations draw from shared worldviews, which in their sociological implications respond to Weber's instruction to consider social worlds as the outcome of cultural frames.

Worldviews do not simply provide a perspective on the world. They also write scripts to those who share them so that they not only perceive the world in certain ways, but value certain forms of action as appropriate and right. The relationship between social action and the natural world is, therefore, mediated by worldviews. If outcomes fail to meet expectations it is to worldviews, especially to the authoritative bearers of knowledge that individuals turn for reassurance concerning their ability to perceive the world. Individuals find within these worldviews explanations for inconsistencies between action and outcome. It is only if they are completely unable to reconcile their worldviews with the outcomes that individuals begin to entertain the possibility of changing their perception of the natural world.

Summarising findings

In the following table 9.1, I present the process of translating hazards into risks in summary form.

Translation takes place when individuals take their natural and social worlds into account as laid down in the social distribution of the stock of knowledge and as brought to bear on the assumptions and expectations that individuals formulate with regard to the outcomes and consequences of their action.

In other words, from a descriptive and analytical point of view, social action does not concern solely the meaning and motivation that individuals have, drawing on a simplified understanding of Weber's methodology, nor the structural constraints upon the individual, to refer to a simplified understanding of Durkheim, but rather the extent to which action can create the conditions of its own possibilities. How do individuals ensure that they will act again? And again, and again? This is the question I tried to answer in the four empirical case studies I presented in chapters five, six, seven and eight.

Table 9.1: Translating hazards into risks in Patrice Lumumba

Dimensions	Relevance	Knowledge		Certainty	
Categories	*Natural*	*Stock*	• Priests, prophets	*Trust*	• Assumptions
			• Elders		• Expectations
			• Healers, lineage members		
	Social	*Status*	• Commitment to worldview	*R. Strategies*	• Individual shortcomings
			• Repertory of action		• Knowledge gaps
			• Patterned responses		

Dimensions	Relevance		Knowledge		Certainty	
Categories	*Natural*	• Floods	*Stock*	• Priests, prophets	*Trust*	• Assumptions
		• Drought		• Elders		• Expectations
		• Civil War		• Healers, lineage members		
	Social	• Repertory of action	*Status*	• Commitment to worldview	*R. Strategies*	• Individual shortcomings
		• Patterned responses				• Knowledge gaps

Contexts of Action

In other words, research in Patrice Lumumba brought me to the view that there is an analytical edge to be gained from conceptualising social action as reflexive in the general sense of action, making further action possible with reference to horizons and constraints it establishes. Beck, Giddens, and Lash (1994) come very close to this conceptualisation in their notion of reflexive modernity. In fact, they may unwittingly be referring to the social action that underlies modernity as such.

I sum up my overarching question here with the idea of taming fate. Indeed, ensuring that one will act again and again is a way of rendering the future predictable and less dangerous. One renders the future predictable and less dangerous through social action that is reflexive and enables itself within clearly defined frameworks. From a methodological point of view the taming of fate is, therefore, the creation of contexts of action. I will illustrate this with a renewed look at the findings of each case study.

In chapter five I presented and analysed two group discussions on the 2000 floods in Mozambique. Drawing from Ralf Bohnsack's documentary method of interpretation I sought to show that the local perception of disaster depended largely on the way in which they had learned over the time to live with the vagaries of nature and to accommodate them into the coping means available to them. To use an ethnomethodological metaphor one could argue that villagers did not make accounts of disaster, rather they 'did' those accounts.

In other words, in drawing the researcher's attention to their lifeworld of patterned and routine responses to floods they were actually performing their experience, i.e., bringing their knowledge of the structure of the world to bear on everyday life. They transformed the interview situation into an occasion to bring their ability to reflect on their experience to bear on the questions I asked them. Their world had a very specific meaning to them and they brought it into the light by providing descriptions of its properties – lived experience, repeated floods, response routines – and eliciting that meaning by producing a coherent account of their present predicament with reference to their lifeworld. Here again, I see the conscious production of a context of action, that is, a normative and structural framework for meaningful action in the future.

In chapter six I expanded on the role of experience in helping people devise ways of translating problematic situations into non-problematic ones. What I found particularly helpful in this undertaking was the analysis of local worldviews and how their nature was central to the constitution of social action and construction of social relations. The main finding here was the existence of local worldviews competing with new technical-scientific influences for interpretive hegemony on the ground. While drawing briefly from a comparison of local and external accounts on the basis of two individual interviews, my attention was drawn mainly to the local side of the equation.

The picture obtained from this focus on local worldviews was that of individuals actively producing normative canopies that imbued their individual actions with meaning at the same time as they rendered them intelligible to others. These local worldviews were not homogeneous in the sense of being shared in a like manner by all relevant groups within the village. This in itself is a significant insight to bear in mind, for it documents in particularly intense ways how much negotiating and tension goes into creating the conditions for social action. Better still, heterogeneous normative canopies document the emergent properties of social action and, as such, reveal precisely the contexts of action underlying what individuals do in their everyday life.

In chapter seven I turned my attention to a very special experience in Patrice Lumumba village, namely the experience of war refugees who moved to the village in the course of the eighties. I used their recollections of the war in their places of origin to trace the process through which, even in the midst of the most extreme form of adversity, people endeavour to create a sense of normalcy in their everday life. They do this by establishing daily routines, which, in their case, consisted in changing the structure of daily chores, that is, altering the time schedule, retreating to the forest, and behaving differently once they arrived there. Faced with uncertainty due to the 'arrival of the war' individuals simply changed their daily routines and sought to carry on with their lives.

Interestingly enough, the war itself and its concomitant violence did not appear to constitute the main criterion for people to define disaster. They simply accepted that it is in the nature of a war that people are killed, that property is ransacked and destroyed, and that people are taken away to join the fighting. The war acquired the status of a disaster the moment individuals became unable to establish routines, that is, to take their world for granted. This proved decisive in compelling individuals to flee, for seeking refuge was bound up with the realisation that it had become impossible to maintain a measure of predictability in their everyday life. Notice how the decision to flee itself conveys the same structural conditions pertaining to the reflexive nature of social action to the extent that it resulted from individuals' attempts at ensuring the conditions of their future action. In a nutshell, even under the most precarious and insecure conditions people are deeply engaged in creating contexts of action.

Finally, in chapter eight I looked at the way in which converts to a Pentecostal sect invest their energy in creating contexts of action which give coherence and legitimacy to their own biographies. I resorted to ethnomethodological and symbolic interactionist ideas about self to argue that performance is central to the production of knowledge about oneself. I tried to show that the way a group of people, bound together by a similar perception of common problems achieves stability over time, depends on the extent to which the individual members can refer to their common world as the background for their own action.

They are because they are in the group, they know what action is appropriate to the group and can reasonably expect other members of the group to react to them in patterned ways born out of their knowledge of who they are. Becoming a member of the Pentecostal sect meant learning how to be a member of the sect and managing to produce a convincing performance of one's Pentecostal self. Similar conclusions can be drawn as far as the two women are concerned who converted to the Swiss Mission. In their accounts they brought to the fore the extent to which individuals need context in order to be able to play out an identity.

Making Sociological Sense of the Findings

In the previous section I tried to show why I think that the creation of contexts of action is an adequate (suitable??) analytical reply to the question concerning how people enable themselves to act again and again. I argued that the creation of contexts of action is the individuals' response to their condition as social beings. If, as generations of sociologists have been saying over and over again, people are social beings and if, as Weber forcefully argued and found qualified support in the work of phenomenological sociologists, the nature of this condition lies in their ability to produce, recognise, and interpret the meaning of what they and others do, then it is fair to suggest that the creation of contexts of action depends to a large extent on individuals' ability to produce meaning. My contention in this regard is that the production, recognition, and interpretation of meaning are crucial moments in the taming of fate, for they, rather tautologically, enable individuals to create contexts of action within which the things they and others do become intelligible.

Intelligibiity, however, is not a function of the intellectual abilities of individuals. Intelligibility is a key property of social reality to the extent that it is based on social action. To put it simply, social reality makes sense to individuals because it makes available to them resources from which they can draw in order to engage meaningfully with others. With these remarks I come back to the explanatory framework I presented at the end of chapter four. I recall that in introducing it I drew attention to the fact that the sense in which the framework should be understood as explanatory was not the natural scientific one of positing a law against the background of which conclusions could be drawn. Indeed, my concern in developing that framework was to build a bridge from the empirical material across to the more or less theoretical discussion I had embarked upon in the first two chapters.

This bridge consisted of two basic sociological assumptions concerning nature as well as our knowledge of the social world. The first assumption rested on the interpretive principle according to which the social world is the outcome of sense-making activities in which individuals engage in their everyday lives. The answers my informants gave me to the questions I asked them on their perceptions of disasters and crises as well as to how they coped with them were themselves interpretive on the part of the informants. Their answers together with whatever inconsistencies, outright lies, inaccuracies, and certainties were not simply drawing from a reservoir of answers that individuals avail themselves of in order to describe their social worlds.

They were also, and most importantly, individual shows of the informants' ability to make sense of their own experience. In other words, for the purpose of describing other worlds, or rather, making the so-called second order observations that interpretive sociology is doomed to make in order to gain access to worlds that are not the world of the researchers concerned, I depended on my respondents' ability to make sense of their own themselves. I had, therefore, to bracket out the empirically existing lifeworld of Patrice Lumumba village and assume that I would be able to recover it through the accounts made by my informants. This attitude corresponds to the explanatory caveat made in chapter three concerning the expressive, or hermeneutic, nature of the data rendered visible by the analytical framework. Indeed, answers to my questions on perceptions of crises and disasters bring to the fore the precarious livelihood context, within which individuals try to make sense of their lives. In so doing, they draw on their empirical relationship with the world, structure it cognitively, and envelope it with the norms and values that define them as a community.

It would be fair to argue that precisely this point renders the description and analysis of African life forms less mysterious than some have been inclined to think. Indeed, studying Africa is neither an adventure into the unknown, nor does it require special conceptual tools. Underneath the symbolically dense world of everyday life we are confronted with in our attempts to approach Africa from a social scientific perspective, there lurks an intelligible world waiting to be made visible by, and retrieved for, analysis with the ordinary tools of the social sciences. This is why it is so important to insist, in the context of phenomenological approaches to sociology, that reality is socially constructed. African reality is no different. Attention to how Africans themselves make sense of their worlds is all that it takes to stay within the bounds of what has enabled important strands of sociology to remain true to its own interpretive roots.

The second element of the bridge consists of the purposeful actions of individuals. Indeed, social reality is not just meaning. Meaning has an origin and consequences. Its origin is what individuals actually do in their everyday life and its consequences consist, again, of what individuals actually do in their everyday life. Individuals take their cue from their own understanding of a given situation, act and, thereby, provoke others into (in)action; in this way they ensure that the social reality that results thereof makes up a world practically accomplished by the individuals themselves. The case studies we looked at in chapters four, five, and six amply demonstrated this by bringing to our attention the extent to which the precariousness of nature was heightened by the nature of social relationships which individuals knit together. They responded to nature by acting and responded to fellow community members also by acting. In so doing they produced outcomes that gave their social and natural worlds their own touch in a never-ending dialectical process.

Central to this dialectic process is what I discussed in chapter five on the relevance of risk sociology to the study of African social phenomena. I recall that I drew attention to the centrality of contingency to social action, quite independently of whether a risk situation obtains or not. The point of drawing attention to the central role of contingency was to stress the fact that central tenets of the sociology of risk are not new to sociological theorising, but actually come on the back of unresolved issues therein. In fact, the strength of the sociology of risk does not lie in its ability to provide a purportedly more accurate description of modern society. Rather, its strength lies precisely in the answers it offers with regard to perennial problems of sociological theorising, such as contingency is. My own suggestion in this connection is that the sociology of risk has broken new theoretical ground, which in turn requires empirically grounded studies to be sure about the sorts of answers it has in stock.

In this connection, the study of Africa acquires a new significance. Precisely because the kinds of situations that the sociology of risk seeks to describe and account for obtain more readily in the present conditions of Africa, the continent offers an ideal empirical background for the further pursuit of the research programme. In the process there may be practical gains to be made, such as developing knowledge that will enable decision makers to find more appropriate ways of intervening into African lifeworlds. However, for the time being, the greater potential is offered by the promise of collecting enough empirical material with a view to testing some of the central hypotheses suggested by the sociology of risk.

In this sense, therefore, the second element of the bridge, that is, the purposeful action of individuals is central. The case studies presented here seem to suggest that individuals' decisions are informed by the judgements they make of the situation. These judgements take into account what individuals did in the past, do at present, and expect to do in the future. More importantly, the consequences of their actions play a fundamental role in the decisions individuals take whether to act or not to act. This makes it imperative to document action and inaction, but also to be sensitive to the kinds of decisions that inform such action and inaction.

Put it differently, the case studies suggest that the intelligibility of the lifeworlds of Patrice Lumumba Village rests on three central aspects. First, the lifeworld is meaningful to individuals because it is of their own making. Secondly, the lifeworld manifests itself through certain properties that individuals can account for. Finally, those properties make themselves felt in the world of individuals. If these aspects ring such ethnomethodological bells as reflexivity, indexicality, and documentation it is because they are, indeed, inspired by ethnomethodology and its invitation to us to see the world as a practical accomplishment of individuals. This is, in the final analysis, what the taming of fate is all about. It is about developing perspectives on the world and ensuring grounds for action.

Daring to Live

Therefore, I end this book on an ambivalent note.

While it is true that in the research process itself I increasingly came to realise that the theoretical and analytical potential of my work could not be found in a description and identification of local perceptions of crises and disasters, nor even in prevention mechanisms and coping strategies, I also found that whatever theoretical interest that could be brought to bear on the studies would end up suggesting answers to that research question. Yes, there are local ways of perceiving, preventing, and coping with crises and disasters. These are based on the existential experience of local populations as well as on their ability to make local worldviews relevant in their attempt to account for their present condition. At the same time, however, the coherence of these local worldviews depends on the locals' ability to assert their relevance prior to the claims voiced by the technical-scientific rationality purveyed by the presence of external forces in their midst.

Indeed, it is the rather fragmented and unreliable presence of this technical-scientific rationality that makes local discourses cogent and legitimate commentaries on local lifeworlds. It is true that, on the one hand, local worldviews are silent commentaries on external 'schemes to improve the human condition …' (Scott 1998), but, on the other, they are also vigorous claims for agency that local actors put forward even though they complain about the inappropriateness of their own ways and deplore life in a world that resists understanding.

Local worldviews notwithstanding, when we take up the teachings of the sociology of risk and those ideas of schools of sociology which view social action as a highly contingent enterprise, then we are forced to realise that we are really concerned with describing and understanding how the villagers in Patrice Lumumba are engaged in taming fate. They do not tame fate by minimising or avoiding risk. They tame fate by daring to live against all odds. And this we all do.

Appendices

Appendix 1: Maps and Figures

Source – Appendices 1-6: Atlas for Disaster Preparedness and Response in the Limpopo Basin, INGC, UEM, FEW/NET, 2003)

Appendix 1.1: Research site (Xai-Xai city)

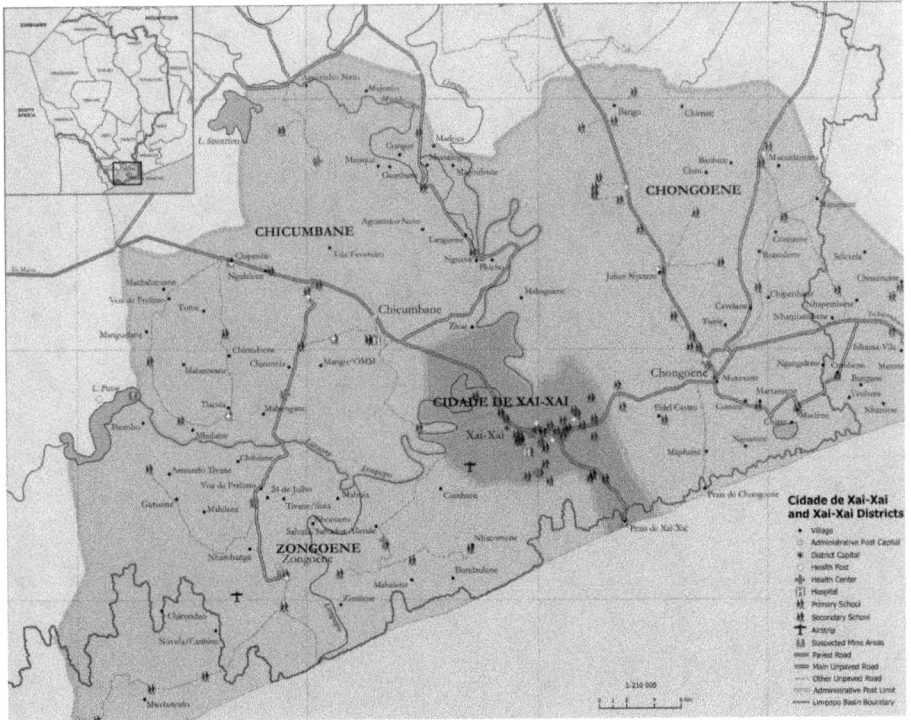

Appendix 1.2: Livelihood zones

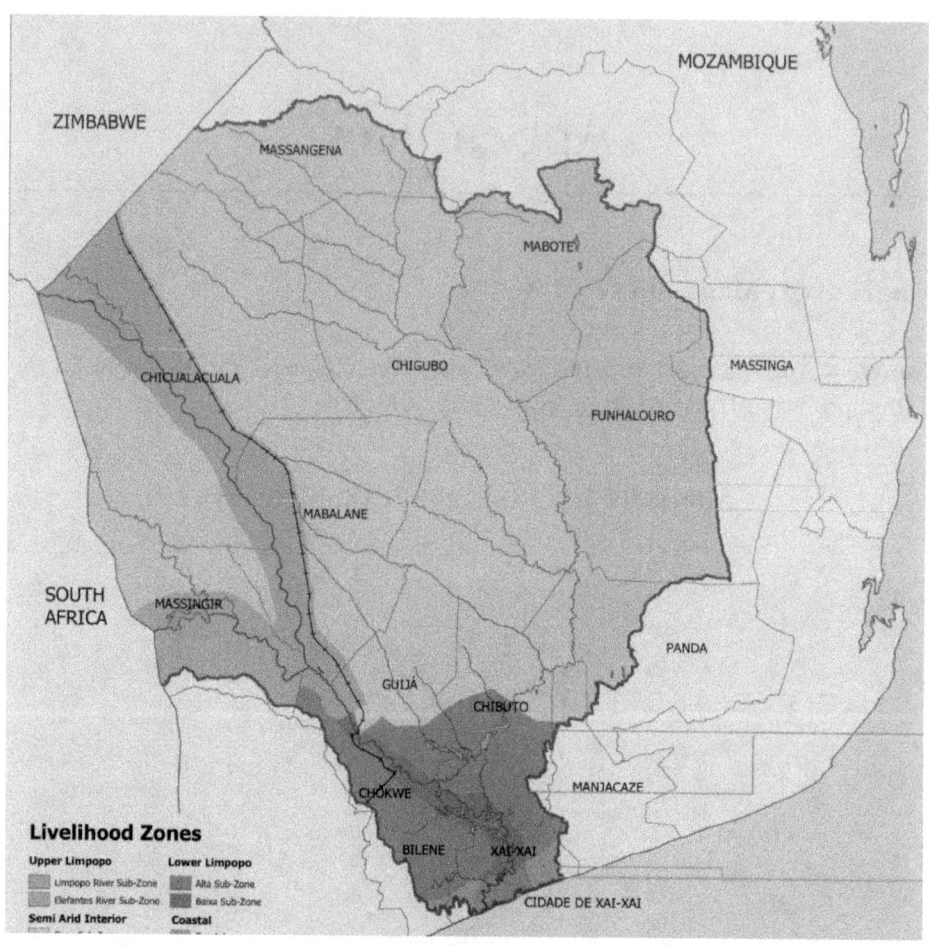

Appendix 1.3: Flood zones

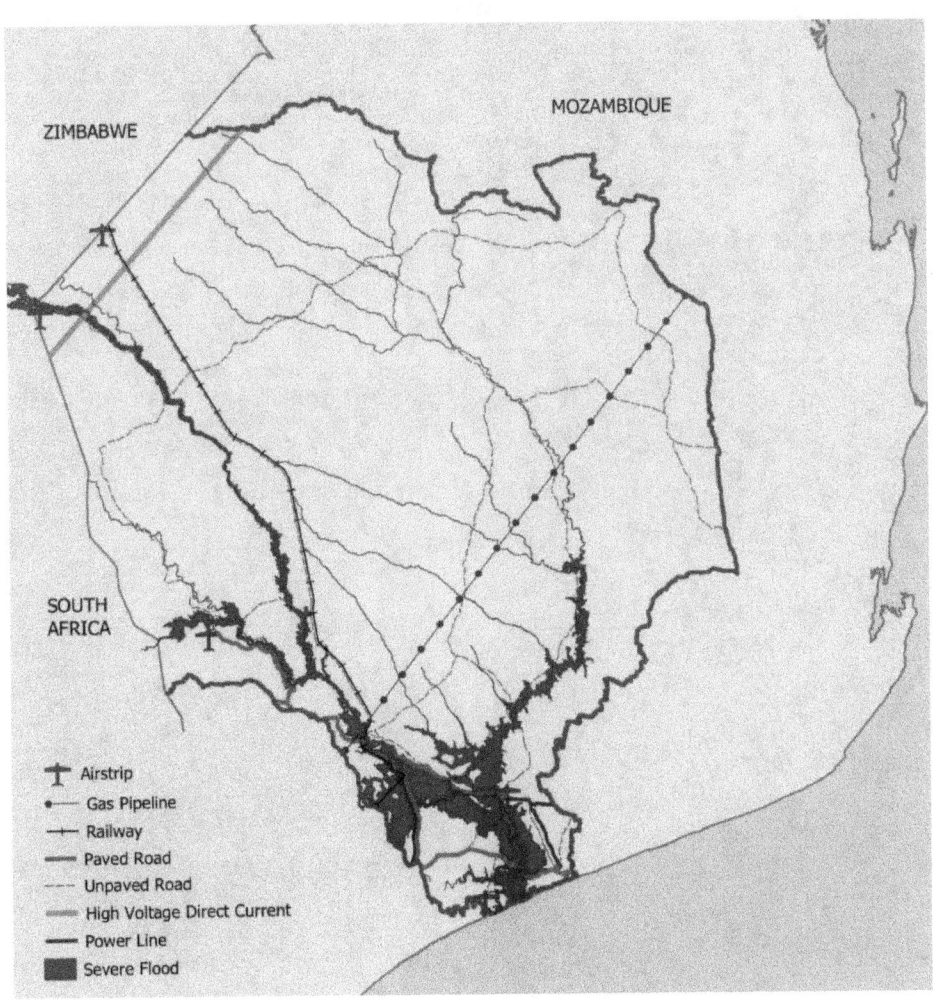

236   The Taming of Fate: Approaching Risk from a Social Action Perspective

Appendix 1.4: Water requirement satisfaction

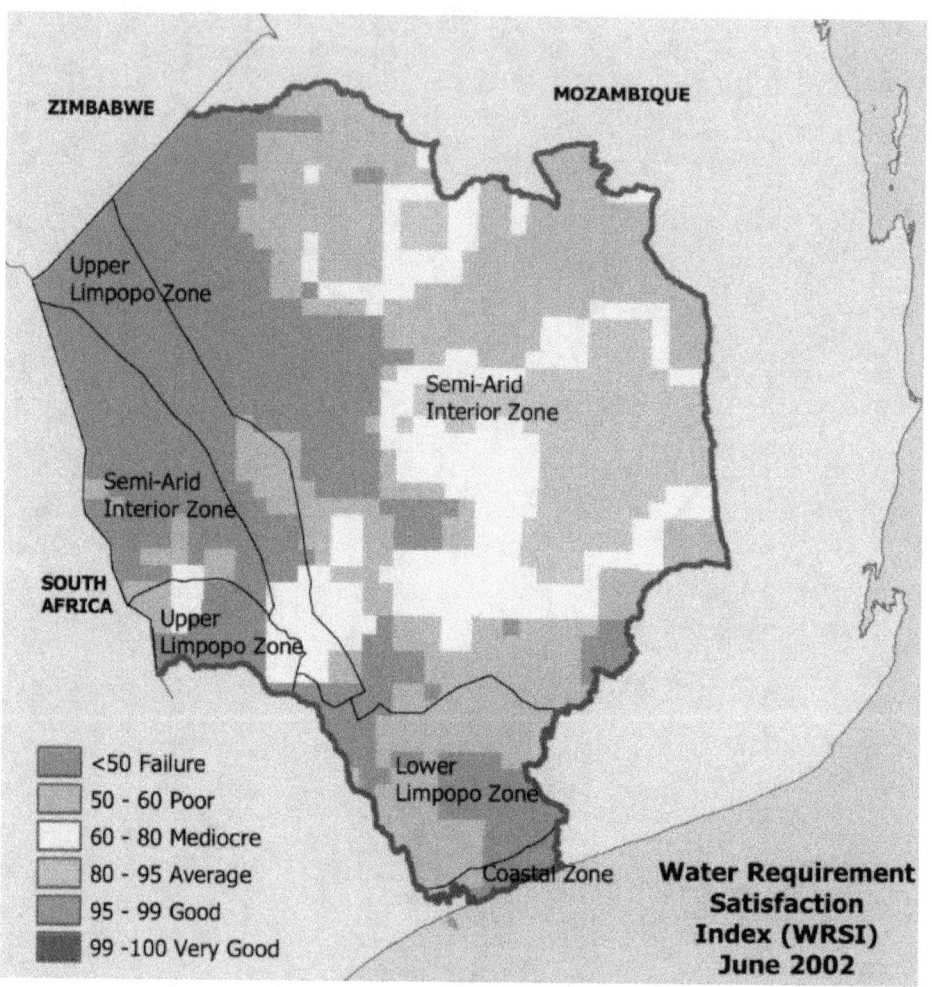

Appendices

Appendix 1.5: Rainfall

Southern Africa

Average Rainfall by Month

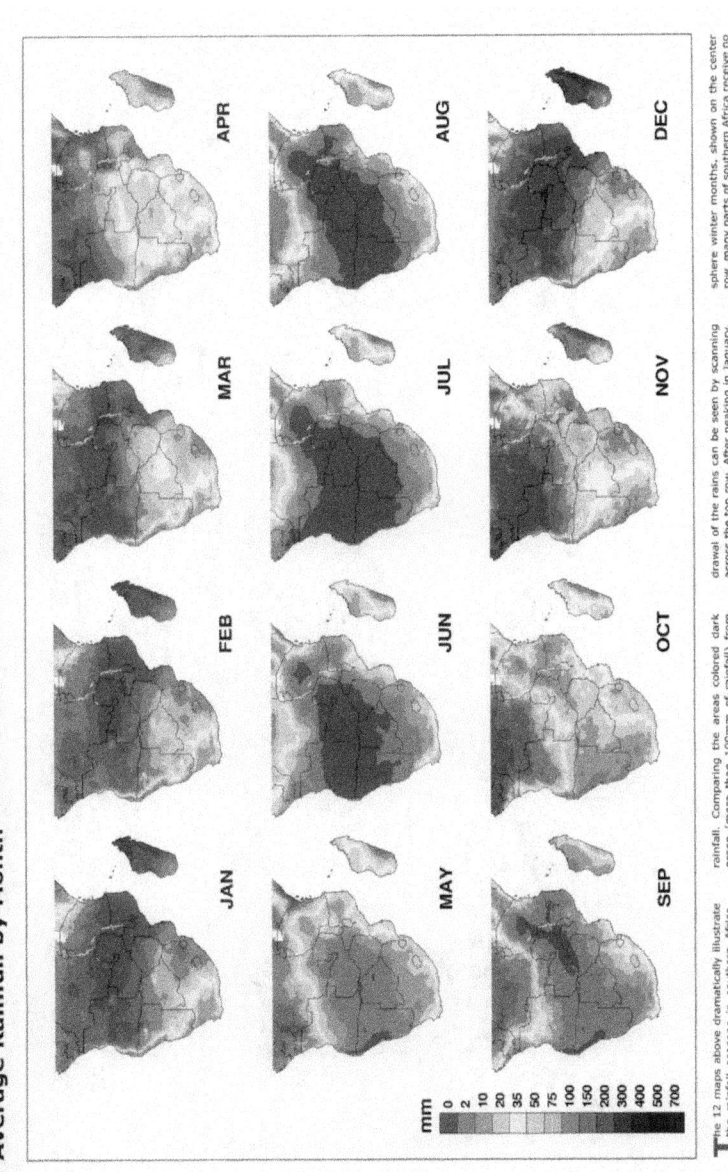

The 12 maps above dramatically illustrate the rainfall seasons in southern Africa. For most of the region, the heaviest rainfall months are December and January, and the driest months are July and August.

The four maps on the bottom row show the gradual southerly progression in seasonal rainfall. Comparing the areas colored dark green (more than 100mm of rainfall) from September to December shows how the rains progress with the southerly movement of the ITCZ (see previous page). In January, rainfall is normally at its peak and the ITCZ reaches its southern most point. The gradual with- drawal of the rains can be seen by scanning across the top row. After peaking in January, the amount of rain begins to lessen and the areas receiving low rainfall (less than 50mm in a month) gradually expand from the extreme southwest of Africa, moving to the north and east. During the southern hemi- sphere winter months, shown on the center row, many parts of southern Africa receive no rain at all on average.

These maps were produced using data from 1600 rainfall stations, over a period from 1961-1990.

Chapter 2: The Geographic Baseline

238 — The Taming of Fate: Approaching Risk from a Social Action Perspective

Appendix 1.6: Limpopo River profile

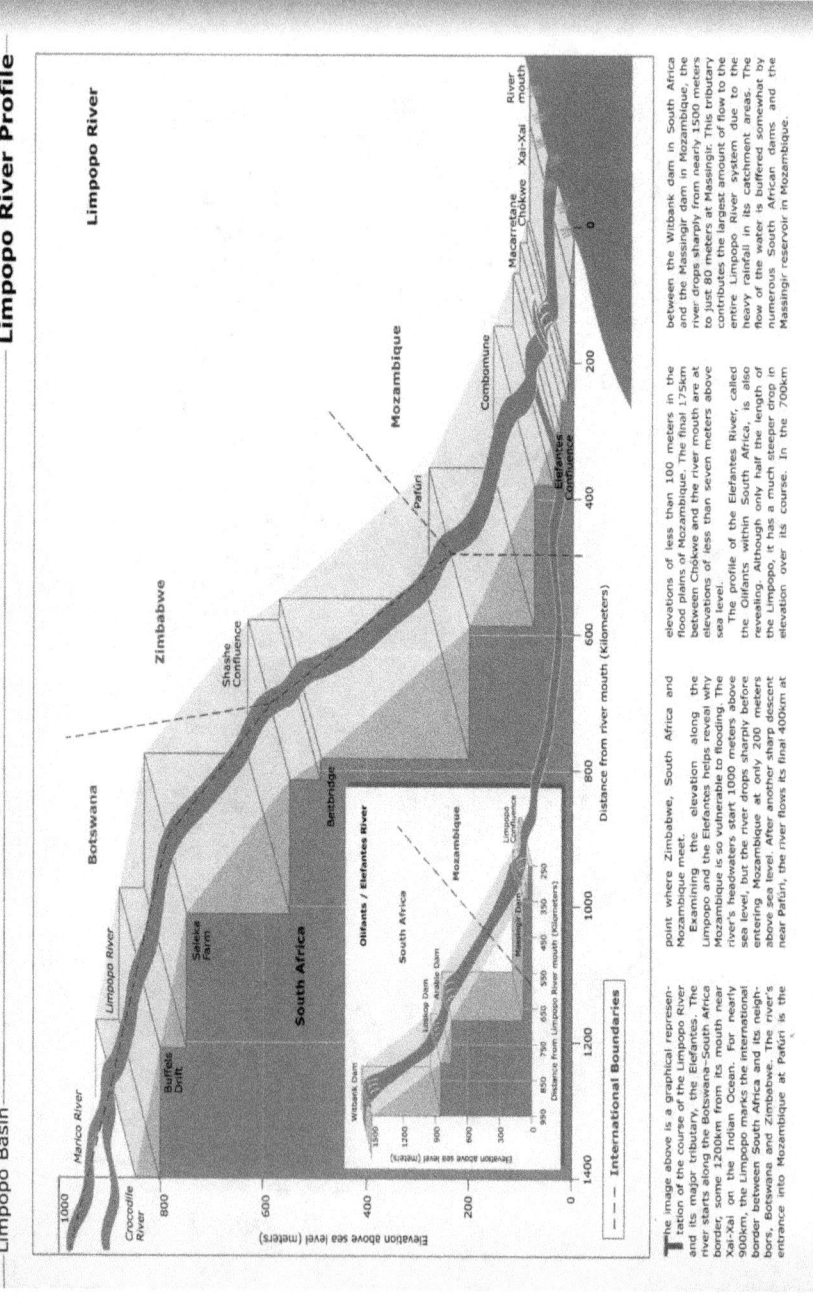

The image above is a graphical representation of the course of the Limpopo River and its major tributary, the Elefantes. The river starts along the Botswana–South Africa border, some 1200km from its mouth near Xai-Xai on the Indian Ocean. For nearly 900km, the Limpopo marks the international border between South Africa and its neighbors, Botswana and Zimbabwe. The river's entrance into Mozambique at Pafuri is the point where Zimbabwe, South Africa and Mozambique meet.

Examining the elevation along the Limpopo and the Elefantes helps reveal why Mozambique is so vulnerable to flooding. The river's headwaters start 1000 meters above sea level, but the river drops sharply before entering Mozambique at only 200 meters above sea level. After another sharp descent near Pafuri, the river flows its final 400km at elevations of less than 100 meters in the flood plains of Mozambique. The final 175km between Chókwè and the river mouth are at elevations of less than seven meters above sea level.

The profile of the Elefantes River, called the Olifants within South Africa, is also revealing. Although only half the length of the Limpopo, it has a much steeper drop in elevation over its course. In the 700km between the Witbank dam in South Africa and the Massingir dam in Mozambique, the river drops sharply from nearly 1500 meters to just 80 meters at Massingir. This tributary contributes the largest amount of flow to the entire Limpopo River system due to the heavy rainfall in its catchment areas. The flow of the water is buffered somewhat by numerous South African dams and the Massingir reservoir in Mozambique.

Chapter 2: The Geographic Baseline — 21

Appendix 1.7: Epidemics and their toll

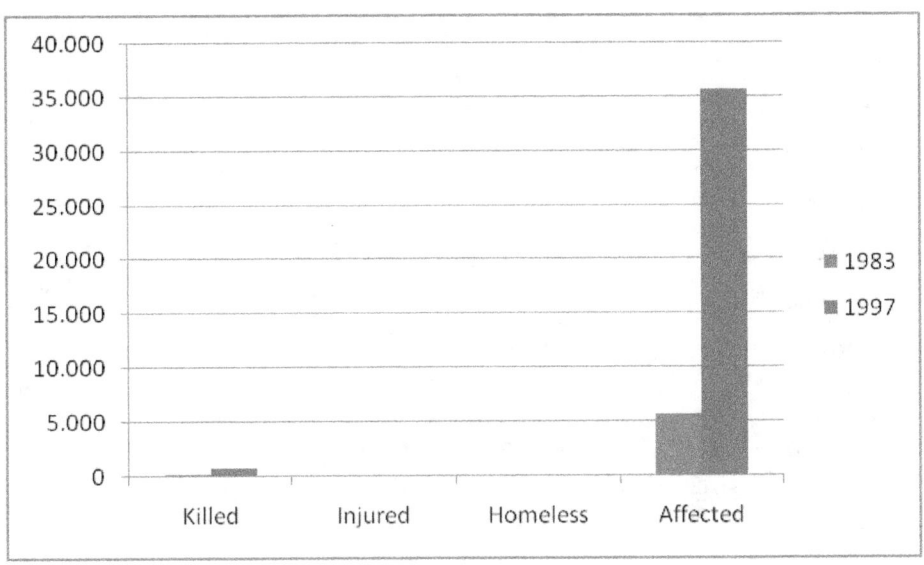

Appendix 1.8: Droughts in recent years

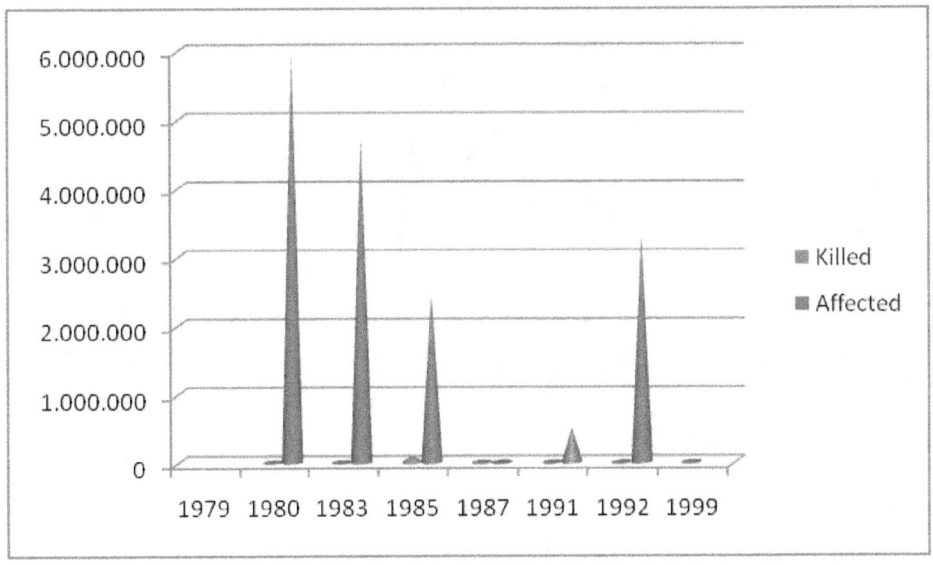

Appendix 1.9: Floods and their toll

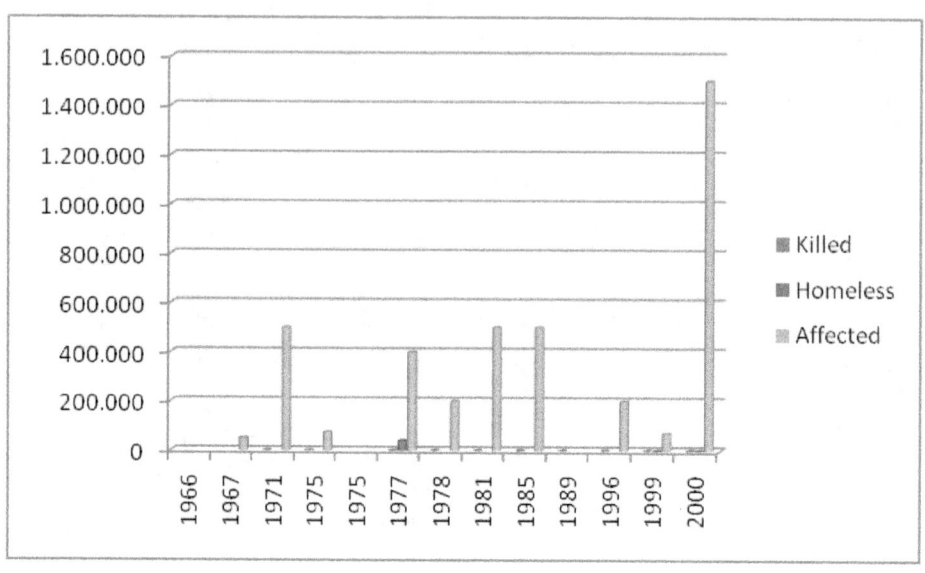

Appendix 1.10: Cyclones / Storms and their toll

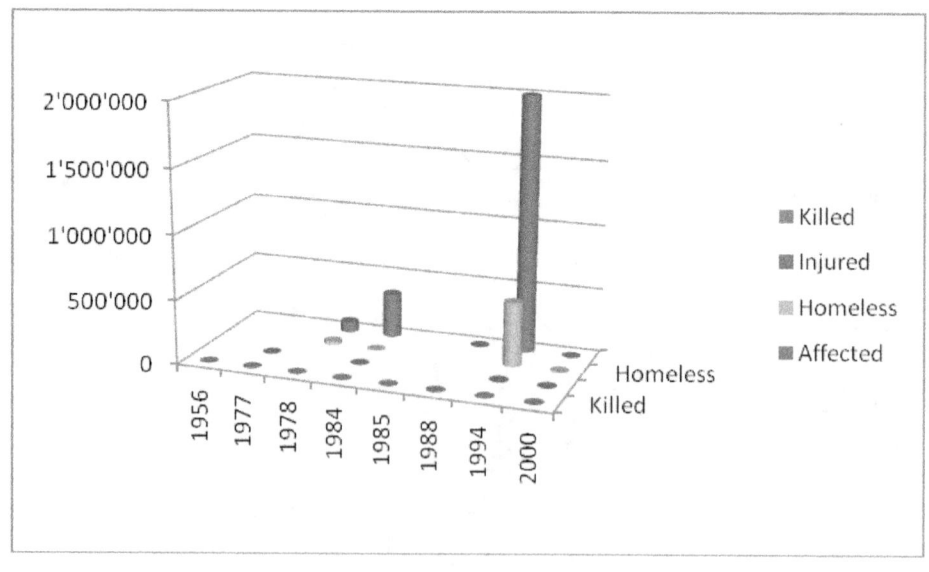

Appendices 241

Appendix 1.11: Age of interview partners

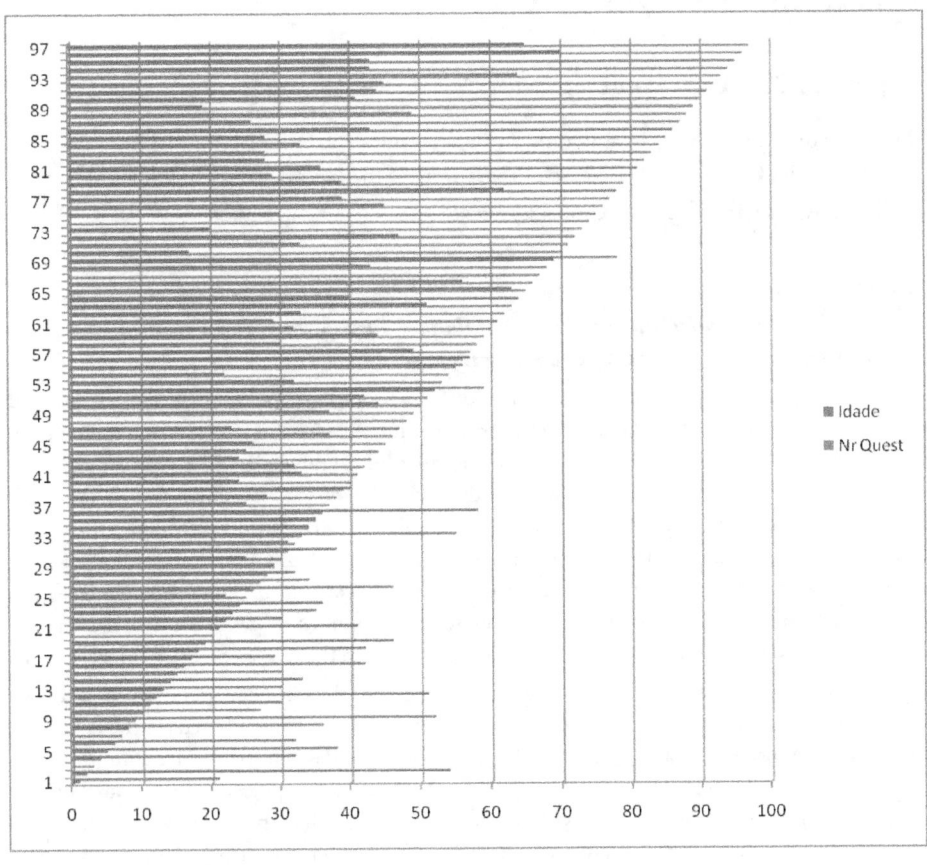

Appendix 2: Interview Schedules, Interview Samples, Field Notes, and Participant Analysis

Appendix 2.1: Project presentation[183]

University of Bayreuth – Federal Republic of Germany
   Humanities Collaborative Research Programme of the Germnan Research Council
   'Local Agency in Africa in a Global Context'

Research Area: Group C – Global reference systems and local knowledge
Project C6: **'Crisis and Disasters in Mozambique: Perceptions, Prevention and Coping Mechanisms within a Context of Global Influences'**

The aim of Project C6 is to collect and analyse information on the perception, prevention and coping mechanisms concerning crises and disasters on the Limpopo Valley. It is a sociological research project, which is interested in knowing how local knowledge on crises and disasters is formed, constituted, and transmitted within a context of global influences. To this end, local knowledge is defined as the whole set of beliefs, practices, and knowledge held and developed in everyday life by the local population. External influences are defined as the whole range of political, economic, and technological interventions from outside the local community following a rationality based on scientific frames of reference (in the case of technical interventions) or on central frames of reference (in the case of political interventions.

The project pursues two analytical objectives. The first objective consists in introducing of a new perspective in the study of disasters in Africa. This perspective is based on the centrality of the notion of risk, that is, on the idea that the everyday life of local communities is characterized by a conscious production of risks. This perspective perceives local communities as actors of their own lives and not as victims following the vulnerability model. In this sense, the study will focus on the systematic collection of the repertory of practices that are part of the local production of risks. The second analytical objective consists in opposing local knowledge systems and global frames of reference. As far as this opposition is concerned, the study seeks to gather information on the interaction between local communities and external actors, drawing on the analytical notion of interpretive hegemony. This notion assumes that everyday life practices are influenced by cultural and scientific frames of reference, which are in constant tension. To this end the project will seek to study the introduction of technical innovations and knowledge into the local context.

The project hopes to contribute towards a better understanding of the cultural and social context of risks, crises, and disasters.

Researcher: Dr. Elísio Macamo

Appendix 2.2: Narrative interview schedule

Issue		Institutional actors	Forms of transmission
Experience	• Have you ever experienced drought (war) in your life? • Can you describe your experience oft he drought (war)?	State	
		Local	
	• What kind of meaning did the drought (war) have to your life? What kind of meaning does it have now? • What kind of meaning does the drought (war) have to your circle of friends, kin and colleagues? • Can you imagine your country and community without drought (war)?	External	
Prevention and coping measures	• What did people do in antecipation of drought (war)? What is sufficient? (Why?) are there other prevention means? • Whose job is it to organise prevention activities? • How much does the danger of drought (war) influence your everyday life?		
Assessment	• What is the situation like today? • How likely is it that drought (war) will strike again?		
Interpretation	• Where does drought (war) come from? How would you explain a drought (war)? • What or who causes droughts (war)?		

Appendix 2.3: Interview schedule – Villagers

- *Since when have you been living in the village?*
    - Aim: Start conversation
    - Alternative: Have you been living in this village for a long time? Are you originally from here?
- *Why did you come here?*
    - Aim: Interview partner should mention his/her experiences.
    - Probe/Alternative: Did you move to this village voluntarily or were there strong reasons for you to move?
- *Can you tell me about your experience of this occurrence/event/phenomenon?*
    - Aim: Appraisal of the event, typical sequence of activities, connections
    - Probe/Alternative: How does one react in such situations? Or: how does one behave in such situations? Or: how did people react in the past?
    - Aim: Transition from objective to subjective appraisal of the event
    - Probe: Would it have been possible to avoid the event or avert its consequences? How?
- *What are the causes of these events in your opinion? Where do such things come from?*
    - Aim: Interpretation and explanation
    - Probe: there are people who said that … [traditional/social/religious explanations] with respect to the floods. What do you think of that?
- *What did you (??)do before, during and after such events?*
    - Aim: Repertories of action, Logic of action
    - Probe: would you say that people who are worse (or less) affected by the event people failed (or succeeded) to take appropriate measures?
- *Are there institutions here that can help you?*
    - Aim: Presence and role of external actors
    - Probe: Can you name the institutions that help you in such events?
- *Where do you get advice on how to behave in such events?*
    - Aim: Who knows what?
    - Probe: Why do you assess suggestions on how to behave in such situations in different ways?

Number of interviews: 25 – 30

Profile of informants:
⇒ Internally displaced people
⇒ Men and women over fifty years of age for information with historical depth;
⇒ Young people for possibly different points of view.

Appendix 2.4: Interview schedule – Institutions

1. Basic information on organisation
   - Field of work, objectives, role of emergency aid (reports?)
   - Since when active in Mozambique/Gaza province
   - Specific cause for work in Gaza province
   - Involved in emergency aid in Gaza province

2. Detecting of crisis/disaster
   - What crises/disasters hit province Gaza during last years/in general (all crises known)
   - Last crises/disasters (flood, drought). When did you realise that a crisis/disaster may come.
   - How was it realised that this may become a crisis/disaster. What information? From whom: media, local public discussions, organisations, state, seen yourself
   - Comparison sudden crisis/disaster (flood 2000) 'slow onset' (drought 2002)

3. Action (last crises/disasters: flood, drought)
   - When did aid start? Special 'kick-off'?
   Request from state, or other organisation, request from local people, need for help obvious
   - What kind of aid (activities)
   - Why specifically these activities?
   - From whom information on necessary type of aid?
   Request from state, or other organisation, request from local people, need for help obvious
   - Was the aid successful? Indicators?
   - What did the local people comment on aid? Did they use the aid offer? Other type of aid requested

4. Role of state and INGC =.... [state co-ordinating body] during crisis management
   - Role of state and INDC during crisis/disaster
   - How access to decisions of INGC
   - How important is INDC or its decisions for your (organisations) work

5. Explanation of crisis/disaster (flood/drought)
   - Reasons for crisis/disaster
   - Where did you find this explanation
   # Statement by state/INGC, aid organisations, # media, # local discussion, # own knowledge
   - Do you know different explanations? – Explanation by local people

6. Local assessment of problems as crisis/disaster (last crises/disasters: flood, drought)
- What was described as crisis/disaster?
- What were the indicators to prove that this special situation was a crisis/disaster?
- What were the main problems from the peoples' perspective?

7. Comments on local perspectives of definition of crisis/disaster and local explanations, that is, flood
- Locally the crisis/disaster was not the flood itself, but the aggravated situation after the flood (hard soil, low yields)
- Local explanations of crisis/disaster differ from scientific analysis (1) traditional: missing respect for 'ancestor spirits'; (2) religious: magic practices express limited respect of God, (3) Social/societal: conflicts missing community spirit.

Appendix 2.5: Interview Protocols

(ACORD/04.09.02, 14.00-15.00)

Respondent: Senhora Isélia Simbine, Programme Assistant (Mid 30)

ACORD is a network of organisations which started its activities in Mozambique in 1989 in Niassa Province. It is run from London and operates in 18 African countries. There are plans to move its headquarters to Kenya to reflect its focus on Africa. It deals with such issues as conflicts, development, HIV-AIDS and does research. Emergency and relief work is not part of its purview, but it was asked by the government of Inhambane to participate in the process of reconstruction after the 2000 floods.

It worked mainly in Panda district. Its activities consisted in the resettlement of displaced people, helping them to initiate agricultural activities, building houses and improving sanitary conditions. In this connection it provided shelter to 59 families, it improved sanitary conditions for 132 families through the construction of improved latrines, it gave assistance to 670 families in their agricultural work and it built bridges with local materials. The main recipients of its assistance were widows, elderly and handicapped who used local materials wherever it was possible. The work was done by the community itself and there was a reward for those who helped. The idea behind the whole programme of assistance was to encourage the local community to be entreprising and to use latrines.

The involvement of ACORD in these activities was partly at the request of the government of Inhambane, but also on its own initiative. This is particularly the case now that there is a severe drought. As soon as the government of Mozambique launched an emergency appeal to respond to drought ACORD undertook to help by introducing drought resistant crops. The impact of its assistance has been positive. The driving force behind it is the idea of helping people to be self-reliant in their everyday life. A particularly positive outcome of this work has been the ability to enable the local community to solve a long standing problem concerning land rights. This is related to land which originally was a re-education camp, then the Mozambique

Cotton Institute and finally was given to a private entity for commercial purposes. For a long time there had been no clarity concerning the local community's access to the land, but thanks to ACORD the local community will soon be constituting itself into a formal association which will be awarded rights over the land to grow vegetables such as cassava, sweet potato, cabbage, onions and a whole host of fast growing vegetables. They are assisted in this by the district agriculture authority (direcção distrital de agricultura), which provides tractors for ploughing while ACORD provides money for the tractors and the local community does the rest.

ACORD thinks that the local community finds its activities very positive. The indicator of this positive attitude is the number of people who join its activities and the enthusiasm with which they work. ACORD gives them many things which they appreciate. It helps them in setting up rice fields, it gives them knowledge, materials, institutional assistance, etc. All the local community has to do is to identify a project and be appropriately organised.

The work done by INGC is good. ACORD works closely with this institution, in fact most of its activities were coordinated with it; ACORD has a seat on the technical commission that deliberates on emergency needs.

Disasters such as the floods that hit southern Mozambique in 2000 and the current drought are natural phenomena. If they were not people would have found a solution to them. Floods and droughts alternate in this part of the world and science has not yet found a way out of the problem. Perhaps it is about time a system were designed to keep rain water for the time of drought. The government is adopting a strategy which consists in building dykes. The floods in 2000 seem to have been related to El Nino to go by what the government and the weather bureau suggested at the time. They may be alternative explanations of this natural phenomenon, but ACORD does not work on the basis of such explanations. Members of local rural communities tend to think in terms of things going wrong as a result of the violation of taboos.

(Frage 6) There are of course traditional explanations for disasters. In fact, it is hard not to be tempted to think in that way, for the soils of Inhambane, for example, are very sandy and shouldn't, in principle, let in too much water. During the 2000 floods there was water shooting up from underground.

As to local Patrice Lumumba accounts (hesitation) it would be much easier to assess them if floods had just happenned there. But they were everywhere. The floods started on the 4th of February, right after a huge traditional ceremony had been carried out in Manhiça (Gwaza-Mthini). The opposition party argued at the time that the floods were a sign that the ancestors had not accepted the sacrifice and were punishing the south. Yet, not too long afterwards there was flooding in the centre and north as well. It is very hard to communicate with the population on these matters, for they know representatives of relief organisations do not give them too much credit. They say 'lava va valungu u nga va byela va nga takuyingela' (you may tell the white people, but they won't listen to you). When ACORD funded the construction of a bridge the local community asked for money to buy a hen, a white sheet and traditional beer for a ritual designed to announce the start of the work to the ancestors. This money was paid out of the pocket of ACORD staff, for the money of the organisation could not be used for that. It was 50.000 Mts.

The interview was conducted in a very friendly atmosphere. Mrs. Simbine spoke very slowly, but seemed very knowledgeable about the work of her organisation. Although she is only a programme assistant, she seems to run the place. She did not allow me to record the interview, so I had to take notes. The questions seemed to have a logical sequence and some were answered without having been asked. There was a slight problem with question 6 concerning alternative explanations of disasters. Mrs. Simbine seemed to be taken aback by the question and I had the impression that she was disoriented for a little while. She seemed to be wondering whether was I was doing was really science. When I then asked her to comment the local interpretations of the 2000 floods she hesitated for some time before answering. Perhaps it would make sense to ask the questions alternatively or at least ask them in a such a way that she does not get the wrong impression I have stepped out of science altogether. Mrs. Simbine gave me the annual report for 2001.

Appendix 2.6: Interview protocol, Sr. Samuel Mondlane, Financial manager, World Vision (Xai-Xai, 9 September 2002)

World Vision International is an American NGO which has been working in Mozambique for some time. More details about its history are available in publications which will be given to me at the end of the week. My interview Partner is a middle-aged man who is an old acquaintance of mine. I could not tape the interview because he said World Vision employees can only do so under permission. I had to take notes.

Basically, World Vision does not do emergency and relief work per se. Before the 2000 floods World Vision activities were limited to the so-called 'development areas', i.e. selected areas where the organisation concentrates its development assistance work. This work consists in supporting long-term development projects (15 years) and child-sponsoring. This is done mainly in Manjacaze in places called Nhluvuko and Txemulane and also in Chidenguele and Chonguene. Child-sponsoring progammes include the whole gamut of development activities (health, education, agriculture), but also missionary work. World Vision also attaches a lot of importance to teaching peasants modern agricultural techniques.

World Vision got involved in emergency and relief work at the request of the government. The government of Mozambique launched an appeal for emergency assistance in the wake of the floods. World Vision basically provided assistance in resettling displaced people, giving them shelter, food and so-called 'agricultural kits'. These kits consisted of seeds, a hoe, a shovel, rake, watering-can and other unspecified implements. In resettling people World Vision provided building materials which consisted of reeds, poles, cement and corrugated iron. People were supposed to build a stable house in the higher part of town while keeping a smaller house in the lower parts near their fields.

It also built schools (7), introduced drought-resistant crops (orange-coloured potato) and encouraged people to plant fruit trees and ordinary ones (árvores de sombra). In its emergency work World Vision placed a lot of emphasis on activities which would help people achieve food security. The mainstay of such activities was accordingly the introduction of modern techniques ('equipar os camponeses com técnicas modernas). Samuel Mondlane insisted on the fact that emergency is not part of the normal work of World Vision, but rather a reaction to a very timely situation.

Because emergency and relief is not part of the normal work of World Vision the organisation only reacted to the floods and to the drought now in the wake of an explicit appeal launched by the government of Mozambique to that effect. In other words, it was not aware of any impending disaster. As soon as it decided it would help it drew up a plan of action which was then funded by the European Union. The latter did not want to channel its emergency funds through the government, but rather through non-governmental organisations. On the other hand, Samuel Mondlane said that even if the government had not launched an appeal his organisation would have intervened, for it is a Christian one. The floods were so devastating that one had to do something. They had such an impact on World Vision that the organisation has now elevated emergency work within its institutional arrangements. There is now an emergency sector within World Vision. This emergency sector works closely with INGC, on which it depends to be able to define priority areas for its activities in this area.

Samuel Mondlane believes that the work of his organisation has a positive impact. He thinks that its role consists in encouraging people to break out of the cycle of dependence on aid. In the past, he argued, non-governmental organisations promoted dependence. Emergency work in the wake of the floods ran the risk of repeating past mistakes, for 'emergency encourages people to be lazy' (a emergência provoca preguiça). World Vision insists even in the context of emergency work that the emphasis should be on development.

It is hard to know what people think of the work of World Vision. He believes, however, that people find the work good. It is true that they find it hard to accept World Vision's principles such as its emphasis on breaking dependence. Some people sometimes say that there are organisations that just offer their aid without asking for anything in return (há organizações que dão de borla). Then again, there are those who think World Vision is taking the place of the government because it builds schools and health centres. There is a joke doing the rounds to the effect that there will be a World Vision candidate for the next presidential elections in the country.

World Vision's philosophy is that the people in the receiving end should play a central role in the definition of the programmes. They have to say what they want to achieve, how much money should be put into the effort and how it should be used. World Vision does not only get requests for assistance from local communities, but also from national NGOs. If these requests are in line with World Vision's priorities they will be supported. A soccer pitch, for example, will not be easily supported. In the whole, however, World Vision follows the government's emphasis on poverty reduction and sets its priorities accordingly.

Samuel Mondlane says that disasters are natural phenomena. The 2000 floods had to do with climate changes, the intensity of the rain, the lack of dams, the geographical position of Mozambique (with rivers washing into the sea), the lack of maintenance of dykes. If Mozambique were able to control its waters – retaining it in dry periods and releasing it in rainy periods – it might not have to experience this kind of disasters.

He is not aware of any significant alternative explanation of the floods. He said that the people say that floods always happen, i.e. they are a normal occurrence. They say floods like those of the year 2000 happen every 50 years.

As for other forms of interpretation Samuel Mondlane heard people who argued that the 2000 floods were the end of the world. They held that the world should have come to an end in 1999, so the floods were the fulfillment of biblical prophecies. When I asked him if such a view was not consistent with World Vision's own religious background he said not quite. People should not mix up religion with nature. Religion is one thing, nature is another. In fact, World Vision trained church ministers to provide 'psycho-training' to people to explain them that floods are a natural phenomenon (é natural, é normal) and that they had nothing to do with God. Some people had been spreading the idea that the floods were a sign God was sending to show that even if people try to ignore him he is still stronger. The training to church ministers was administered by somebody called Tovela who used to work for the social ministry.

Samuel Mondlane insisted on the idea that people should stop making Jesus responsible for whatever goes wrong in their lives. They must accept him and live according to him, but it is not Christ who will solve people's problems, it is people themselves who should fend for themselves. I countered that there might be people who see no contradiction between praying and being successful in life. Mondlane answered that World Vision aims at transforming people (desenvolvimento transformacional do homem). He explained that this approach aims at making people see that it is possible to get out of poverty into wealth. To that effect World Vision tries to build up the potential of communities, helping them to use their resources better. Nothing has ever been achieved by prayer alone without hard work.

Appendix 2.7: Excerpts from the field diary

Local perceptions of disasters

First field day – Patrice Lumumba communal village (15th March, 2002)

We left from Maputo early in the morning at 7 am. We were in two cars, one of which was driven by a student. I took with me six students, one in his final year and five in their fourth year. All of them are studying sociology at the university in Maputo. We met on two afternoons last week to prepare the field trip. At the first meeting we discussed the interviews and tried out the questionnaire. The students seemed to understand what I expected from them. I tried to make them aware of the fact that they should use their judgement to find the best formulation for a question, using as their guidance the objective which I set for which each question.

Some seemed to be apprehensive about the quality of their Shangan, and I encouraged them to try the interviews out with other people. Since not all of us speak the same dialect we agreed that the wording (which I had prepared in advance) should be changed so as to fit the sense of the question.

On arrival we were met by the village head and a few elders. There were about 14 people waiting for us for the interview. The previous week I had been to the village and had conducted a few interviews to test the wording. I took that opportunity to ask the village head to make arrangements for the interviews. I had asked him to invite 12 people selected according to whether they are members of churches, traditional authorities, political organisations or are notable in any way (for example, being the wealthiest farmer, migrant worker, etc.). The idea was to get people who could give us substantial information about the issues which interest us. We did not strive for representativeness in the strict sense.

We arrived at 11 o'clock sharp and this impressed our hosts, for that's the time we'd told them we would arrive. They seemed to appreciate our punctuality. This might have something to do with the fact that officials here do not care much about keeping the time.

We met at the village centre, next to the local primary school. We sat in a semi-circle, each group facing each other, i.e. us (researchers) on one side, and them (villagers) on the other side. The village head said a few words of welcome and took care to mention the fact that we had come at the time we said we would come. He explained that we wanted to interview people in order to know how they live and hopefully find out things which will help the government help them. He mentioned that I had already been in the village asking questions and he wondered whether there was anything that could satisfy me, for last time he thought I had asked everything there was to be asked. In any case, he asked his fellow villagers to answer the questions in all earnest, for we are very clever people and we would know if they were not saying the truth. He then asked me to address the gathering.

I thanked them all for agreeing to come and talk to us. I explained that we had come to find out how they live and learn one or two things about how they think about things of life. I explained that it was important that we speak with them individually, but assured them that we would not be gossiping about anyone. I told them that we would start with the village head and afterwards we would carry out individual interviews. The idea of starting with the village head was for the students to see how I conduct the interview.

We went to a secluded room in what looked like the local administrative office. I had wanted to tape the interview, but I had technical problems with the tape recorder, so I decided to take notes. Later I found out what the trouble was with the tape recorder. I should have activated the Spss. I then interviewed the village head under the attentive eye of the students who were busily taking notes. After the interview we asked the village head to leave us on our own for a few minutes. We told him we would let him know when we could proceed with individual interviews. We then discussed the interview. The students remarked that the interview had been quite short. When we tried out the interviews they lasted more than half an hour. The one

I had just conducted did not take more than 15 minutes, even though I asked more questions than were actually on the questionnaire. We also noted that it was necessary to do some aggressive probing with nearly all the questions, for it was hard to elicit information as readily as we thought our questions would. This seems to be something to do with the nature of the questions themselves, which do not seem to be in line with the way people ask and answer questions here. I will return to this issue.

After this brief discussion each chose a place on the courtyard, where they carried out interviews. For this first day we had set ourselves a target of two interviews each. Two of us did three interviews while the remaining four did two. All in all, then, we did 14 interviews. The idea is to make sure we know where we are going before we go for quantity. We have scheduled a discussion for tonight to review the questions and talk about the problems that occurred. Tomorrow, we are going to increase the interviews, possibly setting a target of three for each. However, this will depend on whether enough people turn up. Those we interviewed today came from different parts of the village and were asked by the village head to bring five people each.

At the end of the interviews we sat down with the men (the women had already left) and exchanged a few words. The men were talking about problems in the village, more particularly about criminals using magic to go about their work. There was a man who seemed knowledgeable about this. He seemed to be some kind of authority and was highly respected by the others. He encouraged people to find interview partners for us and likened us to children being sent to get reeds (va famba va tsema nhlanga). He said people should not be concerned with immediate results from the interviews, but should rather wait. Even if nothing came out of the work we were doing there was no reason for people to be concerned or crossed.

Interview issues

Two issues are worthy of note. First, the questions themselves and secondly the questionnaire as a whole. I had the feeling that the questions are two direct to elicit a clear answer from the interview partners. If a question is not vague, people do not feel compelled to answer in an elaborate manner. They are laconic. If it is vague, then they discuss and speculate. Perhaps this has to do with the fact that they are not quite sure they know what we want from them. I had the feeling that my interview partners were busy trying to interpret the situation (symbolic interactionism).

The second problem is related to the questionnaire itself. Some of the questions do not seem likely to elicit the kind of response that I expect. Two questions in particular should be mentioned. The first question is related to extraordinary events. It seems that everyone knows already that we are interested in floods. So everyone only talks about the floods and about hunger. It seems that the interview partners met beforehand and agreed on what to be said. The second problem is related to the question on what the causes of disasters are. Since interview partners think they know what we want to hear they dish out the story about South African dams. In the discussion we decided that we should not ask them for the causes, but for the reasons why this time things are so different. In this way we hope to get a better response from our interview partners.

Appendix 2.8: Participant analysis – Day One

After dinner, which consisted of grilled fish and mealie-mealie, we sat down in the dining room to discuss the day. I decided that each one should make a brief statement about their interviews and whether there were any interesting pieces of information. Then we should place emphasis on whether the questions were wieldy enough and how the interviewers reacted.

Individual reports

Carmen Bazar

She sent a message to Carlos Bavo warning that if they had the two eldest ladies it would be tough because they could only speak shangan. She ended up with both ladies, who were war refugees. As to whether there was anything extraordinary that had happened in their lives recently they mentioned starvation. Only on insistence did they speak of floods. They couldn't say where the floods came from, but one of them suggested that they might come from South Africa. Later on she said the floods came from the earth (*yi buya hi misaven*), then she said 'god'. They did not get help from anyone and were not directly affected by the floods. They are war victims. They complained that after the flood some of their fields were occupied by flood victims. The ladies complained that assistance only went to flood victims. No development projects with the exception of the Fumo family, which gives them assistance. They say the soils are not fertile. Carmen finds it interesting that the women did not claim any knowledge concerning the origin of the floods. She thinks men are either better informed or knowledgeable. She couldn't fit the answers with the objectives set out for each question. They get information from the radio.

The questions were fine. Probing was only necessary because the interview partners were laconic. When they saw Carmen writing they paused.

Adozinda Sengulane

Adozinda carried out two interviews, the first of which was with a Wesleyan pastor. He's been living in the village since 1977. None of the floods affected him directly, except for the loss of his farmland. The only thing extraordinary that happened was a whale (which looked like a train). On insistence he talked about the floods. He has a religious explanation for the floods. They did not come from South Africa, but were the outcome of prayers because people wanted rain. He has no knowledge of projects; cows were distributed by the women's minister. He compared the 1977 and 2000 floods and said the latter ones were worse because afterwards nothing could be grown. There is only hunger. He was distrustful of the local state officials whom he accused of embezzlment. At the end of the interview he remarked that he thought we were bringing things for them.

The second interview was with a lady who came from Chibuto. She was a war victim. She remarked that after their arrival the fields stopped yielding. She said the only thing extraordinary were the floods, which came from South Africa (the Boers want to kill people in Mozambique). When Adozinda asked her whether the floods might not have been caused by the rains, she said no because the flood water was red and could only have come from SA. The radio is her main source of information. No projects. No support from the government.

Adozinda had trouble with the interpretation of the causes of floods.

D'Bora Carvalho

She was struck by the fact that her interview partner was introduced as a healer who should only talk about matters concerning his trade. He's the head of the healers' league. He's been here since 1977. He heard of the floods in 1955, but can't remember it. The one from 1977 he can just remember and the 2000 he remembers it well. The causes of the floods are the opening of dams in South Africa, but that doesn't wholly satisfy him. It's like we are at war with nature. In the past we could live well after floods, but this time it's different. He recalled an event in 1982. The village head then was sensitive to tradition and listened to the people. People then carried out a traditional ceremony and all was well. So for him starvation now is due to the fact that tradition is not being respected. This is all because the village head is not concerned with tradition. He remarked that rain starts in the village but peters out in Macia. This is local rain which should water the village. As for projects he said sometimes there are white people who come and do a few things, but that's it. War, peace and floods (D'borah thinks he thinks floods are natural). The people are like cattle without a shepperd. There are no experts, for anyone who reveals what he knows ceases to be an expert (?!).

The second interview was in Portuguese. D'borah had the feeling that her partner was concerned to give her a 'politically correct' account of things. He came to the village in 1977. His explanation of the causes of floods was painstakingly geographical. The government warned them. However, he said that he knew floods were coming because they had seen the current swelling, but couldn't tell where he got the information. Later he said the floods have a biblical explanation. God sent them because it's in the Bible. He said he was always astonished to find himself awake in the morning. D'borah was not sure what to make of this all, especially with regard to the conflicting explanations her interview partner gave. He complained about hunger and accused the government of doing nothing. D'borah believes they don't dare criticise the government openly. She thought they were evasive.

Carlos Bavo

He did three interviews, two women and one man. Two of them are from a church. His first interview partner was a woman who came to the village in 2000 because of the floods. The floods are the extraordinary event, but hunger too. Her family and herself are too powerless for the floods, but for hunger there are things which can be done. Life changed slightly after the floods: they got assistance from projects. Children stopped going to school but the government has built schools. She has a religious explanation for the floods. She thinks that the floods come from South Africa as God's punishment for the sins of the people. There are two projects: building a clinic, market. The local authorities are the ones who give her advice on life (madoda).

The second partner was also a lady from Chibuto (war refugee). Floods are the extraordinary thing and hunger. She can't do anything against either because she doesn't have money. Floods brought changes to the worse. The seeds were washed away by the waters. She doesn't know where natural phenomena come from, but she thinks it might be God's punishment. She knows of the plans to build a clinic.

The last partner was a man who has been living in the village since 1977. He doesn't think that the floods in 2000 are any big deal; what worries him most is hunger. There is nothing he can do because he doesn't have cattle anymore. Floods brought many social ills through hunger and homelessness. He thinks hunger is caused by the lack of rain. He thinks the population has good relations with the local authority. He knows of plans to improve the roads. There is some organisation which dug dykes. His church is Velhos Apóstolos and helps anyone who seeks advice.

Patrício Langa

Patrício was struck by the fact that the people think they know what we want from them. They seemed to be concerned with giving us politcally correct answers. The interviews were quite different. The first one was much easier, for the partner spoke more at ease towards the end of the interview. Patrício did not respect the sequence of questions because quite a number of things appeared almost everywhere. He has misgivings about the last question concerning where people seek advice.

The first interview partner was a man who came to the village in 1986 (from Nhanale, north of Gaza). He is a war victim. The floods struck him as extraordinary. They brought hunger and cholera. He doesn't know if these diseases are related to the floods or not, because there are no floods anymore. There is too much malaria (far too much). Could it be God who's causing all this? He's cross with mankind? He spoke of an illness where people dry up to death (a hi yi kume nhloko ya mhaka). He says it's new, it started after the war, but can't explain it. Another aspect is related to people who were victims of the floods. They are stubborn. They did not move because they relied on past experience. He thinks life changed now, not social life but nature. For example, in the past when people took medicine they were healed, but now nothing happens. It's not just with traditional healing methods, but also with hospitals. So God may be a factor. There are too many 12 year old girls suffering from tb. Maybe they get it from elder men. He works for a project in agriculture. He thinks the relationship between project people and government is not clear. He blames the government for it. There was another part to the interview. He said he was a member of Ametramo and a member of the party. He said it's important to distinguish between floods and droughts. There are droughts because there are no ceremonies. These cause rain through a worm. But he says nothing can be explained traditionally today. Things are explained by books (hi ngeneliwile hi mabuku).

The second partner is from the village. The floods (1977 and 2000) are the events he mentioned. They were assisted by the government without any distinction in

1977. In 2000 there was distinction, for locals were not assisted. This was done by NGOs. These were unfair. He doesn't know the origins of the floods but thinks it has something to do with the outside world. The floods changed the look of the village. There are better houses and more people. Many animals died as a result of illnesses caused by the floods. He came back to the causes of the floods and said they came from opening dams in SA. He said this had to do with the rivers of Mozambique. Floods are a natural phenomenon which has to do with God, because God commands nature, just look at Noah's ark. The only thing people can do is to be strong, because nature is just like that. In 1984 they thought by praying they wouldn't change things, but the ensuing rains just damaged more things. Therefore, people shouldn't bother. There is social assistance for the elderly. There is too much Aids. He lost his own daughter who was infected by her husband who used to be a soldier. He can't explain it, but thinks it cam from the USA, Malawi and SA. Miners brought it to Mozambique. Projects are only possible in groups. The government gives them information and advice.

Appendix 2.9: Participant analysis – Day Two

Carlos Bavo

Carlos did three interviews with female partners. The first one is a member of a religious sect (Zione). She is a war refugee. The main event for her was the loss of her husband. Carlos asked her to mention something that affected the whole community and she mentioned hunger. She said that hunger did not change much in the life of the community, she thinks that life goes on as usual. She suggested that hunger was caused by the floods, which swept away the seeds. She does not believe that production will get back to normal, for the soils have changed. People should employ better methods, such as tractors and ploughs, all of which are lacking in the village. Rain, therefore, is not the solution. She has no knowledge of an NGO, and for her the government does not do good work. She believes that local authorities do a much better work, for they liaise with the population. She said that healers have lost ground, but her own church is on the increase (this statement was made without any prompting from Carlos).

The second partner is a catholic war refugee who arrived in the village in 1977, which she then left because of the war. She said that hunger is the main problem as well as thefts. She complained that the community does not get together to try and solve the problem of hunger. Hunger brought suffering in its wake. There is nothing that can be done because there is no money and there are no means. Hunger is caused by drought, but she doesn't know what causes drought. She thinks however that God is responsible for it, though she is not quite sure. She only hopes that when it rains life will get back to normal. She mentioned a few interesting projects such as boreholes and cleaning of drains and cannals. She goes to local authorities for advice.

The third partner is a member of a religious sect called Zione (Betela). She was born nearby and came to live in this village in 1978 in order to stay with those settled in the wake of the 1977 floods. She mentioned floods as the main event, particularly because afterwards things took a shape unheard of in the region. Nothing grows. After the

1977 floods people were able to grow food in big quantities, but now it is different. She does not think hunger is caused by the floods because in her experience it is not like this. She believes that everything took a turn to the worse after the 2000 floods. She added that there is peace in the land, but no welfare. She knows of a few development projects, especially after the 2000 floods. A lot of people were helped by foreigners. Some of them continue to be assisted, especially widows and divorcees, but she does not know who gives them this assistance. Relations between local authorities and the population are good, so much so that whenever people need assistance or advice they approach the authorities.

D'bora Carvalho

D'bora carried out two interviews. Her first partner was very deffident. She arrived in 1982 as a war refugee. She told D'bora that before the interview there was an exchange with the authorities who told her what kind of questions we would be asking, but they did not tell her that notes would be taken. When there floods she was in Makeze and the only reason she stays in the village is because there are schools. Her main complaint is hunger, which is caused by the lack of rain. There is no rain because tradition is no longer respected. However, she thinks such things can only be carried out by the owners of the land (vinyi va tiko). In her own village the owners of the land would carry out traditional ceremonies to propitiate rain. Life changed in the village because of illnesses and death. Life has changed, but she cannot really explain what this means. She does not know of any projects, she can only remember those that operated around the time of the floods. Since 1996 she has been a member of a church and, therefore, she does not go to any witch-doctors. Her only source of advice now are the local authorities. Everything she wants to know she gets it from the authorities. The trouble with people is that they don't believe what the authorities tell them. The other problem is that the elders are dead. After the formal part of the interview was over she said that God knows where the floods come from. If people respect tradition then God will help them. She said floods brought soils with salt which make the land barren. D'bora had to keep asking her about how things were in her own village, because she kept saying that she didn't really know how things are here.

The second partner came in 1977. From the word go the lady complained about hunger; she said she was ill and thin. There is hunger because people don't have money. They can't live off the land because there is no rain. She doesn't know where all these things come from. She says she is too old to speculate about the causes of disaster. She is hungry. When she is ill she goes to hospital, even though she is a healer. The authorities are the ones who give them advice. Since she is not from that village she cannot say anything about the village. She said D'bora couldn't say anything either, because she is not from there (kuni vinyi va muti; mina a ni wa lomo; mina ni tendera svilo sva muti wa mina; nambhi wena ku lava ku tendera svilo sva muti wa wena u ku ntse). She believes that the dead should pick up someone who could tell the village what to do, but this is something which the owners of the land should do. She was quite intrusive about D'bora and advised her to take good care of her own mother; she told D'bora to tell her mother that the lady she interviewed sends her regards and that she is slim and old. D'bora was a bit scared... She also said she has a school.

Adozinda Sengulane

Adozinda had three interviews, two ladies and a man who is a pastor (Igreja Ave Maria de Moçambique). The pastor came in 1977. He mentioned the drought and the lack of opportunities for the kids to get further education. He complained about teachers who ask for money. He says he lost everything in the 2000 floods. They were sent by God. These were announced in the Bible: death and suffering in the year 2000 (A xikwembu si encile mapimu ya xona). He said that the floods brought red soils which are not ok for farming. People need tractors and ploughs because the soils have changed. The only thing that grows is grass, sometimes as high as himself. He complained that religious leaders are not consulted by the authorities because they know people well. He gave the example of orphans, most of whom can only be identified by religious leaders. Churches could help in reducing crime. He remembers asking for money to build a church (just like people need a bathroom to wash). He said that it would be useful to work with the government because the problems his flock has got are bigger than his community. Their main partner is the local village head.

Her second interview partner is a war refugee. She used to be a peasant, but now she does nothing. She mentioned war and hunger as the main events. She was not forthcoming and later she said she wouldn't say much because she was forced to come and give the interview. She didn't feel like saying anything, she only wanted to care about her own things.

The third partner is a female healer who arrived in 1992 (war refugee). She mentioned that there are too many deaths. She finds it strange that in one residential area 2-4 people may die in a row. There is also too much crime. Her family lived in the lower part of the city and she stayed in the village because of her work. The family lost everything, but nobody died. She said she didn't know where floods came from, all she could say was that they had made the land infertile. Later she said 'a mulandi a ni ntumbunuku wa yena'. She gave three explanations for the floods. People stopped respecting tradition and tried to combine religion and tradition. This cannot work. Secondly, she said people destroyed a sacred place (va hahlulile a mimpahlelu; a mimoya a yi hlonipiwanga). She also said that there is no understanding amongst the healers who come from different places. So trees were cut down; when they put watchmen ghosts came who talked to them and killed them. So nobody wanted to do the work and the cutting down of trees went on. Because of that the air could blow unhindered and carry the rain away; she said that it rains further afield, but not here because there are no trees holding it. She said healers should get together, but ultimately the only ones who can really do anything are the owners of the land. She complained that these did not seem concerned. She said there is an elite that presents the problems of the people to the authorities, but the government does not do much. She would very much like to rely on her professional colleagues for advice, but there is no understanding. Now that she knows what it is that we are interested in she will come back tomorrow with more information.

(We paused to discuss the recurring theme of damaged soils; we remarked that this is not just an explanation of the causes of disaster, but rather a plea for better inputs;

Patrício mentioned a study they carried out on behalf of the Presbyterian church where the same thing was said even though people had been given such inputs; so there was an element of empirical experience in the observations they made)

Patrício Langa

Patrício's first interview partner was a lady who was born there. She said before the creation of the village the place was called 'Mbalanin'. She said things were fine in the past, but with the war everything changed, even though the changes have not been too drastic. Now they have to live with war refugees and flood victims. Formerly everything was fine because it was only the Mbalan who were there; originally, those people were seeking refuge. She said that some people say that the problems were brought by the foreigners (non local people), but she doesn't think so. Her list of abnormal things is the arrival of war refugees and flood victims, but she does not have any direct experience of either. Nonetheless, she lost fields and inputs in the lower part because there was no time to remove the things. She says that life changed a lot, especiall hunger and poverty. The government provided some assistance, but mainly in clothing; this was inadequate for fighting hunger. Before the floods tractors would till the land for people, but now there is nothing. As for the causes of the misfortune she said that some people say it is brought by non-locals; she doesn't know. She says people just experience misfortune (war, floods and droughts), but she doesn't know where it all comes from; life simply changed. Non-locals are not to blame, because they too are fleeing misfortune. She doesn't know of any projects; she seeks advice from the local village head.

The second partner was a lady who arrived in 1977. She is a founding member of the residential area. When they arrived they had nearly everything they need to live. She said that people say floods come every five years, i.e. they are normal and regular. What causes them is not rain, but the dams built in SA which are opened when they are full. Floods nowadays cause more damage because of the dams. The primary cause of floods is God because he is the one who causes rain. However, God does not send floods, he only sends rains, so white people in SA are the ones who cause suffering in Moz. The 2000 floods were severe (a mati a ma kota marhefu, which confirms the biblical nature of the floods). She mentioned Noah from the bible and suggested that perhaps these floods are the fullfilment of the prophecy. There are things which show that God caused all this. Boers came by airplane and used cars to reach a point, but couldn't because there was a natural barrier which God had placed there. The floods brought hunger and suffering; in the aftermath there were NGOs which built good housing for the victims, much better than the ones built for those who came in 1977. Some NGOs would only give money to women, perhaps because they thought men would drink. However, she thinks this is not ok and it is a pity that the government didn't intervene; but then again, NGOs don't trust the government. She gets advice from the local village head. After the formal part of the interview she talked about 'Xihumbe', a sacred place where rain ceremonies can be carried out. Only the Mbalan can do this.

The third partner was a young man who has been living in the village since 1995. He is an electrician and was born in 1972. He was asked by the village head whether he knew anything about the floods. He told him to talk seriously, for this was a serious job and he shouldn't bring shame to the village. Patrício explained that he was not really interested in the 2000 floods, but rather in life in the village. The partner said he was born in Chibuto and moved to the village in 1995; after that he wanted to talk about the floods. The abnormal thing that happened recently was breaking his leg; he then went back to the floods and said most people in the village were flood victims. He said they suffer, they lack food. As for the causes he thinks it was rain and water from SA and Zimbabwe. This brought suffering and illnesses.

Carmen Bazar

Carmen carried out three interviews, two women and a mineworker. He lives in South Africa, but has a house in the village. Carmen noticed that her partners were only interested in talking about the floods. Her first interview partner is a war victim. He said he lost his cattle and that the abnormal thing in his life is hunger and illnesses. He said the illnesses, especially malaria, were caused by water pools from the floods. He said the water came from SA and Zimbabwe. He said people lost everything in the wake of the floods, especially cattle and crops. He says there is no project he knows of. He said there are white people who assisted locals in Zimilen.

The second interview partner was a lady who came from Mandhlakazi. She is a war victim. She said her main problem is lack of land, it is not fertile. She also spoke of illnesses and theft. These ills were caused by the floods. She mentioned floods after Carmen's insistence. She was not directly affected by the floods. Only her relatives who lived in the lower part. She herself didn't believe at first that the floods would come. The 2000 floods were different in all respects. She can't explain the causes or origins of the floods. She said the government gives them assistance, but it is not enough. She gets advice from the local authorities.

The third interview partner was a war refugee. She only wanted to talk about the floods. She said they had made the soil infertile. Carmen let her talk about the floods, then asked her about any other abnormal thing. She mentioned thieves. And also the infertility of the soils. She said the floods had brought along red soil which makes the land unproductive. She also said she had no money and, therefore, her children couldn't continue with their schooling. She lacks money to buy farmland (ma ektare). The floods were caused by the dam in Chokwe, which was filled by the dams in SA. She said they gave assistance to flood victims. She said people lost everything during the floods. The radio is her main source of information. The government also. There are no projects now, but during the floods there were some, especially in road construction and housing. Carmen thinks that the preparation they seem to have had prevented people from explaining freely what they thought.

Book Sambo

Book did his interviews in Portuguese because he is not from the region. His first partner was a lady who is a teacher. She's been living in the village for two years. She's from Maleice. She mentioned the 2000 floods as the main event. She was not a direct victim of these floods. She said that pensioners are the main victims of the floods because their papers were lost in the offices. She said the only preventive measure that can be taken is for people to move away from the lower part. People are stubborn, though. They never thought the floods would be like they were. As for the causes she said initially she didn't know. Book had the feeling that she didn't really understand the question and tried to reformulate it. She held fast and repeated she didn't know. She consulted with the elderly to know and promised to search that information to give Book later. She spoke of NGOs which helped people during the floods, but was critical of the criteria used to distribute that assistance. She also said there people among the victims who didn't get any assistance because of corruption. She said NGOs should give their assistance directly and through the local authorities. These are not trustworthy. She gets advice from her relatives (family problems with the parents of the husband).

The second partner was a man. He said there were NGOs which operated during the floods. The government also helped and seemed to be concerned with the situation. Book used the word 'whitemen' in order to get across the idea of NGOs. As for the causes of the floods he said that rumours have it that they are caused by the opening of dams in SA. He doesn't know. He said he'd lost a lot of things as a result of sharing with the flood victims. He didn't complain too much about having to share because the people needed assistance. Book noticed that some answers took care of many questions.

Notes

It seems to have paid off to change the strategy to asking about the reasons why these floods were so different. People reacted differently.

The main problem faced today was the feeling that interviewees seemed to know what to tell us. Some were forced to come and talk to us. All of them came prepared to talk about the floods and hunger.

It seems that we have to be patient. We should let people dish out the official discourse and later insist on personal experiences.

Appendix 3 : Questionnaire

Thank you very much for acepting to talk to us. This interview is part of a research project on certain goods in your lives. We would like to know what role these goods play in your lives, whether they have changed it significantly and whether you yourselves have found new ways of using these goods.

	Questionnaire number	

Survey on 'products of modernity'

Section I: Profile of interviewee

To be filled in by interviewer	Interview Date
Time: From _____ To _____	
Name of interviewer _____	Day
Comments:	Month
	Year
Area: _____	
Profession _____ Gender: M [1] F [2]	2 0 0
Age: _____ Education: _____	
To be filled in by supervisor	Interview checked? [Yes=1; No=2]
Name _____	
COMMENTS.	

Registry

Supervisor	Interviewer	Coded by	Entered by

Section II. Sva mahanyela mutini / domestic matters

1. (a) What type of housing describes the respondent's dwelling best?
   (read aloud and check only **one** answer in the codes column)
   (b) What is the main construction material used for the dwelling?
   (*Observe and ask about the structure and material; check one answer for the roof and one for the walls*)

(1a) Type of housing (check one only)	Code
a. Private dwelling	1
b. Week-End house	2
c. Hut	3
d. Hotel/Boarding house	4
e. Rented room	5
f. Rented hut	6
g. Other (specify):	7

Materials	(1b) Roofing	(1c) Walls
a. Building blocks	1	1
b. Corrugated iron	2	2
c. Reeds	3	3
d. Plastic/cloth	4	4
e. Grass	5	5
f. Mud	6	6

(1d) Water and light (one only)	Code	
	Sim	Não
a. Electricity	1	2
b. Piped water	1	2

2. Which one of these items applies to the housing of the respondent?

(a) Where do you fetch water? (one only)	Code
a. piped water in house	1
b. piped water in the court	2
c. free public tap	3
d. public tap with charges	4
e. Hawked water	5
f. borehole	6
g. rainwater tank	7
h. river or lake	8
i. dam/reservoir	9
j. stagnant water	10
k. well	11
l. source	12
m. other (specify):	13

(b) Housing (one only)	Code
a. Individual property	1
b. Rent	2
c. Comes with job (eg. domestic worker)	3

3. Consummer goods, tools and implements

Products	Code (check as applies)
a. TV	1
b. Radio	2
c. Fridge	3
d. Telephone line	4
e. Mobile phone	5
f. Car	6
g. Motorbike	7
h. Bicycle	8
i. Hoe	9
j. Plough	10
k. Pair of oxen (for ploughing)	11
l. Tractor	12
m. Fertilizer	13
n. Boots	14
o. Motor waterpump	15
p. Table	16
q. Pesticide	17
r. Improved seed	18
s. None	19
t. No answer	20

Section III. Sva uxaka ni svikumiwa ni svihundhla

4. Hi wihi ntirhu wa nwina?

Profession	Code (check as applies)
a. Peasant/farmer	1
b. Mechanic	2
c. Electrician	3
d. Nurse	4
e. Carpenter	5
f. Teacher	6
g. Trader	7
h. Migrant labourer	8
i. Watchman	9
j. Domestic worker	10
k. Office clerk	11
l. Another (specify)	12

5. What kind of tools do you use in your profession?

Tools	Official use

Appendices

6. Do you have these tools?

(not at work, but at home; *if self-employed, then at work*)

Ownership of tools			
Yes	1	No	2

7. What is the importance of the goods listed below?

*(check the strength of the response; only **one** answer is to be checked in each line)*

Importance of goods	Very important	Important	Indifferent	No importance	No importance at all	Don't know
a. Car	1	2	3	4	5	6
b. Piped water	1	2	3	4	5	6
c. Electricity	1	2	3	4	5	6
d. Telephone	1	2	3	4	5	6
e. Mobile phone	1	2	3	4	5	6
f. Bicycle	1	2	3	4	5	6
g. Motorbike	1	2	3	4	5	6
h. Fertilizer	1	2	3	4	5	6
i. Pesticide	1	2	3	4	5	6
j. Drought resistant seed	1	2	3	4	5	6
k. Plough	1	2	3	4	5	6
l. Hoe	1	2	3	4	5	6
m. Table	1	2	3	4	5	6
n. Working boots	1	2	3	4	5	6

8. What would your life be like if you did not have the following items:

*(check the strength of the response; only **one** answer is to be checked in each line)*

| Improve | 1 | No change | 2 | Deteriorate | 3 | Don't know | 4 |

9. What is the importance of the following institutions?

*(check the strength of the response; only **one** answer is to be checked in each line)*

Importance of institutions	Very high	High	The same	No importance	Absolutely no importance	Don't know
a. School	1	2	3	4	5	6
b. Hospital/clinic	1	2	3	4	5	6
c. Government administration	1	2	3	4	5	6
d. Police	1	2	3	4	5	6
e. Army barracks	1	2	3	4	5	6
f. Salary	1	2	3	4	5	6
g. Extension services (agriculture)	1	2	3	4	5	6
h. Post office	1	2	3	4	5	6
i. Civil registration	1	2	3	4	5	6
j. Market	1	2	3	4	5	6
k. NGOs	1	2	3	4	5	6
l. Disaster prevention and relief	1	2	3	4	5	6
m. Vaccination campaign	1	2	3	4	5	6
n. Government	1	2	3	4	5	6
o. Shops	1	2	3	4	5	6
p. High school	1	2	3	4	5	6

Appendices

10. What would life be like if these institutions were lacking:
*(check the strength of the response; only **one** answer is to be checked in each line)*

Improve	1	Unchanged	2	Deteriorate	3	Don't know	4

11. Which goods/products have changed your life most?

Products/goods	Official use

12. Which institutions changed your life most?

Institutions	Official use

Section IV. Disaster prevention and relief

13. What products and institutions exist in the region
(including the city of Xai-Xai)

Products and institutions	Yes	No	Don't know
a. Dam	1	2	8
b. Ditch	1	2	8
c. Irrigation systems	1	2	8
d. Rescue boats	1	2	8
e. Helicopters	1	2	8
f. Early warning system	1	2	8
g. Drought resistant crops	1	2	8
h. NGOs	1	2	8
i. Disaster prevention institute	1	2	8
j. Other (specify)	1	2	8

14. What do you use the following items for?
(use one code on the basis of the list below)

Ditch	Disaster prevention institute (IGC)	Early warning systems (SPA)	Drought resistant crops
(a)	(b)	(c)	(d)
Codes for 'dam' 1=control water volumes 2=keep water for irrigation 3=tourism 4=creating jobs for people 5=other (specify) 98=Don't know	Codes for 'IGC' 1=disaster prevention and control 2=rescue people 3=provide humanitarian assistance 4=seek assistance abroad 5=other (specify) 98=Don't know	**Codes for 'SPA'** 1=hazard warning 2=inform farmers 3=inform IGC 4=climate control 5=other 98=Don't know	Codes for 'drought resistant crops' 1=give people options 2=improve diet 3=respond to circumstances 4=diversify crops 5=other (specify) 98=Don't know

15. When are the following items available?

(check where necessary; only one answer per line)

Availability	All the time	Most of the time	The same	Not all the time	Not available	Don't know
a. Extension services	1	2	3	4	5	6
b. Borehole	1	2	3	4	5	6
c. Disaster prevention institute	1	2	3	4	5	6
d. Ditches	1	2	3	4	5	6
e. Dam	1	2	3	4	5	6
f. Irrigation system	1	2	3	4	5	6
g. Health centre	1	2	3	4	5	6

16. Do you fetch water at the „borehole'?

Yes	1	No	2

(if yes, continue with question 17)
(if no, continue with question 18)

17. How is your life inconvenienced if the borehole is broken? How often does the borehole break down? How long does it remain broken? What do you do when it is broken? Who repairs it? How quickly is it repaired? What are the criteria for eligibility (to fetch water)?

*Use the corresponding codes and check only **one** answer.*

Incovenience	How often	Length		
(a)	(b)	(c)	**Codes for 'incovenience'**	**Codes for 'how often'**
			1 =very strongly 2=strongly 3 =the same 4 =a bit 5 =nothing changes 98 =don't know	1 =once a month 2=twice a month 3 =thrice a month 4 =four times a month 5 =rarely 98 =don't know
Reaction	How quick	What to do	**Codes for 'length'**	**Codes for 'what to do'**
(d)	(f)	(g)	1 =a few instants 2 =1-3 days 3 =one week 4 =two weeks 5 =one or two months 98 =don't know	1 =we repair it ourselves 2 =a local repairs it 3 =we call technicians 4 =nothing/look for alternatives 5 =other (specify) 98 =don't know

Codes for 'quickness':	Codes for 'criteria':
1 = a few instants	1 = to be a resident
2 = 1-3 days	2 = to be a party member
3 = one week	3 = to be a church member
4 = two weeks	4 = if you pay dues
5 = one or two months	5 = other (specify)
98 = don't know	98 = don't know

18. I have come to the end of the interview. Do you have a question or a comment you would like to make?

Questions or comments	Official use
1.	
2.	
3.	

Thank you very much for your time. Everything you told me is important. I am grateful that you shared it with me. I wish to assure you that what you have told will be treated with care and will only be used in the context of research.

Thank you!

Notes

1. Macamo 2001, 2002a, 2003d, 2004.
2. see Macamo 2003c.
3. Cooper 1996; First 1983.
4. First 1983, Harries 1994.
5. The programme ran from 2000 to 2007. Key publications out of this programme are Probst and Spittler 2006, Loimeier et al 2005, Adogame et al 2008, and Cappai 2008.
6. See Liesegang 1967, Smith 1970, Rodney 1971, and Vilhena 1996 for further details on this period.
7. Commenting on Frazer's *Golden Bough*, particularly his ridicule of magical beliefs, Wittgenstein remarked that it was the attempt at understanding itself which produced difference, not necessarily any already existing differences. See Wittgenstein 1995.
8. I have written elsewhere on the mischievous role that can be played by researchers' need to tell plausible stories. See Jöckel and Macamo 2005.
9. One good example of this type of work is Nowotny 1989.
10. See Bonß 1995.
11. See Douglas 1992, and Douglas and Wildavsky 1982.
12. See chapter three and the concluding chapter for an extensive discussion.
13. See chapter one for a statement of this problem.
14. A good illustration of this is Ferguson's analysis of the betrayed hopes of Zambian copper miners which the author appears to take as an indictment of modernity (Ferguson 1999) as such. This suspicious attitude also takes the form of a general lack of precision in using the concept of modernity. In some anthropological writings (see for example Geschiere 1997) modernity is basically used in the sense of something that is simply contemporaneous.
15. A preliminary statement of the problem can be read in Macamo and Neubert 2008.
16. More recently, I have taken up these issues within the context of research projects which doctoral students of mine (at the University of Basel in Switzerland) are conducting on traffic in Burkina Faso and Mali (Pierrick Leu) and water supply systems in Zambia (Stefanie Bishop); a third project on industrially processed foods is likely to be undertaken in Mozambique by Natascha Wyss.
17. Throughout this book I use the word 'agency' as an adequate translation of Max Weber's *soziales Handeln*. However, in discussing Max Weber's concept in later chapters I prefer the translation 'social action' in order to avoid confusion, especially since earlier translations used 'social action'.

18. See chapter seven for a detailed discussion of this concept from phenomenological sociology.
19. See for exemple Appiah 1992: 232–38.
20. Adorno and Horkheimer 1972.
21. See his earlier work, Giddens 1979.
22. See Lepenies 2003 for a useful introduction.
23. See Appiah, 1992 for a critique of the use of this notion in the relevant discourses.
24. [P]our l'Afrique, échapper réellement à l'Occident suppose d'apprécier exactement ce qu'il en coûte de se détacher de lui; cela suppose de savoir jusqu'où l'Occident, insidieusement peut-être, s'est approché de nous; cela suppose de savoir, dans ce qui nous permet de penser contre l'Occident, ce qui est encore occidental; et de mesurer en quoi notre recours contre lui est encore peut-être une ruse qu'il nous oppose et au terme de laquelle il nous attend, immobile et ailleurs (...) L'Occident qui nous étreint ainsi pourrait nous étouffer. Aussi devons-nous, en Afrique, mettre à jour non seulement une compréhension rigoureuse des modalités actuelles de notre intégration dans les mythes de l'Occident, mais aussi des questions explicites qui nous permettraint d'être sincérement critiques face à ces 'corpus (Mudimbe 1982: 12–13).
25. I realise how problematic this adjective might be in the absence of a clarification of what is meant by the noun. In fact, I reserve it for intellectuals from the continent who, through their work and reflection, participate in the definition of a local space that they label 'African'. An extreme version of this understanding of Africanness is constructivist in its elaboration and goes as far as to suggest that no one is born an African, as they become aware of belonging to a community of destiny.
26. These are two articles published in The New York Daily Tribune in its issues of June 25 and August 8, 1853.
27. See Zingerle's critical comments on the reception of Max Weber's historical sociology (Zingerle 1981, especially pp. 28–74)
28. Shorter versions of most of these case studies have been previously published as indicated in the relevant chapters.
29. See eg Kuper 1988, Fabian 1983, and Asad 1973.
30. In his polemics against 'African studies' Kitching argued that the theoretical approaches used to account for African politics had failed to consider Africans' own responsibility for the problems of their continent. Furthermore, he feared that in failing to do this 'African studies' had upheld the colonial paternalist attitude towards Africans, which insisted in seeing the latter as children who could not be made responsible for their actions. This absence of 'adult taking of responsibility' was what depressed him most about 'African studies'.
31. Dieter Neubert (2006) has drawn attention to the pitfalls that litter the way to knowledge about Africa. These pitfalls, as he points out, derive from the assumption that social science concepts are accurate descriptions of European reality. This often leads to the treatment of this reality as the standard against which empirical observations of Africa are measured for accuracy.
32. A similar point is made by Mahmood Mamdani (1996) in his critique of what he calls 'history by analogy'.
33. Frederick Cooper (1996) explores the contradictions of colonial regulation of labour in British and French colonies in considerable detail.

34. Given the structure of this book, I offer descriptions of the background to the research terrain in a piecemeal way and with reference to the immediate methodological interest. I hope the reader will bear with me.
35. James Scott's *Seeing Like a State* (1998), in particular the chapter on Tanzania's forced villagisation programme, picked up familiar themes concerning the responses of post-independence African governments to the challenges of statehood. Those like Tanzania and Mozambique with a somewhat socialist orientation provided the rationale for the manner in which the State reacted to the floods in 1977 – by resettling people in a *communal* village – but the immediate and overarching logic was concerned with the commitment to the belief that it was the state's duty to 'organise' people. There is a controversial debate in Mozambique on this issue (see Casal 1996, Saul 1985, Geffray 1990, Egero 1986, among others), the details of which, for example to what extent villagisation was 'forced' and gave the rebels a social basis, are less important than the social situations it produced. In fact, the transformation of Mbalalen into a communal village brought together people from different regions and clans, all of whom were faced with a new form of life premised on the presence and use of 'products of modernity' as I intend to show in this book.
36. Patrice Lumumba was a Congolese nationalist who led Congo to independence from Belgium and was later overthrown and assassinated by rival Congolese politicians, with external support. His name stands for commitment to the cause of African freedom and self determination and has been adopted by many throughout the continent as homage to what is seen as his martyrdom.
37. See Jacques 1995 [1935] for a good historical description of the region.
38. Fortuna (1993) and Isaacman (1996) offer solid descriptions of the commercial exploitation of this potential. See also Vail and White 1980.
39. The study was conducted by Martin Brandt, a German physical geography student from the University of Erlangen-Nuremberg, whom I helped with contacts in the field (personal communication). Zacarias Ombe, a Mozambican geographer who has worked extensively in the region, argues (personnal communication) that villagers do have ways of ensuring that soils do not become completely degraded. According to him, they simply leave plant roots to rot and replenish the soils with badly needed nutrients (see also Ekblom 2006 for an archaeological description of the formation of the soils).
40. In appendix 3, I reproduce the questionnaire of a survey on 'products of modernity' which I conducted in Patrice Lumumba communal village. I use some of the data from the survey to describe the village and, generally, to inform my own understanding of the context. The case studies I selected for the reflection in this book did not require a closer analysis of the data that the survey yielded.
41. This is only a preliminary introduction to the terrain. I will come back to a more analytical introduction which will integrate elements of phenomenological sociology, seeking to bring to light the different lifeworlds constructed by villagers in their relationship to the natural and social worlds. I will do this in chapter four.
42. I am paraphrasing Marshall Sahlins' memorable critique of accounts of social worlds which fail to acknowledge the agency of the people who make such worlds possible (Sahlins 1995).
43. See Parsons 1964.

44. Wagner (1990) has very insightful discussions of the historical conditions of emergence of the social sciences in Europe.
45. See Durkheim 1988.
46. Raewyn Connell's critique oft he idea of „classical theory" (Connell 1997) is well taken and actually informs my own critique of the normative nature of social scientific approaches to Africa.
47. See Durkheim 1984.
48. See in particular Mudimbe 1988 and Mbembe 2001.
49. See Neugebauer 1989, Ruch and Anyanwu 1981, Wright 1979.
50. Macamo 1999.
51. Irele 1975 uses this expression.
52. Conrad 1975.
53. See the discussion of labour policy by Cooper 1996, Macamo 2002, Vail 1986.
54. Alfred Schütz and Parsons engaged one another passionately by correspondence. See Schütz and Parsons 1977.
55. *Svigonko* is the plural form of *xingonko*.
56. See Barry 1996, Barstow 1994, Scarre 1987.
57. Ahrendt-Schulte 2002, Susini 2008, Segl 1989.
58. The 'bathroom' in the village is usually a construction without a roof and detached from the main building, usually at the back end of the yard.
59. Frédéric Apfell-Marglin has an interesting discussion of these issues in Marglin 1990 and 1996.
60. A recent, useful and topical discussion of Dilthey's thoughts on the matter can be found in Göller 2000 (especially pp. 20–40)
61. Weber 1992: 86–87.
62. Weber writes as much in his discussion of the types of religious association where he draws attention away from the essence of religion towards the conditions and consequences of a very specific form of association (Weber 1980: 245).
63. Zingerle's (1981) discussion of Weber's reception is particularly instructive in this regard.
64. There is more on this in the following chapter.
65. The case study in chapter five deals specifically with this issue.
66. Discussed in the previous section.
67. See also Misztal 1996, Stompka 1999, Hollis 1998, Lagerspetz 1998, Seligman 1997, and Coleman 1990 for the way in which social scientists have sought to place trust at the centre of theorising.
68. Swedberg 1991, 1997; Swedberg, Himmelstrand, and Brulin 1987.
69. Clear examples in Germany are Japp 1996 and Halfman and Japp 1990.
70. Nico Stehr (2001) uses the notion of risk to define modern society as fragile.
71. See also Van Loon (2002) who places the blame on what he considers to be a technological culture and Lash, Szerszynski, and Wynne (1996) who focus on the uncritical use of the social sciences to confer authority to environmentalism.
72. In the meantime, this particular perspective has been further developed in a lively Anglo-American discussion of a so-called 'neo-liberal governmentality'. A good summary of the positions and research questions can be found in a special issue of Economy and Society (2000). In Macamo (2006) I chime in into this discussion.

73. See also Luhmann (1992: 142) and his assertion to the effect that talking about risk is only possible under circumstances in which consequences can be attributed to decisions.
74. See Luhmann (1993: 328).
75. He develops this claim in his 1993 paper on the 'morality of risk and the risk of morality' (Luhmann 1993: 327–28). He writes (translation: EM): 'The distinction between hazards and risks makes it immediately clear that technological progress, even if in itself it is relatively not perilous, leads to an increase in risks. It transforms hazards into risks simply through the creation of possibilities of decision-making that were not there' (p. 328).
76. See Perrow 1999.
77. The German terminology emphasises process. In fact, social relationships are oriented towards the constitution of community or society.
78. See also Lars Clausen's and other contributors' useful introduction into the thoughts of Tönnies (Clausen 1981; 1991).
79. See previous chapter.
80. I draw attention here to Luhmann's definition of risk as something ensuing from a decision.
81. Barbara Misztal stresses in her overview of sociological approaches to trust that this notion is also central to Max Weber's distinction between communal and associative social relationships. Each one of them rests on trust (Misztal 1996: 56–8). See also Geramanis 2002.
82. I borrow this metaphor from Bruno Latour (1991).
83. Particularly Tenbruck 1999; see also Schoreder 1992.
84. Soyinka's, arguably, best play in which a British colonial administrator fails to understand the deeper cultural sources of the action of his African subjects and is reduced to the impotent role of an observer of a tragedy unleashed by his actions at the same time as his actions fail to provide a plausible explanation for what they unleash. A young Yoruba male sent by the district officer to England to study, comes home upon hearing news of his King's death, on the culturally informed assumption that his father, the King's horseman, would have to commit ritual suicide to accompany the King on his last journey. The district officer prevents the ritual suicide by jailing the King's horseman, forcing his son, the medical student, to take his father's place in order to allow tradition and culture to take their course.
85. Thomas Luckmann (2002) came back to the notion of 'communication' and placed it at the centre of his own phenomenological sociology.
86. See also Sen's (1977) critique of rational choice theories in economics.
87. See, for example, Blanchet et al 2000.
88. In connection with this there is an interesting statement by Norman Denzin: 'The interview is a way of writing the world, a way of bringing the world into play. The interview is not a mirror of the so-called external world, nor is it a window into the inner life of the person…" (Denzin 2001: 25).
89. Please, refer to the discussion in chapter one.
90. For this, see Ian Hacking (1999, especially pp. 3–34) and his useful critique and clarification of this much abused concept.
91. At the time when I was conducting my research the local administrator of the village was a lady by the name of Sarifa Amade.

92. Just to give an idea of these numbers, the recent extension of the village to accommodate flood victims consisted of a settlement of close to 500 families.
93. The Gaza-Nguni were Zulu conquerors originating from the Natal area of South Africa in the wake of the so-called Mfecane wars of the first half of the eighteenth century. See Liesegang 1967 and Vilhena 1996 for more details on this period.
94. *Régulo* was the official Portuguese name for a traditional chief.
95. See chapter seven for further details.
96. See chapter seven for further details.
97. See chapter six for a thorough discussion of this issue.
98. See Junod (1924) for more details.
99. See chapter seven for details.
100. There is a saying in Tsonga which goes 'where there is death, there is also a witch.'
101. This notion is at the heart of fundamental differences in the philosophy of the social sciences. See relevant discussions in Knowles 1990 (especially the chapters by Ruben pp. 95–118 and Skorupski pp.119–34) and Longino 1990.
102. I owe this notion of 'scheme of intelligibility' to a French sociologist, Jean-Michel Bertholot (1990, especially pp. 62–82). He offers, to my mind, one of the best accounts of social scientific activity. As my discussion of the explanatory framework will immediately show, I draw considerably from his account. Berthelot's ideas resonate with those of Robert Brown (1970), who, as far as I can ascertain, availed himself of Hempel's very useful discussion of the meaning of 'why' in scientific explanation (Hempel 1970).
103. An earlier version of this case study was published as "Nach der Katastrophe ist die Katastrophe – Die 2000er Überschwemmung in der dörflichen Wahrnehmung in Mosambik" (Macamo 2003).
104. See introduction and chapter four.
105. Bohnsack's distinction can be quite confusing for those who know that Max Weber's notion of 'verstehen' has always been translated as 'interpretation' as in 'interpretive sociology'.
106. On the 'existential determination' of knowledge see Mannheim 1995: 229.
107. See 'hermeneutische Wissenssoziologie' (Hitzler et al 1999), for a closely related approach, and especially Honer's (1994) concept of 'lebensweltliche Ethnographie' (lifeworld ethnography).
108. The drawings depicted two opposing views of disaster. One picture consisted of a flood situation with people drowning and being rescued, respectively, whereas the second depicted a drought situation where peasants were unable to till the soil.
109. See information in transcription symbols in the preliminary pages. VGD stands for 'visualized group discussion'. The attached number refers to either of the two group discussions that were carried out. Participants were coded by order of appearance in the discussion with capital letters of the alphabet. The smaller case letters 'm' and 'f' stand for 'male' and 'female'. The numbers refer to the location on the tape.
110. Reference is to the two drawings depicting the disaster.
111. An earlier version of this case study was published as "Die Flut in Mosambik – Zur unterschiedlichen Deutung von Krisen und Katastrophen durch Bauern und Nothilfeapparat " (Macamo and Neubert 2003b).
112. See in this connection samples of fieldwork notes and discussions in appendix 2.

113. This apparatus includes state institutions as well as cooperating international organisations.
114. See Neubert and Macamo 2003.
115. Evans-Pritchard (1976) drew attention to this several decades ago in his seminal study on Azande witchcraft.
116. See table 1 in the appendix. These are statistics collected and published by Mozambique's National Directorate for Water (DNA).
117. I am quoting from tables provided by the Mozambican Metereological Bureau in Maputo. The full table for Xai-Xai can be found in the appendix.
118. This thesis is stated fully in Ruth First's (1983) study of the Mozambican miner which seeks to show that he is half-proletarian by virtue of the nature of his integration into the capitalist system spawned by mining capital in Southern Africa.
119. This is called the National Institute for Disaster Management. It was set up by CARE International in the early eighties and was known by the official name Department for the Prevention and Management of Natural Disasters until very recently (2002). It consists of chapters in all ten provinces of Mozambique and its brief is to devise strategies to prevent disasters and to help in coping with their consequences.
120. *ndhambhi yi hi kanganyisile.*
121. *mati ma nbhonyile hinkwasvo.*
122. The source of this information is a set of press releases by the state controlled *Instituto de Comunicação Social*, which published this information as a report five months after the floods. The report contains not only weather forecasts but also situational reports written by the provincial government, charting all the measures taken to cope with the floods (Instituto de Comunicação Social 2002).
123. ... der subjektive Ursprung gesellschaftlichen Wissens und das gesellschaftliche a priori – die empirische Priorität des gesellschaftlichen Wissensvorrates gegenüber dem subjektiven Wissensbestand – konstituieren im Aneignungsprozess gemeinsam das Netzwerk der Strukturen der Lebenswelt. Was sich dem Subjekt in der natürlichen Einstellung als Lebenswelt zeigt, was es – subjektiv – als Lebenswelt erlebt und erfährt, zeigt sich ihm zugleich als sozial konstituiert, als Ergebnis gesellschaftlichen Handelns und vergesellschafteter Erfahrungen (Soeffner 1987: 802)
124. I discuss the analytical implications of this question in a joint article with Dieter Neubert (Macamo and Neubert 2003c).
125. It should be borne in mind that the floods are not seen as the problem on account of the fact that they are usually followed by good harvests.
126. During the first two years of my research (2001 and 2002) I carried out fieldwork in the spring and summer of each year. During my first visit to the field I carried out about forty interviews with people of different backgrounds in the village and also with representatives of the relief apparatus, both governmental and non-governmental. My initial interviews with local informants were biographical and aimed at collecting information on the evolution of livelihoods in the region. Theoretically, my main interest was in identifying local concepts for disaster and crisis. In the following year I conducted further interviews with selected informants (20) which I then rounded up with semi-structured questionnaires carried out by students from Eduardo Mondlane University in Maputo who interviewed sixty villagers on my

behalf. Most of these interviews were recorded and have, to a large part, been subsequently transcribed. The two interview excerpts I will look at in this chapter are taken from this pool.

127. These were made available to me by an official at the local radio station.
128. These comprise the following areas: health, agriculture, public works, trade and tourism, transports, police, and disaster relief.
129. I am drawing on interviews with leading members of the clan.
130. This refers to the famous 'Mfecane' towards the end of the first half of the nineteenth century.
131. There are two main rituals: one is *Ku-pahla*, a memorial service to the ancestor spirits which takes place early in the year; the other is *Mbelele*, a ritual exorcism of evil spirits, that is, spirits that cause harm.
132. The level of hostility between prophetic and Pentecostal religious groups and traditional healers is very high, as I was given to understand in the interviews I conducted with representatives of both camps. Traditional healers accused religious groups of using magic spells to undermine their authority in the village. One traditional leader complained to me that the way leading up to his homestead was littered with spells sown by members of a notorious prophetic sect known as 'Zione'.
133. In one informal conversation the need for an explanation was put in this way: 'where there is death, there is a also witch' (*la kunga fiwa kuni noyi*).
134. This place was the sacred forest of the Mbalan clan. At my request the village secretary as well as several other dignataries took me to this forest. To their great astonishment and disappointment, we did not find signs of a sacred forest at the place where they had said it would be. The place had been turned into a small cultivated plot of land with maize, pumpkin, and peanuts growing under the blazing sun. I had been told that the sacred place was guarded by a snake and that any attempt to grow crops there would be magically stalled. There was neither a sign of a snake nor of manipulated fields.
135. '*A loku va fika vanhu a vaha rungulisiwe.*'
136. 'Order' (*nawu*) is recurrent in the conversations. An interview partner said with reference to this: '*Hi biwa hi tindhambi, hi rifu ni jandza hiku a hina nawu*' (we are beaten by floods, death and droughts because we have no order).
137. See discussion of the notion of social relationship in chapter four. Check chapter number!
138. The literal translation of the word would be 'the quality of that which is hard/solid' or 'that which renders something else hard/solid'.
139. This is something that is also known from medieval Europe's stories of witches.
140. An earlier version of this case study was published as "Accounting for Disaster – Memories of War in Mozambique" (Macamo 2006b).
141. They were transcribed by Obede Baloi, a sociologist and Protestant minister. Although Tsonga is one of the most widely-spoken languages in Mozambique, few native speakers, especially the better educated ones, are able to write in it. Among the educated, those more likely to be competent in the language are Protestant ministers, whose churches – mostly offshoots of mission churches – adopted vernaculars as their liturgical languages.

142. See also Sacks 1992a and 1992b, Lena Jayyusi's work (Jayyusi 1984 and 1991), Watson 1994, Hester and Eglin 1997, Silverman 1998, and Sharrock 1974.
143. I use a transcription system largely borrowed from conversational analysis. I indicate my interview partners through the letters of the alphabet in capitals plus a small f or m for female or male, respectively. The transcriptions seek to reflect the flow of speech; for this reason I dispense with punctuation marks. I use italics to indicate foreign words (in this case, non-English words). The sign ":" indicates a stretch in the utterance of a word; the repetition of the sign marks the length of the stretch. Everything between the signs @ indicate laughter in speech. Words between the signs ° indicate that they were uttered in a low voice. Bold indicates loudness. The sign "(.)" indicates a pause and the number of dots within the brackets indicate the length of the pause.
144. This is a Tsonga loan word from Portuguese and means 'father'; it is a generally employed as a form of address for male strangers. In this case it was addressed at me as interviewer.
145. *Titiya* is a Tsonga loan word from the Portuguese and means 'aunt', but is also used to refer to elder women who are not relatives, but command authority. In this case, the interviewee was referring to the lady at whose home the interviews took place.
146. Reference is to demobilised Renamo soldiers as well as Renamo politicians.
147. The original Tsonga word is *usiwana* and has a much wider semantic field than poverty and its suggestion of material deprivation. It means what the interviewee goes on to explain: no relatives, nothing to live on.
148. *Matsanga* was the popular word used to describe Renamo fighters. It is a reference to Renamo's first leader, André Matsangaíssa.
149. There is a widely read book in Mozambique documenting war atrocities. It carries the title *Dumba Nengue*, a Tsonga idiomatic expression meaning literally 'trust your legs'. It can be translated as 'run for your life' (Magaia 1988). Running, *ku tsutsuma*, is the most recurrent word describing what people do during the war. They are always 'running'.
150. This is the story of a kidnapped lady who interceded on behalf of a young girl who could no longer walk from exhaustion.
151. Unfortunately, none of the refugees I spoke with spent any considerable length of time at a Renamo base. They were either never kidnapped or were allowed to return home, or even managed to flee. In the interviews, however, there are references to life on the other side. Young men were basically conscripted into the rebel army; women became the wives of the fighters, and the older men and women lived on the outskirts of Renamo military bases; as soon as the fighters felt that they could be trusted not to flee, they were allowed to accompany the fighters on their looting sprees. One interviewee described these as *ku famba vayiva-yiva*, which means 'stealing around'.
152. Number in brackets indicates frequency of references in the transcripts.
153. The interview partner uses the Portuguese word *vizinho*.
154. Hester and Eglin (1997) argue that talk is 'culture-in-action'.
155. Renamo fighters.
156. Josina Machel is a national hero and was the wife of the first Mozambican Head of State, Samora Machel, against whose Marxist politics Renamo claimed to be fighting.

157. Samora Machel was Mozambique's first Head of State and Frelimo leader.
158. These were members of the local community with no special training, but with authority in the village.
159. An earlier version of this case study was published as « Biographical knots » (Macamo 2002).
160. Igreja Assembleia de Deus, 1984.
161. Jonah 2:8-11: 'They that observe lying vanities forsake their own mercy. But I will sacrifice into thee with the voice of thanksgiving; I will pay that that I have vowed. Salvation is of the LORD. And the LORD spake into the fish, and it vomited out Jonah upon the dry land' (Stirling 1960).
162. I borrowed this idea from Benetta Jules-Rosette, an American sociologist of religion, who presented it at a conference at the École des Hautes Études en Sciences Sociales in Paris in May 1999 during a talk entitled 'La reconstruction des traditions religieueses et le dialogue hermnenéutique en(vers) l'Afrique: nouvelles perspectives'.
163. I published results of this work in Macamo 2001, 2002a, 2003c, 2003d, and 2004.
164. In several interviews members of nearly all Pentecostal sects I spoke with mentioned St. Mark 16:15-18: 'And he said into them, Go ye into all the world, and preach the gospel to every creature. He that believeth and is baptized shall be saved; but he that believeth not shall be damned. And these signs shall follow them that believe; In my name shall they cast out devils; they shall speak with new tongues; they shall take up serpents; and if they drink any deadly thing, it shall not hurt them; they shall lay hands on the sick, and they shall recover'. (Stirling 1960).
165. See Macamo 2000 for more information on the Swiss Mission in Mozambique.
166. Dr. Gagnaux is meant who was murdered by the rebels during Mozambique's civil war in the eighties.
167. 'Coming out' is the literal translation of the Tsonga word (a Bantu language spoken in Southern Mozambique), *ku huma*. The idea behind it is that some spirits have taken possession of a person and want to reveal themselves. In the context of witchcraft and magic spirit possession this is one of the main qualifications for the practice of witchcraft. A person with spirit possession is expected to learn to control them and use them for divination. Often illness, misfortune, and social problems are signs that a person has been elected as an abode for spirits.
168. The 'Zion' church is a highly decentralised prophetic sect which is very popular among the economically weaker urban groups in Mozambique (see Cruz e Silva 2002, Pfeiffer et al 2007 and, for a more historical perspective, Anderson 2000).
169. The complete interview, as well as other interviews from the same research, is stored in a personal archive of the author.
170. These are well described by Teresa Cruz e Silva (2001) as important carriers of African nationalism in Mozambique.
171. See Macamo 2004.
172. They even became known as *ceux de la prière* (those who pray), (van Butselaar 1984).
173. A Swiss missionary, Henri-Alexandre Junod had already drawn attention to the fact that women worked more than men in Tsonga societies (Junod 1913).
174. See Biber 1987 and Harris 1959.

175. See Silva Rego 1960 and Schädel 1984.
176. On colonial labour legislation see Lopes Galvão 1925 and Aurillac 1964.
177. For more on this see Macamo 2003d.
178. Keith Thomas' (1980) work is in this respect highly enlightening.
179. Reference should be made of Zingerle's (1996) discussion of Durkheim's analysis of magic, which is consistent with the kind of reading that the missionaries applied to their own mission. See also his earlier edited volume on the relationship between magic and modernity (Zingerle 1987).
180. Mpapele 1967. There is a slightly different version of the same book, but in another language, namely Xitswa, with the title *Wutomi gi nene* (the right conduct of life) written by Navess and Bartling (1979).
181. Sometimes he would listen in on the conversations, but usually he simply went to look for a place in the shade a few metres away from us and patiently wait for me to finish.
182. The fieldnotes in Appendix 2 give a few hints about his influence on interview partners.
183. See some thoughts on this in a short paper I co-authored with Andrea Jöckel (Jöckel and Macamo 2005a). See also Oevermann (2008) and Macamo (2008) for more on the problem of validity of my interview material.

Bibliography

Adogame, Afe/Echtler, Magnus/Vierke, Ulf (eds.) (2008): *Unpacking the New – Critical Perspectives on Cultural Syncretization in Africa and Beyond.* Hamburg/Münster: Lit.
Ahrendt-Schulte, Ingrid (ed.) (2002): *Geschlecht, Magie und Hexenverfolgung.* Bielefeld: Verlag für Regionalgeschichte.
Aijmer, Karin/Stenström, Anna-Brita (2005): Approaches to Spoken Interaction. *Journal of Pragmatics* 37, 11, 1743-1751.
Alden, Chris (2001): *Mozambique and the Construction of the New African State: From Negotiations to Nation Building.* Basingstoke: Palgrave Macmillan.
Anderson, Allan (2000): *Zion and Pentecost – The Spirituality and Experience of Pentecostal and Zionist/Apostolic Churches in South Africa.* Pretoria: University of South Africa Press.
Anderson, David/Johnson, Douglas (eds.) (1995): *Revealing Prophets: Prophecy in Eastern African Prophecy.* London: James Currey.
Appiah, Kwame A. (1992): *In my Father's House – Africa in the Philosophy of Culture.* London: Methuen.
Asad, Talal (ed.) (1973): *Anthropology and the Colonial Encounter.* New York: Humanities Press.
Augé, Marc (ed.) (1974): *La construction du monde: religion, représentations, idéologie.* Paris: Maspéro.
Augier, Mie (1999): Some Notes on Alfred Schütz and the Austrian School of Economics: Review of Alfred Schütz's Collected Papers, Vol. IV. Edited by H. Wagner, G. Psathas and F. Kersten (1996). *Review of Austrian Economics* 11, 1-2, 145-162.
Aurillac, M. (1964): Les provinces portugaises d'outre-mer ou la 'force des choses'. *Revue Juridique et Politique, Tome XVIII,* 1, 239-262.
Austin, Kathi/Minter, William (1994): *Invisible Crimes: U.S. Private Intervention in the War in Mozambique.* Washington, DC: Africa Policy Information Center.
Azarian, Reza (2000): *The Basic Framework in the General Sociology of Harrison C. White.* Stockholm: Department of Sociology, Stockholm University.
Barnes, Barry (1985): *About Science.* Oxford: Blackwell.
Barry, Jonathan (ed.) (1996): *Witchcraft in Early Modern Europe – Studies in Culture and Belief.* Cambridge: Cambridge University Press.
Barstow, Anne L. (1994): *Witchcraze – A New History of the European Witch Hunts.* New York: Pandora.
Baudrillard, Jean (1992): *L'Illusion de la Fin ou la grève des évènements.* Paris: Éditions Galilé.
Bayart, Jean-François (2000): Africa in the World: A History of Extraversion. *African Affairs* 99, 217-267.

Beattie, John/Middleton, John (1969): *Spirit Mediumship and Society in Africa*. New York: Africana Publishing Corporation.
Beck, Ulrich (1992): *Risk Society: Towards a New Modernity*. Thousand Oaks/London/New Delhi: Sage.
Beck, Ulrich/Giddens, Anthony/Lash, Scott (1994): *Reflexive Modernization: Politics, Tradition and Aesthetics in the Modern Social Order*. Cambridge: Polity.
Becker, Gary (1976): *The Economic Approach to Human Behavior*. Chicago: The University Press of Chicago.
Beckert, Jens (1996): What is Sociological about Economic Sociology? Uncertainty and the Embeddedness of Economic Action. *Theory and Society* 25, 803-840.
Beckmann, Jörg (2004): Mobility and Safety. *Theory, Culture & Society* 21, 4-5, 81-100.
Behrend, Heike (ed.). (1999): *Spirit Possession, Modernity & Power in Africa*. Oxford: James Currey.
Berard, Tim J. (2005): Evaluative Categories of Action and Identity in Non-Evaluative Human Studies Research: Examples from Ethnomethodology. *Qualitative Sociology Review* 1, 1, 5-30.
Berger, Peter/Luckmann, Thomas (1966): *Die gesellschaftliche Konstruktion der Wirklichkeit*. Frankfurt: Fischer.
Bernstein, Peter (1996): *Against the Gods: The Remarkable Story of Risk*. New York: John Wiley.
Berthelot, Jean-Michel (1990): *L'Intelligence du social – Le pluralisme explicatif en sociologie*. Paris: Presses Universitaires de France.
Berthoud, P. (1888): *La Mission Romande a la Baie de Delagoa*. Lausanne: Georges Bridel.
Biber, Charles (1987): *Cent ans au Mozambique – le parcours d'une minorité*. Lausanne: Editions du Soc.
Bierschenk, Thomas/Schareika, Nikolaus (eds.) (2004): *Lokales Wissen - Sozialwissenschaftliche Perspektiven*. Hamburg/Münster: Lit.
Billig, Michael (1996): *Arguing and Thinking: A Rhetorical Approach to Social Psychology, Revised Edition*. Cambridge: Cambridge University Press.
Blanchet, Alain/Ghiglione, Rodolphe/Massonnat, Jean/Trognon, Alain (2000): *Les techniques d'enquête en sciences sociales*. Paris: Dunod.
Bloor, David (1997): *Wittgenstein, Rules and Institutions*. London: Routledge.
Blumer, Harold (1986): *Symbolic Interactionism – Perspective and Method*. Berkeley: University of California Press.
Boden, Deirdre (1990): The World as It Happens. Ethnomethodology and Conversation Analysis. In: Ritzer, George (ed.): *Frontiers of Social Theory: The New Synthesis*. New York: Columbia University Press, 185-213.
Boden, Deirdre/Zimmerman, Don H. (eds.) (1991): *Talk and Social Structure*. Oxford: Polity Press.
Bohnsack, Ralf/Nentwig-Gesemann, Iris Nohl, Arnd-Michael (eds.) (2001): *Die dokumentarische Methode und ihre Forschungspraxis – Grundlagen qualitativer Sozialforschung*. Opladen: Leske und Budrich.
Bohnsack, Ralf (1992): Dokumentarische Interpretation von Orientierungsmustern. Verstehen-Interpretieren-Typenbildung in wissenssoziologischer Analyse. In: Meuser, M./Sackmann, R. (eds.): *Analyse sozialer Deutungsmuster – Beiträge zur empirischen Wissenssoziologie*. Pfaffenweiler: Centaurus.

Bohnsack, Ralf (1993): *Rekonstruktive Sozialforschung – Einführung in Methodologie und Praxis qualitativer Forschung.* Opladen: Leske und Budrich.

Bohnsack, Ralf/Nentwig-Gesemann, Iris/Nohl, Arnd-Michael (2001): Einleitung – Die dokumentarische Methode und ihre Forschungspraxis. In: Bohnsack, R./Nentwig-Gesemann, I./Nohl, A.-M. (eds.): *Die dokumentarische Methode und ihre Forschungspraxis.* Opladen: Leske und Budrich.

Bonß, Wolfgang (1995): *Vom Risiko – Unsicherheit und Ungewissheit in der Moderne.* Hamburg: Hamburger Edition.

Brown, Robert (1970): *Explanation in Social Science.* Chicago: Aldine Publishing Company.

Burt, Ronald S./Guilarte, Miguel/Raider, Holly J./Yasuda, Yuki (2002): Competition, Contingency, and the External Structure of Markets. *Advances in Strategic Management* 19, 167-217.

Cabrita, João M. (2000): *Mozambique: the Tortuous Road to Democracy.* New York: Palgrave Macmillan.

Camic, Charles/Gross, Neil (1998): Contemporary Developments in Sociological Theory: Current Projects and Conditions of Possibility. *Annual Review of Sociology* 24, 453-476.

Cappai, Gabriele (ed.) (2008): *Forschen unter Bedingungen kultureller Fremdheit.* Wiesbaden: VS Verlag für Sozialwissenschaften.

Casal, Adolfo Yanez (1996): *Antropologia e desenvolvimento – As aldeias comunais de Moçambique.* Lisbon: Instituto Nacional de Investigação Científica Tropical.

Chan, Stephen/Venâncio, Moisés (1998): *War and Peace in Mozambique.* Houndmills/Basingstoke/Hampshire/New York: Macmillan Press/St. Martin's Press.

Chilcote, Ronald H. (1972): *Emerging Nationalism in Portuguese Africa: Documents.* Stanford: Hoover Institution Press, Stanford University.

Chriss, James J. (2002): Bogen on Social Theory, Rules, and Order (Book Review). *Human Studies* 25, 2, 241-249.

Clausen, Lars (ed.) (1991): *Hundert Jahre „Gemeinschaft und Gesellschaft" – Ferdinand Tönnies in der internationalen Diskussion.* Opladen: Leske und Budrich.

Clausen, Lars (ed.) (1981): *Ankunft bei Tönnies – Soziologische Beiträge zum 125. Geburtstag von Ferdinand Tönnies.* Kiel: Mühlhau.

Clausen, Lars/Dombrowsky, Wolf R. (1983): *Einführung in die Soziologie der Katastrophen.* Zivilschutzforschung Bd.14, Schriftenreihe der Schutzkommission. Bonn-Bad Godesberg: Bundesamt für Zivilschutz.

Coleman, James S. (1990): *Foundations of Social Theory.* Cambridge: Harvard University Press.

Coleman, James S. (1994): A Rational Choice Perspective on Economic Sociology. In: Smelser, N./ Swedberg, R. (eds.): *The Handbook of Economic Sociology.* Princeton: Princeton University Press.

Comaroff, Jean/Comaroff, Joan (eds.) (1993): *Modernity and Its Malcontents – Ritual and Power in Postcolonial Africa.* Chicago: Chicago University Press.

Connell, Raewyn W. (1997): "Why Is Classical Theory Classical?" In: *The American Journal of Sociology*, Vol. 102, No. 6. 1511-1557.

Conrad, Joseph (1975): *Heart of Darkness.* Harmondsworth: Penguin Books.

Cooper, Frederick (1996): *Decolonization and African Society – the Labor Question in French and British Africa.* Cambridge: Cambridge University Press.

Cooper, Frederick (2001): What is the Concept of Globalization Good for? An African Historian's Perspective. *African Affairs*, 100, 189-213.
Corbrigde, Stuart (2007): The (Im)possibility of Development Studies. *Economy and Society* 36, 2, 179-211.
Coulter, Jeff (1979): Beliefs and Practical Understanding. In: Psathas, G. (ed.): *Everyday Language*. New York: Irvington Press.
Coulter, Jeff (1983): Contingent and *A Priori* Structures in Sequential Analysis. *Human Studies* 6, 4, 361–76.
Coulthard, Malcolm (1977): *An Introduction to Discourse Analysis*. London: Longman.
Crossley, Nick (2001): The Phenomenological Habitus and Its Construction. *Theory and Society* 30, 1, 81-120.
Cruz e Silva, Teresa (2002): Entre a exclusão social e o exercício da cidadania – Igrejas 'zione' do Bairro Luís Cabral na cidade de Maputo. *Estudos Moçambicanos* 19, 61-88.
Cruz e Silva, Teresa (2001): *Protestant Churches and the Formation of Political Consciousness in Southern Mozambique (1930 – 1974.)* Basel: Schlettwein Pub.
De Moraes Farias, Paulo F. (2003): Afrocentrism: Between Crosscultural Grand Narrative and Cultural Relativism (Review Article). *Journal of African History* 44, 2, 327-340.
De Oliveira Teixeira, Márcia (2001): A ciência em açao: seguindo Bruno Latour. *História, Ciências, Saúde* 8, 1, 265-289.
Dean, Mitchell (1997): Sociology after Society. In: Owen, D. (ed.): *Sociology After Postmodernism*. Thousand Oaks/London/New Delhi: Sage, 205-228.
Deflem, Mathieu (2003): The Sociology of the Sociology of Money. Simmel and the Contemporary Battle of the Classics. *Journal of Classical Sociology* 3, 1, 67-96.
Della Rocca, Roberto (1997): *Mozambique: de la Guerre à la Paix – Histoire d'une Médiation Insolite*. Paris: L'Harmattan.
Denzin, Norman K. (2001): The Reflexive Interview and a Performative Social Science. *Qualitative Research* 1, 1, 23-46.
Dombrowsky, Wolf R. (1996): Falsche Begriffe, falsches Begreifen, schädliches Zugreifen vor Ort: Über die Folgen verkehrten Denkens beim Gutgemeinten. In: Hanisch, R./Moßmann, P. (eds.): *Katastrophen und ihre Bewältigung in den Ländern des Südens*. Hamburg: Deutsches Übersee-Institut.
Douglas, Mary (1992): *Risk and Blame: Essays in Cultural Theory*. London: Routledge.
Douglas, Mary/Wildavski, Aaron (1982): *Risk and Culture: An Essay on the Selection of Technological and Environmental Dangers*. Berkeley, CA: University of California Press.
Drew, Paul (1978): Accusations: The Occasioned Use of Members' Knowledge of 'Religious Geography' in Describing Events. *Sociology* 12, 1, 1–22.
Drew, Paul/Heritage, John (1992): *Talk at Work: Interaction in Institutional Settings*. Cambridge: Cambridge University Press.
Durkheim, Émile (1984): *The Division of Labor in Society*. New York: The Free Press.
Durkheim, Émile (1988): *Les règles de la méthode sociologique*. Champs: Flammarion.
Economy and Society, (2000): Configurations of Risk. Vol.29, Nr.4.
Eder, Klaus (2006): The Public Sphere. *Theory, Culture & Society* 23, 2-3, 607-611.
Egero, Bertil (1986): *Mozambique: The Dream Undone – The Political Economy of Democracy 1975-1984*. Uppsala: Nordic African Institute.

Eisenstadt, Shmuel N. (1998): Modernity and the Construction of Collective Identities. *International Journal of Comparative Sociology* 39, 1, 138-158.
Eisenstadt, Shmuel N. (2000): Multiple Modernities. *Daedalus* 129, 1, 1-30.
Elster, Jon (1989): *Salomonic Judgements: Studies in the Limitations of Rationality*. Cambridge: Cambridge University Press.
Ericson, Richard (2005): Governing Through Risk and Uncertainty (Review Article). *Economy and Society* 34, 4, 659-672.
Etzioni, Amitai (1973): The Crisis of Modernity: Deviation or Demise? *Journal of Human Relations* 21, 4, 371-394.
Evans-Pritchard, Edward E. (1976): *Witchcraft, Oracles and Magic Among the Azande*. Oxford: Clarendon Press.
Evers, Hans-Dieter (1999): *Globale Macht. Zur Theorie Strategischer Gruppen*. Working Paper No. 332. Bielefeld: Fakultät für Soziologie, Universität Bielefeld.
Evers, Hans-Dieter (2001): Macht und Einfluss in der Entwicklungspolitik. Neue Ansätze zur Theorie Strategischer Gruppen. In: Thiel, Reinold E. (ed.): *Neue Ansätze zur Entwicklungstheorie*. Bonn: Deutsche Stiftung für Internationale Entwicklung, 164-172.
Ewald, François (1993): *Der Vorsorgestaat*. Frankfurt am Main: Suhrkamp.
Fabian, Johannes (1983): *Time and the Other. How Anthropology Makes Its Object*. New York: Columbia University Press.
Fedderke, Johannes/De Kadt, Raphael/Luiz, John (1999): Economic Growth and Social Capital. A Critical Reflection. *Theory and Society* 28, 5, 709-745.
Ferguson, James (1999): *Expectations of Modernity – Myths and Meanings of Urban Life on the Zambian Copperbelt*. Berkeley: University of California Press.
Fevre, Ralph/Thompson, Andrew (eds.) (1999): *Nation, Identity and Social Theory: Perspectives from Wales*. Cardiff: University of Wales Press.
Fine, Ben (2002): It Ain't Social, It Ain't Capital and it Ain't Africa. *Studia Africana* 13, 18-33.
Finnegan, William (1992): *A Complicated War: the Harrowing of Mozambique*. Berkeley: University of California Press.
First, Ruth (1983): *Black Gold - The Mozambican Miner: Proletarian and Peasant*. Sussex: The Harvester Press.
Fligstein, Neil (1996): Markets as Politics: A Political-Cultural Approach to Market Institutions. *American Sociological Review* 61, 656-673.
Fortuna, Carlos (1993): *O fio da meada – O algodão de Moçambique, Portugal e a economia-mundo 1860-1960*. Porto: Edições Afrontamento.
Foucault, Michel (1991): Governmentality. In: Burchell, G./Gordon, C./ Miller, P. (??): *The Foucault Effect - Studies in Governmentality*. London: Harvester, 87-104.
Fourcade-Gourinchas, Marion (2003): Economic Sociology and the Sociology of Economics - What is Sociological About the Sociology of Economics? Some Recent Developments. *Economic Sociology - European Electronic Newsletter*, 4, 2.
Fried, Mirjam/Östman, Jan-Ola (2005): Construction Grammar and Spoken Language: The Case of Pragmatic Particles. *Journal of Pragmatics* 37, 11, 1752-1778.
Garfinkel, Harold/Sacks, Harvey (1970): On Formal Structures of Practical Actions. In: McKinney, J.C., Tiryakian, E.A. (eds.): *Theoretical Sociology*. New York: Meredith, 338-366.

Garfinkel, Harold (1967): *Studies in Ethnomethodology*. Englewood Cliffs: Prentice Hall.

Gawley, Tim (2007): Revisiting Trust in Symbolic Interaction: Presentations of Trust Development in University Administration. *Qualitative Sociology Review* 3, 2, 46-63.

Geenen, Elke (2003): Katastrophe, Terror, Revolution – Gemeinsamkeiten und Unterschiede. In: Clausen, L./Geenen, E./Macamo, E. (eds.): *Entsetzliche soziale Prozesse*. Münster: Lit.

Geertz, Clifford (1973): *The Interpretation of Cultures*. New York: Basic Books.

Geffray, Christian (1990): *La cause des armes au Mozambique. Anthropologie d'une guerre civile*. Paris: Karthala.

Geramanis, Olaf (2002) : *Vertrauen – Die Entdeckung einer sozialen Ressource*. Stuttgart: Hirzel.

Gersony, R. (1988): *Mozambique Refugee Accounts of Principally Conflict-Related Experiences in Mozambique*. Washington: State Department.

Geschiere, Peter (1997): *The Modernity of Witchcraft: Politics and the Occult in Postcolonial Africa*. Charlottesville: University of Virginia Press.

Ghaziani, Amin/Ventresca, Marc J. (2005): Keywords and Cultural Change: Frame Analysis of *Business Model* Public Talk, 1975-2000. *Sociological Forum* 20, 4, 523-559.

Ghiglione Rodolphe/Blanchet Alain (1991): *Analyse de contenu et contenus d'analyses*. Paris: Dunod.

Giddens, Anthony (1979): *Capitalism and Modern Social Theory - An Analysis of the Writings of Marx, Durkheim and Max Weber*. Cambridge: Cambridge University Press.

Giddens, Anthony (1985): *The Constitution of Society – Outline of the Theory of Structuration*. Cambridge: Polity Press.

Giddens, Anthony (1990): *The Consequences of Modernity*. Stanford: Stanford University Press.

Glaser, Barney G./Strauss, Anselm L. (1967): *The Discovery of Grounded Theory – Strategies for Qualitative Research*. New York: Aldine de Gruyter.

Glasersfeld, Ernst von (1997): *Radikaler Konstruktivismus – Ideen, Ergebnisse, Probleme*. Frankfurt am Main: Suhrkamp.

Goffman, Ervin (1974): *Frame Analysis*. Cambridge: Harvard University Press.

Goffman, Ervin (1994): *Interaktion und Geschlecht*. Frankfurt am Main: Campus.

Goldthorpe, John (1998): Rational Action Theory for Sociology. *British Journal of Sociology* 49, 167-92.

Gubrium, Jaber F./Holstein, James A. (1998): Narrative Practice and the Coherence of Personal Stories. *Sociological Quaterly*, 39, 1, 163-87.

Güth, Werner/Kliemt, Hartmut (2007): The Rationality of Rational Fools – The Role of Commitments, Persons and Agents in Rational Choice Modeling. In: Peter, F./Schmid, H.B. (eds): *Rationality and Commitment*. Oxford: Oxford University Press, 124-149.

Guzzini, Stefano (2001): *Another Sociology for IR? An Analysis of Niklas Luhmann's Conceptualisation of Power*. Paper presented at the 42nd Annual Convention of the 'International Studies Association' Chicago, 21-25 February 2001.

Hacking, Ian (1990): *The Taming of Chance*. Cambridge: Cambridge University Press.

Hacking, Ian (1999): *The Social Construction of What?* Cambridge: Harvard University Press.

Halfmann, Jost and Japp, Klaus P. (eds.) (1990): *Riskante Entscheidungen und Katastrophenpotentiale.* Opladen: Westdeutscher Verlag.

Halkowski, Timothy (1990): 'Role' as an Interactional Device. *Social Problems* 37, 564-577.

Hall, John R. (1999): *Cultures of Inquiry. From Epistemology to Discourse in Sociohistorical Research.* Cambridge: Cambridge University Press.

Hall, Margaret/Young, Tom (1997): *Confronting Leviathan: Mozambique Since Independence.* Athens: Ohio UP.

Hammersley, Martyn (2005): Should Social Science Be Critical? *Philosophy of the Social Sciences* 35, 2, 175-195.

Hanson, F. Allan/Martin, Rex (1973): The Problem of Other Cultures. *Philosophy of the Social Sciences* 3, 1, 191-208.

Hardin, Russell (2003): If It Rained Knowledge. *Philosophy of the Social Sciences* 33, 1, 3-24.

Harries, Patrick (1994): *Work, Culture and Identity: Migrant Labourers in Mozambique and South Africa, c.1860-1910.* London: James Currey.

Harris, Marvin (1959): Labour Emigration among the Moçambique Thonga: Cultural and Political Factors. *Africa* 29, 1, 50-66.

Hegel, Georg W. F. (1959): *Einleitung in die Geschichte der Philosophie.* Hoffmeister, J. (ed.). Hamburg: Meiner.

Hempel, Carl G. (1970) *Aspects of Scientific Explanations and Other Essays in the Philosophy of Science.* New York: Free Press.

Hester, Stephen/ Eglin, Peter (1997): *Culture in Action: Studies in Membership Categorisation Analysis.* Washington, DC: University Press of America.

Hester, Stephen/ Francis, D. (2001): Institutional Talk Institutionalised? *TEXT* 20,3,391-413.

Hester, Stephen/ Housley, William (2002): *Language, Interaction and National Identity.* Aldershot: Ashgate.

Hilbert, Richard A. (1992): *The Classical Roots of Ethnomethodology. Durkheim, Weber, and Garfinkel.* Chapel Hill/London: The University of North Carolina Press.

Hindess, Barry (1988): *Choice, Rationality, and Social Theory.* Boston: Unwin Hyman.

Hitzler, Ronald (1994): Wissen und Wesen des Experten – Ein Annäherungsversuch – zur Einleitung. In: Honer. A./Hitzler R./Maeder, C. (eds.): *Expertenwissen – Die institutionalisierte Kompetenz zur Konstruktion von Wirklichkeit.* Opladen: Westdeutscher Verlag, 13-30

Hitzler, Ronald/Reichertz, Jo/Schröer, Norbert (eds.) (1999): *Hermeneutische Wissenssoziologie – Standpunkte zur Theorie der Interpretation.* Konstanz: Universitätsverlag Konstanz.

Hitzler, Ronald/Honer, Anne/Maeder, Christoph (eds.) (1994): *Expertenwissen – Die institutionalisierte Kompetenz zur Konstruktion von Wirklichkeit.* Opladen: Westdeutscher Verlag.

Hollis, Martin (1998): *Trust within Reason.* Cambridge: Cambridge University Press.

Honer, Anne (1994): Einige Probleme lebensweltlicher Ethnographie – Zur Methodologie und Methodik einer interpretativen Sozialforschung. In: Schröer, N. (ed.): *Interpretative Sozialforschung – Auf dem Wege zu einer hermeneutischen Wissenssoziologie.* Opladen: Westdeutscher Verlag, 85-106.

Horkheimer, Max/Adorno, Theodor (1972): *Dialektik der Aufklärung - Philosophische Fragmente*. Frankfurt am Main: Fischer.
House, Juliane (2006): Text and Context in Translation. *Journal of Pragmatics* 38, 3, 338-358.
Housley, William/Fitzgerald, Richard (2002): The Reconsidered Method of Membership Categorization Devices. *Qualitative Research* 2, 1, 59-83.
Housley, William (2000a): Category Work and Knowledgeability within Multidisciplinary Team Meetings. *TEXT* 20, 1, 83–107.
Housley, William (2000b): Story, Narrative and Teamwork. *Sociological Review* 48, 3, 425–443.
Hume, Cameron (1994): *Ending Mozambique's War – the Role of Mediation and Good Offices*. Washington: US Institute of Peace Press.
Igreja Assembleia de Deus (1984) (7th edition): *Tinsimu ta Mhalamhala ya Evangeli*. White River: Emmanuel Press.
Instituto de Comunicação Social (2002): *Lista de Processos*. Xai-Xai: Delegação Provincial de Gaza.
Isaacman, Allen (1996): *Cotton is the Mother of Poverty – Peasants, Work and Rural Struggles in Colonial Mozambique 1938 – 1961*. Portsmouth: Heinemann.
Japp, Klaus Peter (1996): *Soziologische Risikotheorie – Funktionale Differenzierung, Politisierung und Reflexion*. Munich: Juventa.
Jayyusi, Lena (1984): *Categorization and Moral Order*. London: Routledge & Kegan Paul.
Jayyusi, Lena (1991): Values and Moral Judgement. In: Button, G. (ed.): *Ethnomethodology and the Human Sciences*. Cambridge: Cambridge University Press, 227-251.
Joas, Hans (1996): *The Creativity of Action*. Chicago: University of Chicago Press.
Jöckel, Andrea/Macamo, Elísio (2005a): Mitspielende Zaungäste und kompatible Geschichten. SIETAR Journal 1, 27-30.
Jöckel, Andrea/Macamo, Elísio (2005b): Andere Länder, andere Katastrophen: zur lokalen Wahrnehmung und Erfahrung von Krisen und Katastrophen am Beispiel von Mosambik und Sudan. *International Textbook Research* 27, 389-402.
Kaufmann, Franz-Xaver (1973): *Sicherheit als soziologisches und sozialpolitisches Problem. Untersuchungen zu einer Wertidee hochdifferenzierter Gesellschaften*. Stuttgart: Enke.
Kersten, Fred (2002): A Stroll with Alfred Schutz. *Human Studies* 25, 1, 33-53.
King, Gary/Keohane, Robert O./Verba, Sidney (1994): *Designing Social Inquiry – Scientific Inference in Qualitative Research*. Princeton: Princeton University Press.
Ki-Zerbo, Lazare (2001): Schütz and the Rational Choice-Debate in African Economics. *The Review of Austrian Economics* 14, 2-3, 157-172.
Klinenberg, Eric (1999): Denaturalizing Disaster: A Social Autopsy of the 1995 Chicago Heat Wave. *Theory and Society* 28, 2, 239-295.
Knorr-Cetina, Karen (1981): *The Manufacturing of Knowledge – An Essay on the Constructivist and Contextual Nature of Science*. Oxford: Pergamon Press.
Knowles, Dudley (ed.) (1990): *Explanation and its Limits*. Cambridge: Cambridge University Press.
Kollock, Peter (1998): Social Dilemmas: The Anatomy of Cooperation. *Annual Review of Sociology* 24, 183-214.
Konecki, Krzysztof T. (2005): The Problem of Symbolic Interaction and of Constructing Self. *Qualitative Sociology Review* 1, 1, 68-89.

Koppl, Roger/Whitman, Douglas G. (2004): Rational-Choice Hermeneutics. *Journal of Economic Behavior and Organization* 55, 3, 295-317.
Krippner, Greta R. (2001): The Elusive Market: Embeddedness and the Paradigm of Economic Sociology. *Theory and Society* 30, 775-810.
Krüger, Gesine (2002): *Die Verbreitung der Schrift in Südafrika. Zur Praxis des Schreibens in alltags- und sozialgeschichtlicher Perspektive 1830 – 1930.* Manuskript der Habilitationsschrift, Universität Hannover.
Kuper, Adam (1988): *The Invention of Primitive Society – Transformations of an Illusion.* London: Routledge.
Kurrild-Klitgaard, Peter (2001): On Rationality, Ideal Types and Economics: Alfred Schütz and the Austrian School. *The Review of Austrian Economics* 14, 2-3, 119-143.
Lacey, Nicola (2006): Analytical Jurisprudence Versus Descriptive Sociology Revisited. *Texas Law Review* 84, 4, 945-982.
Lachenmann, Gudrun (1994): Systeme des Nichtwissens – Alltagsverstand und Expertenbewußtsein im Kulturvergleich. In: Honer A./Hitzler, R./Maeder. C. (eds.): *Expertenwissen – Die institutionalisierte Kompetenz zur Konstruktion von Wirklichkeit.* Opladen: Westdeutscher Verlag, 285-305.
Lagerspetz, Olli (1998) *Trust: The Tacit Demand.* Dordrecht/Boston/London: Kluwer Academic Pub.
Lash, Scott, Szerszynski, Bronislaw & Wynne, Brian (eds.) (1996): *Risk, Environment and Modernity – Towards a New Ecology.* London: Sage.
Latour, Bruno (1991): 'Technology is Society Made Durable'. In: John Law (ed.) *A Sociology of Monsters – Essays on Power, Technology and Domination.* London: Routledge.
Latour, Bruno (1984): *The Pasteurization of France.* Cambridge: Harvard University Press.
Laurier, Eric (2001): *The Region as a Socio-Technical Accomplishment of Mobile Workers.* Edinburgh: Institute of Geography, University of Edinburgh.
Law, John/Singleton, Vicky (2005): Object Lessons. *Organization* 12, 3, 331-355.
Leiris, Michel (1996): La possession et ses aspects théatraux chez les Éthiopiens de Gondar. In: Leiris, M. (ed.): *Miroir de l'Afrique.* Paris: Gallimard, 921-946.
Lemke, Thomas (1999): The Critique of the Political Economy of Organization as a Genealogy of Power. *International Journal of Political Economy* 29, 3, 53-75.
Lepenies, Wolf (ed.) (2003): *Entangled Histories and Negotiated Universals – Centers and Peripheries in a Changing World.* Frankfurt am Main: Campus.
Lerner, Daniel (1964): *The Passing of Traditional Society – Modernising the Middle East.* New York.Free Press of Glencoe.
Levinson, Stephen (1997): *Pragmatics.* Cambridge: Cambridge University Press.
Lewis, J. David/Weigert, Andrew G. (1985): Social Automism, Holism, and Trust. *Sociological Quarterly* 26, 4, 455-471.
Lie, John (1997): Sociology of Markets. *Annual Review of Sociology* 23, 1, 341-360.
Liesegang, Gerhard (1967): Beiträge zur Geschichte des Reiches der Gaza Nguni im südlichen Moçambique 1820-1895. PhD Dissertation, Universität zu Köln.
Loimeier, Roman/ Neubert, Dieter/ Weissköppel, Cordula (eds.) (2005): *Globalisierung im lokalen Kontext – Perspektiven und Konzepte von Handeln in Afrika.* Hamburg/Münster: Lit.
Longino, Helen E. (1990): *Science as Social Knowledge.* Princeton: Princeton University Press.

Luckmann, Thomas (2002): Der kommunikative Aufbau der sozialen Welt und die Sozialwissenschaften. In: Luckmann, T. (edited by Knoblauch, H./Raab, J./Schnettler, B.): *Wissen und Gesellschaft – Ausgewählte Aufsätze 1981-2002*. Konstanz: UVK Verlagsgesellschaft, 157-182.

Luhmann, Niklas (1993): *Risk – A Sociological Theory*. New York: De Gruyter.

Luhmann, Niklas (1992): *Beobachtungen der Moderne*. Opladen: Wiesbaden.

Luhmann, Niklas (1993): 'Die Moral des Risikos und das Risiko der Moral'. In: Gotthard Bechmann (ed.): *Risiko und Gesellschaft*. Opladen. Westdeutscher Verlag.

Luhmann, Niklas (1988): 'Familiarity, Confidence, Trust'. In: Diego Gambetta, *Trust*. Oxford: Oxford University Press.

Lupton, Deborah (1999): *Risk*. London: Routledge.

Lynch, Michael (1999): Silence in Context: Ethnomethodology and Social Theory. *Human Studies* 22, 2-4, 211-233.

Lynch, Michael (1993): *Scientific Practice and Ordinary Action*. Cambridge: Cambridge University Press.

Lynch, Michael (2000): The Ethnomethodological Foundation of Conversation Analysis. *TEXT* 20, 4, 517–532.

Lynch, Michael/Bogen David (1994): Harvey Sacks's Primitive Natural Science. *Theory, Culture and Society* 11, 1, 65–104.

Lynch, Michael/Bogen, David (1996): *The Spectacle of History: Speech, Text and Memory at the Iran-Contra Hearings*. Durham, NC: Duke University Press.

Macamo, Elísio (1999): *Was ist Afrika? Zur Kultursoziologie eines modernen Konstrukts*. Berlin: Duncker & Humblot.

Macamo, Elísio (2001): Die protestantische Ethik und afrikanische Geister. In: Bauer, U./Egbert, H./Jäger, F. (eds.): *Interkulturelle Beziehungen und Kulturwandel in Afrika. Beiträge zur Globalisierungsdebatte*. Frankfurt am Main: Peter Lang.

Macamo, Elísio (2002a): Biographical Knots. In: Krastev, I./Elkana Y./Macamo E./Randeria, S. (eds.): *Unraveling Ties – from Social Cohesion to New Practices of Connectedness*. Frankfurt am Main: Campus, 147-159.

Macamo, Elísio (2002b): Plus ça change, plus c'est la même chose: Wandel und Politik in Mosambik. In: Augel, J./Meyns, P. (eds.): *Transformationsprobleme im portugiesischsprachigen Afrika*. Hamburg: IAK, 67-92.

Macamo, Elísio (2003a): Nach der Katastrophe ist die Katastrophe: Die 2000er Überschwemmung in der dörflichen Wahrnehmung in Mosambik. In: Clausen, L./Geenen, E./Macamo, E. (eds.): *Entsetzliche soziale Prozesse*. Münster: Lit.

Macamo, Elísio (2003b): Da disciplinarização de Moçambique: Ajustamento estrutural e as estratégias neo-liberais de risco. *Africana Studia* 6, 231-255.

Macamo, Elísio (2003c): Work and Societal Order in Africa – Negotiating Social Change. In: Lepenies, W. (ed.): *Entangled Histories and Negotiated Universals*. Frankfurt am Main: Campus, 281-309.

Macamo, Elísio (2003d): Frauen als moralischer Körper der Gesellschaft. Schweizer Mission in Mosambik und die Erfindung der Tsonga. In: Lienemann, C./Strahm, D./Walz, H. (eds.): *Als hätten sie uns neu erfunden – Beobachtungen zu Fremdheit und Geschlecht*. Lucern: Edition Exodus, 153-164.

Macamo, Elísio (2004): Schweizer Mission, Kolonialismus und die Bewältigung der Moderne in Mosambik. In: Bogner, A./Holtwick, B./Tyrell, H. (eds.): *Weltmission und religiöse Organisationen – Protestantische Missionsgesellschaften im 19. und 20. Jahrhundert*. Würzburg: Ergon, 571-588.

Macamo, Elísio (2005a): Über die Produktion des Lokalen: Was ist Afrika? In: Loimeier, R./Neubert, D./Weißköppel, C. (eds.): *Globalisierung im lokalen Kontext – Perspektiven und Konzepte von Handeln in Afrika*. Hamburg/Münster: Lit, 125-146.

Macamo, Elísio (2005b): Negotiating Modernity – From Colonialism to Globalization. In: Macamo, E. (ed.): *Negotiating Modernity – Africa's Ambivalent Experience*. Dakar: CODESRIA/Zed Books, 1-18.

Macamo, Elísio (2006a): The Hidden Side of Modernity in Africa – Domesticating Savage Lives. In: Costa, Sérgio/Domingues, J. Maurício/Knöbl, Wolfgang/Da Silva, Josué P. (eds.): *The Plurality of Modernity: Decentring Sociology*. München: Rainer Hampp, 161-178.

Macamo, Elísio (2006b): Accounting for Disaster – Memories of War in Mozambique. In *Afrika Spectrum*, Vol.41, Special Issue: Memory cultures; S.199-219.

Macamo, Elísio (2008): Wenn nichts verborgen bleibt – Ein Kommentar zur objektivhermeneutischen Auslegung *meiner* Gruppendiskussionen. Eine Stellungsnahme zum Beitrag von Ulrich Oevermann. In: Cappai, Gabriele (ed.): *Forschen unter den Bedingungen kultureller Fremdheit*. Wiesbaden: VS Verlag für Sozialwissenschaften, 235-241.

Macamo, Elísio/Neubert, Dieter (2008): The New and its Temptations: Products of Modernity and their Impact on Social Change in Africa. In: Adogame, Afe/Echtler, Magnus/Vierke, Ulf (eds.): *Unpacking the New: Critical Perspectives on Cultural Syncretization in Africa and Beyond*. Hamburg/Münster: Lit, 267-299.

Macamo, Elísio/Neubert, Dieter (2003a): The Politics of Negative Peace: Mozambique in the Aftermath of the Rome Cease-Fire Agreement. *Portuguese Literary & Cultural Studies 10*, 23-48.

Macamo, Elísio/Neubert, Dieter (2003b): Die Flut in Mosambik – Zur unterschiedlichen Deutung von Krisen und Katastrophen durch Bauern und Nothilfeapparat. In: Schareika, N./Bierschenk, T. (eds.): *Lokales Wissen – Sozialwissenschaftliche Perspektiven*. Hamburg/Münster: Lit, 185-209.

Maffesoli, Michel (1996): *Ordinary Knowledge - an Introduction to Interpretative Sociology*. Cambridge: Polity Press.

Magaia, Lina (1988): *Dumba Nengue, Run for your Life: Peasant Tales of Tragedy in Mozambique*. Trenton, N.J: Africa World Press.

Mahoney, James (2000): Path Dependence in Historical Sociology. *Theory and Society* 29, 4, 507-548.

Mamdani, Mahmood (1996): *Citizen and Subject - Contemporary Africa and the Legacy of Late Colonialism*. Kampala: Fountain Pub.

Mannheim, Karl (1995) (8th edition): *Ideologie und Utopie*. Frankfurt am Main: Vittorio Klostermann.

Manning, Peter K. (1997): Organizations as Sense-Making Contexts. *Theory, Culture & Society* 14, 2, 139-150.

Marglin, Frédéric A. (ed.) (1990): *Dominating Knowledge – Development, Culture and Resistance*. Oxford: Clarendon Press.

Marglin, Frédéric, A. (ed.) (1996): *Decolonizing Knowledge – From Development to Dialogue*. Oxford: Clarendon Press.
Marx, Karl (1978): On Imperialism in India. In: Tucker, R. (ed.): *The Marx-Engels Reader*. New York: W.W. Norton, 653-664.
Mason, Ian (2006): On Mutual Accessibility of Contextual Assumptions in Dialogue Interpreting. *Journal of Pragmatics* 38, 3, 359-373.
McCarthy, E. Doyle (1996): *Knowledge as Culture - the New Sociology of Knowledge*. London: Routledge.
McHoul, Alec/Watson, D. Rod (1984): Two Axes for the Analysis of 'Commonsense' and 'Formal' Geographical Knowledge in Classroom Talk. *British Journal of the Sociology of Education* 5, 3, 281–302.
Mingione, Enzo (1991): *Fragmented Societies: A Sociology of Economic Life Beyond the Market Paradigm*. Cambridge:Basil Blackwell.
Minter, William (1994): *Apartheid's Contras: an Inquiry into the Roots of War in Angola and Mozambique*. Johannesburg/London/Atlantic Highlands, N.J: Witwatersrand UP/Zed Books.
Misztal, Barbara A. (1996): *Trust in Modern Societies – The Search for the Basis of Social Order*. Cambridge: Cambridge University Press.
Mitchell, Jeff (2000): Living a Lie: Self-Deception, Habit, and Social Roles. *Human Studies* 23, 145-156.
Monnier, Nicolas (1995): Stratégie Missionnaire et Tactiques d'appropriation indigénes: La Mission Romande au Mozambique 1888-1896. *Le Fait Missionnaire*, Cahier Nr.2.
Moore, Mick (1999): Truth, Trust and Market Transactions: What Do We Know? *The Journal of Development Studies* 36, 1, 74-88.
Mpapele, M. R. (1967): *Mahlayisele ya Miri*. Braamfontein: Sasavona Publishers and Booksellers.
Mudimbe, Valentin Y. (1982): *L'Odeur du Père – Essai sur les limites de la science et de la vie en Afrique Noire*. Paris: Présence Africaine.
Mudimbe, Valentin Y. (1988): *The Invention of Africa – Gnosis, Philosophy and the Order of Knowledge*. London: James Currey.
Myhre, Knut Christian (2003): Conference Report. Uncertainty in Contemporary African Lives (conference organised by the Nordic Africa Institute, 9-11 April 2003, Usa River, Tanzania). *African Affairs* 102, 409, 651-652.
Navess, B. T./Bartling, Clara (1979): *A Wutomi gi Nene*. Braamfontein: Sasavona Publishers and Booksellers.
Neubert, Dieter/Macamo, Elísio (2003): Wer weiß hier was. „Authentisches' lokales Wissen und der Globalitätsanspruch der Wissenschaft. In: Schareika, N./Bierschenk, T. (eds.): *Lokales Wissen – Sozialwissenschaftliche Perspektiven*. Hamburg/Münster: Lit, 93-122.
Neubert, Dieter (2003): The 'Peacemakers' Dilemma'. The Role of NGOs in Processes of Peace-building in Decentralised Conflicts. In: Foblets, M.-C./Trotha, T. v. (eds.): *In Search of Peace: Contemporary Processes of Ideological, Social and Legal Reconstruction after War and Disruption*. Hart Onati Series on International Law and Society. Oxford: Hart.
Neugebauer, Christian (1989): *Einführung in die afrikanische Philosophie*. Europäische Hochschulschriften. München/Kinshasa: African University Studies.

Nowotny, Helga (1989): Sicherheit und Komplexität: Über den Umgang mit Unsicherheit. *Zeitschrift für Wissenschaftsforschung* 5, 3-12.
O'Malley, Pat (2000): „Uncertain Subjects – Risks, Liberalism and Contract'. In: *Economy and Society*. Vol.29, Nr.4, 460-484.
Oevermann, Ulrich (2008): Zur Differenz von praktischem und methodischem Verstehen in der ethnologische Feldforschung – Eine rein textimmanente objektiv hermeneutische Sequenzanalyse von übersetzten Verbatim-Transkripten von Gruppendiskussionen in einer afrikanischen lokalen Kultur. In: Cappai, Gabriele (ed.): *Forschen unter Bedingungen kultureller Fremdheit*: Wiesbaden: VS Verlag für Sozialwissenschaften, 145-234.
Park, George (1990): Making Sense of Religion by Direct Observation. In: Riggins, Stephen H (ed.): *Beyond Goffman - Studies on Communication, Institution and Social Interaction*. Berlin: Mouton de Gruyter. 235-276.
Parsons, Talcott (1964): *The Social System*. New York: The Free Press.
Parsons, Talcott (1967): *The Structure of Social Action*. New York: The Free Press.
Paul, Axel T. (2001): Organizing Husserl. On the Phenomenological Foundations of Luhmann's Systems Theory. *Journal of Classical Sociology* 1, 3, 371-394.
Pels, Dick (1997): Mixing Metaphors: Politics or Economics of Knowledge? *Theory and Society* 26, 5, 685-717.
Perez-Gonzalez, Luis (2006): Interpreting Strategic Recontextualization Cues in the Courtroom. Corpus-Based Insights into the Pragmatic Force of Non-Restrictive Relative Clauses. *Journal of Pragmatics* 38, 3, 390-417.
Pettenkofer, Andreas (2003): Erwartung der Katastrophe, Erinnerung der Katastrophe: Die apokalyptische Kosmologie der westdeutschen Umweltbewegung und die Besonderheiten des deutschen Risikodiskurses. In: Clausen, L./Geenen, E./Macamo, E. (eds.): *Entsetzliche soziale Prozesse*. Münster: Lit.
Pfohl, Stephen, J. (1985): *Images of Deviance and Social Control: A Sociological History*. New York: McGraw-Hill.
Plummer, Ken (1996): Symbolic Interactionism in the 20th Century: Rise of Empirical Social Theory. In: Turner, B. S. (ed.): *The Blackwell Companion to Social Theory*. Oxford: Blackwell.
Polanyi, Karl (2001): *The Great Transformation: The Political and Economic Origins of Our Time*. Boston: Beacon Press.
Pomerantz, Anita M. (1978): Attributions of Responsibility: Blamings. *Sociology* 12, 115–21.
Radford, Gary P. (2000): Conversations, Conferences, and the Practice of Intellectual Discussion. *Human Studies* 23, 211-225.
Ritzer, George (2004): *The Globalization of Nothing*. Thousand Oaks/London/New Delhi: Sage.
Rodney, Walter (1971): The Year 1895 in Southern Mozambique: African Resistance to the Imposition of European Colonial Rule. *Journal of the Historical Society of Nigeria* 5, 4, 509-536.
Rorty, Richard (1992): *The Linguistic Turn – Essays in Philosophical Method; with Two Retrospective Essays*. Chicago: Chicago University Press.
Richard Rorty (1989): *Contingency, Irony, and Solidarity*. New York: Cambridge University Press.

Ruch, E. A./ Anyanwu, K.C. (1981): *African Philosophy – An Introduction to the main philosophical trends in contemporary Africa.* Rome: Catholic Book Agency.

Rutter, Jason (2001): *From the Sociology of Trust Towards a Sociology of 'E-trust'.* Manchster: ESRC Centre for Research on Innovation and Competition, University of Manchester.

Sacks, Harvey (1992a): *Lectures on Conversation,* Vol. I. Oxford: Blackwell.

Sacks, Harvey (1992b): *Lectures on Conversation,* Vol. II. Oxford: Blackwell.

Sahlins, Marshall D. (1995): *How Natives Think – About Captain Cook, for Example.* Chicago: Chicago University Press.

Saul, John S. (ed.) (1985): *A Difficult Road: The Transition to Socialism in Mozambique.* New York: Monthly Review Press.

Scarre, Geoffrey (1987): *Witchcraft and Magic in Sixteenth and Seventeenth-century Europe.* Basingstoke: Macmillan Education.

Schaedel, M. (1984): *'Eingeborenen- Arbeit' - Formen der Ausbeutung unter der portugiesischen Kolonialherrschaft in Mosambik.* Köln: Pahl-Ruggenstein.

Schegloff, Emanuel A. (1992): Introduction. In: Sacks, H. (ed.): *Lectures in Conversation,* Vol. I. Oxford: Blackwell.

Schneider, Wolfgang Ludwig (2000): The Sequential Production of Social Arts in Conversation. *Human Studies* 23, 2, 123-144.

Schroeder, Ralph (1992): *Max Weber and the Sociology of Culture.* London: Sage.

Schütz, Alfred/Luckmann, Thomas (1984): *Strukturen der Lebenswelt.* Frankfurt am Main: Suhrkamp.

Schütz, Alfred & Parsons, Talcott (1977): *Zur Theorie sozialen Handelns – Ein Briefwechsel.* Edited by Walter Sprondel. Frankfurt am Main: Suhrkamp.

Schütz, Alfred (1964): The Well-Informed Citizen. An Essay on the Social Distribution of Knowledge. *Social Research* 13, 463-478.

Scott, James C. (1998): *Seeing Like a State: How Schemes to Improve the Human Condition Have Failed.* London: Yale University Press.

Segl, Peter (1989): *Hexenglaube und Hexenverfolgung – eine kritische Bilanz.* Augsburg: Akademie-Publikationen.

Seligman, Adam (1997): *The Problem of Trust.* Princeton: Princeton University Press.

Sen, Amarty K. (1977): Rational Fools: A Critique of the Behavioral Assumptions of Economic Theory. *Philosophy and Public Affairs* 4.

Sharrock, Wes (1974): On Owning Knowledge. In: Turner, R. (ed.): *Ethnomethodology.* Harmondsworth: Penguin.

Sharrock, Wes/Button, Graham (1999): Do the Right Thing! Rule Finitism, Rule Scepticism and Rule Following. *Human Studies* 22, 193-210.

Sift, Peter (1999): *The Silent War – South African Recce Operations 1969-1994.* Alberton: Galago.

Silva Rego, A. Da (1960): *Alguns problemas socio-missionários da Africa Negra.* Lisboa: Junta de Investigações do Ultramar.

Silverman, David (1998): *Harvey Sacks: Social Science and Conversation Analysis.* Oxford: Polity Press.

Smith, Alan K. (1970): *The Struggle for Control of Southern Mozambqiue, 1720-1835.* Berkeley: University of California Press.

Soeffner, Hans-Georg (1987): Rezension von Schütz & Luckmann: Strukturen der Lebenswelt. *Kölner Zeitschrift für Soziologie und Sozialpsychologie* 39.

Spittler, Gerd (1989): *Handeln in einer Hungerkrise – Tuaregnomaden und die große Dürre von 1984.* Opladen: Westdeutscher Verlag.
Sprondel, Walter M. (1979): ,Experte' und ,Laie': Zur Entwicklung von Typenbegriffen in der Wissenssoziologie. In: Sprondel, W. M./Grathoff, R. (eds.): *Alfred Schütz und die Idee des Alltags in den Sozialwissenschaften.* Stuttgart: Enke.
Srubar, Ilja (1998): Phenomenological Analysis and Its Contemporary Significance. *Human Studies* 21, 2, 121-139.
Stallings, Jerry (2003): „Soziologische Theorien und Desaster-Studien'. In: Clausen, L./ Geenen, E./ Macamo, E. (eds.): *Entsetzliche soziale Prozesse. Theoretische und empirische Annährungen.* Hamburg: Lit.
Stehr, Nico (2001): *The Fragility of Modern Societies – Knowledge and Risk in the Information Age.* London: Sage.
Stirling, John (ed.) (1960) (7th edition): *The Bible.* London: The British and Foreign Bible Society.
Stokoe, Elizabeth H. (2003): Mothers, Single Women and Sluts: Gender, Morality and Membership Categorization in Neighbour Disputes. *Feminism and Psychology* 13, 3, 317-344.
Susini, Marie-Laure (2008): *Éloge de la corruption.* Paris: Fayard.
Swedberg, Richard (1991): Major Traditions of Economic Sociology. *Annual Review of Sociology* 17, 251-276.
Swedberg, Richard/Himmelstrand, Ulf/Brulin, Goran (1987): The Paradigm of Economic Sociology: Premises and promises. *Theory and Society* 16, 169-214.
Szreter, Simon (2002): The State of Social Capital: Bringing Back in Power, Politics, and History. *Theory and Society* 31, 573-621.
Sztompka, Piotr (1999): *Trust: A Sociological Theory.* Cambridge: Cambridge University Press.
Tambiah, Stanley J. (1990): *Magic, Science, and the Scope of Rationality.* Cambridge: Cambridge University Press.
Temple, Bogusia (2006): Representation Across Languages: Biographical Sociology Meets Translation and Interpretation Studies. *Qualitative Sociology Review* 2, 1, 7-21.
Tenbruck, Friedrich, (1999): *Das Werk Max Webers. Gesammelte Aufsätze zu Max Weber.* Edited by Homann, Harald, Tübingen: Mohr Siebeck.
Thomas, Keith (1980): *Religion and the Decline of Magic - Studies in Popular Beliefs in Sixteenth and Seventeenth Century England.* London?: Weidenfeld & Nicolson.
Toulmin, Stephen (1990): *Cosmopolis – The Hidden Agenda of Modernity.* New York: The Free Press.
Tucker, Kenneth H. (1998): *Anthony Giddens and Modern Social Theory.* Oxford: Polity Press.
Turner, Bryan S. (2006): Classical Sociology and Cosmopolitanism. A Critical Defence of the Social. *The British Journal of Sociology* 57, 1, 133-151.
Turner, Bryan S. (2006): Hospital. *Theory, Culture & Society* 23, 2-3, 573-579.
Vail, Leroy/White, Landeg (1980): *Capitalism and Colonialism in Mozambique.* London: Heinemann.
Vanderstraeten, Raf (2002): Parsons, Luhmann and the Theorem of Double Contingency. *Journal of Classical Sociology* 2, 1, 77-92.

Van Dijk, Teun A. (1997): *Discourse as Social Interaction*. Thousand Oaks/London/New Delhi: Sage.

Van Loon, Joost (2002): *Risk and Technological Culture – Towards a Sociology of Virulence*. London: Routledge.

Viehöver, Willy (2003): Die Klimakatastrophe als ein Mythos der reflexiven Moderne. In: Clausen, L./Geenen, E./Macamo, E. (eds.): *Entsetzliche soziale Prozesse*. Hamburg/Münster: Lit

Vilhena, Maria da Conceição (1996): *Gungunhana no seu reino*. Lisbon: Edições Colibri.

Vines, Alex (1996): R*ENAMO: from Terrorism to Democracy in Mozambique*. York: Centre for Southern African Studies, University of York.

Vines, Alex. (1991): R*ENAMO: terrorism in Mozambique*. London: James Currey.

Wagner, Gerhard (1997): The End of Luhmann's Social Systems Theory. *Philosophy of the Social Sciences* 27, 4, 387-409.

Wagner, Hans-Josef (1999): *Rekonstruktive Methodologie*. Opladen: Leske und Budrich.

Wagner, Peter (1990): *Sozialwissenschaften und Staat – Frankreich, Italien, Deutschland 1870-1980*. Frankfurt am Main: Campus.

Warde, Alan (2004): *Practice and Field: Revising Bourdieusian Concepts*. CRIC Discussion Paper No 65. Manchester: Department of Sociology, University of Manchester.

Watson, D. Rodney (2006): Tacit Knowledge. *Theory, Culture & Society* 23, 2-3, 208-210.

Watson, D. Rodney (1978): Categorizations, Authorization and Blame-Negotiation in Conversation. *Sociology* 12, 1, 105–113.

Watson, D. Rodney (1994): Harvey Sacks' Sociology of Mind in Action. *Theory, Culture & Society* 11, 169–186.

Watson, D. Rodney (1983): The Presentation of 'Victim' and 'Motive' in Discourse: The Case of Police Interrogations and Interviews. *Victimology* 8, 1/2, 31–52.

Watson, D. Rodney (1997): Some General Reflections on 'Categorisation' and 'Sequence' in the Analysis of Conversation. In: Hester, S./Eglin, P. (eds): *Culture in Action: Studies in Membership Categorisation Analysis*. Washington, DC: University Press of America.

Watson, D. Rodney (2001): The Character of 'Institutional Talk': A Reply to Hester and Francis. *TEXT* 20, 3, 377–391.

Weber, Max (2007): Politics as a Vocation. In: Hans H. Gerth/Wright Mills, C. (eds.): *From Max Weber: Essays in Sociology*. London: Routledge.

Weber, Max (2007): Science as a Vocation. In: Hans H. Gerth/Wright Mills, C. (eds.): *From Max Weber: Essays in Sociology*. London: Routledge.

Weber, Max (1980): *Wirtschaft und Gesellschaft*. Tübingen: J.C.B. Mohr.

Weber, Max (1991): *Schriften zur Wissenschaftslehre*. Stuttgart: Phillip Reclam.

Weber, Max (2002): *The Protestant Ethic and the Spirit of Capitalism*, edited by Stephen Kalberg, S. Blackwell: Oxford.

White, Louise (1993): Vampire Priests of Central Africa: African Debates about Labor and Religion in Colonial Northern Zambia. *Comparative Studies in Society & History* 35, 746-772.

White, Louise (1995): Tsetse Visions: Narratives of Blood and Bugs in Colonial Northern Rhodesia . 1931-9. *Journal of African History* 36, 219-245.

Whitford, Josh (2002): Pragmatism and the Untenable Dualism of Means and Ends: Why Rational Choice Theory Does Not Deserve Paradigmatic Privilege. *Theory and Society* 31, 325-363.

Wieder, D. Lawrence (1974): *Language and Social Reality: The Case of Telling the Convict Code*. The Hague: Mouton and de Gruyter.
Wilshire, Bruce (1997): Pragmatism, Neopragmatism, and Phenomenology: The Richard Rorty Phenomenon. *Human Studies* 20, 1, 95-108.
Winch, Peter (1987): *Trying to Make Sense*. Oxford: Basil Blackwell.
Winch, Peter (1972): *Ethics and Action*. Oxford: Routledge and Kegan Paul.
Wittgenstein, Ludwig (1995): Remarks on Frazer's Golden Bough. Ed. By Rush Rhees. Harleston: The Brynmill Press.
Wittrock, Bjorn (2000): Modernity: One, None, or Many? European Origins and Modernity as a Global Condition.In: *Daedalus*, 129, 1, 31-60.
Wright, Richard (1979): *African Philosophy - an Introduction*. Washington D.C.: The University Press of America.
Wynne, Brian (1996): 'May the Sheep Safely Graze? A Reflexive View of the Expert-Lay Knowledge Divide'. In: Scott Lash, Bronislaw Szerszynski & Brian Wynne (eds.) (1996): *Risk, Environment and Modernity – Towards a New Ecology*. London: Sage.
Yin, Robert K. (1989): *Case Study Research. Design and Methods*. Thousand Oaks/London/New Delhi: Sage.
Zafirovski, Milan (1999): Unification of Sociological Theory by the Rational Choice Model: Conceiving the Relationship between Economics and Sociology. *Sociology* 33, 3, 495-514.
Zeleza, Paul T. (2003): *Manufacturing African Studies and Crises*. Dakar: CODESRIA.
Zelizer, Vivian A. (1997): *The Social Meaning of Money*. Princeton: Princeton University Press.
Zingerle, Arnold (1996): „Der ‚moralische Körper' der Gesellschaft und sein magischer Schatten – Zur Perspektivität von Magiebegriffen, am Beispiel von Emile Durkheim'. In: *Jahrbuch für Volkskunde* (Sonderdruck). Würzburg: Görres-Gesellschaft.
Zingerle, Arnold (ed.) (1987): *Magie und Moderne*. Berlin: Guttandin & Hoppe.
Zingerle, Arnold (1981): *Max Webers historische Soziologie. Aspekte und Materialien zur Wirkungsgeschichte*. Darmstadt: Wissenschaftliche Buchgesellschaft.
Zukin, Sharon/Dimaggio, Paul (eds.) (1990): *Structures of Capital: The Social Organization of the Economy*. Cambridge: Cambridge University Press.

Index

A

abduction, 107–8, 185
ability, 6–8, 21, 44, 47, 49, 58, 61–66, 75–76, 156, 158, 173–74, 213, 224, 226, 228–31
　people's, 96, 112
absence, 14, 33, 65–66, 69, 94, 125, 174, 187, 209, 276
accounts, 32–33, 40–42, 46–48, 50–53, 62, 74–76, 80–82, 140–41, 159–60, 173–77, 180–83, 185–89, 211–13, 220–22, 228–31
　local, 153, 159–60
　refugee, 180–81, 187, 190, 193–95
　traditional, 155
acknowledgement, 42, 54, 155
ACORD, 246–47
act, 15, 31–32, 34, 42–43, 52–54, 56, 73, 79–80, 84–87, 104–5, 107–8, 125, 205, 210–11, 228–30
action, individual, 42, 53, 85, 109, 221, 227
activities
　bound, 181, 184–85, 187–90
　floods World Vision, 248
actors, 26, 60, 63, 81, 89, 112, 150, 165, 169, 171–73, 177, 181–82, 191, 203, 242
Adozinda, 253–54, 258
advice, 244, 255–61
Africa, 7, 9, 11–16, 19–20, 25–27, 31–32, 34–37, 44, 86, 137, 217, 242, 276, 287–88, 296–98
　study of, 1–2, 16, 35, 37, 50, 54, 220, 230
African Christian, 197, 199, 201, 203, 205, 207, 209, 211, 213
African community, 36, 200
African experience of modernity, 13, 67
African lifeworlds, 75, 212, 230
African natives, 68–69

African Philosophy, 12, 36, 300, 303
African reactions, 69
African reality, 25–26, 229
Africans, 3, 12–16, 28, 35–36, 39, 44, 68–70, 113, 197, 208–10, 212, 229, 276, 287
　individual, 3
African social action, 14
African social phenomena, 44, 55, 86, 230
African social reality, 7, 12–13, 15, 20, 25, 27, 31, 33–35, 37, 46, 66–67, 220
African social reality sets, 75
African societies, 13–14, 25, 28, 33, 45, 209
　traditional, 209–10
African studies, 7, 16, 25, 27, 33, 37, 44, 75, 220, 276
African traditional society, 3, 209
African Weltanschauungen, 68–69
Africa's experience of modernity and colonialism, 14
Africa World Press, 297
Afrika, 295–97
agency, 8, 11–12, 21, 77, 80, 85, 105, 188, 217, 220, 231, 275, 277
agreement, 121–22, 124, 129, 161, 170
Alexander, 32, 42
ambivalence, 13–14, 28
analytical approaches, 18, 25–27
analytical framework, 13, 15, 18, 75, 79–80, 82, 85, 92, 104–11, 117, 124–25, 128, 173, 222, 229
Analytical Framework for Descriptive Inference, 105
Analytical Integration, 124, 173, 212
Analytical Integration Accounting for Disaster, 193
ancestors, 100, 123, 132, 135, 155, 158, 247, 282

ancestor spirits, 101, 103, 154–56, 159, 174, 246
Anderson, 284, 287
Andrea/Macamo, 294
angels, 156, 201
animals, 38–39, 44–45, 49, 84, 101, 161, 170, 256
Annual Review of Sociology, 289, 294–95, 301
answers, 44–45, 49, 51, 57–58, 80, 83–84, 163, 217–18, 220–21, 223–24, 229–31, 251–53, 263, 267–69, 271–72
apparatus, 151, 153, 281
  emergency assistance, 138–39
  local problem solving, 171–72
  problem-solving, 111, 153, 155, 157–58
appeal, 100, 152, 157–58, 248–49
Appendices, 233, 235, 237, 239, 241, 243, 245, 247, 249, 251, 253, 255, 257, 259, 261
appendix, 138, 233–46, 248, 250, 253, 256, 262, 277, 280–81, 285
approaches, 11, 13–16, 18, 42, 44, 59, 61, 66, 69, 83, 87, 109–10, 118–19, 122, 137–40
Approaching Risk, 2, 4, 6, 8, 10, 12, 14, 16, 18, 20, 26, 28, 30, 32, 34
area, non-problematic, 119–20, 128
army barracks, 183, 185, 188, 268
arrival, 90, 138, 183, 186–88, 191, 195, 205, 251, 253, 259
artefacts, 3, 8, 20, 25, 51, 68, 74, 90, 103, 171, 214, 221
  technical, 163–64, 171, 177
Assembly of God, 198, 201, 203
assistance, 95, 122–23, 131–34, 152–53, 162, 188, 246, 248–49, 253–54, 257, 259–61, 270
association, 159–60, 278
assumptions, 1–2, 32–33, 52–55, 61, 65–67, 70–71, 81–82, 85–86, 88, 95–97, 109–11, 139–40, 175, 190, 224–25
  empirical, 139
Authorisation, 96–97
authorities, 28–29, 50, 90–91, 97, 148, 152, 156–58, 175, 180, 201, 252, 257–58, 278, 282, 284
  colonial, 95, 154, 209
  local, 89, 255–57, 260–61

B

background, 8, 42, 44, 47, 70, 73, 110–12, 121–22, 124–25, 128, 138–39, 210, 212–14, 221–22, 228
background assumptions, 72
background assumptions individuals, 71
basis, 5, 9, 61, 63, 68, 73–74, 92, 107, 110, 125–26, 128, 150–52, 156, 181–82, 200–201
Bayreuth, 7–8, 217, 242
beasts, wild, 100, 193
behaviour, 41, 43–44, 62, 71, 74, 76–77, 82, 84, 86, 97, 103, 126, 174
  human, 76–77, 221
belief, 10, 21, 34, 38–40, 44, 49–50, 61, 95, 148, 175–76, 197–98, 201, 220, 277, 287
  basic, 88, 102
believers, 100, 156–57
Berger, 47–48, 87, 288
Berkeley, 288, 290–91, 300
bible, 100, 174, 199, 201, 204, 254, 258–59, 301
big disasters, 123, 133–34
  floods are a, 123
biographies, 17, 73, 111–12, 119, 198, 200, 202–5, 208, 210, 214, 227
  individual, 199, 205, 212, 214
Blackwell, 287, 299–300, 302
blessing, 197, 202–3
Bohnsack, 19, 117–18, 120–22, 288–89
bones, divinatory, 161, 170
boreholes, 29, 256, 264, 271–72
bridge, 75, 152, 228–30, 246–47, 291
Budrich, 288–89, 302
bush, 100, 183–85, 188, 190–92
  sacred, 100–101

C

CA, 146, 290
California Press, 288, 290–91, 300
Cambridge, 287–90, 292–98, 301, 303
Cambridge University Press, 287–96, 298, 301, 303
Campus, 292, 295–96, 302

Index

capitalism, 10, 14, 301–2
care, 65–66, 68, 135, 206, 211, 217, 219–20, 251, 258, 261, 273
Carlos, 256, 291
Carmen, 253, 260
categories, 9, 16, 20, 62, 66, 106–8, 112, 124, 127, 173–74, 181, 184–85, 187–93, 213, 222–24
categorisation devices, non-personal membership, 181, 186, 188
category-bound activities, 190–93
category collections, 181, 189
cattle, 28, 90, 94, 99, 133, 162–63, 166, 185, 187–89, 191–92, 254–55, 260
ceremonies, 100–101, 161, 170, 255
  traditional, 100–104, 247, 254, 257
ceremony people, 161, 170
Chicago, 288–89, 292, 294, 299–300
Chicago University Press, 288–89, 299–300
child, 182, 184–85, 189–90, 208
children, 29, 48, 90, 135, 184, 190, 194, 197, 202–3, 206, 254, 260, 276
children's mass, attended, 207–8
choice, 18–20, 82, 223, 293
Chokwe, 161–62, 165, 260
Christians, 17, 156, 206–8, 210–12, 249, 292, 298
church, 100, 156, 158, 198, 200–201, 203, 206–9, 211, 251, 254–58, 282, 284
  prophetic, 153, 156
civil war, 4, 91, 111–12, 154, 157–58, 179, 194, 201, 218, 222, 225
claim, 11, 13, 15–17, 25–26, 39–40, 45–46, 51–52, 54, 79, 81–88, 108, 110, 139–40, 153–54, 172
clan, 29, 89, 154–56, 158, 277, 282
Classical Sociology, 290, 299, 301
Clausen, 119, 279, 289, 292, 296, 299, 301–2
clues, 105–7, 149, 181, 186, 193
code, 89, 133, 160, 163, 202, 263–66, 270, 272–73, 303
CODESRIA, 303
coherent accounts, 32, 74, 101, 186, 226
colonialism, 11, 13–15, 35–36, 69, 207, 297, 301
colour, 97, 99, 148
commission, 151–53
  provincial floods, 151–52

communal village, 28, 90–91, 153–54, 183, 187–88, 193, 277
community, 26, 34, 77, 122, 128–29, 153–59, 174, 187, 193–95, 198–99, 201–2, 204–5, 208–13, 221–22, 256
  human, 6, 8, 195
community life, 38, 44
Community Lifeworld, 157
community of fate, 11, 35–36
community worldview, 174–75
concepts, 1–2, 13–14, 25, 27, 33, 50–51, 58–60, 63, 72, 75–76, 81–82, 84, 86, 176, 275–76
  analytical, 8, 88
conditions, 11–12, 14–15, 31, 33, 35–36, 41, 44–46, 63, 85–86, 118–19, 127, 129, 202–3, 221, 227–28
  existential, 11, 36, 86
connection, 17–18, 38, 58–59, 64, 66, 69, 82, 84, 95, 171, 218, 221, 230, 244, 246
consciousness, 106, 126
constitutive role, 43, 45, 65, 75
constraints, 54, 65, 87, 128, 208–10, 223, 226
  external, 33–34, 188, 191
construction, 48, 65–66, 118, 120, 149, 155, 202, 204, 208, 210, 212, 214, 246–47, 287, 290–91
  interactional, 69–70
  social, 46, 48–49, 54, 120, 122, 124, 128, 159, 292
constructionist approaches, 59–60, 87
constructionists, 19, 32, 51, 87
contamination, 162, 168
Context of Research, 2, 88, 273
contexts, 1–3, 7–8, 17–21, 41–44, 63, 79–80, 83–87, 104–6, 108–9, 111–12, 118–20, 122, 124–25, 212–13, 226–29
  historical, 25–26, 208
  local, 65, 242
  producing, 111, 113
contexts of action, 15, 17, 31–32, 55, 79
  creation of, 1, 18–19, 56, 58, 124, 226, 228
contextualisation, 40
contextualise, 163, 219
continent, 11–14, 25, 35–37, 55, 230, 276–77
contingency, 15, 26–27, 31, 38, 40, 45, 54–55, 57, 60, 63, 66–67, 75–76, 107, 127, 230

double, 42, 53
Contingency and Social Action, 41
contingency of social action, 66–67, 69–70, 74
contingency problem, 53, 107
  double, 53
contours, 37, 82, 90–91, 122
coping, 1, 3, 5, 7, 9, 11, 13, 15, 17, 19, 21, 109, 163–64, 226, 231
coping strategies, 124, 158, 171, 217–18, 221, 231
country, 91, 93, 98, 112, 135, 154, 179, 183, 201, 208, 210, 243, 249
creating contexts, 17–18, 176, 227
creation, 15, 92, 111–12, 175, 197, 199, 201, 203, 205, 207, 209, 211, 213, 259, 279
crises, 1, 4–5, 8, 17, 20, 26, 95, 109–10, 115, 118–20, 162, 166–67, 209, 242, 245
  big, 162, 166–67
crises and disasters, 27, 54, 109–10, 218–19, 231, 242
  local perceptions of, 138, 217–19, 221, 231
  perceptions of, 220, 229
Crises and Disasters in Southern Mozambique, 1, 3, 5, 7, 9, 11, 13, 15, 17, 19, 21
crises/disasters, last, 245–46
crisis/disaster, 245–46
critics, 37–39, 61
critique, 12, 14, 20, 40, 43, 63, 103, 276, 278–79, 295, 300
cultivation, 122–23, 132–34, 155
Culture, 20, 60, 64, 104, 279, 287, 290, 292–93, 296–98, 300, 302
Culture & Society, 288, 290, 301–2
customs, 101, 103, 158

D

dams, 98, 138, 148, 152, 161, 163, 165–66, 250, 254, 256, 259–61, 270–71
daughter, 72, 186, 190, 202–3, 205, 209, 256
death, 64, 103, 123, 131, 134, 157, 163–64, 179, 185, 189, 255, 257–58, 280, 282
debates, 10–13, 32, 36, 52, 60, 220
decisions, 6, 17–18, 59–60, 80–81, 84, 125, 128, 139, 185–86, 189, 194–95, 227, 230, 245, 279

demons, 197, 201
denial, 13, 27–28, 209
development, 10, 16, 26, 33–35, 37, 52, 57, 61, 80, 163, 246, 249, 297–98
Die institutionalisierte Kompetenz, 293, 295
Dieter, 281, 295, 297–98
differences, 5, 20, 27, 30, 49–50, 59, 86, 106, 139–40, 150–51, 156, 159, 177, 205–7, 211–12
dimensions, 2, 92, 106–8, 124, 127, 148, 173, 222, 224
disagreement, 122, 124
disaster prevention, 268, 270
disaster prevention institute, 270–71
disasters, 7–9, 95–96, 109–11, 117–24, 128–30, 132–35, 156–59, 180, 193, 195, 217–21, 226–27, 242, 247–50, 280–82
  doing, 195
  interpretations of, 111, 173–75
  natural, 157, 179, 201, 281
  second, 123, 135
disasters and crises, 1, 4–5, 8, 17, 20, 26, 77, 109, 115, 119, 229
Disaster Strikes, 117, 119, 121, 123, 125, 127, 129, 131, 133, 135
discipline, 32–33, 37, 59, 61, 66
discourse, 85, 121–22, 125–26, 172, 276, 293, 302
diseases, 31, 38, 212, 255
displaced people, 121, 162, 167, 244, 246, 248
distances, long, 31, 90–92
distribution, 106, 112, 126–27, 151, 155, 162, 174, 213, 223
ditches, 148, 270–71
doctors, 202–3
documentary evidences, individual, 74
Douglas, 60, 275, 287, 290, 295
drink, 101, 162, 167, 259, 284
droughts, 95, 100–101, 123, 125–29, 133, 135, 153–54, 171, 173–74, 222, 243, 245–47, 255–56, 258–59, 270
droughts and floods, 100, 106, 222
Durkheim, 19, 32, 35, 52, 54, 57, 76, 224, 278, 290, 292–93
dwellings, 183, 188–89, 200, 217, 263
dwellings and cattle, 189

Index

E

earth, 100, 135, 156, 201, 253
economic sociology, 54–55, 288–89, 291, 295, 301
elaboration, secondary, 88–89, 98, 102–4
elders, 101, 127, 175, 194, 223, 225, 251, 255, 257
electricity, 29–30, 263, 267
elements, discursive, 200–202
Elísio, 294, 296–98
emancipation, individual, 3
emergency, 129, 163, 247–49
emergency work, 249
emerging properties, 70–72
empirical realities, 1, 33–34
employment, 30, 90
Enter Disasters and Crises, 4
Entsetzliche soziale Prozesse, 292, 296, 299, 301–2
environment, 7, 89, 92, 103, 105, 154, 295, 303
ethnomethodologists, 43, 47–48, 60, 62–64, 70–74, 76, 88
ethnomethodology, 8, 19, 55, 67, 70, 72, 74, 112, 180–81, 200, 220, 288, 292–93, 296, 300
Europe, 10, 12, 20, 27, 33–37, 218, 278
Europeans, 10, 12, 14, 36, 65, 68–70, 210
events, 45, 47, 98–99, 102, 107–8, 119, 122, 124, 126, 128–29, 151, 156, 158, 244, 254–55
  extraordinary, 118, 124, 252, 254
  main, 256, 258, 261
  problematic, 128
everyday life, 65–67, 70–71, 88, 112, 117–18, 120, 123–25, 138–40, 149–51, 153, 155–57, 202–4, 226–27, 229, 242–43
  routine of, 119, 195
everyday life knowledge, 150, 153
everyday life situations, ordinary, 2, 21
excerpts, 96, 103, 121, 160, 163–64, 206–8, 211, 250
existence, 9, 12, 28, 33, 36, 38–39, 41, 44–45, 49, 87, 126, 174, 176, 203, 207
  objective, 72–73, 88, 125
expectations, 42–43, 46, 60, 63, 68, 71, 105, 107, 111, 122, 127, 139, 148, 175–77, 224–25
experience, 47–50, 63–69, 72–73, 96–97, 111–12, 117–21, 123–24, 126–28, 149, 180–83, 185–87, 189–90, 219–20, 226–27, 243–44
  existential, 66, 139, 153, 231
  lived, 67, 73, 196, 226
  people's, 94, 112
Expertenwissen, 293, 295
experts, practical, 150–51, 153, 155
explanations, 38, 42, 83–84, 98–99, 102, 108–9, 138–39, 148, 157, 187, 244–45, 247–48, 250, 254, 258
external actors, 138, 163–65, 171–73, 177, 187, 191–92, 242, 244
External Problem-solving Structure, 151
external world, 6, 51–53

F

facts, social, 32, 34, 88
failure, 25–27, 30, 45–46, 96, 98–100, 102–3, 122, 127, 148, 155, 175–76, 195, 199, 209, 220
families, 4, 29–30, 34, 101, 162, 168, 187, 194, 199, 207, 209, 211, 246, 254, 258
farming, 28, 30, 92, 95, 99, 141, 147, 158, 191, 194, 258
fate
  tame, 4, 231
  the taming of, 1
father, 72, 180, 186, 193, 203, 205, 207, 279, 283
female shepherds, 80–81
fields, 4–6, 16, 18–19, 25, 28–29, 49, 94, 96, 99, 129, 132–35, 138, 183–85, 217–18, 253
fieldwork, 2, 18, 38, 90, 100, 154, 176, 217, 281
findings, 1, 14, 17–20, 49, 52, 72, 137, 171, 220–22, 224, 226, 228
firearms, 188–89
fish, 96, 192, 219, 284
flee, 122, 129, 185, 189, 194–95, 227, 283
flight, 16, 126, 182–83, 186, 189, 192, 195
flooding, 98, 247

floods, 28, 90–103, 117–19, 121–24, 128–29, 131–35, 140–41, 148–49, 151–67, 171, 218–19, 222, 244–50, 252–61, 281–82
　big, 98, 100, 161, 165
　major, 90–91
　normal, 98, 129
　previous, 123–24, 131, 133, 135
floods and droughts, 4, 163, 171, 173, 247, 255, 259
floods overtook, 123, 135
floods people, 133, 257
flood victims, 90–91, 118, 153, 253, 259–61, 280
floodwaters, 132, 148, 218
floodwaters recede, 127
flood zones, 235
focus, 6, 19, 54, 61, 85–86, 92, 102, 105, 107, 111–12, 140, 171, 200, 242, 246
followers, 66, 157, 201, 213
food, 47, 80, 93, 125, 132, 134, 152, 162, 167, 183–85, 198, 202, 248, 257, 260
forces
　natural, 163–64, 169
　transcendental, 138, 163–64, 171, 177
forests, 131, 161, 170, 193–94, 227, 282
formula, 109, 160
Forschungspraxis, 288–89
fragility, 57, 64, 67, 71–72, 75, 104
framework, 2, 4, 7, 12–15, 26, 28, 46, 53, 82, 85, 104–5, 107, 212–14, 223, 228
Frankfurt, 288, 291–92, 294–97, 300, 302
Free Press, 290, 293, 299, 301
frelimo, 179, 183, 186–87, 192–93
functions, 5, 12, 25, 39, 48, 59, 63, 66, 96, 174, 180–81, 193–94, 201, 228

G

Garfinkel, 9, 48, 60, 63, 70–71, 74, 291–93
Gaza-Nguni, 90, 154, 280
Geenen, 95, 119, 292, 296, 299, 301–2
Gesellschaft, 62, 289, 296, 302–3
Giddens, 10, 33, 48, 58, 63, 67, 85, 226, 276, 292
Global Context, 218, 242
God, 13, 61, 95, 102–3, 132, 156–57, 159, 197–98, 201–4, 210, 246, 250, 254–59, 288

goods, 162, 166, 189, 262, 267
government, 247–49, 254–56, 258–61, 268
government of Mozambique, 201, 246, 248–49
group, 111, 119, 121, 123, 125–28, 153, 156, 174, 176, 181, 183, 197–98, 200–204, 213, 226–28
　religious, 121, 201, 282
　youth, 207–8
group interviews, 119, 121
guest, 31, 99, 121, 123, 128, 131, 133–34, 148

H

Hamburg, 289–90, 293, 296, 301–2
Hamburg/Münster, 287–88, 295, 297–98
harvest, 131, 133–34, 147
harvests, good, 101, 122, 127, 154–55, 281
hazards, 1–2, 6, 15, 53, 58–60, 76, 104–5, 125–26, 128, 173–74, 193, 195, 213, 222, 279
healers, 45, 90, 225, 254, 256–58
heaven, 156, 201
Hester, 283, 293, 302
history, 4, 10, 12, 20, 36, 61, 68, 84–85, 90–91, 100, 105, 107, 222, 296, 301
Hitzler, 150, 280, 293, 295
home, 30–31, 36, 39, 45, 96, 101, 132, 134, 183–84, 188–89, 200, 205–6, 211, 279, 283
Honer, 150, 280, 293, 295
hospitals, 30–31, 90, 184, 200, 210, 255, 257, 301
hours, 29, 100, 162, 167, 183, 198, 202, 204, 251
houses, 94, 99, 132, 134–35, 158, 162, 166, 183, 185, 189, 205, 248, 256, 260, 264
housing, 30, 163, 260, 263–64
Housley, 40, 293–94
Humanities Collaborative Research Programme, 4, 7–8
humans tame fate, 221–22
Human Studies, 290, 294, 296, 298–301, 303
hunger, 95, 142, 182, 218, 252–61
husbands, 48, 186, 188–89, 194, 203, 209, 256, 261

Index

I

identity, 11–12, 17, 112, 199, 201, 204, 207–10, 213, 228, 288, 293
   new, 204, 213
idiom, 88–89, 92–94, 96–101
illnesses, 18, 162, 167, 201–2, 255–57, 260, 284
indexicality, 72–75, 118, 121, 231
individuals, 1–5, 7–9, 31–34, 40–50, 52–55, 62–77, 83–89, 96–97, 104–13, 125–28, 139–40, 173–77, 211–14, 220–25, 227–31
   acting, 46, 71
   experiences, 47
   interacting, 181, 186, 195–96
individuals act, 53–54, 63, 77, 79
individuals act in order, 15, 20, 56, 77, 84–86, 110
individuals and communities, 11, 20, 26, 77, 221
individuals experience, 11, 66, 213
individuals group experiences, 47
individuals repair, 67, 72
individuals structure, 3
industrial society, 6, 33, 35–36
informants, 147, 155, 158, 160, 163, 171, 217–20, 229, 244
information, 47, 49, 63, 83, 161–62, 165–66, 242, 244–45, 251, 253–54, 256, 258, 261, 280–81, 284
INGC, 233, 245, 247, 249
inhabitants, 20, 91–92, 96, 141, 157, 200
Inhambane, 147, 246–47
inputs, 258–59
insecurity, 4–6, 17, 28, 53, 58–61, 89, 147, 182, 186, 218–19
insistence, 10, 119, 163, 206, 253
institutions, 8, 35, 70, 158, 208, 244–45, 247, 268–70, 288
insult, 206–7
intelligibility, 105, 109–10, 137, 210, 219, 228, 231
interaction, 62, 65, 67–69, 71–72, 74, 118, 181, 187, 189, 192, 242
   human, 70–72
interpretations, 8–9, 72–73, 75, 111, 117–21, 124, 137–41, 147–49, 151, 153, 155–59, 161–63, 171, 173, 199

documentary, 74
   local, 111, 117, 153, 248
   religious, 156
interpretations people, rejecting, 44
interpretive approach, 26, 45, 51–54, 67
interpretive hegemony, 139, 177, 226, 242
Interview Code, 93–94, 96–104
interviewee, 93, 182, 187, 206, 208, 261, 283
interview excerpts, 105, 140, 160, 184, 282
interview partners, 100, 117–19, 121–22, 160, 181, 187, 191, 196, 241, 244, 248, 252–54, 260, 282–83, 285
   first, 254–55, 259–60
Interview Protocols, 246, 248
interviews, 89, 110, 138, 154, 160, 163, 165, 169, 179–80, 182, 186–87, 248, 250–62, 279, 281–84
   individual, 227, 251
   informal, 198
   recorded, 89
   second, 253–54
Interview Schedules, 242, 244–45
   narrative, 118–19, 243
introduction, 1, 3, 25, 27, 76, 79, 85–86, 209, 217–18, 242, 249, 290, 297, 300, 303
items, following, 268, 270–71

J

James, 289, 291–92, 297, 300
John, 180, 288, 290–93, 295, 300–301

K

Kanana, 198–99, 201, 203–5
Katastrophe, 280, 292, 296, 299
killing, 190–91
knowledge, 16–17, 25–26, 39, 48–49, 84–85, 96–98, 106–8, 124–28, 140, 149–53, 155–56, 173–75, 222–28, 242, 297–301
   expert, 151, 153
   local, 138, 150, 242
   sociology of, 12, 52, 73, 87, 123, 149–50, 153
   stock of, 17, 49–50, 96, 99, 106, 126, 149, 151, 224
   tacit, 71, 302

technical-scientific, 139, 150
knowledgeable people, 45
knowledge base, 96–97
knowledge claims, 92, 96–97
knowledge dimension, 106–7, 213
Konstruktion, 293, 295

L

labour
  migrant, 30, 92, 147, 154, 182
  regulation of, 3–4
lady, 157, 213, 253, 255, 257–61, 279, 283
land, 29, 91, 95, 122, 131, 133, 135, 154, 158, 161–62, 166, 170, 174, 246–47, 257–60
leader, 95, 192, 198–99, 203–6, 213
leader of Kanana, 203–5
length, 9, 19, 48, 96, 179, 272, 283
levels, 19, 26, 49, 53, 83–84, 194, 202, 204, 211, 282
lifeworld, 28, 31, 86–87, 104–6, 110–12, 117, 149, 174, 181, 196, 201, 220–21, 226, 229, 231
life-world, 47–49, 63, 91, 149, 181, 187, 190, 204
lifeworld
  everyday, 9, 31
  local, 86, 103, 110–11, 175, 210, 231
  traditional, 154, 157
Limpopo Valley, 28, 90–91, 138, 141, 242
linkage, 163, 165, 169
livelihood, 4, 30, 92, 103–4, 119, 125, 140–42, 147, 151, 156, 189, 200, 219–23, 281
loads, heavy, 185, 191
local actors, 7, 138, 163–64, 169, 171–73, 177, 187, 191, 231
local African community, 2, 110, 210
local agency, 5, 8–9, 31, 177, 191, 217–18
local communities, 1–4, 49, 110, 112, 121–22, 124, 127–30, 147, 150–53, 210, 221, 242, 246–47, 249, 284
local coping capacities, 154–55
local experience, 5, 65, 105, 126–27, 175
local informants, 138, 163, 171–72, 281
Locality, 111–12, 197, 199, 201, 203, 205, 207, 209, 211, 213
local people, 245, 259

local perceptions, 4–5, 8, 118, 219, 226
Local perceptions and interpretations of disasters and crises, 5
locals, 8, 148, 206–7, 231, 243, 256, 260
local village head, 258–59
logic, 3, 10, 14, 46, 175, 244
London, 246, 287–88, 290–91, 293–96, 298, 300–303
Luckmann, 48–49, 54, 63, 66, 87, 120, 149, 181, 296
Luhmann, 6, 53, 58–60, 63, 76, 279, 296, 301
Lumumba, Patrice, 15, 17, 19, 28, 30–31, 38, 91–92, 95–99, 102, 104, 138–39, 153–54, 222–23, 225–27, 277

M

Macamo, 3, 11, 27–28, 35, 150, 156, 209, 275, 278, 280–82, 284–85, 292, 296–97, 299, 301–2
magic, 10, 39, 41, 60, 150, 252, 282, 285, 291, 300–301
magnitude, 141, 148, 161–62, 165–66
maize, 29, 93, 123, 133–34, 282
Major disasters, 95
Making Risk Relevant, 75
Maputo, 30, 138, 143, 147, 162, 250, 281, 290
marriage, 207–8, 220
Mbalalen, 9, 28, 277
Mbalan, 9, 90, 154, 174, 259
Mbalan clan, 9, 28, 30, 154–55, 158, 174–75, 282
Mbalan lineage, 90–91
Mbalan territory, 90–91
MDCs, 180–81
meat, 118, 183, 192, 218–19
members, 28, 30, 90–91, 121, 153–56, 158, 194, 198–99, 201–6, 208–9, 213, 228, 255–57, 282, 284
  individual, 222, 228
membership categories, 180–81, 187, 207
membership categorisation devices, 18, 112, 180, 182, 184–93, 205–6
members of society, 150, 181
member steps, 198
memories, 105, 111, 154, 156, 196, 296–97
methodological implications, 37, 79–80

Index   313

Methodological Issues, 79–81, 83, 85, 87, 89, 91, 93, 95, 97, 99, 101, 103, 105, 107, 109
methodologies, 79, 81, 110–11, 289
methods, documentary, 18, 73–75, 117, 120–22
Michael, 288, 296
migrant workers, 31, 147, 188–89, 251
mission, 3, 198, 209–12, 285
missionaries, 64, 208–11, 285
missionary work, 68–69, 211, 248
misunderstandings, 64–66, 68, 75
modernisation theories, 7, 13, 27, 69
modernisation theorists, 13–14
modernity, 7, 9–11, 13–15, 27–28, 58, 175, 177, 214, 275, 289, 291–92, 295, 297, 301, 303
  notion of, 7, 27, 221
  products of, 7–9, 29, 277, 297
modern society, 20, 34–36, 57–58, 60–61, 220, 230, 278, 298, 301
  nature of, 20, 60–61, 76
moments, 36, 120, 154, 156, 186, 199, 202–3, 228
Mondlane, Samuel, 248–50
money, 30, 63, 131, 133, 247–49, 255–60, 290, 303
Mosambik, 280, 294, 296–97, 300
mothers, 111, 180, 186, 189–90, 192, 211, 257, 294, 301
motives, 46, 63, 83, 85, 302
Mozambicans, 158, 179–80, 208–9
Mozambique, 3, 89, 91, 141, 179–80, 201, 208–10, 246, 248–50, 256, 277, 281–84, 287–93, 297–98, 300–302
Mozambique Refugee Accounts of Principally Conflict-Related Experiences, 292
Mudimbe, 12, 26, 68–69, 276, 298
Mundane Reason, 88–89, 92–94, 96–105

N

name, 9, 26, 28–29, 36, 90, 95, 203, 205, 207, 219, 244, 277, 279, 284
natural environment, 87–88, 92, 95, 98, 102, 222–23
natural events, 9, 99, 102, 119, 140–41, 171
natural phenomena, 17, 47, 111, 126, 156, 163, 173, 195, 247, 250, 255–56
natural sciences, 40, 210

natural world, 87, 97, 106, 125–28, 140, 173–76, 193–94, 222–24, 230
natural world category, 106, 194, 222
natural world challenges individuals, 125, 223
Negotiating Modernity, 297
neighbours, 123, 134, 147, 186–88, 194
Neubert, 150, 275, 280–81, 295, 297–98
New York, 287–93, 296, 298–301
NGOs, 161–63, 168, 171, 256, 259, 261, 268, 270, 298
non-Christians, 206–8, 211–12
non-members, 205–6
normality, 93, 119–20, 124, 183, 191, 194–95
norms, 33, 37, 42, 53, 55, 64–65, 82–83, 159, 184–85, 210–11, 229
Nuclear disasters, 5, 59
nyimpi, 183, 186–88, 191–92

O

objective world, 40, 84
objects, 32–33, 39–40, 42, 47–48, 51, 72–74, 76, 110, 125, 160, 163, 165, 169, 172, 177
  grammatical, 171
  natural, 39–40, 43
occurrence, 95, 98–99, 101–2, 119, 121
  reported, 187–88, 190
opinion, 119, 123, 131, 133, 172, 182, 244
Opladen, 288–89, 293, 295–96, 301–2
opposing horizons, 122–24
  negative, 121–23
organisations, 112, 245–46, 248–49, 255
Organization, 147, 295, 297
outcomes, 8, 12, 45, 51, 63, 66, 87, 89, 109–10, 181, 186, 201–3, 220, 224, 229
owners, 257–58
Oxford, 287–88, 291–92, 294, 296–303

P

pair, standardised relational, 181, 186, 189–90
Paris, 284, 287–88, 290, 292, 295, 298, 301
Parsons, 32–33, 40, 42–43, 48, 52–53, 64, 277–78, 299, 301
Participant Analysis, 242, 253, 256
partner, 254–56, 258–60

second, 255–57, 259, 261
past experience, 96–98, 105, 111, 255
Patrice Lumumba Communal Village, 4, 13, 17, 20, 28, 30, 59, 89, 92, 129–30, 138, 151, 154, 182
Patrice Lumumba Village, 117, 222–24, 231
Patrício, 255, 259–60
Pentecostal worldview, 213
people, 30–31, 89–102, 104–5, 122–27, 131–35, 147–48, 151–59, 161–63, 165–70, 183–87, 192–97, 218–20, 227–28, 243–44, 247–61
 encouraged, 249, 252
 helping, 226, 246
 interview, 251
 making, 191, 250
 white, 218, 247, 254, 259–60
people act, 79–80, 97, 222
perceptions, 4, 8–9, 33–34, 47–48, 71–72, 87–89, 105–6, 161–63, 165–66, 190–91, 222, 224, 227, 229, 242
periods, colonial, 2, 89, 98, 154, 200–201, 206
person, 38–39, 44, 74, 161, 163, 170, 176, 181, 192, 206, 279, 284, 292
perspectives, 39–40, 43, 51–52, 67, 69, 73, 130, 173–74, 187, 221, 224, 242, 246, 288, 291
 ethnomethodological, 73–74, 76
Peter, 254, 288, 292–95, 297, 300, 302–3
Pfohl, 72–75, 299
phenomena, 16–18, 38, 40, 47–49, 59, 72–73, 84, 86, 103–4, 106, 108–10, 117, 119, 125–26, 147–48
phenomenal world, 50
phenomenological sociology, 106, 128, 140, 276–77, 279
Philosophy, 39, 280, 293, 298, 300, 302
ploughs, 131–32, 256, 258, 265, 267
political power, 90–91
politics, 68–69, 105, 161, 165, 288, 291–92, 297, 299, 301–2
Pollner, 88–89
population, 90–91, 141, 152–53, 201, 247, 255–57
Portuguese, 89–91, 200, 254, 261, 283
position, 14, 36, 44, 69, 71, 77, 90, 128, 154–55, 158–59, 176–77, 190–91, 209–10, 212, 278

positivist accounts, 44, 52
possibility of social action, 45–46, 76, 86, 113
power, 12, 26, 36, 58, 69, 91, 154, 156, 188–89, 198, 289, 292, 295, 301
Pragmatics, 287, 291, 294–95, 298–99
pray, 102, 198–99, 202–4, 284
prayers, 156–57, 197–99, 202–5, 250, 253
 fasting, 198, 202
 ritual, 203–4
praying, 198, 203–4, 209, 250, 256
preachers, 174–75, 223
pre-condition, 48, 51
predicates, 163, 165, 169, 171–73, 184–85, 187–93, 208, 212
 frequent, 171–73
predictability, 53, 57–58, 62–65, 104, 112, 159, 195, 227
Presbyterian Church of Mozambique, 206, 208
press, 151–52, 281, 287, 289, 292, 295, 301, 303
prevention, 119, 129, 164, 242–43, 281
prevention mechanisms, 217–18, 221, 231
problem, 15–17, 25–27, 32–34, 37–38, 53, 55, 66, 94–98, 119, 131–33, 150–53, 157–58, 161–63, 203, 256–59
 health, 202–3
 individual, 213
 main, 161, 165, 246, 256, 260–61
 people's, 250
 second, 252
problematic nature, 92, 96, 155
problematic situations, 9, 92, 95–96, 102, 140, 149–50, 226
procedures, authorisation, 89, 92, 95–96, 102
process, 7–12, 17, 35–36, 47–49, 68–69, 88, 104, 119–22, 128, 149–50, 163, 168, 204–7, 213–14, 221–22
programmes, 16, 54, 246, 249, 275
projects, 132, 181, 210, 217, 242, 247, 253–57, 259–60, 275, 289
promise, 3, 13, 27–28, 155, 230, 301
promissory notes, 11, 13
properties, 64, 72–73, 81, 84, 106, 120, 127, 163–64, 173, 193, 195, 206, 212, 226–27, 231
prophets, 156–57, 174–75, 223, 225, 287
propositions, 163–64, 176

Index

punishment, 95, 174, 255
puzzle, 32, 81, 83

Q

questionnaire, 250, 252, 262, 277

R

radio, 253–54, 260, 265
rain, 95, 101, 104, 125, 131, 135, 138, 142, 161–65, 168–69, 184, 222, 250, 253–60
rainfall, 126, 141–42, 237
rationality, 39, 41, 147, 210, 242, 291–93, 295, 301
  technical-scientific, 147, 231
realise, 84, 172, 220, 231, 245, 276
realist approaches, 59
reality, 12, 51–52, 65, 67–68, 70–74, 80–82, 84–85, 87–88, 106–9, 119–21, 137–41, 149, 177, 180–81, 199–201
  retrieve, 84
Reality of Uncertainty, 92
reasoning, mundane, 18, 88–89, 92, 97
reasoning practices, 88–89, 92, 97–103
rebels, 179, 183–85, 189, 277, 284
reconstruction, hermeneutic, 199–201, 204
reference, 8–9, 15–16, 45–47, 68–69, 89, 91, 111, 161–63, 165–66, 175–77, 186–89, 211–14, 226, 242, 282–83
  central, 160, 163–64
reflexivity, 9, 43, 48, 63, 72–75, 231
refuge, 93, 124, 133, 180, 185–86, 193, 195, 222, 227, 259
refugees, 90–91, 112, 158, 179, 182–93, 283
Refugees-Ef Code, 183–84, 188–89
Refugees-Hm Code, 182, 187–88, 190
Refugees-Jm Code, 192
region, 7, 86, 89, 92, 95, 103–4, 141, 147, 157, 198, 256, 261, 270, 277, 281
regulation, 3, 27–28
relatives, 260–61, 283
relevance, 16, 19, 47, 50, 52, 57, 66, 105–6, 108, 111, 148, 150, 219, 222, 230–31
  analytical, 1, 41
relevance areas, 153

relevance dimension, 106–7, 125–26, 173–74, 193, 222
reliance, 21, 97–98, 126–27
relief work, 246, 248
religion, 10, 41, 68, 91, 150, 250, 258, 278, 284, 287, 299, 301–2
Renamo, 179, 183, 187, 283, 302
Renamo fighters, 183, 185–87, 283
repair strategies, 107–8, 127, 175, 213, 224
  community worldview, 175
repertoire, 92, 95, 126, 147–48
representations, 12, 25–26, 73, 81
request, 192, 198, 204, 245–46, 248, 282
research, 2, 4–8, 18–20, 86, 88–89, 110–11, 118–19, 137–38, 141, 197–200, 218–19, 273, 279, 281, 284
  empirical, 31, 75, 87
  qualitative, 19, 40, 86, 180, 290, 292, 294
research area, 65, 87, 89, 95, 102, 242
researched social world, 18
researcher, 80–81, 218, 242
research process, 18, 231
research programme, 17, 49, 54, 58, 61, 230
research question, 219, 231, 278
research terrain, 28, 79, 86, 89, 105, 277
resources, 3, 50, 63, 72–73, 86, 91, 104, 111–12, 181, 183, 186, 207–8, 210, 228, 250
  cultural, 42, 66
responses, 17–18, 33–34, 37, 51–52, 60–61, 67, 69, 92–93, 96, 98–100, 102, 104, 138, 252, 267–69
  conscious direct, 67
  routine, 93–94, 226
Retrieving Social Reality, 186
Richard, 291, 293–94, 299, 301, 303
Risiko, 289, 296
risk, 1–2, 5–8, 15–17, 57–62, 75–77, 104–8, 110–13, 124, 173–74, 176, 222–25, 242, 279, 290–91, 295–96
  notion of, 6, 21, 64, 75, 77, 220, 242, 278
  production of, 1, 6, 17–18, 60
  sociology of, 1–2, 5–6, 15, 18, 20, 55, 57–59, 61, 67, 75–77, 79, 86–87, 107, 220–21, 230–31
  understanding of, 60, 75–76
risk and hazards, 1, 59

risk and social reality, 15, 57, 59, 61, 63, 65, 67, 69, 71, 73, 75, 77
risk calculation, 61
risk sociologists, 60, 76
rituals, 39, 103, 204–5, 213, 247, 289
rivers, 93, 96–97, 99, 101, 148, 256, 264, 298
Rodney, 275, 299, 302
room, 2, 133–34, 195, 197–98, 204
routines, 63, 93, 95, 120, 124, 126, 183–85, 194–95, 227
Routledge, 288, 290, 295–96, 298, 302–3
rules, 8, 39–40, 71, 83, 90, 109, 123, 135, 174–76, 184–85, 189, 200, 210–11, 288–89
 colonial, 3, 27, 35, 208–9, 212

S

Sacks, 9, 181, 283, 300
Sage, 288, 290, 295, 299–303
salvation, 91, 95, 202–4, 284
scare people, 38
schools, 30, 90, 205, 210, 221, 231, 249, 254, 257, 268
Schütz, 46–50, 63, 66, 87, 106, 149–50, 278, 294–95, 300
Schütz, Alfred, 37, 43, 46, 63, 76, 83–85, 106, 149, 278, 287, 301
science, 10, 21, 26, 35, 39, 42, 52, 58–59, 139, 150–51, 247–48, 287, 293–95, 298, 301–2
scientific knowledge, 6, 60–61, 125
search, 5, 46, 52, 59, 61, 64, 80–81, 93, 98–99, 101, 112, 200, 202, 219, 221
seeds, 94, 162, 248, 255–56
shepherdesses, 81, 83–84
signs, 148, 154–55, 163, 212, 247, 282–84
sing, 104, 161, 169, 198–99
situations, 45, 66–68, 70–71, 73, 91, 94, 97, 139–40, 149, 151–52, 163, 193, 195, 230, 243–44
 general, 152
skills, 106, 126–27, 150, 194, 207
snake, 93–94, 100–101, 282
social action, 1–2, 5–9, 15–17, 26–27, 40–54, 58–62, 64–67, 74–77, 82–87, 104–5, 137–40, 200, 219–21, 224, 226–28
 centrality of, 4, 59
 circular nature of, 77, 87
 conditions of possibility of, 45, 76, 86, 113
 constitution of, 31, 160, 226
 instance of, 41
 interpretive understanding of, 82–83
 nature of, 6, 15, 77
 properties of, 16, 64, 85
 property of, 63–64
 structure of, 17, 32, 62, 104, 139, 299
 subjective meaning of, 82–83
 understanding of, 41, 51, 64
Social Action and Meaningfulness, 46
Social Action Perspective, 2, 4, 6, 8, 10, 12, 14, 16, 18, 20, 26, 28, 30, 32, 34
social change, 3, 7, 90, 113, 119, 205
 rapid, 34–35, 86
social context, 41, 54, 72–73, 176, 187, 214, 242
social distribution, 17, 48–50, 96, 149, 194, 224, 300
social encounters, problematic, 67
social environment, 6, 75, 77, 87–88, 91, 106–7, 154, 180, 199
social interaction, 48, 65–67, 71–72, 74, 87, 120, 186, 299, 302
social life, 15, 20, 39–45, 50–54, 60, 65, 75, 79, 84, 86, 103, 119, 175, 193, 214
Socially Constructing Disaster, 121
social order, 33, 35, 38, 69–70, 72, 74–75, 298
social phenomena, 2, 8, 16, 19, 27, 41, 44–45, 51, 57, 72, 74, 109, 113, 119
social reality, 12, 14–17, 19–21, 25–27, 44–46, 48–49, 51–52, 57–59, 63, 65–75, 108–9, 149, 180–81, 198–203, 228–30
 communicated, 50
 constructing, 49
 local, 50, 89
 properties of, 70, 73
 stable, 92
social relations, 17, 20, 33–34, 44–46, 48, 106, 126–27, 137, 139–40, 156, 159, 177, 219–20, 223, 226
social relationships, 42, 44, 54, 62–64, 104, 159, 195, 279, 282
social sciences, 14–15, 25–27, 34, 40, 42, 45, 52, 75, 81–82, 84, 278, 289, 293, 300, 302

Index 317

social scientists, 16, 20, 52, 59, 64, 82, 84, 137, 217, 221, 278
social stock, 71, 85, 106, 126–27, 149–50, 153, 174, 213, 223
social theory, 7, 11, 13, 26, 46, 55, 63, 110, 113, 219–20, 288–89, 291, 293, 296, 299
social world, 8–9, 16, 18–20, 26, 86, 88–89, 106–7, 125–26, 173–76, 190–91, 194, 212, 219, 222–24, 228–29
social world category, 106, 194
society, 1–3, 6–7, 10, 25, 32–35, 48–50, 57–61, 63–64, 120, 149–51, 220–21, 288, 290–91, 294–99, 301–2
  individual members of, 181
  science of, 33
  study of, 16, 32
sociological, 50, 59, 76, 113, 200, 202, 220, 230, 288–89, 291
sociological accounts, 33, 55
sociological theory, 44, 76, 296, 301, 303
sociological understanding, 4, 6, 46
sociologists, 6, 16, 26, 32–33, 43, 46, 52, 58, 60, 67, 71, 76, 82, 181–82, 199
  positivist, 52–53
sociology, 15–16, 32–37, 40, 51, 53–55, 57–58, 61–62, 75–76, 84–85, 219–20, 229, 289–90, 292, 294–95, 299–303
  emergence of, 33
  grounding of, 41, 53, 62–63
  interpretive, 48, 52, 54, 81, 229, 280
sociology of religion, 41
sociology studies, 33–34
sociology Weber, 41, 43
soils, 29–30, 101, 122–25, 129, 131–35, 162, 168, 183, 247, 253, 256–58, 260, 277, 280
solution, 33, 53, 83, 119, 150–51, 155, 157, 203, 213, 247, 256
South Africa, 30–31, 138, 141, 147, 154, 161, 165, 189, 205, 208, 253–54, 260, 280, 287, 293
South African, 30, 219, 252
Southern Africa, 3–4, 281
Southern Mozambique, 1–5, 7, 9, 11, 13, 15, 17, 19–21, 139, 147, 151, 158, 197, 284, 290
Sozialwissenschaften, 289, 296–97, 299, 301–2
specialists, 155–56

special knowledge, 150, 153
speech, 160, 283, 296
spirits, 10, 100, 160, 182, 201, 203, 282, 284
  evil, 156–57, 197, 202–3, 282
Sprondel, 150–51, 301
state, 37, 53, 62, 90, 147, 152, 154, 158, 180, 185, 243, 245, 277, 281, 283–84
statements, 25, 34, 41, 109, 121, 123, 160, 163, 171–72, 176, 208, 245, 253, 256, 275
state relief apparatus, 147, 151–53
status, 34, 36, 76, 82, 106–8, 126, 147, 160, 163–64, 172, 174, 213, 223, 225, 227
Stephen, 293, 295, 299, 301
story, 20, 31, 38–39, 41, 44, 64, 80, 182, 201–3, 252, 283, 294
strength, 53, 99, 122–23, 133, 135, 182, 197, 230, 267–69
stretch, 92, 283
structural constraints individuals, 53
structure, 2–3, 8–9, 20–21, 25–28, 32, 47–48, 63, 74, 76–77, 149–53, 186–87, 193–94, 200–201, 220–21, 226–27
  discursive, 202
  propositional, 171–72
  social, 70–71, 121, 288
students, 138, 250–51, 281
Studying Africa, 15–16, 25, 27–29, 31–33, 35, 37, 39, 41, 43, 45, 47, 49, 51, 53, 55
Suhrkamp, 291–92, 300
Swedberg, 278, 289, 301
Swiss Mission, 208–12, 228
Swiss Presbyterian Mission, 2–3
system, social, 33, 44, 52–53, 63, 299

T

Table, 141–43, 146, 164–65, 169, 171, 173, 190, 197, 225, 265, 267, 281
table 6.6a, 171–72
Talcott, 299–300
taming fate, 20, 113, 226, 231
technology, 3, 5, 7, 57, 295
tension, 13, 19, 21, 27, 77, 81, 105, 121, 139, 208, 227
terms, 2–3, 9–11, 13–15, 36–37, 39–40, 61–62, 68, 82–83, 85–87, 161–62, 166, 180–81, 213, 219–20, 222–23

text, 93–94, 96–104, 121, 131, 133, 182–85, 187–93, 293–94, 296, 302
thematic fields, 121–22
Theory, 288, 290, 296–97, 301–2
Theory and Society, 288, 290–91, 294–95, 297, 299, 301–2
Thomas, 288, 295–96, 300–301
tilling, 124, 133–35
title, 19–20, 25, 46
Tönnies, 159, 279, 289
tools, 19, 25, 33, 76, 82, 85, 94, 110, 122, 140, 210–11, 265–67
tractors, 122, 129, 131–33, 247, 256, 258, 265
tradition, 6, 13, 83, 101, 126–27, 150, 161, 170, 209, 254, 257–58, 279, 288
traditional society, 3, 14, 33–34, 37
translating hazards, 1, 105, 108, 111–13, 225
  process of, 106–8, 112, 124, 126, 173–74, 193, 223–24
translation, 12, 128, 149, 176, 213–14, 222, 224, 275, 279, 294, 301
trees, 98, 101, 176, 185, 258
trust, 27, 53, 57–58, 62–65, 96, 104, 107–8, 126–27, 194, 213, 224–25, 278–79, 292–93, 295–96, 300–301
  community worldview, 175
trust and predictability, 62–65, 104
truth, 61, 82, 139, 175–76, 223, 251, 298
  regime of, 210–11
Turner, 299–301
typifications, 48–50, 66, 74, 149, 181, 190
  process of, 48–49

U

uncertainty, 6, 27–28, 30, 42–43, 45–46, 54–55, 57, 60, 66, 75–76, 92, 107, 110, 127, 181–82
understanding, 25, 27, 33–35, 40–43, 51–53, 63, 69–70, 76, 80–81, 83–84, 110–11, 117, 139–40, 219–20, 275–77
  individual's, 67
  shared, 50, 69, 71
  simplified, 224
understandings individuals act, 69
University of California Press, 288, 290–91, 300

V

valley, 28–30, 91, 93–94, 99, 122–23, 125, 131–35, 141–42, 148, 152, 154, 200
village, 9, 28–31, 44–45, 89–91, 102–3, 105–6, 118–19, 153–58, 174–75, 183–85, 200–201, 222–23, 244, 250–61, 277–82
village community, 44, 49
village context, 159
village head, 158, 251–52, 254, 259
village lifeworld, 87, 92
villagers, 4–6, 28–31, 38–39, 41, 44–45, 49–50, 87–92, 104–7, 117–19, 174–76, 184–85, 189–92, 195, 217–18, 220–22
  lifeworld of, 127, 221
villagisation policy, 154
violence, 112, 193, 195
vitamins, 31, 90–91
voices, 197, 199, 204, 220, 284

W

Wagner, 117, 278, 287, 302
war, 111–12, 153–54, 179–80, 182–83, 185–86, 189, 193–95, 227, 243, 254–56, 258–59, 282–84, 287, 289, 297–98
  context of, 181, 188–90, 194
  experience of, 17, 180–81, 185–86, 188, 190, 193, 195
warnings, 148, 152, 220
war refugees, 17, 179–81, 183, 185, 187, 189, 191, 193, 195, 227, 253, 255–60
war victim, 253, 255, 260
Washington, 287, 292–94, 302–3
water, 29, 93, 99, 101, 122–24, 127, 131–35, 148, 151–52, 161–64, 166–67, 247, 250, 254–55, 260
  big disaster, 123, 133
  dirty, 162, 167
  fetch, 264, 271–72
  flood, 162, 254
  piped, 29–30, 263–64, 267
water levels, 93, 96–99, 102, 122, 124–26, 133, 148, 162
water recedes, 131
Watson, 283, 302

wave, 57, 90–91, 158, 161, 165
Weber, 10, 20, 32, 41–44, 46–48, 50, 54, 57, 62–65, 67, 76, 82–83, 159–60, 278, 302
Weber, Max, 1, 6, 10, 15, 40, 43, 52, 82–83, 159, 275–76, 292, 300–303
Weber's conceptualisation, 45
Weber's notion of social action, 40, 46, 50
Weber's theorisation of social action, 41, 44
Weber's understanding of social action, 83
well-being, 154–56, 158
West, 7, 12, 68–69
Westdeutscher Verlag, 293, 295–96, 301
William, 287, 291, 293–94, 298
Wirklichkeit, 288, 293, 295
witchcraft, 38–39, 95, 156–57, 210, 284, 291–92, 300
Wittrock, 11, 303
woman, 147, 176, 184, 189–90, 197–98, 202, 205–7, 254
women, 29–31, 174, 180, 184, 189, 194, 197, 200, 205, 208–12, 218, 244, 252–54, 259–60, 283–84
  position of, 209
work, 2–3, 7, 63–64, 67–68, 87–88, 127, 133–34, 156–57, 162–63, 199–201, 203, 206–7, 245–50, 252, 258
  emergency and relief, 246, 248
  routine, 122
Work and Societal Order in Africa, 296
worker, domestic, 264, 266
work ethic, 2, 4, 17, 197, 200
world, 3–5, 14, 39–41, 50–52, 72–74, 81–84, 100–102, 104–8, 125–27, 137, 171–77, 205–7, 211–14, 219–21, 229–31
  non-problematic, 120
  orderly, 52
  possible, 82, 219
  referential, 105, 160
  routine, 95, 120, 191
World According, 199
world accounts, 172
worldviews, 104, 140, 147, 156, 160, 173–77, 200–202, 204, 213–14, 218, 223–25
  local, 138, 226–27, 231
  religious, 174–75
  scientific, 139

  traditional, 174–75, 223
World Vision, 147, 248–50
  normal work of, 249
  resettling people, 248

X

xingoko, 38–39, 41

Z

Zingerle, 276, 278, 285, 303

www.ingramcontent.com/pod-product-compliance
Lightning Source LLC
Chambersburg PA
CBHW052133010526
44113CB00035B/1994